THE MIND IS MIGHTIER

Reflections on the Historic Rise of Cognition and Complexity

PART I

Bar-Giora Goldberg

AUTHORS PLACE
—PRESS—

Published by Authors Place Press
9885 Wyecliff Drive, Suite 200
Highlands Ranch, CO 80126
AuthorsPlace.com

Manufactured in the United States of America.

ISBN: 978-1-62865-781-4

Dedicated to Pnina, Amit, Dror, Ronen, Avalyn, Gracyn and Declan

And to the memory of Moshe and Shoshana

CONTENTS

1. PREFACE

"We are all in the gutter, but some of us are looking at the stars."

Oscar Wilde

L ife is a gigantic mystery and while we are starting to decipher few of the secrets, we find out that the path is leading to rising complexity and the cognization of our lives, sciences, technologies and arts.

This reflective historical study, representing mostly western thought, is a set of observations, perhaps a conjecture on the swift evolution of cognition and complexity in human history; a review of our languages, ontologies, the forces that drive us to scientific and artistic heights and the make-believe mythologies and biases we adapted on the path we have taken so far into the cognitive, artistic, scientific, social and political dimensions. History is our mirror and guide, a vast chronicle and ontological canvas that is not neutral and must therefore be interpreted every generation anew.

Animals are born to survive, but humans evolved to explore, learn, create, reflect, ponder and understand. We are here to be inquisitive, curious - a thinking species. In time, our knowledge reveals the world and human affairs to be immensely complex; it seems that complexity is a feature of the universe and of the phenomena of life. As we progress, we find out that by opening new vistas in our understanding or describing the world, we enter new and higher complex models. This seems to be a destination, an endless path of continuous rising cognition and complexity.

The rise of complexity and the centrality of cognition in our modern world-view, define the fundamental drivers, intellectual progress, advances and affluence of western societies. These cognitive developments, the outcome of our high language and the abstract and symbolically oriented world-view, coupled with the rapid advances in the science of computers - especially Machine-Learning, AI and Biology (specifically in genetics) are by now quite progressive. They have created the potential to approach soon and maybe tinker with some of the fundamental building blocks of the nature of life and its differentiation from inanimate matter, issues that could not have been pondered even a few decades ago. This capacity is possible due to our ability to analyze and model complex scientific, social, political and abstract conditions. Also, to comprehend myriad of spiritual disciplines, mythologies, symbolism, changes in our world-view, advanced communications and the rapid rise of thinking machines. We are absolutely in the age of Idea, Data and Cognition.

However, in-spite of our advanced capabilities and fantastic cognitive progress, we have never learnt to tame the beast within us. With knowledge came the realization of the matters we do not know and the others that are perhaps unknowable. Our body and mind still command most of what we do - as automata! We act and behave without knowing how, why or for what purpose. Our grasp of life's riddles is largely limited. Many fundamental life's enigmas may forever stay in the realm of philosophy. Steven Weinberg, winner of the Nobel prize in Physics, stated: "*The more the universe seems comprehensible, the more it seems pointless.*" Life that is pointless, without purpose, is a great challenge to the human mind. We seek purpose in a universe brimming with secrets. Among our many riddles is the nature of the mind and consciousness, the origins of our language, the correlation between matter and spirit, life's purpose or direction and our destiny, or purpose.

Few principles are guiding our modern perception of life and complexity. Material Darwinism defines life's drive only in "survival" and "success" in the reproduction of genetic copies[108]. But then, it seems that life in its marvelous branching and diversity has also evolved towards higher complexity - from Cyano-bacteria (the Photosynthesis pioneers) to Dinosaurs and then mammals; this manifestation of complexity allowed in time human evolution, with our cognition. The mind, consciousness, complexity and cognition have not yet been incorporated into Darwinism, a fact that even Darwin recognized and agonized over. It is our Cognition that has taken us well beyond the boundaries of material natural-selection and farther towards symbolism and abstraction. Human evolution is no more strictly Darwinian; there might be a struggle for respect, or recognition, for position in the social order, even a continuous slow genetic change; but Darwinian survival is receding as a force in the evolution of humanity. Our progress is now definitely directed, motivated and accelerating on the cognitive path. Our brains conquered brute force. ***The Mind Is Mightier.***

We have evolved from the early dominating belief of God's hand in every matter, into better understanding of nature, history and ourselves. Religion is an important component of the human affair, but its interpretation changed in modernity, perhaps towards a more complex, abstract forms - the philosophical God.

There is no doubt that language, our cognitive cradle, has grown in complexity over time and become richer in its expressive, nuance and descriptive-communicative power. The lingual ability allowed us to imagine, to speculate, to build imagined worlds. Indeed, we dwell in universes we mostly produce, part of our mythologies, imagination and "make belief".

The book's focus is indeed the rise of cognitive complexity across the apace of our intellectual activity. There is no doubt that the human brain, in size and wiring complexity, has grown beyond proportion to other creatures. The physical resources our brains demand and the burden of a heavy organ, held high by an erected ape, are very taxing but have paid off. We are feeble creatures in comparison and can't compare in muscle, strength or speed to apes or large cats, but our cognition, language and social assembly gave us the advantage to take dominion over the earth. Biologists tell us that success depends on adaptation to a niche; we defy the odds, we adapt to every niche because of our cognitive capacities.

The evolution of our civilizations, only a few thousand years since the agricultural revolution, has not been uniform. Historical records tell us that, while certain human societies enjoyed a rapid rise in Cognition and complexity - Mesopotamia, Egypt, ancient Greece, Greco-Roman, the Renaissance among them - they were usually followed by decline: the Barbarians, the Plagues, the Dark Middle-Ages, Fascism, among them. We are capable of reaching the summit but tend also to take great steps backwards. We are good students of history but fail to learn its lessons. The horrors of the 20th century, when we hoped to be enlightened after the scientific revolution and the promise of the Enlightenment, will never be forgotten. Our knowledge is cumulative, we have learned to record our progress. Thus, even after the "Barbarians" visit us, as they do from time to time, we learn to recover. The past continues to beckon and eventually helps direct and enable us to return and surpass what has been achieved in the days of yore. And knowledge easily multiplies, one person can teach many! Education is our salvation.

Historians, religious leaders and thinkers tried over the generations, and specifically in the last few centuries, to formulate a general theory of History, in both material and intellectual spheres. Some of them will be reviewed herein (chapter 3) as a background for the formulation our world views in modernity. The puzzle of life's purpose has been a frustrating enigma throughout history and its solution is not likely to emerge soon or maybe ever. To ponder such questions, perhaps requires religion and this is not a religious work. To the non-believer, purpose is not given. Otherwise, life has no known purpose, except perhaps following the religious or Epicurean maxims. Within the Darwinian philosophy, the one that commands the modern paradigm, Evolution, the process of gradual change and adaptation in living matter, has no direction or purpose. If there is a direction, a "force", it is only survival and procreation; these alone are not satisfying to the inquiring mind!

The rise of our abstract thinking has immensely accelerated at a rate that is unique and unprecedented. These are not driven by genetic mutations, rather by mental processes and our mysterious innate drive for knowledge. The scientific investigations of cognition, what we came to call the Cognitive Sciences, are rather young. Among them are Linguistics, Artificial Intelligence (AI), Psychology and Philosophy of the mind. Both modern Linguistics and AI have advanced mightily in the second half of the 20th century and today, some of the leading scientists are speculating about "solving the issue of intelligence" within the next half century. The reference is to thinking machines (AI) that can make better decisions than humans; and yet, machines do not think, definitely not like us. Our language vastly enhanced our ability to communicate, accumulate and transfer knowledge to other minds. In particular, following the invention of writing, language enabled another level of extra-bodily memory and inter-generational communication. Thus, we seem to evolve on other lines; the Darwinian brutal, cruel struggle has given way to civilization. Civilization, the concepts of morality, humanity and social responsibility are by nature anti-Darwinian. We support, cure and encourage the sick, the weak and the unfortunate. We have reversed the cruel, apathetic course of nature. Consequently, we have conceived concepts like The Rights of Man, Charity and Liberty; we have taken dominion and started to assume responsibilities for the earth and the biosphere.

The social order has always been held together by a combination of cognitive mechanisms and coercion. The progress humanity has made during the span of civilization (some 400 generations) most probably with little fundamental genetic changes, has to be found and understood only within the Cognitive space. There are strong reasons to believe that our brain capacity has not altered much, due to Darwinian selection changes during this period, just some 10K years. It means our "progress" - let's define it temporarily as the rise of our knowledge, thinking faculties, abstraction, humanity, freedoms and communications - is driven by self-organizing or directed-organizing cognitive processes. This revolution is so amazing that even in the material world of wealth and power, the greatest assets today are Data and Ideas. Not the traditional land, gold, machinery or natural resources, but cognitive concepts that can be translated into both the material and spiritual domains.

The terms Cognition, Complexity & Consciousness are used abundantly in the work; we have little knowledge about the dawn, mechanisms, nature and evolution of these traits that are quite universal in the animal Kingdom and perhaps in all living matter. Our brain, as far as we can tell, is a vast collection of some 100 billion neurons with many more interconnections (Synapses). We have no knowledge of the internal-language the brain uses or our eventual capacity to model such a vast organ. What we do know is that we are making fantastic progress in the understanding of brain chemistry, functionality, communications and behavior; we try to model our "thinking machines" on the way we think our brain works (neural networks).

We can adapt one of two general hypotheses for the nature of our experience. Einstein summarized this in one of his aphorisms, "*There are only two ways to live your life. One is as though nothing is a miracle. The other is as though everything is a miracle.*" Otherwise:

- The totality of our being is derived only from the material world; thus all can be explained by material processes. This world-view is sometimes termed "reductionist materialism."
- There is something else inherent in the phenomena of life beyond the material – the spiritual, emotional, the ineffable. This world-view is sometimes termed "Idealism."

At the dawn of civilization, almost everything was explained on a spiritual-mythical level. The world and humans were a total mystery, forever in the hands and whims of the gods. In time, we are explaining more and more, while the religious, spiritual and ineffable are left to occupy other corners of our being. Still, while our understanding improves, the ineffable part of our lives, be it religion, art or mystical experiences and life's irrationality, are fundamental to our being. Those spiritual experiences and mythologies are central to the human condition, but we have no language, except the arts and music perhaps, to describe them. Our experiences teach that human affairs are definitely more complex than just material and reasoning. Much critique has been leveled on the materialistic viewpoint, our dependence on the natural sciences and worldly experiences alone. No doubt, we have made vast progress in the physical sciences, probably the pinnacle of human intellectual achievements. Still, there is much mystery and irrationality in our long story.

If throughout history our main concern was food, we seem to have arrived in the *Age of the Idea*. When the largest taxi company (Uber) owns no cars, when the largest social media company (Facebook) provides no contents, or the largest hospitality company (Airbnb) owns no real estate, it is time to ponder the meaning of it all and what this rise of cognition and complexity means to the future of the social-order.

The purpose of this work is to demonstrate our unique evolutionary path and its cognitive trajectory. Progress has been driven by our ability to operate as a complex and very large cognitive-social structure. This structure invented, for the purpose of its cooperative endeavors, complex languages, abstract conventions, symbols, systems of coercion and systems of make-believe (or shared-believe[4]). These allowed us to operate beyond the real, in imaginary realities, while continuously improving communications between the members of the community and the efficiency of its labor pool. The rise of our cognition and large social structures gave us dominion over the elements; we are continuously shaping the environment to our needs, not otherwise. Soon, software (SW) controlled DNA technologies might accelerate these processes to levels unthinkable until recently, ushering in a possible new era of mental evolution[333], and with them new social, ethical and moral challenges. The work starts with a short discussion on the history of cognition and its evolution, and the definition and evaluation of the "Cognitive-Cloud" (chapter 2). It will then continue to briefly review the history of Historiosophy (or historiography, chapter 3) - the perceptions of human history, future and its nature by a few important thinkers, from the standpoint of its chronology and driving forces. The main body will follow by presenting various hypotheses for the forces that drive the social structure and what we call progress, substantiating the claims for our model of rising cognition and complexity by following certain progress made in the arts, music, politics, economy, social order and the sciences (chapters 4, 5, 6).

People who write history are much better at predicting the past than the future. This work shall mostly focus on historical analysis.

I have borrowed from many and am indebted to them all.

Bar-Giora Goldberg

San-Diego, CA

2. INTRODUCTION

"The past is a foreign country; they do things differently there."

L.P. Hartley

The world as we know it is not far from the Platonic model (matter & form). There is a reality out there (matter), but the world is also our idea (form). We alone live in a homo-centric universe; monkeys, dogs or microbes live in a completely different one. Language, religion, nationality or art, are unique to us because our mind is so unique. Our brain is situated inside a quiet chamber, an odorless dark box. This organ, beyond managing our bodily functions, also receives information from our sensors and via elusive cognitive-processing builds its own world, the one we envision. From the sensory information, influenced by the social order, with the aid of our history and abstract thinking, a whole world is born and made up of civilization, traditions, mythologies, the material universe, science, art, math, music, religion, the social order and our world-view. This is mostly possible because of all our gifts, the one that shines brightest is our language – the expression of our cognitive capacity and the cognitive "instrument". Because of our ability to express ourselves intricately and communicate in such a rich manner and thus influence others, store information and conceive ideas and beliefs, we had the ability to create large communities and create a cognitive world-view; this cognitive capacity gave us dominion over the earth.

Our civilization is about 10,000 years old; half of this time was dedicated to the Neolithic revolution, the end of which earned us cities - congregation in large numbers, agro-technology, animal husbandry, a certain civic behavioral code and writing. Thereafter, our mental evolution within the congregation accelerated enormously and brought us to the threshold of knowledge. We developed a moral code, acquired good models for the evolution of the universe and living matter and generated an immense body of science and art. We have a rudimentary understanding of the chemistry of our genetics and developed the concepts of Right-of-Man and Civic Liberties. Our artistic expressions are phenomenal and of great variety. Our achievements are immense, but one field, related to our consciousness, the mind and the interaction of the mind with the physical world, is still lacking. All we can say is that consciousness seems to be a feature of life, but we cannot explain what it is or how it emerged. We are now approaching a new cognitive threshold, the result of our technology and thinking machines. We are ready to pass into other unknowns of immense complexity in all our faculties; we might have the tools to play with the very building blocks of Life via genetic manipulations[333]. Artificial Intelligence (AI) experts aspire to solve the matter of intelligence and create machines of impressive functionality that behaves like "thinking", but machines do not think like us. Machines perform functions, algorithms; they do not know, they have no consciousness, emotions or morality. They might beat us in Chess, but they know not that they play Chess. There is a difference. And yet, it seems that a certain "intelligence", not consciousness, is emerging from silicon, that is not carbon based.

However, we are still ignorant; life and the universe continue to be a great puzzle. The phenomena of life continue to amaze us as we learn more; and with technology come risks. We still lack self-understanding of motives that drive humanity, sometimes to the threshold of self-annihilation. On the threshold of the greatest achievements, we still face hatred, fanaticism and other primeval, beastly risks.

THE COGNITIVE-CLOUD

Ideas, even more than know-how, inventions or discoveries are the engine of our cognitive evolution. Ideas require a language. Of the many differences between man and beast, the most fundamental is expressed in our highly developed language. We have passed many critical evolutionary thresholds: upright mobility, modified our skin for perspiration, evolved saliva that can digest starch, developed tools and grew a very large brain, among many others. However, the evolution of our language is singular and gave us our current dominant position and the capacity to achieve our intellectual, social and artistic expressions. The wealth of words and complex syntax enabled our species to express, record, communicate and congregate in large groups. Thus, we create social orders, mythologies, shared conventions and specialized in communications; these help us in sharing and spreading knowledge, understanding and abstract thinking. Abstraction is just one of the attributes of our high language, one allowing us to venture into the cognitive universe and create a sense of time and experience, far more than just the physical elements we share with our surroundings. Other creatures live mostly in the material world alone and they survive, while we are here to understand, to experience, to model, to change the world. Humans actually live in two universes, the real material world and the universe of our invention, our mythologies, imagination and beliefs - what we have termed the Cognitive-Cloud. For the purpose of this work, the "Cognitive-Cloud" is rather an allegorical term for a hyper-reality where the repository of our systems of beliefs, myths, memories, intellect, knowledge, religions and conventions reside. This Cloud is continually evolving and changing with our knowledge, ideas and the spirit of the time (*Zeitgeist*). The creation of the Cognitive-Cloud, which allows us abstract thinking beyond reality, is possible only because we can cooperate and communicate in very large ensembles and enjoy a fruitful combined imagination due to our lingual skills. The creation of such hyper-realities, the make-believe worlds and the symbolically oriented world-view, are essential to human society. The Cognitive-Cloud is a system always in flux, always changing and adapting. Change however is difficult; imagine 2000 years of the best minds looking at the Greek model of planet orbiting in perfect circles, at constant speed, in the face of contradicting data. Even Galileo refused to follow Kepler because Kepler's geometry was so "unattractive". Still, contradiction and critic are the fuel of our evolutionary cognition. Every opinion or thought, scientific or artistic, is subject to review, critic and opposition; dialectic, sometimes critic, is the central force of our intellectual progress. And we gained the sense of time. We do not live only in the now. Our long history is loaded with various evolutionary achievements that separate us from other animals, among them are bigger brains, walking upright, thus freeing the hands, and the structure of our dexterous hands, which allow us to use tools extensively. The domestication of fire, plants and animals, were critical to our ascent as was our ability to congregate. Thus, the bigger brain defeated its cost of very high energy consumption and a heavy load, carried high above the ground (the upright position also cost us in speed and muscle power); eventually, we evolved to become a species that specialized in Knowledge, Reasoning and Communication, otherwise Information. As we developed a complex social order and acquired the eventual ability to record, first in speech, some 70-100K years ago, then writing, our ancestors evolved to dominate the earth. Our language is also the most fundamental expression of our Cognition. Many other species use lower languages to exchange information (warning, territorial marking, mating rituals, etc...) by sound, smell, gesture or visuals, but humans are distinct. Our language is different, it transcends corporeality; we can imagine far beyond the real world. Speech is the fundamental property of language no doubt, but writing was the instrument that enabled the extra step - the extension of our memory, recording capacity and eventual artistic expressions and education - the spreading of knowledge. Then came the print, one of our greatest cognitive revolutions. Our memory is immense and complex, societies can somehow run without extensive writing system - some large South-American Empires had very primitive writing. Without a recording system, something was amiss; societies without writing could not compete with the "writers". When they came in contact with the literate world, they were quickly overwhelmed. Consequently, and in time, we have developed other hyper-languages, be it math, artistic expressions, music or computing. Math, the abstract invention of reasoning, became the language we attribute to nature and our tool for expression of nature's laws. Other languages became avenues for expressing human emotions that the spoken language could not express (art).

About 10,000 years ago, humans started to congregate in small settlements, mainly in the area of the Middle East and the Yellow river basin in China. The Agricultural revolution was underway. With bigger settlements, humans came close to the foundation of what we call "civilization," a social-order that requires, as a minimum: a larger community/town, high languages, some socio-political organization and a ceremonial code. These societies were ready to take off, their advantages - at least in social efficiencies, reproduction, protection and food production - over the hunter-gatherer soon showed. However, the real breakthrough, the ability to grow the communities to substantial numbers with a strict social order, happened around the invention of writing, some 5500 years ago. The tools to organize sizable societies run by code-of-laws, ruling order, social structure (classes), accounting (keeping records), tax collection and ritualistic mythologies was already available and ready to be utilized.

INVENTION OF WRITING

What drove humans to write? Writing was not even seen as a blessing by all. Socrates thought that the right way to communicate was via a dialog; consequently he did not write; but on this, like so many other issues, Socrates was wrong. Writing was a unique evolutionary step because it allowed humans, for the first time in all of history, to record and store data outside of their brain memory and send written messages, thus, shorten distances and improving communications. There are certain types of data that fits our brain-memory well, while others (like number records) do not and require external storage mechanisms. Moreover, writing allowed the singularly "brilliant brains" that statistically existed in the community, to make advancements and leave their legacy for the community and the following generations, beyond the personal contact of teaching. Once one person records an idea, a method, a piece of art or a discovery, the whole community can learn it forever! A ten-year-old child need not be as smart as Archimedes, to comprehend and understand his teachings. This represents an immense lever in the evolution of a social order and the accumulation of knowledge and understanding. Writing is more than just a method of recording, but rather a method for thinking, creating and organizing. The accelerated rate of our cognitive advancement after writing is clear. We have fantastic memory capacities - certain animals record their whole geography and can navigate immense distances, but many social functions: counting, storage, number crunching, and cataloging are tough. With writing, we overcame this difficulty and information could be stored and propagated quickly across the community and not mainly from parents to offspring (as animals do). Through writing, memory became a shared human commodity and the amount of recorded data exploded in size and quality. Initially, written letters were pictographic by nature, and evolved into wedge-shaped lettering called "cuneiforms," but the number of symbols gradually grew into a vast alphabet. A quick cognitive evolution transformed writing into phonetic-syllabic, a much more efficient system of writing, just 3500 years old, and then alphabetic, similar to the lettering system we use today. The load on our memory shrank immensely, as letters went from thousands to a few dozens. Many more individuals became literate in comparison to few scribes; when the raw number users increase, the probabilities of creating extra talent or genius improve. Today, our cognitive progress rate is so high that the PC or WEB revolutions, happened in less than a generation and their spread is practically immediate! The mechanisms for propagating information improved exponentially via electronic media and the Web.

Records of storage management by accountants are already apparent in the Sumerian civilization more than 5000 years ago. Accounting records are not data our brain can store efficiently but are absolutely necessary for inventory control and the management of large databases, as in a city with thousands. These records are marked on clay and are abundantly available in museums. Early text of literary contents appeared in the 24th century BCE (Before the Common Era). A code of law, the concept and method that organize human society to this day, appeared around 1800 BCE (Hammurabi), but such codes may have existed even earlier. With the invention of the Alphabet, great masterpieces of literature and mythology, like the Bible, Homer, or the Eastern mythologies, appeared in languages we command today. The rate of the development of the expressive written language (in the phonetic alphabet) borders on the impossible, even if most of these masterpieces (Gilgamesh, Homer, Bible) were records from mythology, carried long before, by memory in folklore stories. While most members of these early societies were not literate, it seems that the social order was already capable of creating and appreciating such great masterpieces. The poetic, psychological, lingual and descriptive power of those works stand at the zenith of human intellectual achievement. Thus, it is fair to assume that the intellectual capacity of these people, as individuals, was not less than those of modernity. Interestingly enough, the study of language in the past was mostly of aesthetics, syntax or style. The science of philology was only born late in the Renaissance and the study of the essence and lingual origins started only one hundred years ago.

THE RISE OF THE TOWN

Nobody knows the exact reasons or origins for the shift from hunters to settlements at the time and anthropologists and psychologists have debated the issue. It seems natural that human societies were not static, that many forms of congregations were tried over the generations. However, the settlement is so advantageous in comparison to the gatherers (see below) that when it was tried, and it was tried in many places and many times, there was no turning back. The settlement, the village/town, is absolutely the foundation of civilization. Settling also requires certain technologies to liberate the congregation from the constant movement of the gatherers, among them the domestication of animals and plants.

The root of the word civilization (definition: a large enough settled community, under a social order that is capable of writing and producing surplus food supply; some historians add the required erection of architectural monument and domination of its environment) is the Latin *civitas*, a congregation that is large enough to be defined as a town, or village/town. Congregation and settlement have the following advantages:

a.   Somewhat "predictable" food supply.

b.   Allowing a much larger and growing group - strength in numbers.

c.   Bigger groups lead to organization, politics and civilization.

d.   Efficient defense - numbers and wall.

e.   Capacity for fermentation.

f.   Ability to create and accumulate property.

g.   Stability enabled much bigger family.

Some of the disadvantages:

- Male dominated family and society subjugated half of us; women hunter/gatherer were responsible for gathering and were probably more partners and with fewer children. In the settlements, they became more homebound, played 2nd role and produced the larger families or at least many more pregnancies.

- Settling and density increase the risk of propagating disease.

- The emergence of a strict, mostly coercive social order.

- The hunter-gatherer enjoyed a more diverse, healthier diet.

The early cities, with perhaps a thousand souls, transformed itself from hunting-gathering to settling and developing agro-technology. Soon property and wars over the land ensued, the origin of agricultural society. The process was possible because humans learned, specifically in river-valleys, to produce excess food by domesticating certain grains, cereals and animals and planning and storing this excess for future distribution in times of need. This could be done only with a sufficient social size (hunter-gatherer society consisted of small groups, less than 200) that required the emergence of a social order. This social order, when structured, enabled a large group to cooperate efficiently, divide work, provide some protection and manage this structure in a reasonable social manner. The social structure immediately required organization and a social hierarchy of sorts. The social ladder, classes in later days, was born and solidified. The creation of a stratified society - a class of warriors, leaders, administrators and workers - is a complex process, conditioning and coercion being its main forces.

The small towns that evolved some 9,000 years ago (like Jericho) did not develop to a large size. They consisted of about 1000 souls and evolved slowly until the time of the invention of writing, some 5000 years later. The bigger congregations created social pressure because of the social dimensions and organizational needs. This social involvement, interaction with the many, was shown to create rising cognition (not only in humans), towards bigger brains. We do not have the capacity to socialize with thousands; to do that, other imaginary social-mechanisms (family, tribe, nation) were at work, enabled by our language and conveyed through chatter and writing. The imaginary social structures of such mechanisms (myth, history) usually transcend reality, they enable the magnification of events, leaders, mythologies and religions. The town had to be able to defend itself from the marauding gatherers and supply itself with enough resources for hard times. This was achieved by cultivating and domesticating food and labor resources and by evolving a social structure, which allowed division of labor, control of resources, storage management and strict civil authority. Society became more efficient. Life back then was very violent, with an especially high mortality rate for adult males. The social organization, must have had an interest in the growth, protection and pacification of the population; also the conversion of more hunter-gatherers into its ranks to grow its population. Large congregations develop an appetite for expansion - there is no doubt strength in numbers. In time the cities grew to many thousands. The earliest pyramid in Memphis, a vast project of immense dimensions is estimated at 4,600 years old. It is almost inconceivable that such a structure was planned and managed without records, writings, drawings or a strict social structure (or for that matter, the domestication of cereals, animals, or the vast underground mines) with highly disciplined labor management and workforce; maybe already a form of slave-labor[64]. The number of workers who built an average pyramid is estimated at up to 100,000. This required very sophisticated organizational skills, material management, mobility, planning and accounting, especially as some materials had to be brought from far away, using complex tools. In the days of Hammurabi (3,800 years ago), the social structure was already set for a large community that was equipped with a written legal code.

VILLAGE, TOWN LEAD TO CIVILIZATION

Certain social forces glue us together, most of them are our inventions. There is obviously a certain sense of responsibility and sharing association that comes with *proximity* - neighbors, friends. But the connection of thousands requires a social imagination: family, tribe, nation, shared history, gods, leadership and mythology, part of our vast "make-believe" systems[4] we created. While neighbors are well known to develop a certain natural affinity due to proximity, the idea of tribe and nation is a fundamental part of the glue of the social order; it is a cognitive concept that transcends reality. On a large scale, such bond of millions (nations) can only be done cognitively. The ideas of nation, of common heritage, shared history and faith, are absolutely mostly in our mind, a concept of "togetherness" - one of our powerful make-beliefs.

The emerging villages that require order, work management and social structure must have applied pressure for the development of a social structure to form a certain civility or minimal code of behavior, both civil and economical. Those were necessary for living together in a big community, both behavior and to set merchandise value. It must have been a catalyst for the further evolution of the language, simply because so many functions and interactions were added to the city, hence the need for expanding terminology - very much like we have today, with the rising of new professions, disciplines and overall complexity of life. This led to the pressures of the evolving social structure and leadership that naturally enjoyed privileges and already sought leisure and glory beyond the day-to-day survival of the hunter. A leisure class, central to civilization, was born. This required, at least for the leadership, a new world-view of life, lifestyle and vision of the future. Even if this group was a small minority, their position in the community was, still is, decisive; they become the model that the social order aspires to emulate and drive its style. Hence leisure, leisure products and their creators, expectations, monuments and lifestyle that support artistic expressions and rituals formalizing the social structure.

Some historians[4, 28] argue that the transition from hunting/gathering to city dwelling was a catastrophic process for most, converting them from "free" wanderers to "slaves." That the "slavery" of labor, social classes and specifically the stratification of the social order into "masters" and "laborers," caused loss of freedoms and misery. This view-point, although humane and with certain reasoning - history, until modernity was a story of untold misery for most - must be questioned, even if just on principle. The hunter/gatherer could not have developed civilizations, which are eventually our destiny. If we could choose today, what would our decision be, settle or wonder? In addition, the "romantic-idealization" of the hunter-gatherer is also coming into question. The lifestyle of "just a few hours of work a day" is questionable as is the "equality" of the members. Evidence emerged that it was not equal after all. Leadership even in small tribe creates privileges, no matter in what social order; even in the animal kingdom. Rousseau's primitive and happy man, before the dawn of civilization, is also very naïve. Fact is that civility and civility alone, our ability to congregate in large numbers and develop civilizations, brought us to where we are. And while most history was miserable for so many, the last few centuries saw a vast improvement in the lot of many and the improvements continue to spread. The importance of the city/town cannot be overstated, it is the only place where civilization could hatch and evolve. The congregation of substantial population centers and the rise of the Cognitive-Cloud brought upon us the conveniences and safety of more organized life and eventual civilization. The congregation of a larger community forces an increased pressure on its organization towards more complexity, more diversity and more order. A certain level of work division, a rudimentary set of rules of civility, a formation of political hierarchy - its early version could have been already in early existence for the hunters - and even rudimentary hygiene rules, must have intensified. Large congregations without hygiene and allocation of "restrooms" facilities, sometimes outside the community (some mammals do it naturally), was impossible due to the quick spread of diseases. The interaction between so many settlers required a much higher level of communication and social interaction than for hunter-gatherers. It also required an increase in vocabulary and the refinement of language, thus a more complex brain. Where would we be today as hunter/gatherers? There are still few nomad tribes left and nobody would trade places with them! Increased complexity is the fuel of reasoning, problem-solving, critic and higher Cognition. Urbanization is one of the major drivers for increased complexity. We were driven out of Eden - the allegorical "enjoy life by doing nothing"; thank God for that. The process of "general urbanization" (today, in the developed societies, some 65-70% live in large cities) was actually slow, gradual; most of humanity did not reside in large urban centers until recently. For example, during the American Revolution, most Americans resided in villages, even if antiquity already had its large population centers, such as Babylon, Rome, Byzantium or Cordoba. These were the seats of government that managed the Empires, its brain trust, commercial and cultural center. In the beginning of the 20th century, just a century back, most people of the world still worked the land and resided in villages. However, the large city was indeed where progress was made in learning, organization, art, science and civilization. Knowledge became available to many through the formalized educational system that started in cities and eventually propagated to the land. The continuous urbanization of humanity is now a historical fact that is quickly intensifying. In the next 50 years, some billion people in Southeast Asia will continue to migrate from villages into the many new megalopolises that are on the drawing board today. Pericles, the famous 5th century BCE mayor of Athens observed that "*all good things flow into the city;*" even if only allegorically, it expresses a great truth for the evolution of civilization.

There is no doubt that the "Cognitive Cloud" was initiated in the town/city, where the exchange of ideas and the challenges that the community creates must be sorted out, discussed, resolved and propagated.

RELIGION

We seem to have a natural longing for belief and worship, but religion is also an acquired traditional discipline, mostly from the family and the community. The same religious Muslim from Cairo would have been Christian or Jewish or Hindu, had she been born to a Christian, Jewish, or Hindu family in Alexandria. We adapt our religions from family and only few ever convert out of their religion or tradition, to adapt a new ritual and faith. We seem to inherently wish to worship, to find something above humanity steeped in the deep past that comes with a rich tradition and ritual. Religion also serves deep social needs and means for congregation. There was sufficient mystery and fear in the early life, to create a yearning for something above humanity, greater than us. Death, disease, the elements and violent natural occurrences, must have created a certain reverence or respect and fear for "superior powers" much even before the age of settlements. The gods provided answers, order and solace. The creation of religions with orderly rituals required both a community and a preserved tradition; rituals are a mechanism of relief but also of conformity. Religious rituals are natural as the voice of the individual drowns in the majority and swept by its conformity. Many scientists speculate that organized religion must have followed the origins of language because its transmittal requires a certain level of symbolism, or higher cognition. Others think that religious rituals must have predated the language. Whatever the age, the invention of the gods was a unifying process for the emerging communities because the mythologies that are inherent in every religion must have already been residing in the Cognitive-Cloud. Those easily propagated throughout the settled community and the crowd that later chose to join it. There are various commonalities in mythologies and there is a good corollary between the various mythologies in the various geographies, either from copying, influence or common human emotional drivers. For example, the mythology of the Bible can be found in other earlier Mesopotamian sources. The "real world" was as difficult to comprehend then as it is today. The social structure required an imagined world, a hyper-reality for its co-existence. The myths, the religions, and the common beliefs and conventions of a forming society had to be erected, an imagined reality had to emerge. Those beliefs alleviated fears and fostered cohesion that provides security, confidence; these acted to cement the social structure and form it. It provided solace, hope, and promise, even a possibility of meeting the dead in the afterlife. These beliefs were powerful beyond our comprehension; readiness to self-sacrifice was sometimes seen as abiding the will of the gods for the service of the self and the community.

A social structure of the many, without personal acquaintance, requires a common system of beliefs, mutual trust, civility, structure and common interests. The myth created a common denominator, a sense of belonging to something greater. Such order must also be based on certain fundamental morality, the natural law of group self-preservation. Murder and betrayal were always the greatest offences. The Bible provides Sodom and Gomorrah as an allegorical society lacking morality; these communities were destined for destruction or otherwise, punished by the gods.

Many of our shared beliefs—religion, nationality, mythology, are genuine, at the core of the social order; they are also more perceived than real, they resided in the imagination of the folks. They are the product and fashion of the physical and cognitive needs of the specific shared community. Humans are born with comparatively little instinct, the reason humans require such long upbringing and the reason we are so heavily fashioned by our family and civilization. The way we look at the world, from its material features, to the relationship we hold to this reality, to our people or to others, depends very much on our family background, education, the Cognitive-Cloud we share. This characteristic, so individual to our community, is also one of the fundamental reasons for world conflicts and the lack of understanding between civilizations or traditions[6]. People from different civilizations, religions or languages live in different universes, hence the difficulties.

OTHER LANGUAGES, THE ARTS

During our evolution of the last 100,000 years, the human experience started to develop other languages in matters related to economy (counting), aesthetics and emotions (arts) and science (mathematics). We developed a need for expressing what cannot be expressed in words. Specifically, in the visual arts, inspired by the need for religious and emotional devotions and then, in theater and music, new ways to express and reflect our emotions. Expressions like lullabies, singing or prayers (ritual) emerged, as did paintings, specifically on cave walls or carving on stones (both figures and early jewelry). It is hard to speculate the materialistic value of aesthetics for an emerging species, but we have ample evidence that the visual arts - cave paintings existed 30,000-60,000 years ago, sculpture, dance - probably starting with religious rituals, existed even before the establishment of steady settlements. From the Darwinian standpoint, these must have had a survival value. Alas, our aesthetic needs and expressions might pose a challenge over the modern technological postulate that *"we are a bunch of algorithms."* One suspect that we are more and that human irrationality and spiritually are windows into other domains not yet fully understood. Many of our emotions cannot be expressed by words or reason. The arts became supplementary languages. The codification of these languages - colors, writing style, spatial configurations and written music - appeared just a few millennia after the invention of the lettering systems. Musical notations, maybe the latest language for the most abstract artistic expressions of the human intellect, came even later.

THE LAW

As the community increased in size, a more efficient political, social and moral structure was necessary to hold it together. This social process led to the formulating of a code of Law, the organization and arbitration of social cohesion. One of the first written codes of Law, Hammurabi's, was mainly concerned with material (economy) exchange and social infractions. The Law was written in stone or clay and acted on a stratified social order. It became, until this day, the foundation of every social order. Our law is so central that US presidents, during their inaugurations swear, or affirm that they *"will to the best of my Ability, preserve, protect and defend the Constitution of the United States."*

When the Mosaic Law appeared, some 3,000 years ago, it was already within a religious framework. The Law was established within a religious book and God was its ultimate authority, Lawmaker (or Lawgiver) and its last arbiter. Satisfying God and obeying His commands became life's purpose. God took possession of life's centrality for millennia. Of the Ten Commandments, the first three are dedicated to the relationship between humans and God, one has social bearings (the Sabbath) and the rest are dedicated to the social structure (Thou shall not murder, etc...). The Biblical Law has been broad in its scope, covering life's essential issues. The Pentateuch is as much a law book as it is a chronicles, written down around the middle of the first millennium BCE when the Jewish scriptures started to codify, around the time Cyrus the Great commissioned the return from Babylon (circa 538 BCE).

About half a millennium later, the Roman code of Law matured and later became the foundation of Western Law. Many historians consider the Roman code to be the crown of the great Roman Empire, which had great political, architectural, military and social achievements. The Roman code of Law (*Corpus Juris Civilis*) was secular, known today as mainly formulated in the age of Justinian, middle 6th century CE (Common Era). This intricate law served as a basis for legal practice throughout Western continental Europe and later in most former colonies of these European nations, including Latin America. English and North American Common Law was also heavily influenced by this canon as well as the Bible. However, many of the social-political principles of the more modern constitutions, like the US, have been influenced by the ideas of the Enlightenment and are secular in nature. The separation of church and state, so central to the US constitution, came later.

Since the Middle Ages, the Canon (religious) Law continued its sharing authority with the Civil law and during the Renaissance, attorneys had to study this law because all documents of Will or Trust, or related to the church (then a rich, powerful land owner of vast political muscle) had to be dealt with inside this law. Canon law is still applicable in many cases (marriage, family, burial, etc.).

PROGRESS THROUGH IMPERIALISM

Political leaders had growing appetites and some of the early cities grew to become empires and empires played a significant role in the development of our histories. Their civilizations were cross-fertilized by their components and they influenced others, especially neighbors and later, conquered lands. The integration of many nationalities and traditions, sometimes via mass exile of the conquered nobility, gave rise to advanced ideas and opened roads to commerce and cross-fertilization. Empires allowed cross-cultural exchange, within and without, providing advantages for commerce: standards, currency, and roads. The Roman Empire was the political marvel of antiquity and perhaps, with the Greek, the whole of western history. Rome was the largest city of its kind, a vast center of authority, commerce, military, law, planning and artistic expression. The Empire, with an estimated population of some 60 million, endured because it was managed so efficiently with a well-organized military and a reasonably meritorious system. Because of the prohibitive distances, the cross-fertilization with the eastern Empires of the time, China for example, was still limited. However, this would be overcome later when transportation technology improved and merchants started to travel wide (Marco Polo or Ibn-Battuta are examples of the 13-14th centuries). On the other hand, the isolation of the south-central American Empires before

1492CE left them without metal tools, metal arms, the wheel and immunization that developed in the Euro-Asian area. Consequently, these impressive Empires fell easily when they came in contact with western invaders. With the integration of large territories, the bureaucracy and protocols of management, the complex economic system, already moving goods and services across lands, then continents, was evolving; consequently, a monetary system (coins) to support it was also evolving and providing the ease of currency economy. Initially the Roman army consisted of citizen-soldiers, but as the Empire grew to eventually contain millions, the army grew to immense dimensions, perhaps close to 500,000. Such an organization had to quickly professionalize and use mercenaries from across the whole Empire. The erection and maintenance of a powerful military, partly using mercenaries to coerce the conquered territories, was in time too expensive; such economic burden, coupled with decadence, consequently caused Empires to fall.

LEADERSHIP

The social order has a pyramidal structure and at the head of the structure there is always one. In time, this one became the King (or Queen), sometimes with super-natural powers. Until today, even the corporate structure is eventually led by one person, the CEO, or in the government, the President or Prime Minister. Pharaoh (or Queen Victoria for that matter) might have emerged from charismatic, powerful origins of dynastic founders, later inherited by their progeny, as a part of a tradition or ritual. Alas, the heredity system could not produce great leadership in perpetuity. The obvious lack of charisma in progeny was a serious challenge to the institution from time immemorial. This was earlier overcome by the power of the nobility who was always interested in the preservation of the social order. In most cases, these upper strata supported the elevation of the monarch to an almost super-human status. In the case of a very weak monarch, there were, not often, changes in leadership. These happened by overthrowing the monarch and replacing him/her by another member of the family or by a new noble family in a "court coup d'etat." Interestingly enough, the concept of the King's person and position were already separated during ancient times; the monarch was divine as was his position. This brilliant cognitive advance, separating the Monarchy from the individual King, led to the concept of *the King is dead, long live the King*.[24]" Hence, the monarchy is eternal even if the person of the King is temporal. In time, the hereditary position of the king weakened towards a chosen leader. In modernity, the monarchy is a traditional, ritualistic body lacking political authority.

MODERNITY: A COGNITIVE-DRIVEN SOCIETY

Some components of the paradigmatic cognitive progress, since the end of the Middle Ages and the rise of modernity, can be affirmed herein:

1. Religion and dogma lost its political and scientific grip. As a consequence, after a long struggle, human Cognition was given, in certain civilizations, the freedom to soar. Cognition, ambition and acumen started to replace birthright and tradition.

2. The affairs of the state run for the benefit of majority, not just a small privileged minority. The position of the dynastic monarch/ruler and the controlling apparatus around them started to waver, leading to social upheaval and the resurrection of the Republic and Democracy. The concept of "The Rights of Man" was born. The absolute monarch was replaced by a constitutional one or mostly by Republics.

3. Science and technology raced forward at a break-neck pace. The scientific revolution is our greatest achievement, but also one that presents high risk because some of the means we developed can also destroy.

4. Scientific concepts have become very abstract and deal with probabilities, rather than certainties. The world models we build are complex beyond the understanding of the majority and this complexity continues to rise.

5. Artistic expression that evolved first towards heavenly beauty to serve nobility, democratized towards humanity, abstraction and complex structure. The artist became central to the art.

6. Universal education was preached and supported. Education became one of the fundamentals of government responsibilities.

Perhaps the greatest modern leap of the Cognitive-Cloud happened in the west, during the Enlightenment (17-18th century). Aristotelian-Scholastics was replaced by the new methods that looked for knowledge in the natural world and abstract thinking. Descartes found a way to turn geometry (literally meaning "measuring the earth") into abstract algebraic expressions in his Analytical

Geometry. Experimentation and the behavior of the natural world, not scriptures, became the data upon which the mind acted. Empiricism was replacing traditional, orthodox thinking of the church. The Bible contains much wisdom, but not all knowledge. The search for the behavior of the natural-world had to be looked for in the working of nature. This is how Voltaire[165] described it allegorically, "*Inoculation was not born in the mind of a brilliant philosopher; rather the masters of the eastern harem noticed that by exposing the young women to light cases of small-pox, they can provide a lasting protection and women without scars fetched a better price. The English ambassador noticed and in England the theory was tested and verified. It took France forty years to adopt the procedure because the theology faculty objected, for this constituted "intervention in the divine order" and the medical faculty forbade the procedure because 'the Hippocratic oath forbade doing harm.'*"

The consequences of Empiricism were revolutionary and world-changing. While Luther challenged the authority of Rome and changed religious rituals, the philosophers of the Enlightenment challenged the authority of the Bible in matters that were not religious. Our scientific and technological advances are the consequence of this new world-view. The concept of natural data introduced skepticism, instead of absolute confidence; skepticism (or criticism) became the foundation of modern science and eventual progress. It was also obvious to the Enlightenment philosophers (John Locke for example) that our knowledge is limited, specifically because it is derived from natural occurrence and analyzed by a limited human mind. Critique and better observation of nature became the directive method. Consequently, all previous knowledge came under scrutiny, everything had to be learned and tested again. The prerogative of the eternal institutions, churches, started to be suspect. So was their authority, as new data was forcing new models (Brahe-Kepler-Galileo-Newton) not found in old books or the teachings of ancient sages. It is hard for us to imagine the momentous revolution this caused in western thought simply because we are now living within the new paradigm.

To many, our coupling to the world looks mysterious; our senses, our functionality, the arts and sciences all seem to fit perfectly a complex world. And then, math that is supposed to be the invention of our mind, can describe and predict the behavior of the world so well. How can this be? However, we are not some outside observers, we act from within. We are "of the world", indeed a product of the world. All the matter we see around, including our bodies, has been created out there, sometimes in processes that took billions of years, in far away galaxies. And the processes that fashion this matter to become our body and mind, they are also all natural processes. When viewed this way we become part of the universe and therefore an extension of its being and therefore fit so well. The exceptions could be our morality that demand behavior that seems unnatural, definitely not Darwinian in the "struggle for survival" fashion that we see around us. Maybe this secret will be revealed too one day.

MAKE-BELIEVE

"The King is Dead, Long Live the King." We live within a vast system of make-believes[4]. Civilization is impossible, maybe incomprehensible without these make-believe illusions (such as money, religion, social order, nationality, authority, mythology, tradition and codes of behavior). It is essential we believe in central ideas, even if most of them are only the products of our minds and fruitful imaginations. And as we progress, we continue to move deeper into the cognitive universe and away from reality. With the evolution of history in modernity and the increase in social complexity, our world-view has become more and more attached to the fabrications of the Cognitive-Cloud and the symbolic world-view. The concept of ruling by the direct spoken word, which seems natural in modernity, is actually only a recent phenomenon. Only in the last century, when modern media started to afford mass distribution, did leaders understand that the substantiation of their authority before a nation of tens of millions could only be achieved by words - the ultimate transformation of politics into the Cognitive sphere. Before modernity, the word was propagated to some extent via messengers, but more importantly by daily interaction, gossip, chatter. Today, the distribution of the word is instant to millions via technology, we have devised marketing and political propaganda, sometimes manipulations, that are possible on a vast scale. Political races are performed on media platforms, with tens of millions listening (TV, radio, web) and participating, in messaging, town-hall meetings or social media feedback. Some linguists speculate that messaging and social media are actually creating a new version of the language as well. Some of it is understood only by the participants that use the tools of social media (messaging uses many abbreviations not available before, like SMI, SMIM, LOL, etc.). Today, our society is ruled by Cognitive means, be it money (the standard of value that is only a symbol, having no value itself), symbols, words (media) and religions (many of our economic, social models are also somewhat "religions"). Our arts and sciences are also expressed in symbols; math and therefore the physical sciences are ruled by symbols and abstractions. Some of the modern sciences lack any intuitive quality and can be understood only thru their mathematical expressions. All modern art is practically symbol and abstraction.

PLACEBO

Another demonstration of the effect the brain has on our perception is the Placebo-effect - an inert preparation or prescription having no therapeutic value, prescribed to effect the mental condition of the patient and thus, his/her overall health. While the Placebo is known to be neutral, the effect we find on the treated condition can be immense, because of the power of our perception. There are cases in which 35% of the treated with Placebo find significant relief, not only for medications, even for certain medical operations. Placebo has been proven to have significant affect on a wide range of medical conditions. So powerful is the effect that modern pharmacology requires testing all new medications to be compared to the Placebo and to prove that they are significantly superior. New explanations exist for brain function and chemistry but for us, the point is the power of Suggestion, sometime Auto-suggestion, to affect our world-view, feelings, pain, health and view of the world. Because of ethical issues, Placebo is used only in research and not as a treatment.

PROMISES AND RISKS

Republics and Democracies started to offer, at least in principle, states that serve the majority and equal opportunities to all. A dream of meritocracy, rejecting the class and "noble birth," social order became viable to the majority. The gene pool for Cognitive potential grew immensely, from the privileged few to the many, on its way to majority participation via education and opportunities. This is a key point, because Darwinism operates on the individual, but human society is a social structure and its Cognitive-Cloud operates on the aggregate order. History shows that great talent emerges equally from all social strata. This social force, our talents, so intangible yet so central to our being, is the core energy of modern progress; modern progress is predicated on the democratization of knowledge. The fast political-techno evolution of the last half millennium was possible because the Cognitive-Cloud, now powered by a more significant part of the population, could advance much faster than the Darwinian process of slow genetic change allows. The process of knowledge building is directed and driven by intelligence and reason, its evolutionary path is swift. When more are exposed to knowledge, the probability of rising talents improves.

While the natural world with its immense balance, convergence, symmetry, is also driven to disorder (rising Entropy), humanity acts in an opposite manner. We are "correcting" nature. Nature is oblivious, indifferent to pain, cruel, unjust, and follows the power of the muscle and the luck of the draw; we are not! Civilization is really an "anti-natural" force, one based on **ordering**, compassion, morality and good-will. This might seem a contradiction, but is an exciting concept, because civilization, the better-angel of our being, evolved specifically as anti-Darwinian. Darwinism is the individual struggle, while Civilization is about the communal organization to support the majority. The essence of Civilization is morality, compassion, helping the poor and the sick and humanity; these concepts are unknown to Darwinism where the weak is eliminated. Indeed, when science was applied to the extreme in the form of Social Darwinism, the results were monstrous. The essence of true Civilization is otherwise.

Our artistic expressions progressed in a similar manner of increased abstraction. From the ideal of creating art-imitating nature, we have progressed to abstraction, symbolism and cognition. Music turned inward, the artist became central, as did painting, literature and sculpturing. Art became available to many (actually to all), not just a noble minority, and artists started to create the world-view and artistic tastes not subject to nobility's taste or religion. Abstraction took over and with it a higher level of complexity. The sweet melody or clear line was not sufficient to express a world of growing complexity. Consequently, past conventions have been breached towards a freer mode of expression in all artistic expressions. More cognitive tools had to be employed and these increased the arsenal, the tools available to the artist and with them our expressions.

At the beginning of the 21st century we face a future of great potential, but one pregnant with much peril and risks. Interestingly enough, in the last few decades, we invented new machines, computers of sorts that, unlike the previous mechanical apparatus - engines, cars, planes, mechanical contraptions - are now enabling our intellect. We start to call them computers, "thinking machines" or AI (Artificial Intelligence), and they have the potential to again change everything. These machines "think" unlike us, but could potentially emulate (or complement) our thinking and help regulate a planet growing in complexity. The world today is unthinkable without computers and they continue to penetrate and integrate into our lives. Together with our technology, comes the ability to destroy ourselves, either in wars or via the abuse of the environment. We are violating the environment in many ways; it is not certain that we are taking our responsibilities, as the masters of the Earth, seriously enough.

With all the new technology we devised, emotionally we have not changed. Social risks, emerging religious fanaticism and technological mayhem have increased exponentially as the last century taught us so painfully. Our cognitive powers are significant, but the human affairs is not all reason; our tendency to act on emotions remains both a risk and a promise.

COMPLEXITY

The term is somewhat elusive and even scientists find it difficult to agree on a definition, and overall, many of us believe that "we know complexity when we see it." This is not exactly so,[171] perhaps because there is no total correlation between Complexity and Disorder (Entropy). While entropy has been defined mathematically in statistical terms, the correlation between the two might look more like suggested by Sean Carroll (see ref 171). More popular definitions suggest that *High complexity is achieved in systems that exhibit a mixture of order and disorder (randomness and regularity) and that have a high capacity to generate emergent phenomena.* Emergent phenomena usually require non-linear behavior, like in weather systems or biological models. It seems we are becoming capable of thinking in more complex models. Herbert Simon offered a concise definition that seems to encompass much in a simple fashion: system *Complexity manifest itself in the difficulty to predict its future behavior.*

Thus, we continue to reveal the complexity of the universe and our nature. They seem to be much more complex than we can understand now but our knowledge and complexity continue to evolve exponentially. Complexity is not always beneficial; there are many evolutionary mistakes that led to extinction or reversals. Nature is oblivious to extinction; it is how life is recycled!

Human cognitive complexity is rising for reasons we do not fully understand and do not seem to control the process. We have an insatiable thirst for knowledge, mostly for the purpose of knowledge. Knowledge or information and complexity are basic human needs. And knowledge keeps growing, as we know. We seem to have arrived at a point when we know enough to really understand how little we know, how ignorant we are before the great mysteries.

3. HISTORY AND HISTORIOSOPHY

In God we trust.

Official motto of the United States.

Man is the measure of all things.

Greek philosopher Protagoras.

History writing is never objective, the historians' background and world-view biases, sometimes nationality have always influenced their work or thesis. The methodical study of history, or Historiosophy, was born only in modernity, when the concept of progress, evolution or even historical direction had been adapted. Historians and poets have recorded history and mythology since antiquity, but Historiosophy was mostly the domain of religion then, not a scientific discipline. Protagoras' statement (above) must be astonishing, considering it was written more than 2,500 years ago. In antiquity, the Hebrews and the Greeks stood out for their consciousness of history. For the Hebrews, the past had a significant meaning for their evolution as a civilization and of their relationship with the one God. For the Greeks, the motives were similar except for the religious component. The Greeks searched for reasons, logic and explanations of history and are, therefore, considered to be the Fathers of history.

Thinking has a history too. It is hard to imagine that people thought differently in the past or that they actually think differently across civilizations today. This is one of the reasons for the difficulties and conflicts between civilizations. Across just one hundred generations, human thought has gone through an amazing revolutionary process; eventually in modernity we are challenging every aspect of our thought from the Law to Politics and the source of Intellectual authority. In the meantime, as modernity dawned, thinkers asked questions about the nature of history writing, the driving order of humanity and speculated on the direction of the path we took or might take. The following is a short review of what some original thinkers thought on the matter and how the concept of history continues to evolve along the lines of cognition and rising complexity.

3.1 WHAT IS HISTORY?

"The one duty we owe to history is to rewrite it."

Oscar Wilde

In its most general terms, history was defined as the "story and study of the sum of human collective chronicles" - the story of our annals, the accounts of our past. Since Herodotus, the "father of history," it is much more. In addition to chronicles, we wish to analyze and understand the historical forces, the reasons, perhaps formulate "historical laws," and thus interpretation. Perhaps the first question we should ask about history: is history the story of past events or is it the way we remember and wish to tell it? If it is the latter, then history is not just a bunch of stories-telling or past chronicles; rather History becomes a study, sometimes scientific methodical study, a continuous research, given to various interpretations of how and what we wish to see in the past.

All past cognitive monuments were subject to changes. Scriptures, mythologies or codes of law were constantly edited, changed, added or subtracted and eventually interpreted. While Scriptures were frozen, or rather canonized at a certain time and given a Holy status, other documents, including History, have been constantly and continually researched, edited, explained, celebrated and reinterpreted. We know that history is viewed differently when written in different times or by different people and civilizations. History is always subjective, there is no objective history. What then is History? It becomes immediately evident that the definitions offered herein are too broad for many reasons, as follows:

a. Our collective chronicles (family, tribe, social network, nation or humanity) are too vast and too detailed. Too many events happened and most of them bear no relevance of value for our understanding. As a famous historian noted, *"millions have crossed the Rubicon, only one is remembered."*

b.   Our collective memories are loaded with legends, mythologies, gossip, lies, traditions, and even religion, and these must be sorted out accordingly.

c.   History is not written in a vacuum or neutrality, nor do impartial observers scribe it. People who write history usually bear certain biases, which can be nationalistic, ideological, opinionated or otherwise.

d.   History is created by Historians! This fact might be contested of course, but specifically in modernity, the professionals, the experts, command all areas of knowledge, history too. This does not make History an arbitrary game, but the interpretation by historians is always somewhat personal, not neutral. It should become immediately clear that History "is not out there" to find, like uncovering a statue from the marble stone; rather, it is for every generation to interpret anew. There is no "absolute historical truth" - one history that upon discovery will be eternal; rather history is changing in time, like looking at a landscape from different angles, space and time. As we evolve, history is changing with us, constantly receding into our world-view. History is by its nature a pick-and-choose process and the historian will always gravitate to choosing for his ideology, her world-view.

The process of writing history started with our epics, our mythologies, to tell our past and perceived origins. Some of it came with certain purposes, mostly tribal or mythological (Egyptians, Mesopotamian, Hebrews). The "Father of history," Herodotus, broke with this tradition and formed History as a "scientific" discipline. He wanted, not only to tell the chronicles, but also ask, why did they occur in such a way? He wanted to understand the other side too. Reasoning history then became a science, the methodical explanation of the past, its cause and effect. Herodotus obviously had an ideology, he thought that "free men," like the Greeks, would always be able to defeat the "enslaved," based on the social order he witnessed in Persia. He wrote history from the "Greek angle". The search for a framework for what happened and the influence of our ideology on history - be it national, moral, ideological or universal is a study by itself. In modernity, the expert professionals dominate the field as they do in all fields. Since history is always a matter of discourse, critique is an integral part of this discipline. Historians come with biases and will try to arrange the data to their cause. Just collecting data about the past does not make history and the historian usually comes to the material already biased with a framework that emerged from his studies, teachers, community and cultural biases. This is a central point—the amount of historical data is so vast that a professional can somewhat, sometimes pick what fits their theory to support it. Unfortunately, this has sometimes led to horrific racial, cultural and scientific distortions. In most professional cases, the purpose is a certain genuine coherent theory, as expressed by the individual historian. Consequently, there is no singular history, nor is one history better or more true than another (assuming it was written professionally and with a purpose to be loyal to the facts as the historian sees them), as the endless heated discussions between historians demonstrated.

History writing has a history itself, view the below or the evolution of our biblical interpretation, from the godly authorship to the historical and archeological research that includes both writing style analysis and archeological evidence. It has also been noted that the "victors write history", not much neutrality there. The various historical theories, themselves evolving, are by nature contradictory sometimes (for example, when written from different nationalistic viewpoints). History is, after all, the study of humanity and humanity is not driven by reason alone; and "truth" can be biased. In his seminal book "What is History[3]," the English historian E. H. Carr, opined well why history must be subjective and why, in the end, history is also made by the interpretation of the historians. A classic classical example is the current liberal interpretation of history - as if we can judge people who lived hundreds of years ago according to our current standards. Must we condemn Thomas Jefferson or George Washington as "slave owners" or tear down Robert E. Lee's monuments because he was the brilliant commander of the Confederate Army of Northern Virginia (not the winning side) during the Civil War? Can we judge people's behavior in the past based on our modern world-view?

THE GREAT MAN

The discourse about the centrality of the "Great Person" in history and mythology, will probably never end. Traditionally, history was about the tales and deeds of "great men." These are the powerful personalities, leaders, artists, thinkers, warriors that transformed historical events and thought. The "great man" as historical trailblazer was the thinking from time immemorial and Thomas Carlyle's (1795–1881) book about *The Heroic in History* provides his theoretical baseline for the claim. The opposition, which has mostly developed recently, disputes the theory on the bases that these individuals, while exceptional in their capabilities, were always the result of a long process in which very many participated. If not them, someone else would have risen; thus the process and the many who contributed, are more important than the singular personality. Herbert Spencer (1820–1903) disputed the claim that "history is the history of great men" toward recognition that all these great men, or women, were the result of social conditions; the outcome of a long previous process and eventually the Cognitive-Cloud of their time. For example, Newton was indeed an incomparable genius with immense contribution and influence in physics and math; but Newton's world was the result of very many who came before him, some with larger contributions, others with minor, that helped build the tension of the paradigm to a boiling point. All these, and the Cognitive-Cloud (we know for example that the inverse square-law was pondered by few before Newton and during his times), led to the possibility of sublimation of new science (see later in Hegel) in the person of Newton; and if it were not Newton, others would have found same theories.

Also, until recently, history writing was mostly the privilege of the "Patricians" because it was the leisurely intellectual exercise of those who were interested and could afford it. In modernity, this privilege passed to the academic dons, the majority of modern history writers, mostly emerging from the middle-class. With them the interest in the life of the people grew, not only the tales and gossip of palaces and nobility. History evolves with our world-view and constantly supported by new archeological evidence and new findings, due to modern theories and technology, our ability to accurately date, analyze, decipher and project, using scientific tools.

Oscar Wilde quipped a century ago, "*The one duty we owe History is to rewrite it.*" History is changing in step with our world-view, as do all sciences. In modernity, all sciences are given to the professionals and this was mainly E. H. Carr's point. The professionals in every discipline are so dominant that their influence is almost total. They decide the current paradigms, specifically as the amount of data is mounting and every field of knowledge becomes so vast.

The following short survey will not only point out few major historiosophic theories, but also demonstrates how the process is meandering and accelerating. The rate of change and the abstraction of historical concepts, together with the growing variety of thought and speculations, indicate the explosive process of rising cognitive awareness of the world and its increasing complexity.

3.2 RELIGIOUS INTERPRETATIONS

Religion had a commanding influence on our historical views from time immemorial. Indeed, most of our early histories were written under the religious paradigm. The early religious institutions presented the first coherent written history in mythological fashion; they built complete chronologies that were ancient with peoples and gods and magnificent stories. More people believe in this interpretation than in any other, for most people are religious. Specifically, we can point to the Bible, the most influential book of western civilization that attempted a tale of Creation, Genealogy, Chronology and Morality by the hand of the one true God. This God was initially tribal and then, in later books, more accommodating; and then in the Christian New Testament, became a true universal God. A God who incarnated to suffer and eventually, self-sacrificed for all humanity and specifically invites all humanity to join under the universal Christian tent. The Biblical Creation narrative (told more than once in Genesis) takes but a single chapter to describe the creation of the universe, until the appearance of man. Interestingly, the world is created by divine words, "*And God said…*" a cognitive divine function, God's word. God first created Light, then the Firmament, Earth, Vegetation, the Sun & Moon and the Stars - all these in four days. On the fifth, he created sea creatures and the birds and on the sixth day, the land creatures. Toward the end of the sixth day, God created Man in his image - even if God has no image according to the Jewish religion (and images are strictly forbidden in Judaism and Islam). And then, immediately, he gave man dominion over the earth and all its creatures.

Although there were many other mythologies in other civilizations, this account has been the dominant history that most western people believed in, until very recently. From a vista of more than 2,500 years, even if the document is taken at its face value and not as an allegory, the biblical view is quite astonishing. It points to a moment of creation, chronicles the order of creation in a rather fitting way, from the void to celestial order, then from the lower to higher animals and, eventually, places humans at the top of creation, giving them dominion over the earth, its resources and its creatures. This order fits the Anthropo-centric world-view shared by most of us until today, in the religious context. God, the perfect cause and the infinitely good and benevolent creator, gave us the best possible world - a thesis later challenged only by the Enlightenment Deists (18 century). Even now, with all the knowledge we have acquired over the last two millennia, a single "Creation" chapter, from Big Bang to the evolution of humans, would have a similar order of events but use different terminology and time span. Over billions of years, there will be "Big Bang" instead of "Let there be light," and "evolution" instead of "creation;" particles and waves with unknown causes following universal quantum laws, substituting for the "will of God". The appearance of various life forms actually show in the right order. In the following chapters, Adam and Eve disobeyed God's command, tasted the forbidden "fruit of Knowledge," became wise thus responsible, therefore punished; hence disgraced and expelled from the Garden of Eden. The good life in Eden of "fun without work" was condemned to sweat and toil - the hard life. Original sin was born, even if it was discovered by Christianity a millennium after its origination in the biblical narrative. For the purpose of this short exposition, suffice it to note in the biblical account that:

- Man has been created in the image of God (which gives the narrative a moral dimension) and placed at the top of the creation pyramid. Consequently, the medieval world-view ordered the pyramid structure: God, Angels, Man, Animals, Plants, and Inanimate matter.

- The biblical narrative presumes that life has a purpose, even if it is divine and a mystery to us. It ascribes purpose to living the righteous life and obeying God's command. Within the story of creation, the only divine command given to us in Genesis Chapter 1 was "*be fruitful and multiply…*" - a command we managed to obey diligently, now counting more than seven billions, and fast growing.

- We are commanded to the righteous life, a common purpose in all Abrahamic religions. The promise of after-life is a later invention, not a biblical device.

The God, being perfect, created the best world and placed us in it to worship and conduct a moral, god-fearing life. Indeed, the Bible must be read first as a religious book with these specific purposes.

Let us note that traditionally, the Bible was considered divine inspired scriptures, written by holy men (Moses, Samuel, St Paul, etc...); its authenticity beyond doubt. Modern Bible-research is different and is mostly critical. It is based on: a. Studying the text - language, style, interpretation. b. Weaving the Bible into the evolving study of history of the middle East and Mediterranean. c. Archeology. This study is new (about 1.5 centuries), evolving and exciting but sometimes tells very different stories[335] which scientists try to somewhat weave into the biblical story.

3.3 RELIGIOUS HISTORIOSOPHY

"Epicurus' old questions are still unanswered…"

David Hume

The major religions that influence the world today were founded within close time proximity (Mesopotamian, Egyptian, Judaism, Hinduism, Greek mythology). Judaism, the Abrahamic parent of Christianity and Islam, was probably born more than three thousand years ago. Its scriptures started to formalize only after the Babylonian exile—6th century BCE, where much local (Babylon then the great power) mythology influenced the thinking and contents of the first chapters of Genesis and some of its laws. The Hebrew Bible was canonized in the beginning of the 2nd century CE. This is also the estimated time of the writing of the Christian Bible, the New Testament that was canonized first some two centuries later (late 4th century CE). The Greek mythology is also of similar age; Homer is 8th century BCE. The birth of Hinduism and Buddhism is estimated at about 500 BCE. Islam was born in the 7th century CE.

Religious Historiosophy is somewhat simpler than the philosophical because of the presence of God(s) or divinity and the divine plan. While the Greeks created a system of Gods not too interested in our day-by-day existence, the Abrahamic

God is very much concerned with humanity and with every detail of our being. Calvin used to say, *"Not a blade of grass, not a leaf of the tree will move without the will of God."* God is axiomatic in the philosophy of religion, the monument of its mystery and the standard bearer of the moral code. Therefore, the questions of purpose, good and evil or morality, questions that plagued the human intellect from time immemorial, are mostly pointed towards the God; their solutions exist, but forever unknown to us. Why is there evil in the world, or why is it that the wicked are frequently rewarded? This is perhaps the most difficult, most tortured question for all religions, and religious thinkers engaged many "acrobatics" for a mystery with no answer. Jewish prophets already asked these questions; the philosophers of the Enlightenment (17-18th century) started to question the *"what is - is good"* (Alexander Pope, 1688-1744) in the light of so much misery, injustice and natural disasters. Religious philosophy also deals with the mysteries of the ineffable, morality and human behavior, but the centrality of the view with regard to evil is answered by "God's presence;" we simply cannot comprehend the divine plan. Thus we have to submit to reality as the will of God.

Religions also created "purposes" for life's goals, which have to do with goodness, moral behavior and submission to God, in addition to strictly following the ritual. The virtuous life is its own reward or will be rewarded after we pass the short passage (life) into the eternal punishment or bliss of Paradise - the Kingdom of heaven. All Abrahamic religions preach righteousness and specifically morality before God. The statement, *"I am your God"* occurs frequently in the Jewish Bible, *"And that you may remember and do all My commandments … I am the Lord your God"* (Numbers 15:40, 41). God's presence and attention are constant and eternal, he is watching us! In the Jewish tradition, life's purpose beyond the Mitzvot (righteous behavior) is about studying scriptures, the word of God, *"vehagitabo"* – thou shall study (scriptures) day and night.

Epicurus thought otherwise, he is quoted (we have no direct writings from him) as saying, *"God either wishes to take away evil and is unable; or He is able and is unwilling, or He is neither willing nor able, or He is both willing and able. If He is willing and is unable, He is feeble, which is not in accordance with the character of God; if He is able and unwilling, He is envious, which is equally at variance with God; if He is neither willing nor able, He is both envious and feeble, and therefore not God; if He is both willing and able, which alone is suitable to God, from what source then are evils? Or why does He not remove them?"* Epicurus did not develop a new religion, rather a different world-view and lifestyle. If avoiding pain and seeking pleasure (his *Aponia & Ataraxia*) can turn into a religion, then it would be Epicurean. In Hebrew, the word Epicurus is synonymous with "heretic."

The Messianic concept, that of the end-of-days, might have arisen in Judaism (Messiah-King, the anointed one, from the house of David), but became central only later in Christianity. Islam recognizes the concept, but with no central importance. The concept of the Mahdi, the redeemer, does not appear in the Quran.

In Christianity, the focus of worship has shifted toward Love and Redemption in Christ. Judaism and Christianity, two religions with similar roots, are fundamentally different; the term Judeo-Christian is somewhat confusing. The Christian God incarnated in the womb of a woman, was born and suffered like a man, crucified and then achieved divinity. Jesus' Crucifixion and Resurrection are central to the Christian dogma and are the primary focus of the four gospel books. This is almost the opposite of fundamental Judaism, with the abstract one-God and its highest religious commitment already demonstrated by the Patriarch Abraham, who was ready to sacrifice his son to God! Really the total opposite. In Islam, the most iconoclastic religion, the religious focus is on Submission and the Haj (the Pilgrimage). The fundamental elements of Muslim life include: creed, prayer, alms-giving, fasting (during Ramadan), and the Haj - pilgrimage to the holy places.

Religion may also resort to the afterlife as part of life's purposes, as a reward system, or the universal "solution" for injustices during life. However, the afterlife is a later development in all religions. In Christianity, beyond the resurrection of Christ, the concept of human resurrection already appears in the Nicean Creed, early 4th century CE, where Christianity was first canonized in the Roman Empire. By the time of the birth of Islam, the after-life was already ingrained in the human imagination.

In the Hindu religions, reincarnation is a central belief.

Life's purpose is a universal riddle to all religions, but follows a similar scheme, which is to live a righteous life devoted to God's commands. History then, is the unfolding of our goodness or wickedness and God's rewards or punishments, because he has endowed us with intelligence and free will while endlessly watching us.

The western religions believe in an end to history with the coming of a Messiah, forecasted to defeat evil and establish a lasting Kingdom of Justice forever. The vision is beautifully described in Isaiah 2, of peace and justice and God's benevolent presence in human affairs. There are obviously other Messianic interpretations; some of us understand that the figure or concept of the Messiah must always be interpreted only as a **futurist** concept of a hopeful humanity.

In most religions, the significant part of history is already behind us because the truth has been already revealed via prophets or scriptures. The future, the end of days, the Apocalypse or the resurrection are only a matter of interpretation. All religions, specifically through their mystical interpretations, eventually place the heart, the faith, and the mystery, beyond or above Cognition. True belief must be a-priori, unshaken. Questions, even certain doubts, are allowed only after the believers have wholly accepted and confessed to their faith.

Most of humanity declares itself "believing," but religious authority (the church) has been precipitously declining in the west in the last two to three centuries. This is actually what Nietzsche meant when he declared, *"God is Dead,"* that religion lost its centrality, no more able of taking over our lives as it was traditionally. Still, religion is one of the most powerful forces in human affairs. Indeed, in-spite of the historical conflicts, most world religions actually conform to the same fundamental principles.

3.4 GREEK CIVILIZATION

This being the greatest and most influential of western civilizations, the Greeks set the models for most of our cognitive foundations and were the first to be Humanist, placing man at the center of creation and interest. Although the ancient mind could not be expected to ponder some of the modern concepts, the early Greek genius already postulated a universe in a state of constant flux that obeyed math laws (geometry for the Greeks), order, and physical laws. Indeed, if the world is believed to follow a certain order, not just the whim of the gods, we can and should learn this order, learning which the Greeks started to ponder. However, Greek history was provincial, mostly engaged with Greece and its affairs. The universal God and world-view came later.

A mighty exchange developed in regards to the nature of the universe. Permenides (and Plato later) held an eternal, timeless, unchanging universe, subject to the laws of reason (Pythagoras). Indeed, one of the great revolutions the Greeks gave us was the concept of a regulated world (not chaos), one behaving orderly according to natural causes. This led immediately to the belief that the world is knowable! Science was born because if the world is subject to natural laws that are knowable, we can and must know these laws. Early in the 5th century BCE, Heraclitus (and Aristotle later) speculated that the universe is in a constant state of change (flux), also known as *panta rhei,* thus "everything flows," or as the Greeks rephrased it, "*you cannot go down twice to the same river.*" Modern philosophy of science is still struggling with these concepts. We may interpret Heraclitus as the hypothesis of evolutionary, even if the proposition does not specify a definite process; rather the existence of change and dynamics in time, in every element of the universe. The small Greek states also comprehended the importance of personal freedom in politics and gave us the principles of Democracy. Greeks also held the principle of the power of Fate, which they called *Moirai* - the independent power, incarnation of predetermined Destiny, certain fatalism with regard to the sequence of events and the future. See Schopenhauer later.

Herodotus is considered the "father" of history because his method and his inquiries into the nature of events, beyond the narrative, was the first to consider history as a cognitive science thus seeking reason and motives for what has happened in people's character and motives and the unfolding of history. Herodotus and his followers turned history into a methodical, analytic study. Soon Plato asserted similar principles in his writings. In his Timaeus dialogue, he wrote, "*everything comes to be and passes away, but never really is*" - indeed, what is the present but the contact, the instant point between the past and the future? Plato together with Aristotle set the groundwork for all future western philosophy. Plato's Epistemology

(Idealism & his theory of Forms), theory of knowledge, consists of two worlds, the literal that we approach via our senses and the Ideal, which we approach only through our minds. Aristotle was more pragmatic and set in motion the natural sciences, from Physics to Botany. In modernity, we realize how dominant this imagined Platonian world is, the invention of our cognitive thinking about reality. In certain ways, Plato's Idealism is the story of humans' evolution of Cognition. We rely on our mind's models to describe the world as much as we rely on reality. Modern cognitive sciences demonstrate how the brain is modeling and extending our reality; modern science builds mathematical models that sometimes wait decades to be verified (such as the Higgs-Boson particle or the theory of General Relativity) but can sometimes also predict! Our trust in such models is so unshaken that it took fifty years of dedicated, continuous search, to reveal the Higgs particle, at great expense; all this because we are no longer ready to abort the **standard model** (quantum mechanics), the mathematical model of the world.

Aristotle developed a complete world-view on the matter of creation and the flow of time. In his writings, the Prime Mover (God) created the universe because "everything must have a cause," a mover. Therefore, this world must have had a beginning, but no end. To Aristotle, a perfect being cannot be involved with the imperfect world and therefore, God is mostly engaged with his own perfect thinking. Aristotelian logic was later integrated into the Scholastic-Aristotelian system that held sway throughout the Middle Ages. Both Aristotle and Plato were Teleological, they believed that processes (the world for example) are driven by a cause, by a purpose.

Epicurus (341–270 BCE) formed a school that formalized another path to history and the purposes of life. For Epicurus, the purpose of life (and therefore history) was to attain a happy, tranquil life with peace and freedom from fear, living a self-fulfilling life. Therefore, life has a purpose, even if it is but temporal. He postulated pleasure and pain to be the measures of good and evil and death as the end of body and soul. Epicurus believed that the universe is infinite and eternal; he accepted the atomic concept as the basic structure of the universe. The Roman philosopher Lucretius (99–55 BCE), a follower of Epicurus, suggested in his De Rerum Natura[154], the possibility of evolutionary changes as a fundamental nature of the world.

The Greek religion centered on a polytheistic godly hierarchy, but the Gods were not all good or all powerful. They were subject to their own rules and possessed human character, even vices. How else can we imagine them?

3.5 AUGUSTINE/MEDIEVAL ERA

Towards the end of Late Antiquity, more than a millennium after the Bible writing and Greco era, a giant Christian figure emerged in the person of St. Augustine. Augustine (354–430 CE) was born a pagan in North Africa but was later converted to Christianity by Saint Ambrose (387 CE) and, for a millennium, became the authority on matters of religion, philosophy and history in the Christian world. A thousand years after Augustine, when Petrarch wrote his autobiography (the first after Augustine's *Confessions*), it took the form of a dialog with Augustine, at a time when Augustine's grip over western thought started to loosen. Augustine was also one of the first integrators of early Christianity and neo-Plationism.

For Augustine, history was totally providential. He was the bleakest philosopher, but believed in progress, albeit giving little hope to humanity. He was one of the originators of predestined grace, an idea that found much sympathy with Calvin and others a thousand years later. Augustine rejected the literary biblical narrative of creation. He speculated that God created the universe in one instant, but grasped the allegorical nature of the biblical narrative and was ready to leave the matter for the future, when we might know more. Augustine also questioned issues like primary matter, first principle, or the beginning and end of all things. He divided history into six ages, according to the biblical narrative:

1st age – Adam to the Flood

2nd – Flood to Abraham

3rd – Abraham to David

4th – David to the Babylonian exile

5th – The Exile to the birth of Jesus

6th – Jesus to the current time.

Augustine assigned approximately a millennium for every age and expected the imminent coming of the 7th age, which he deemed destined to bring the end of the world when humanity shall come to its eternal rest with God. Eschatology (our final destiny) was one of his theological innovations and concerned the end of time, the last stage and the final judgment. Although Augustine saw history as a continuum, he also thought it comes to an end, a kind of an "Omega (last) Point" that was expanded in the writings of many later philosophers, among them the Jesuit Teilhard de-Chardin[15] (discussed subsequently).

The millennium of the Middle Ages between Augustine and the Humanists witnessed the ascent of the church and a very slow change of world-view, based mainly on Christian dogma (such as Augustine's) in the west. This dogma captured the mind of the west and most history writing was about the lives of saints or monarchic biographies (like Einhard (775–840 CE) about the life of Charlemagne), while Muslim thinkers absorbed and interpreted Aristotle and reintroduced him later to the emerging 12th century Renaissance in the west.

Seven hundred years after Augustine, the mystic monk Joachim of Fiore (1132–1202), said to have been visited by Richard Lion-heart during his visit to Sicily on the way to the crusade (1190 CE), challenged Augustine and produced a new historical timeline, based on three religious stages. Alas, the holy man (a saint to some, a heretic to others) made the Apocalypse (his third stage) a staple of western life to this day - nuclear wars in the 1960s, pollution in the 1980s, global climate change (GCC, GW) and environmental catastrophe today.

The Renaissance Humanists, starting with Petrarch (then on to Bracciolini[27], Pico dela Mirandola, Bruni and Albertini) made a decisive break from medieval thinking and criticism was born. They harkened back to the ancient Greco-Roman sources and placed Man, not God, at the center of creation (hence the Humanist moniker). They were mostly highly educated and started to mark history by cultural, not religious, events. Although deeply religious, they grasped that humanity is at the center of the cognitive world, while God helps cast a shadow of authority, morality or social behavior. In addition, they started to question antiquity and old sages, from Galen, Aristotle, or even the Bible, and started to put their faith in experiments, rather than blind belief in the superiority of the past. They speculated that God's work is revealed by his world, with the many contradictions and errors they found in the biblical narrative. Their ideal became the *studia humanitatis*, specifically comprising grammar, writing style, rhetoric, history, poetry, and moral philosophy. The Humanists were obsessed with past writings and set out to find lost ancient texts. Among many other old masterpieces, Ficino (1433–1399 CE) translated Plato into Latin, Pogo Bracciolini rediscovered Lucretius and Petrarch uncovered some of Cicero's letters. The west was slowly waking up from Medieval thought to the Renaissance because the Humanists wanted the past (Greek-Roman) to inspire, but also looked for modern, fresh, original thinking. The Age of Reason started to dawn - an anthropomorphic world-view was in the making as man, not religious dogma, again became the measure of all things. A new life-philosophy was developing, anchored more in fact-finding and data manipulation than in religion and dogma. Fibonacci imported the Arab numerals early in the 13th century, architecture became a study (Alberti, 1404-1472) and the art and science of Perspective - the projection of the three-dimensional world into a two-dimensional plane (demonstrated already by Masaccio (1401-1428), later formulated by Brunelleschi) appeared at the beginning of the 15th century. A hundred years later, Luther would divide the Catholic system and brew a mighty revolution of thought; even the religious ritual would change. Through linguistic analysis, Lorenzo Valla (1407–1457) proved that the "Donation of Constantine" (supposedly a 4th century document giving the Papal States to the Pope) was fraudulent, a forged Roman decree written in the 8th century. Valla was just a symptom of the larger movement - the Humanists started to develop criticism as a method of history writing. A certain method started to appear (Jean Bodin, see ref. 161) towards authenticity, to stop the exaggerating glories or crediting magnificent orations to have occurred during past episodes that could not have happened. Some of the Christian communities started to doubt and critic the authority of the Pope. Print was invented (1453 CE); Copernicus, Brahe, Kepler, Galileo, and Newton would successively discover and found modern science. They propelled the western world into the Age of Reason, even if the old regimes - both Church and monarchy - were still very powerful. In-spite of the magnificence of the early scientific revolution, Humanist thinkers were still somewhat medieval focused; even Newton was still an alchemist and fanatically religious; the church continued to claim ownership of Knowledge. This traditional pattern was about to be challenged with the inquiry into the nature of knowledge and science (Bacon, Descartes). In addition, a significant historical chasm happened due to the Reformation. Doubts emerged over Rome's 1,500-year-old ritual, religious style and authority. Luther even burned his excommunication letter and called the Pope "a Satan". A new historical page dawned in the west, together with the discoveries of a new continents and the rise of the maritime empires of the 16th century. The Reformists challenged the authority of the Pope and declared God personal.

In the beginning of the 17th century, Galileo challenged Aristotelian physics and when one article is questioned, skepticism rises about others, even if the source were the venerable Aristotle, or even the Bible. Soon, Newton would prove that nature behaves according to strict laws, which he could prove mathematically. And if the heaven obeys laws, perhaps we should also seek laws that govern man's behavior. A new history was brewing; the Enlightenment soon arrived.

Four historical luminaries of the post-medieval age made a decisive impression on our view of history. These four included the trio that defines the historical view of Romanticism (Giambattista Vico, 1668–1744; Johann Gottfried von Herder, 1744–1803 and Johann Georg Hamann, 1730–1788) and historian Edward Gibbon. They already saw history as a rationally progressing process that the historian must decipher; even more, they already saw history as a product of civilization and language and Herder even dismissed "universal history" altogether. We can only yearn nostalgically at the Enlightenment, so naïve in its confidence in the power of reason and science. We learned quickly that history behaves otherwise, but the above were crucial for our better understanding of the historical process. The middle of the 19th century started to shift history studying from the "great men" towards the people; Jules Michelet (1798-1874) is an indicative example.

The other great historical luminary of the Enlightenment, whose influence is steady, was Edward Gibbon. Vast in scope and detail, secular, magnificent in writing style, Gibbon was a true son of his age. His voluminous book (*The Decline and Fall of the Roman Empire*) is a vastly researched study that combines all the preceding elements of history writing and serves as a guide to future historical reference. The work is also a frontal attack on Christianity; Gibbon blames the fall of the Empire partly not for deserting Christian morality, but for accepting it. Thus, he claims, the Empire was reduced to (in his terminology) effeminate, apathy and relegation of duties away from the personal, because of Christian morals!

Enlightenment and Romanticist historian pre-modern thinkers were the trailblazers that changed our view on history writing, scope and meaning.

3.6 AMERICAN AND FRENCH REVOLUTIONS

These two revolutions symbolize the change in the western world-view by unshackling the *ancient regime* and towards personal freedom, human rights, and democracy. They comprise the foundation of the first modern state - the USA, the concept of self-rule by elected representatives and a Constitution; the concept of rule by Law, by procedures, not by people, was also established. In-spite of a long political and spiritual tradition, these ideas were fresh, mostly from the revolutionary philosophers of the Enlightenment. The 17th and 18th centuries' age of reason (the Enlightenment), with its vast naval explorations and the establishment of huge overseas empires, was aided by magnificent scientific discoveries, Newton's being first among them. These shifts were followed by the philosophers of Enlightenment (such as Didero, Voltaire, and Rousseau) and the west was set on a path of scientific reasoning and a revolutionary world-view based on reason and critique.

In France, a very long period of stable monarchy (practically since the late 9th century CE) came to a temporary end. Grand monarchs like Louis XIV (1638-1715CE), a King by "Divine Right" and the one daring to state "*L'etat c'est Moi*" (I am the State), became symbols of the past. The 18th century brought upheaval to the French people with economic stagnation and horrible poverty. The French economy continued to modernize and grow during the reigns of Louis XV and XVI, but was plagued by financial mismanagement and scandals that led to ruin[290]. The introduction of mechanization and the development of factories only increased the social gap (as is the case in our own time's Gap). The costly Seven Years' War (1754-1783) and ongoing conflicts with Great Britain over North American territories, which cost the French treasury a fortune, and scandals like the Mississippi Bubble (1718-1720) brought the monarchy to a boiling point. The rise of empires, and specifically "corporate empires" produced an illusion as well as a growing economic gap. In the meantime, at the beginning of the 18th century, rampant capitalism revealed it had its limits (in particular, Scottish financier John Law's pivotal influence on France's affairs in its American colonies). Although

Capitalism might be the most efficient economic system we have devised so far, it also has had its excesses and risks, booms and busts. Proponents of unregulated Capitalism demonstrated the system's ability to destabilize markets by catering to the greed of a few powerful men who would manipulate markets. The capitalistic system fueled the rise of mercantilism and quickly created bubbles that had to burst; they still do. Market bubbles had happened before - the "Tulip mania" speculative bubble (in the 1630s) a century earlier in Holland was a shining example; but these are usually ignored. Therefore, it was not surprising (in hindsight) in the 1700s (or in 2008) that unregulated capitalism showed instability on a global stage as a global integrated economy was forming; it was also a tragedy and ruin for many. When coupled with the rise of the middle class, the ideas of the Enlightenment and a hesitant monarch, it fomented the Revolution. Citizens proclaimed that France was a Republic and overthrew King Louis XVI (he was guillotined in 1793)[290]. The humane albeit idealistic slogans of the revolution can now be found on every public French building, *Liberté, Egalité, Fraternité*. Liberty, Equality, Fraternity - an idealistic dream we continue to struggle with. The feudal system was supposedly swept away and new socio-political ideals, at least in theory, were established.

Thomas Paine published his damning critique of the monarchy (*Common Sense*). The concept of the Bill of Rights was born, the idea that every citizen had civil and property rights. It was a statement of Republic vs. Monarchy, Liberalism vs. Conservatism and Feudalism and Secularism vs. the yoke of the Church. Documents like France's 1789 "*Declaration of the Rights of Man*" established citizens' basic rights and acknowledged them against Despotism, Slavery, and a view towards Democracy.

Few years earlier (1776 CE) the United States, then a young country of some three million inhabitants across the ocean, had thrown off the British monarch's yoke and declared independence. It also declared Liberty and a determination for a classless society. The preamble of the U.S. Declaration of Independence has become one of the iconic, monumental statements of humanity.

"*IN CONGRESS, July 4, 1776. The unanimous Declaration of the thirteen united States of America, ... We hold these truths to be self-evident, that all men are created equal, that they are endowed by their Creator with certain unalienable Rights, that among these are Life, Liberty and the pursuit of Happiness. To secure these rights,*

Governments are instituted among Men, deriving their just powers from the consent of the governed. That whenever any Form of Government becomes destructive of these ends, it is the Right of the People to alter or to abolish it, and to institute new Government, laying its foundation on such principles and organizing its powers in such form, as to them shall seem most likely to effect their Safety and Happiness."

The consequences of the American Revolution and U.S. Constitution were profound; future society of a growing power will be governed and regulated by laws (a regulated elective process) and not by persons (e.g., despotism). They constituted revolutionary human concepts of a new social order. Unlike the Greek democracy, modernity gave us Liberal Representative Democracy, of freedom with compassion and responsibility. Eventually, after a bitter struggle, the US legally abolished slavery and the concept of social responsibility evolved, as the constitution adapts to modernity. A government of limited authority was established on the basis of a certain meritocracy (18th century style). It was a unique event in history, stemming from a unique generation of learned and enlightened leadership.

Europe was not yet ready and even in France, reversal to old monarchy came in the near future. But, the concepts of freedom became carved in the Cognitive-Cloud, never to be erased. No matter how many tyrannies will be thrown our way, we now know better. What should have been evident has been immortalized; people are ready to pay any price for freedom. On the other hand, this new world-order requires a more complex, educated society. The people have to be better educated to make the right choices, the social structure more complex. We are responsible to choosing our leaders and their path! In this category, we have not yet arrived at the promised land. The concept of *"one man one vote"* that came later, comes with responsibilities. The American Declaration of Independence even declared citizen's right to be happy, an absolutely unprecedented assertion in human annals. It solidly inferred that merit and social position must not be based on birthright, but on personal achievements. It is predicated on citizenship that must assume more responsibility, for themselves and for the social order. Many of the common folks did read and learn much (English publishers realized the unusually large size of the U.S. market for their books, they sold more books in the US than in England) and became engaged in the process. This rise in complexity and responsibility has been a conflicted issue that has not yet been resolved. In time, we witness the rise of many democracies around the world, built on the concepts of the Enlightenment and the Rights of the people. There were/are continuously attempts at nationalistic, despotic regimes; the horrors of the 20th century will not be forgotten soon, but overall, the human Cognitive-Cloud has been enriched by concepts of freedom and freedom to choose. In recent years we witness an attempt along national and sometimes cultural fault lines. The UK just declared its impending withdrawal from the EU through Brexit, and other European groups, be they Catalans, Basques, or Lombards, aspire for independent nationhood! Rising modern empires (specifically China) are challenging the democratic ideology altogether and even the capitalistic method of free-market and short term profits, as opposed to the long term "guided-from-above" planning. Even if these ideas were proven more efficient, alas they come at the cost of personal freedoms!

The world today is more peaceful than ever before. When many are empowered, educated, and trusted with opportunities, we increase the size of the talent pool, thus improving the opportunity and probabilities of rising talents. Though not yet a panacea, the French and American revolutions cleared a path for the future, establishing natural rights that perhaps existed only in the Cognitive - Cloud (otherwise, what is the meaning of "unalienable rights"?); consequently these became etched into our laws and world-view.

3.7 HEGELIAN HISTORIOSOPHY

Georg Wilhelm Friedrich Hegel's (1770 - 1831) method and dialectics not only revolutionized historical philosophy, but also paved the way for so many thinkers who followed him, including Karl Marx. Hegel's Historiosophy (he is sometimes described as the "Protestant Aquinas") was spiritual, comprehensive and all-encompassing. For Hegel, history became an evolutionary, logical process that continued forever, fueled by the force of contradictions. And history is eventually the evolution of the universal Spirit that became a science to be reasoned and explained. Conflict is inherent in history, which has a direction and purpose in the sublimation of the Spirit. The dialectics are central to Hegel's world-view: thesis, anti-thesis, and synthesis, which he coupled with the concept that mind, or spirit - **Geist** in German - manifested in an evolving spiral of contradictions and oppositions that ultimately converge and unite without eliminating or reducing either. His fundamental concept of "Zeitgeist," the "spirit of the time," can be interpreted as the "combined consciousness" of the era that was both creating and affected by the "consciousness of the epoch;" thus, a social-intellectual phenomenon, the culture or the intellectual fashion of the time (definitely associated with the concept of the Cognitive-Cloud).

Hegelian History is a continuous process of contradictions based on the refutation and integration of two opposing systems, in a continuous process of resolution by synthesis that never ends. Let us demonstrate the concept with a historical example. At the end of the American Revolutionary War, the thirteen colonies were a loose confederation held together by a certain tradition, the war and the Articles of Confederation (ratified on March, 1781). These articles comprised the first U.S. constitution, which did not yet defined "nation" or "government," but instead carefully stated, *"The said States hereby severally enter into a firm league of friendship with each other, for their common defense, the security of their liberties, and their mutual and general welfare, binding themselves to assist each other, against all force offered to, or attacks made upon them, or any of them, on account of religion, sovereignty, trade, or any other pretense whatever."* Although the articles allowed a common congress, they contained no central executive or judicial authority. Consequently there arose clashing opinions: the Federalists wanted to foster the union (thesis); the anti-Federalists, objected to a powerful central authority and suggested certain modifications for the Articles of Confederation (anti-thesis) that still left the states powerful enough. Eventually, the debate (well demonstrated in The Federalists papers) led to a compromise that the majority could agree on and the Constitution, a compromise between the two forces, with authoritative if moderate at the time central government, was ratified by a majority vote (synthesis) in 1789. The constitutional process was subject to intense debates among legal experts and citizens, and eventually yielded a necessary compromise—the synthesis[119, 300]. The foundation of an authoritative, central, federal government was established. This was by no means the end; the anti-Federalists demanded a Bill of Rights, which after great debate was ratified in 1791. The process of amending the U.S. constitution continues to this day. The constitution continues to be interpreted by opposing opinions and constantly modified (by bringing laws and amendments up for a vote by legal experts and the people). The nature of cognitive progress, always involves opposing forces that eventually contribute to the new synthesis, which soon will be challenged again as the spiral continues.

For Hegel, Christianity was the sublimation of the process, from the primitive religions toward its zenith in the Christ. Later in his career, Hegel wrote in a more abstract, obscure, and sometimes heavy - esoteric style. Consequently, others have interpreted his theories. After his death—Alexander Kojeve's exegesis has proven popular, specifically in the matter of "the end of history." Hegel divided history into several distinct stages, comprising the Oriental, the Persian, the Greek, the Roman, the German and the Modern. Each of these civilizations is defined by its relationship to the Geist. From the Oriental, to the Modern stage, this relationship with the Spirit has expanded and become more subjective. Each civilization grew up from a dialectical clash with the next. The result of this dialectical opposition was a new relationship with the Geist that was more complex but had not yet reached the ultimate subjective individuality. This, according to Hegel, will be resolved when the German world and the Catholic Church bring individuals back to a contemplation of the subjective relation to Spirit, while promoting the objective Universal through its ecclesiastical structure.

Writing about understanding history, Hegel maintained that, "*The owl of Minerva spreads its wings only with the falling of dusk;* " otherwise, humanity's wisdom or understanding of history comes at the end of a cycle, (Minerva the Roman goddess of wisdom). Thus, the study of history became the central method of our growing understanding, beyond the physical universe. Hegel also coined the term "*End of History,*" perhaps with Bonaparte - his sublimation of the Geist - in mind. He asserted that history is progressing toward a true completion, a complete unfolding of the Universal, which he calls the "*absolute end of history,*" a concept later interpreted by Kojeve and Fukuyama[5] in political terms. Today, this absolutist maxim, such "end of history" may be difficult to accept (it can be religious, utopian or on the Fukuyama model - descending to democracy and market economy), especially for modern and post-modern thinkers. How can we imagine the end of the cognitive spiral in a world that is, like never before, cognitively so active and dynamic? How can the "end of history" be anything but the idealistic, futuristic dream that was featured in the Omega Point (see below) or similar concepts?

3.8 SCHOPENHAUER'S PESSIMISM

When the Romantic era dawned on artists and intellectuals in the 19th century, many ideals of the Enlightenment were rejected. We already mentioned Herder's rejection of "universal history"[21] and Romantic-era artists started to create new styles and ideals beyond the natural or reasonable. Mary Shelley's Frankenstein's monster or Victor Hugo's Hunchback were new, outer-world creatures, sometimes of malevolent nature. For them and some of us, the Romantics devised a new solution that touched into the spiritual and religious - redemption. It colored their philosophy, view of history and art; other human features were pointed out beyond reason and the artist grew to become a "hero".

Arthur Schopenhauer (1788 - 1860) was a younger contemporary of Hegel and less popular during his time, but ultimately with a significant influence on the history of thought, on philosophers and on the arts. Schopenhauer was born into a privileged family, he studied at the University of Gottingen and subsequently in Berlin. Later, he lectured in Berlin at the same time as Hegel, but to a much smaller audience. When the cholera epidemic erupted in the city, it claimed Hegel; Schopenhauer fled to Frankfurt, survived and led a rather long if lonely life. Schopenhauer developed original ideas that encompass many disciplines, such as music, art, ethics and sexuality - his notoriously misogynistic opinions are well known. He summarized his philosophy in a single influential, rather short and very accessible book, **The World as Will and Idea**[9] (1818-1819). Contrary to Hegel and his Zeitgeist, Schopenhauer chose to focus on the individuals and what drives us. In Schopenhauer's mind, this mystical force - the Will - controls the universe. Consequently, humans are motivated and driven by their own basic desires, or "*Wille zum Leben,*" - the "will to live," which for Schopenhauer, directs and drives all living matter. Nietzsche later expanded the idea into his "Will to Power". This insatiable force, the endlessly hungry Will, the driving force of human desire, is futile, illogical, voracious, malevolent and directionless; by extension, so is all human action in the world and throughout history. Perhaps his most famous aphorism expressed this idea about humanity and the internal forces that operate on us: "*Man can indeed do what he will, but he cannot will what he will*"; a "force" that cannot be diverted or distracted is driving our actions even beyond ourselves. For Schopenhauer, the extreme pessimist and misanthrope, this force is evil and acting illogically, with no purpose, direction or logic, just a driven appetite and ambition. This Will is a malignant, universal, metaphysical force that controls, not only the actions of the individual, but ultimately all observable phenomena. For Schopenhauer, Will is what Kant called the "thing-in-itself," the intuitive knowledge or "knowledge without senses," the original and moving force. Like so many of his contemporary thinkers, Schopenhauer believed that the essence of life is in conflict, struggle (dialectics in action) and that the fundamental nature of the universe is in conflict - somewhat like the third law of Newton's mechanics. Although Hegel could see progress through his process of integration, Schopenhauer maintained a dramatically pessimistic view on world evolution through the struggle of ambitions and the endless conflict of the Will. Consequently, his philosophy contrasts with Hegel's; the Zeitgeist cannot affect our behavior because other, more powerful forces drive us.

Schopenhauer revived a complete philosophy of craving, ambitions, suffering and pain - *"when one observes the cruelty of nature, one can't believe in God"* - that can be relieved only through aesthetic contemplation, of which music is its ultimate expression because of its very cognitive and abstract nature. Thus the aesthetical experience, especially in music, enables a respite from the strife of life, desires and the force of the Will. His views on the arts and specifically on music, were extremely influential (Thomas Mann, Nietzsche, Proust), specifically on the thought and music of Richard Wagner - only through sublimation of the will can we achieve peace and resolution, as epitomized by Wagner's ultimate redemption by self-sacrifice (the cathartic fate of the Wagnerian heroine). Schopenhauer had a decisive influence on many philosophers, artists and scientists. Among them: Nietzsche, Weininger, Wagner, Ibsen, Wittgenstein, Campbell, Shaw and even Einstein's philosophical and artistic views.

3.9 CAPITALISM

"Under capitalism, man exploits man. Under communism, it's just the opposite."

J K Galbright

Capitalism is a system of private ownership, profit, minimal government intervention and opportunity. It has been exercised for long but formulated only during the 18th century, Adam Smith being its prophet. Capitalism initially developed as an economic theory about private ownership of labor and means of production for profit. It later developed into a materialistic world-view of history and eventually, an economic paradigm (perhaps a form of "religion") during the 2nd half of the 20th century. Capitalism preaches an economy managed by free markets, minimal necessary regulations, competition and wage labor cost, private property and a price system. Today, practically all world economies are practicing various forms of capitalism, including Communist China.

The old world was steeped in economic concepts that posited an economy of finite and limited scope, perhaps growing apace with population size. Capitalism proved otherwise, rather, that wealth could grow much faster than population and that the economy is *not* a zero sum game; that wealth can grow to limitless dimensions. It is estimated that the world's wealth has grown by x1,000 times in the last 500 years while population growth was about x10.

Capitalistic theory arose with the beginning of the European overseas Empires and at the dawn of the industrial revolution. Adam Smith, 1723-1790; published his *Wealth Of Nations*[134] in 1776; it became a classical book, especially for economists and political theorists. The concept of growing wealth did not exist in antiquity, wealth was steady or mostly robbed from neighbors. Consequently, the concept of growing wealth, consumerism and the division of labor did not exist, at least not as an economic theory before the 18th century. Although credit always existed, its usage was very limited when compared to modern times. Credit and debt were shown to be critical to economic development and growth. In the old days, credit was a source of much agony, especially when it could not be paid on time (the Merchant of Venice is but one example of predatory "loan-sharks"). Today debt is so prevalent, we even have legal mechanisms to erase debt (bankruptcy) and governments habitually manipulate their debt via instruments like inflation or taxation. Debt was shown to allow business growth and consumerism, both central factors in economic development and growth can grow endlessly without robbing anybody.

The science of Economy, like myriad other scientific disciplines, was not yet born before the 18th century. An economy fueled by entrepreneurs and the majority working folks, as consumers, could simply not be imagined when the wealth of the nation was practically in the hands of hereditary few. During the 16th and 17th centuries, enormous wealth arrived from the Americas and the East; to fund European monarchs' various adventures (for example, Spain in the low countries) the banking system was already mature and the concept of investment had already fueled the maritime Empires, even before an Economics theory had formed. However, the rise of banking, commerce and corporate Empires did not change the ancient thinking about the economy. Adam Smith (and other contemporaries) conjured a few revolutionary ideas stemming from the fruits of their observation and from theoretical considerations. Their efforts birthed the concept of the division of labor. In Adam Smith words "*The division of labor, by reducing every man business to some one simple operation and by making this operation the sole employment of his life necessarily increases very much the dexterity of the worker.*" Two hundred years later, Henry Ford extended the principle with his *production line*, by which work was divided and mechanized along a sequential line of workers and operations. By then, he hoped that not only mechanical parts would be interchangeable (thus, standardize production rather than the slow fitting each part by hand), but also the workers who produced and put them together! It worked.

The concept of consumerism, contrary to the frugal Old World belief that "*thou shalt not waste*" has been shown to be a necessary condition for economic growth. Indeed, the Industrial Revolution enabled mass consumption (by lowering cost and rising wages) and consumption fueled growth. Consumption was placed at the center of capitalism, as was the assumption that the economic pie can and must endlessly grow. Economic growth became the centerpiece of economic success and indeed, until today, no good models for a shrinking economy exist. Businesses must grow to survive and flourish. This has proven to be a blessing but might in the future become a curse. The concept of capitalism is that we can all live better and the economy can continue to grow, practically with no end, particularly as technology enables new machinery, automation and efficiencies. Automation and productivity are already so immense that, for example, in the facility pictures below (Figure 1), just 30 employees produce 21 percent of Iceland's tomatoes, on a 5,000 - square-meter, computerized and fully automated facility. The facility is driven 100% by computers and technology, light is artificial, CO_2 is pumped to expedite growth, water delivery is optimized (water conservation is a mail goal in many such facilities, the Netherlands has a $100B industry of such technology) and every parameter is tightly monitored and controlled by automation.

Figure 1: Fridheimar, Iceland, producing tomatoes

Another concept, which rose during this period, was "*The Invisible Hand - self interest as an optimal economic force*" - Adam Smith's promise of social-benefit of the self-interested individual acting in a free economy. Capitalists are certain that such self-interest is an optimal measure of total efficiency, advising the individual to be free to pursue his/her own interests. Smith promised that such action would result in free markets that would create an economic "optimum". Even more significantly, capitalism was the harbinger of the massive credit system, the true base of modern economy, and with it the rise of the mass-consumption individual, the force of economic growth, rather than the monarch or the political authorities of the past. Credit is so central to capitalism that the U.S. federal government has now accumulated debt of some $20 Trillion (2016), already greater than the nation's GDP. This debt is now growing at a rate of almost a trillion dollars a year with no relief in sight (in the last 10 years, between presidents Obama and Trump, the U.S. federal debt increased by more than $10 Trillions). US total debt stands now at about $80 Trillions. Simple calculation shows that the per-capita national federal debt alone is now $60,000 for every person. This number is almost equal to the average net worth of the American ($70,000 in 2017). Recently, the interest payment on federal debt was on the threshold of default because Congress would not authorize the government to borrow more and this caused serious tremors in the world economy and financial markets. Most economists are not yet alarmed and consider favorably, temporarily growing debt for the benefit of economic growth. Capital has assumed a very complex cognitive interpretation, beyond being an instrument of exchange; financial instruments are also growing and becoming very complex. Capitalism being a system with loose controls, allows also periods of Boom and Bust cycles that might, in the extreme, even collapse of the banking system, as we witnessed in 2008.

Historically, opposition to capitalism arose immediately. Although prophets and idealists had called for social-economic justice since time immemorial, Socialism as a discipline and political movement became evident only during the 19th century. The allure of organized society, with an organized and planned economy, was attractive for the utopians (for example, early socialists like Robert Owen or Saint-Simon) later expanded by Karl Marx into a social revolution theory. They believed that such a system would be more just and efficient. Today, practically the whole intellectual class of the West deems itself "Socialist," mostly for the better social justice the stance promises - more just, more meritorious society, managed by a central government, is attractive intellectually. The current drive towards universal health-care, education or guaranteed income, also known as "Universal Base Income" (UBI), is enticing for those seeking better meritocracy, and perhaps is economically possible. The welfare state is already acting similarly. UBI which provides guaranteed income, whether one is working or not, is now being tried in Finland, soon might be in India too.

Capitalism's overall success during the last 400 years is undeniable and became a modern-day paradigm. For some it suggests a panacea for almost all financial maladies. Needless to say, we have become addicted to the fruits of consumerism, as we hope for eternal economic growth. On the other hand, this economic success, with its polarized wealth distribution, has fueled excesses that threaten our environment and the social system. In modern times we have realized that the economy - a rather vast chaotic system - is more efficient when not organized from the top. Certain amounts of chaos are beneficial (see work by Friedrich Hayek and Tversky-Kahneman[336]). Yet today the free capitalist system is challenged by China's top-down economy, capitalism that is managed from the top. Time will tell.

3.10 MARXISM

The Industrial Revolution gave us engines, cheap cotton, trains, cars, planes and mass consumerism. Its benefits for humanity are countless. It also brought exploitation, tragedy and misery. Suffice it to listen to the testimonies of 6-8 year-old boys and girls, from the mills and factories of Manchester, circa 1830-40, working 15-16 hours a day and with life expectancy below 20 years to understand the Socialist and later Communist movements. The industrial revolution started with rising working class of modernity not yet enjoying labor laws, no working conditions, no children labor law; they were just exposed to what we can do to one another in the name of profit. But it must be admitted that the horrific price they paid paved the path to modernity and much better work, health and wage conditions. Did the low worker of the farm or manor of the past, before the industrial revolution, fare better?

Karl Marx (1818 - 1883) was a German historian, economist and philosopher. The most influential Hegelian that turned Hegel's spiritual "*Weltgeist*" ("world-spirit") into cold Materialism. For Marx, the concept of materialistic-dialectics drives the world and the economy is the driving force of history, rather than Hegelian spirituality. He was a Hegelian adherent, but also turned Hegel's viewpoint on its head. If Hegel saw history as the manifestation of the evolution of Spirit, Marx saw it in the evolution of the economy. He called on philosophers to stop merely interpreting history and start to change it. So he did. Marx was one of the more influential personalities of the 20th century. His investigation into the nature of money (e.g. Capital) and the history of class struggle, led to his formulating Communism, as an alternative to Capitalism. Marx's Historiosophy continues to have a commanding influence on politics, economic theory, history, and thought, in the last century and today. Marxism is still popular in many intellectual circles.

Marx was educated in Germany and influenced by Hegel and Feuerbach, but was exiled (1849) due to his revolutionary political activities. After a short sojourn in Paris he settled in London, where he wrote his monumental work, *Das Kapital*. Marx's ideas about economics and the history of money - labor, capital, markets, and classes are still influential. To Marx, the essence of human history is human's struggle to realize their potential. Being a materialist, Marx rejected the ideas of Romanticism, towards a belief that human history obeys knowable, discoverable laws and history could be treated as an exact science. For Marx, the proletariat has a destiny because labor transforms man's world during the course of his activity and labor is central to Marx's view of history. Thus, the history of society is the history of inventive labor that alters man's outlook, relationships and habits. Among man's inventions is the division of labor, which leads to class struggle, exploitation, and coercion. Drawing from fundamental Hegelian concepts of dialectics, Marx held that human societies progress through class struggle; the conflict between an "ownership class," which controls the wealth and means of production and a "proletariat class," that supplies the labor for production. He deemed Capitalism the "dictatorship of the bourgeoisie," run by the wealthy classes who exploit the poor for their own selfish benefits. He predicted that, like previous socio-economic systems, capitalism produce internal tensions, which would lead to its self-destruction. In Lenin's interpretation, *we will hang the last capitalist by a rope he produced* - and be replaced by a new system he called Socialism. Marx argued that under socialism, society would be governed by the working class in what he called the *"dictatorship of the proletariat,"* the "workers - state" or "workers - democracy." He believed that socialism would eventually give rise to a somewhat universal, stateless and classless society, which he termed Communism, one that would unite humanity. Alas, history showed that Nationalism proved to be a more powerful force. Along with believing in the inevitability of socialism and communism, Marx actively fought for their implementation, arguing that social theorists and underprivileged people alike should carry out organized revolutionary actions to topple capitalism and bring about socio-economic change. Marx expected the revolution to erupt in the developed countries, fueled by the desperation of factory workers and the victims of the industrial revolution, as he saw it. This did not happen; the revolution that broke in Russia, then with very little industrial base, was led not from the bottom, rather by a group of intellectuals, from the educated class.

Marx had little personal charisma or a special aptitude for rhetoric, but he was practical. He wisely forced the Anarchists out of his International (the first international meeting in London in 1864). Marx ignored Nationalism and other emotional forces that proved so powerful during the twentieth century. In reality, during August 1914, French and German workers put on their national uniforms and marched to the trenches to slaughter one another by the millions. There was no workers-brotherhood. For Marx, all of history can be interpreted and forecasted according to materialistic considerations (another mistake) and thus, he rejected religion as *"opium for the masses."* Marx was familiar with Darwin's theory of evolution and adapted it. The Darwin-Marx integrated theory became the hallmark of some thinkers for the following century. It spells a combination of material-evolutionary process that is based on continuous struggle, to be resolved in the Marxian fashion.

Although Marxism is still a favorite ideology, especially in certain intellectual circles, it must be acknowledged that as a social-economical-political system, it has failed. Its two mighty proponents, Russia and China are no longer preaching Marxism to the world and China, while despotic, runs a modified (managed from the top) Capitalist economy.

3.11 DARWINISM

"I have called this principle, by which each slight variation, if useful, is preserved, by the term of Natural Selection."

Charles Darwin

"Speech ended not only the evolution of man, by making it no longer necessary for survival, but also the evolution of animals."

Tom Wolfe[178]

Alfred Russell Wallace (1832-1913), the English naturalist, was the first person to publish a principle of Evolution by natural selection. In a paper he mailed in February 1858 to, of all people, Charles Darwin (1809-1882) from the Malay Archipelago, he spelled the Darwinian ideas as a speculation of the evolutionary process. Darwin submitted the letter to the London Linnean society, however along with his own quickly assembled brief, claiming that the idea had come to him some twenty years earlier. Darwin was the senior and more accomplished scientist at the time and his detailed work on Evolution eventually earned him the primacy. In time, this theory became known as Darwinism and, when later integrated with genetics, as Neo-Darwinism. Darwin's theory was revolutionary and causes controversy to this day. It was the first attempt to describe a natural process that required no divinity, was malleable and based on much field data. Such concept of ongoing process, or adaptation of living matter, a concept for gradual change and evolution, became the successful paradigm of the science of biology and more. There is really no scientific challenge to this paradigm today.

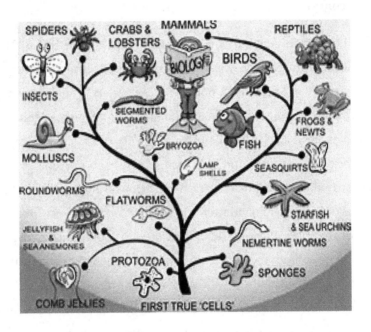

Figure 2: Conceptual tree of life

During the 17th and 18th centuries, contemporary scientists have collected much field data and enormity of species on geological and biological matters. When Carl Linnaeus (1707-1778) introduced his revolutionary system of biological-geological binomial-taxonomy (two-word), he already called us Homo-Sapiens (1758). Thus, he inferred we descended from apes more than a hundred years before Darwin published. Malthus published his seminal work on population, *An Essay on the Principle of Population,* in 1798. This work, which demonstrated life as a struggle of too many survivors for not enough food, greatly influenced both Wallace and Darwin. Later, following the works of previous geologists, Charles Lyell published his *Principles of Geology* (1830-33); it became increasingly evident that earth was very old (they were still thinking millions, not billions of years), and so were living creatures. The slow evolution of any of these processes, biological or biological, requires a very long time, though the age of the Earth was not yet established. Lord Kelvin (1824 - 1907), the great physicist of the era, estimated the age of the earth at about 20 million years, and later extended the range to 80 million years. Darwin somehow intuited that even such age of the Earth was not sufficient to support the tedious and gradual process he had posited. His daring theory was a grand and daring speculation, framed a new universe that was somewhat outside the religious paradigm. Wallace was a more religious and excluded human from the Darwinian process; he considered us to be "divinely inspired".

When Darwin joined the voyage of the HMS *Beagle* in 1831, to chart the shores of South America, he was only 23 years old. The ship's captain, Fitzroy, gave him a copy of Lyell's first book, *The Principles of Geology*, postulating an enormously old earth and a gradual geological change across eons. It influenced Darwin and enabled a scientific baseline for a very old Earth. Prompted by daring new publications by famous and respected scientists about geology and the Earth's age (as compared to the biblical narrative), various thinkers started to toy with the idea of the evolution of living matter that stretched across a very long time. Millions of years, not the biblical thousands. The French naturalist Jean-Baptiste Lamarck (1774-1829) presented the first comprehensive theory of evolution (1809). In addition to being logical and intuitive, Lamarckism presented a mechanism that is much expedited in comparison to Darwinism, because it assumed "acquired characteristics," hence certain directivity, comprising an active force in the evolution of living matter. It postulated an evolutionary mechanism, driven by need that can be inherited quickly. For example, if the tall tree presents a challenge (and opportunity), the giraffe will quickly resolve it by growing a long neck and the following generations will continue the process to its ultimate conclusion. Therefore, Lamarckism assumed a certain level of "intelligence" and "directivity" in the nature of living matter's evolution; then the process continues "*an organism can pass on characteristics that are acquired during its lifetime to its offspring.*" Specifically, characteristics will be acquired by necessity and if "beneficial," inherited by offspring; the process is directed and thus accelerated. Given the later meteoric acceptance of Darwinism, Lamarckism was initially rejected, but later became part of the vast body of evolutionary theory (even by Darwin).

Darwin possessed a genius mind but was forced to publish before he was ready (galvanized by Wallace's 1858 letter); it was a monumental paradigm shift that scared him for its divorce from tradition. Darwin developed his theory carefully and methodically, based on the myriad facts he studied during his long career. The scientific community quickly adopted his concepts. Darwinism was an attractive theory from the start; it was the scientific path for "*design without a Designer*," but took time to be established and expanded (for example, Neo-Darwinism). Because of its daring and originality and the controversy with the established religious paradigm, even Darwin's position wavered in later editions of his first and famous book, "*On the Origins of Species*[1]." The essence of Darwinism, the completely materialistic view of the development (not the origin) of life on Earth, is briefly outlined herein:

- Nature is endowed by immense diversity.

- Change is inherent in nature, due to inheritance variations and environmental pressures. Change is a random process (random mutation, or spontaneous variations in Darwin's time) with no purpose or direction and occurs naturally and continually. No directivity in Darwinism.

- Species are capable of generating much more offspring than the environment can support (in Bertrand Russell's words, "if all offspring survived, the ocean would become solid fish in no time"). This pressure creates competition, even within the species.

- The engine of evolution is "survival of the fittest." Due to limited resources, offspring constantly struggle for survival among themselves and the environment. If the change (see above) is beneficial, they will better survive. The survivors pass on their new, advantageous changes (genetic characteristics) to their progeny. The process is continuous.

- Life is never dormant, it is an active force that changes and adapts constantly. The changes are random, few of them beneficial; such beneficial characteristics in individuals within the group help their survival; eventually they take over the species, until the next evolutionary step occurs.

- The evolution of life will be explained by the scientific method alone. The process is natural, there is no divine necessity nor are we different; we are just another, smarter species, with no divine blessings.

Naturally, such materialistic theory, requiring no divine intervention, was controversial from its inception; conservatives and creationists reject it to this day. Even the Deist view of a world charged by god and left alone was violated. Darwin opined that the world is in constant change, of incremental adaptations forced by the elements, not by a divine plan. For so many, the concept of the natural marvel with its intricacies (even Darwin was bothered by the intricacies of the eye and other organs) being created from chaos without a guiding hand, is genuinely fraught with difficulty. In addition, such departure from religious interpretation and postulates, and the conclusions that life has no direction or purpose, is challenging. Darwin did not attempt at the origins of life or how life might have started, only to explain the process once it got going.

DARWINISM AND SOCIETY

Darwinism had far-reaching socio-political implications. The whole concept of "survival of the fittest" brought various dangerous ideas to the surface. Specifically, it gave "scientific" excuses to various racial theories and eventually led to the tragic and sometimes criminal exercise of Eugenics.

Darwin was not a racist as shown in his book, *"The Descent of Man."* He actually rejected racism as a scientific principle. However, Darwin was also the product of his time (European domination with great empires and belief in superiority) and such statements as: «*At some future period, not very distant as measured by centuries, the civilized races of man will almost certainly exterminate and replace throughout the world the savage races*" can be found in the Descent. The theory fomented multitudinous new thinking, starting with Herbert Spencer (whose sociology was compared to Social Darwinism). There were other issues, emerging from Darwin's philosophical implications:

- The evolution of life is 100% materialistic. Darwin did not deal with our mental or spiritual evolution.

- Nothing is special about us, we are just another animal. A notion offensive to our homocentric world-view.

- Life has no purpose, just the meandering of living matter in time, trying to survive and propagate.

- Survival of the fittest eventually means no compassion. Such ideas gave rise to the philosophies along Spencer's line; e.g. let the fittest survive as nature commands. This will later lead to certain monstrous conclusions (Racism, Nazism, Eugenics).

- Conflict is essential to life.

DARWINISM AND COGNITION

The swift evolution of human cognition cannot be Darwinian. By its nature, our mental evolution is directed and knowledge can be acquired and multiplied within a very short time, often much shorter than a single generation. Moreover, what we learn cognitively is not through genetic mutation or from our parents. Most of what we learn comes from strangers (our teachers), experiences and books; our learning is swift, just note the mental rate of change in babies. Freeman Dyson, a modern prophet of Darwinism, recently opined, *"The epoch of Darwinian evolution based on competition between species, ended about ten thousand years ago when a single species, Homo Sapiens, began to dominate and recognize the biosphere. Since that time, cultural [cognitive] evolution has replaced biological…"*

Darwin tried unsuccessfully to incorporate the evolution of language into his theory. He understood his theory was somewhat lacking as it pertained to the cognitive space. Today, the field of cultural-evolution is attempting to formulate explanation to our rapid cognitive progress in Darwinian lines. Some die-hard Evolutionists try to explain the difference by calling our "material evolution" a type of Hardware that takes a long time to evolve, but that our "Cognitive evolution" is likened to Software and therefore far more agile (Pinker[71]). Put another way, the evolution of our consciousness and the accelerated rise of our Cognition cannot be explained, at least not yet, within the pure Darwinian paradigm. Perhaps it need not be forced to fit into Darwinism; Cognitive evolution, lingual or otherwise, is highly directed and not a matter for the tedious random genetic process. Or, other researchers suggest, perhaps a modification to Darwinism is waiting to happen. Overall, our ignorance about our consciousness and thought prevents us from making more detailed comments on the matter. Another central point is that civilization, as mentioned already, is altogether anti-Darwinian. We cure the sick, help the weak and have developed personal and institutions sympathy for civility and humanity. Civilization is about morality and therefore, not about "survival of the fittest," hence anti-Darwinian.

Perhaps in due time, the Darwinian theory shall be supplemented by extensions to accommodate the issues of consciousness, cognition and language.

3.12 PIERRE TEILHARD DE-CHARDIN

The French Jesuit-Philosopher Pierre Teilhard de-Chardin (1881-1955) was born near Clermont-Ferrand in central France. After a formal education in the sciences, he became a life-long naturalist and avowed Darwinist. The naturalistic tendencies of this very religious man employed by the church, fomented conflict with his employer for most of his life. As a consequence, many of his publications were forbidden and he was "exiled" to China; but this exile did not deter his fertile mind. Some of his books were only published posthumously. From reference 18, *"In 1925, Teilhard was ordered by the Jesuit Superior General to leave his teaching position in France and sign a statement withdrawing his controversial statements regarding the doctrine of original sin. Rather than leave the Jesuit order, Teilhard signed the statement and left for China. This was the first of a series of condemnations by certain ecclesiastical officials that would continue until long after Teilhard's death. The climax of these condemnations was a 1962 **monitum** (reprimand) of the Holy Office denouncing his works."*

Published posthumously, de-Chardin's magnum opus, *The Human Phenomenon*[15] developed a popular cult following, the "Teilhard cult," because of his positive, spiritual and idealistic vision for the evolution of humanity and its destination. In 1912, while he was in England, de-Chardin formed an excavating team with academic paleontologist Arthur Smith Woodward and amateur archeologist Charles Dawson. They excavated the Piltdown site (in east Sussex, around 20Km northeast of Brighton, England). At the time - the beginning of the 20th century - Nationalism was rampant and the English (as well as others) were eager to demonstrate that the "first man" originated in their geography, not in other competing world powers' (like Germany or France). The result was the famous "Piltdown Hoax", perhaps the most infamous in the history of

Paleontology. Dawson claimed that he had recovered human skull fragments at Piltdown. De-Chardin was associated with Dawson and, when they came back to excavate later in 1912, they found extra specimens, among them a human jaw. Woodard published the findings in December 1912 and the resulting controversy continued, until 1953, when the specimen was revealed to have been fabricated, hence a hoax. Stephen Gould[15] described these chronicles as a mystery story with very fine details and analysis and concluded that de-Chardin was the possible culprit!

De-Chardin was a prolific writer. He revealed his philosophical-historical future vision in his concept of the Omega Point, first in his book *The Future of Man* (1950) and then in *The Phenomenon of Man* (*Le Phenomene Humain*), in 1955. Although Teilhard was definitely an avid Darwinist, he was deeply religious and could not accept one of the Darwinian tenets, postulating that evolution has no direction and no purpose; that the totality of the evolution of matter (and spirituality) is fueled by a pointless random process and driven only by the mechanism of "selection." Teilhard looked for a way to fuse matter and spirituality into a larger canvas of Evolution. Either because of his religiosity, or by observing the historical and Paleontological data available to him, he concluded that humans and cognitive history must have a time arrow - indicating a purpose or direction. Like so many before him, Teilhard observed that in the universe, both matter and spirit are in a state of constant flux and develop constantly towards higher levels of "material complexity and consciousness". Teilhard called this process the Law of Complexity-Consciousness. He believed (along with many other modern followers, like Soleri, Tipler, and Kurzweil[17]) that the universe must move in the direction of higher complexity and increased consciousness, or towards a higher Cognitive level. For de-Chardin, the universe and humanity are being drawn by an active supreme point of consciousness, which he called the Omega Point (Omega being the last letter of the Greek alphabet and symbolizes an endpoint). The Omega Point, which Teilhard posited as an active "pulling force," is not very different from the Augustinian Seventh Day and might be interpreted as an end-of-days vision of humanity merging into the Christ even if the book does not mention the word God. Teilhard described his Omega Point as Autonomous, Irreversible, Eternal and Active. Various modern thinkers, inspired by him, used the metaphor more than the theory. The concept is attractive, idealistic and exciting - a vision of an integrated cognitive-humanity coming together as a cosmic concept, perhaps naïve, but also beautiful. The below is an illustration from de-Chardin's book *The Phenomenon of Man*, and further elucidates his concept of his concept of our cognitive Evolution.

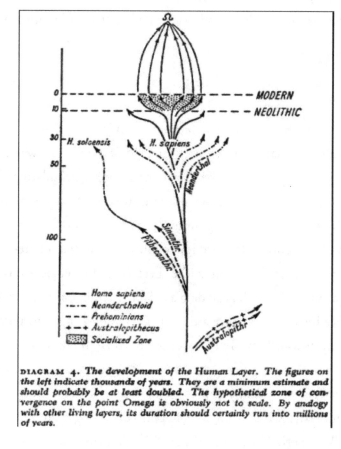

DIAGRAM 4. The development of the Human Layer. The figures on the left indicate thousands of years. They are a minimum estimate and should probably be at least doubled. The hypothetical zone of convergence on the point Omega is obviously not to scale. By analogy with other living layers, its duration should certainly run into millions of years.

Figure 3: Teilhard's concept of the human evolution from The Phenomenon of Man

3.13 HUNTINGTON & FUKUYAMA

During the last quarter-century, historians have proposed new visions of evolutionary futurist history. We will focus herein on two political representatives, one from the standpoint of conflict and one of hope. Huntington and Fukuyama (who studied under Huntington) developed conflicting visions of the future and Fukuyama ventured beyond the near future. Both departed from the Marxist-

Darwinist materialistic Historiosophy that dominated the views of the intellectual classes in the last century.

Samuel Huntington (1927-2008) was an American political scientist. From 1963, until his death, he was a tenured professor at Harvard University, where he taught and published prolifically. His last and perhaps most influential popular book, "*The Clash of Civilizations and the Remaking of World Order*[27]" was published in 1993. Although it did not contain a comprehensive Historiosophy, Huntington speculated on the near future (post-WWII, the Cold War era and after the collapse of the Soviet Union), specifically on fundamental features of human conflict. He proposed that, even though the age of ideology might have ended, the post-Cold War world seemed to have reverted to exhibiting a natural civilization clash. He argued that the primary axis of conflict in the future would be along cultural and religious lines. By extension, he posited that the concepts of different civilizations - the highest rank of cultural identity, would become increasingly useful in analyzing the potential and drive for conflict. Huntington wrote, "*It is my hypothesis that the fundamental source of conflict in this new world will not be primarily ideological or primarily economic. The great divisions among humankind and the dominating source of conflict will be cultural. Nation states will remain the most powerful actors in world affairs, but the principal conflicts of global politics will occur between nations and groups of different civilizations. The clash of civilizations will dominate global politics. Hence, the fault-line between civilizations will be the battle lines of the future.*"

Huntington went even further and delimited the borders of these civilizations, the West, Latin America, the Muslim world, the Orthodox world, the East (China, Japan, India), sub-Sahara, and a few smaller groups. He also offered some reasoning for his postulates, among them:

- Differences among civilizations are too fundamental to reconcile. Civilizations are differentiated from each other by history, language, culture, tradition, and most importantly - religion.

- The world is becoming a smaller place. Proximity causes friction.

- Due to economic modernization and social change, people are separated from their longstanding local identities. Instead, religion has filled this gap.

- The growth of civilization-consciousness is enhanced by the dual role of the west, which is not only at a peak of power and wealth; it is also rejected by return-to-the-roots phenomena among non-Western powers.

- Cultural characteristics and differences are less mutable and hence, less easily compromised and resolved than political and economic ones.

- Economic regionalism is increasing.

Huntington forecasted the continuous evolution of humanity as an extension of the concept of struggle, but along ideological, geographical, cultural or religious lines.

Francis Fukuyama (1952-) comprehensively described a very different vision in his famous book, "*The End of History and the Last Man*[5]" (1992). He was educated at Cornell University with Allan Bloom[235] and later in Harvard with, among others, Huntington himself. Despite the horrors of the 20th century, Fukuyama formulated a positive vision of the future, although he was critical about the growing influence of our technology and its threats. Fukuyama began *The End of History* with a short review of the Kojevan (Alexandre Kojeve, 1902-1968) interpretation of Hegelian Historiosophy. Fukuyama's goal is to establish a history with direction and demonstrate that economic interpretations of history (e.g. Karl Marx) are insufficient because humans are much more than solely economical. The Hegelian interpretation demonstrates that humans, unlike animals, have a fundamental need for spiritual life and to be recognized by their peers, in Hegel's terminology: "*to desire the desire of other men.*" In this view, human struggle is not for "physical survival" but for "recognition, respect;" not a physical, but a cognitive force. It follows that civilization has turned into "a battle for prestige." The "universal and homogeneous state," which Fukuyama interpreted as the liberal democracy, based on the ideals of the French and American revolutions, puts an end to the master-slave relationship in history - the cause of conflict according to Marx/Kojeve, because, at least in principle, modern Democracy offers universal and equal recognition (a function of the meritorious society). Fukuyama opines that history has nowhere to go because its fundamental conflict has been resolved. Thus, "*What we may be witnessing is not just the end of the Cold War, or the passing of a particular period of post-war history, but the end of history as such. That is, the end point of mankind's ideological evolution and the universalization of Western liberal* *democracy* (meaning Democracy and free market economy*) as the final form of human government.*" Specifically, Fukuyama forecasts world politics methodical conversion to the style of western democracies and economies' convergence into various forms of "free-market economies." Fukuyama does not deny the possibilities for local despotism or atrocities that might occur as time elapses, but his vision for humanity is a gradual descent into the "western style democracies and laissez-faire economies."

In light of the events of the last 15 years, specifically in Arabia, Islam and the West's rising conflict with China and Russia, in the Ukraine and along the border with NATO, Huntington's forecast seems, at least in the short term, to have the upper hand. Only time will tell. Fukuyama presented a beautiful dream but in the 20 years that passed since its publication, we are realizing a different historical evolution of nationalism, isolation and the rise of despotism.

3.14 OTHERS

Many world-view interpretations have emerged, some fomented by the immense technological progress we have witnessed, others are age old, yet few due to the rise of the "machine" and advances in Artificial Intelligence (AI) and cognitive sciences. I allow limited room for the occult, as representing a different type of thought. The occult occupies a vast domain in people's thoughts, beliefs and mythologies, even though it is not a scientific or even logical discipline.

RUPERT SHELDRAKE

The human affair contains much that is not scientific nor logical. The occult has always been attractive to many believers. From Mesmerism to séances summoning spirits or even Astrology, the occult provides solace and a certain supportive belief system. So much of life is left unexplained that other, non-scientific or Pseudo-Scientific explanations have found wide currency throughout history and various spiritual theories have developed that explain what we cannot.

Rupert Sheldrake (1942-) is an English biochemist, plant physiologist, and somewhat of a Para-Psychologist. He received his education at Cambridge and

Harvard universities. Based on certain animal behavior and biological observations, he developed his theory of "Morphic Resonance," detailed in his book, "*The Presence of the Past*[19]". Based on various observations, he arrived at the conclusion that the biological mechanisms we have devised are not sufficient to describe all phenomena of life. Instead, he speculated on the "Morphic Resonance," a phenomenon that Sheldrake turned into a certain philosophy of science and life. He expressed it as, "*the basis of memory in nature…the idea of mysterious telepathy-type interconnections between organisms and of collective memories within species.*" Sheldrake added that memory is inherent in nature, and what we think of as the laws of nature may be more like "*universal habits.*" The basis of this memory process comprises his "Morphic Resonance," which is an influence through or across space and time. Its implication for heredity is that inheritance depends not only on the chemistry of coded DNA, but also on such "Morphic Resonance" from past members of a species. Other implications indicate mechanisms for accelerated rate of evolution and forms of behavior. Memory in individuals thus is based on self-resonance (perhaps stored in some universal cloud) and not only in the brain. Sheldrake postulates the existence of a "collective memory" we all contribute to and we all draw on, which also provides mechanisms for understanding of past-life memories, the ability to survive bodily death, telepathy, and ritual (myth). Such hypothesis is part of a wider change in the paradigm by which all of nature (not only Earth), throughout the entire universe, is a living organism (not only the Gaya hypothesis - viewing planet earth as an integrated living organism, see reference 302). Sheldrake asserts that regardless of the ultimate validity of Morphic Resonance, our return to a sense of nature as alive and animate is absolutely essential to achieving a better relationship with the environment on which we depend, and therefore, vital for our very survival.

In comparison to the so many pseudo-sciences we developed, Sheldrake is actually benign, just remember that few states still oppose teaching Evolution or require teaching Creationism instead or besides it; indeed, who decides what science is, Scientists? Politicians? The Public? Sheldrake has assembled following enthusiasts, but his thinking is not part of scientific discipline and is included here as just one example of many pseudo-sciences. To the observant, life presents immense enigmas and mysteries. It is not surprising that such theories have broken through the Hegel-Marx-Darwin paradigm to suggest new speculations on the mysteries of life.

Carl Gustav Jung (1875-1961) was a Swiss psychiatrist and psychotherapist who founded analytical psychology. Jung proposed and developed the concepts of the collective unconscious, perhaps correlated to some degree, with the Hegelian *Zeitgeist*. His work has been influential in psychiatry as well as in the study of religion, literature, and related fields. Jung started as a Freudian disciple but later broke off and developed the concept of analytical psychology as individuation - the psychological process of integrating opposites, including the conscious with the unconscious, while still maintaining their relative autonomy. Jung considered individuation as the central process of human development. He posited that, in addition to our immediate consciousness, whose nature is thoroughly personal, a second psychic system exists. This parallel system, distinguished from the personal, is collective, universal and impersonal, and shared by all individuals. The collective unconscious does not develop individuality but is inherited and shared. It consists of pre-existing forms, which Jung termed "*The Archetype.*" The Archetypes constitute the structure of the collective unconscious—they are psychic innate dispositions that represent basic human behavior and situations that affect our experiences. For example, the mother-child relationship is governed by the mother's Archetype. The collective unconscious appears to consist of mythological motifs or primordial images, and Jung reasoned that the myths of all nations are their real exponents. He asserted that the whole of mythology could be seen as a sort of projection of the collective unconscious. We can, therefore, study the collective unconscious in two ways, either through mythology or by analysis of the individual. Consequently, Jung disputed the Lockian (John Locke, 1632-1704) concept of *Tabula Rasa* (that we are born with a "clean slate") in favor of a universal system of consciousness (like a "Cognitive-Cloud") that has a profound effect on our minds and behavior. Jung definitely believed in our yearning for religion and worship, and opined we possess a "religious instinct" toward a relationship with something higher that transcends humanity.

TELEOLOGY & THE ANTHROPIC PRINCIPLE

The concept of an Anthropic (*the universe has properties that are shaped by the observation of intelligent, sapient life*) universe was born within the scientific community, posited mostly by Astrophysicists and Cosmologists. This bold conjecture (actually somewhat Platonic, after all he already opined that every orderly system must have been designed; the universe is quite an orderly system; what is the mind that designed it?) arose from the realization that life is possible because of the infinitesimal ranges of physical constants that allowed the universe and life. Any tiny deviation of these, would have made life impossible. As we continue to make increasingly accurate observations of the universe, we continue to be amazed by the beauty of its unfolding, the symmetry and even mathematical (math after all is the invention of sapient minds) perfection of its design for the emergence of reality as we know it and specifically life and the complexity of life forms. The razor-thin cosmological constants range, that enables life, the immensity of the DNA molecules and the puzzle of its creation, cause certain doubts about it all emerging from "chaos." Even certain ratios of cosmological constants, (such as the gravitational constant, the estimated age of the universe, and the mass of elementary particles) seem to fit "too well" into the possibilities of creating conditions that are conducive to support life, according to Krauss and others[100]. Despite all the improbabilities of creating a DNA molecule randomly, we are here, the awesome improbabilities against us notwithstanding! As we know more, we are increasingly amazed. Semantically, the principle should not be called "Anthropic" because it specifies *intelligence*, not specifically "humans." Also, it must be noted as a related curiosity that Alfred Wallace Russell, a father of Darwinism, already speculated in 1904, "Such a vast and complex universe as that which we know exists around us, may have been absolutely required... to produce a world that should be precisely adapted in every detail for the orderly development of life, culminating in man." He definitely had unusual insights; he was also very religious. Additionally, perhaps the principle can be further interpreted as: *life and intelligence are inherent in the universe.* The originators and supporters of this theory drew on many previous thinkers; they do mention and ubiquitously us terms like, "Omega Point," "the absurd universe" and such.

In the last few decades, the "Gaia hypothesis" has taken root[326]. Observations of the planet operating in a certain tandem as an integrated life form that supports life, has risen as a possibility. Is our planet as a whole, a living organism? Lovelock (Gaia originator) opined: "*It may be that the destiny of mankind is to become tamed, so that the fierce, destructive, and greedy forces of tribalism and nationalism are fused into a compulsive urge to belong to the commonwealth of all creatures, which constitutes Gaia.*" What indeed is the meaning of "evolution from the world of the early thermo acidophilic and methanogenic bacteria towards the oxygen-enriched atmosphere today that supports more complex life[326]?" Is it possible to extend the definition of life and living beyond the individual or the species, into a planetary complex? It is definitely a healthy view of our position in the universe.

KURZWEIL, VENTER – SINGULARITY & LIFE AS A SET OF ALGORITHMS

Raymond Kurzweil (b. 1948) is an American technologist, author, inventor and futurist; he is a leading scientist in the fields of artificial intelligence, text-to-speech, character (pattern) recognition, print to speech, music synthesizers and speech recognition. Kurzweil was born in New York City and educated at MIT. After various ventures and numerous inventions, he focused on educational systems and speech recognition and even produced a movie, *The Singularity Is Near: A True Story About the Future.* Kurzweil derived his technological singularity concept from its originator, Vernor Steffen Vinge (now retired American professor of Mathematics, b.1944). "*It is a theoretical (and maybe imminent) moment in time when artificial intelligence will have progressed to the point of a greater-than-human intelligence that will "radically change human civilization, and perhaps even human nature itself." Since the capabilities of such intelligence may be difficult for an unaided human mind to comprehend, the technological singularity is often seen as an occurrence (akin to a gravitational singularity) beyond which—from the perspective of the present—the future course of human history is unpredictable or even unfathomable.*"

This is a post-modern technocratic view of history as a cognitive process that evolves to a point that our machines' intelligence will exceed their creator's. In retrospect, history is seen as marching toward an intelligence level that has been developed by the human mind, yet can exceed its potential; a silicon-mind that exceeds the biological! Can the machine be smarter than its creator? For this outcome, we'll have to wait, but some of the leading technologists promise that this potential is already around the corner![222] Technocrats and even some historians are also advancing the notion that life might be viewed as a set of Algorithms (see below), that if we can decipher these algorithms, we can decipher the secrets of life, take control of our genetics, improve our conditions and, maybe, our cognition through genetic or implant manipulations.[291]

Craig Venter (1946 -) is another brilliant scientist and futurist whose achievements in genetics are of historical caliber. He operates in another pole of technology - genetics, which are the fundamentals of life or, as he calls it: DNA, the fundamental software of life. Venter believes humans are now infinitesimally close to an evolutionary revolution due to technology and capacity to manipulate our genetics.

We have evolved to the brink of being able to model and manipulate the very basic building blocks of life itself, the DNA. A great revolution is at hand. This process, probably inevitable, is fraught with both promise and risks[333]. The ideology underpinning the process, is *that life, our mind, our being comprises a set of biochemical algorithms that can be learned and improved.* If we can comprehend and model the DNA, we can find, not only cures, but also understand and manipulate our total behavior. It is possible that better algorithms can be devised outside of the Darwinian process merely by employing the computational power of our machines and our cognition. Thus the possibility of vastly improving our being, both intelligence, health and longevity, are least in principle, within striking distance of life becoming a cognitively controlled process, rather than one controlled by the whims of the environment and our DNA chemistry[333]. Venter points to such potential in his book[51], and forecasts it's happening rather soon, within just a few decades. "*DNA as digitized information is not only accumulating in computer databases, but can now be transmitted...to re-create proteins, viruses and living cells...with this new understanding of life...the door cracks open to reveal exciting new possibilities. As the Industrial Age is drawing to a close, we are witnessing the dawn of an era of biological design. Humankind is about to enter a new phase of evolution.*"[51]

Again, the exact implications of such bold prediction will be tested in time. The process is not only chemical; we have to find and understand the total mechanisms that turn an organism. And with the promises come vast challenges.

Summary: The preceding short review, demonstrates the relentless drive of rising human cognition and the acceleration of recent cognitive history. We have progressed from the naïve belief that the universe is driven by mysteries and the hands of gods, to searching physical, historical and mental-emotional laws that provide certain explanations about, and possible predictions for, the behavior of nature and humans. Even the possibilities of manipulating human behavior, function and intelligence are now considered. These include our longevity (already rising by better hygiene, certain drugs, medical procedures and preventive medicine), replacements of parts, biotechnology sensors monitoring our bodies constantly, improved intelligence (this is a complicate issue that will require manipulation of hundreds of genes, but not impossible) and preventive medicine. And with this came a relentless rise in the complexity of our models and understanding.

The world and humans, by our nature, always have been complex and this complexity keeps rising. We are discovering that even as our understanding and our ability to make certain prediction improve, such knowledge comes at the cost of increased complexity. Complexity seems to be an extricable feature of the universe and the human experience.

NOTE:

The foregoing comprises a set of predominantly modern Western views. Inclusive world-history is rather a new discipline and some historians are scrambling to integrate worldwide-history into the heavily biased western canvas. Other civilizations have viewed history differently; only some of their ideas have been integrated into western thought. We will do well to remember Arnold Toynbee on the matter, *"We have to remember that the annals of warfare between "civilization" and the "barbarians" have been written almost exclusively by the scribes of the "civilized."*

4. SOCIAL FOUNDATIONS: RELIGION, LAW AND ECONOMY

People fashion their God after their own understanding.

I think that God, in creating man, somewhat overestimated his ability.

Oscar Wilde

4.1 RELIGION

"My religion consists of a humble admiration of the illimitable superior spirit who reveals himself in the slight details we are able to perceive with our frail and feeble mind."

Einstein

"For centuries, theologians have been explaining the unknowable in terms of the not worth knowing."

H. L. Mencken

Religion is a universal phenomenon, shared by all societies and civilizations. We have a natural passion for believing, following and worshiping, a yearning to be part of something greater than us. It is also a source of social cohesion - especially in a hostile world; you and me being Baha'i, Jewish, Muslim or Zen-Buddhist, makes us somewhat a part of a "family," a bigger family. It is also natural that people were always looking at the universe and finding it hard to believe that all this happened without a designer, a prime mover. Or as it was referred to by so many: *a watch without a watchmaker?*

Others will claim that the belief is "absurd," baseless. Even saints (perhaps St. Paul, perhaps Tertullian) sometimes reflected, "*I believe because it is absurd!*" Maybe it is. During most of our history, religion was anything but absurd, one of the greatest forces in all of history, to this day. Religion is a powerful human emotion and world-view; the result of our cognitive mind and ability to abstract and our ability to follow our "make-belief." As a central spiritual expression, religion - both its ritual and belief systems - has changed and modified in response to the evolution of the social order and our cognition. Since the dawn of civilization, human's concept of the gods has progressively evolved into greater abstraction and the gods gradually vanished into the depths of mythology, spirituality and even philosophy. New organizations and concepts arose to aid the people to follow and comprehend what we perceive as godly commands and religious rituals. The gods were initially communal, and then became individual, then communal or national again; then they became universal. Today, with the success of the Reformation, a certain personal god is again gaining in Christianity. A large portion of the believing community has no "Pope," rather direct contact is encouraged (Islam, Judaism, Protestant Christians and Hinduism).

The God, or gods, are only one component of religion, though a central one. The deity is after all one of the most powerful make-belief systems that engage the discourse of human thought, imagination and emotions. God is infinite and cannot be described by our language. God can only be worshipped and usually by an a-priori belief. God is beyond reality or experience and, although universal and all goodness, not all the myriad attributes ascribed to the gods were positive. The benevolent one-God, the infinite Goodness, is mostly a Jewish-Christian concept, but even in our civilizations the God can be punishing and destructive. God is the ultimate mystery of being, the supreme manifestation of reality and beyond. Because language is not sufficient, our approach to the deity always involved emotions, ritual, prayer and the arts, especially music, poetry and symbolism. Through music, our supreme abstract artistic form, many have found the path to ecstasy and a deeper connection with the divine.

Initially, the polytheistic gods were represented as material icons, and access was only through kings, prophets, or priests. After a time, the pantheon converged into a single God. This God, once personal, receded in time. From present and available to early Patriarchs, it became elusive, for selective few and only in vision even for them. God's commands derived from ancient, divine scriptures, ritual, and the moral code, which gods came to represent. Individual's access eventually became possible through prayer, ritual or particular church. As times advanced, the abstract God became spiritual, personal - the ineffable moral guardian. Religion became a way of life, rife with ritual and tradition. The receding-disappearing god, once accessible to prophets, became a symbol, an abstraction, sometimes a philosophy.

Throughout the centuries, the churched demanded and conditioned us to uniformity. Individual, personal contact with God was mostly rejected, given to only chosen few. Religion, especially via the church, supplied answers to the many mysteries of life and death and became central to people's mythologies and lives everywhere. Religion also helped the political leaders organize and control society, always critical to keeping the peace, enabling stability, exercising social classification and avoiding chaos. It was therefore a very convenient tool in the hands of the leaders, as a unifying force. The church mostly complied, specifically with the traditional order.

Religion has two faces, the personal and the communal via the church. Personal religion is a profoundly powerful force in human affairs, it generates dedication, following, a way of life, spiritual wealth and sometimes fanaticism almost unparalleled by any other system. Personal religion is a spiritual journey of many qualities and degrees of commitment. For many deeply religious folks, their religion has practically taken over their lives. Alternatively, the church produced a different experience and history; as an organization it fashions the ritual, the rules, structure, and hierarchy of the believers and its institutions and monuments. It also aspired political power. Religion is very much present in every life. Even if we lead secular existence, still we are born into the rituals (baptism, circumcision, holidays, rituals, marriage and death among them) that most of us still practice and adhere to. Most people describe themselves today as religious even if not praying regularly or belonging to a church. When the going gets tough, most resort to religion and wish to believe in something bigger than we are, higher than humanity.

THE MYSTERY OF DEATH

Anthropologists have speculated about the origin of religion since its inception, estimated at more than 50,000 years ago. Such rituals seem to be initially associated with making sense of the mystery of the world and especially of death, as demonstrated in burial sites and the various favored fetish rituals. All animals possess instinctive fear, a fundamental requirement for survival, but for us, death is an entirely different, enigmatic concept. We can conceptualize our demise, even death itself, but the nothingness conceived with death, is a much greater enigma. It is not surprising that our concept of death arose at about the same time we acquired language, just as our cognition rose by our ability to communicate and express ourselves. The inevitability of death and our fears became driving forces in the formation of our ritual, world-view and beliefs. Art and symbolism have long been useful tools to negotiate the riddle too. Symbols we find in archeological sites also indicate a deep capacity for abstraction already tens of thousands of years ago, the sign of growing cognition and awareness of the great enigma. Some have speculated that the origins of religious behavior primarily stemmed from an emotional connection, our wish to continue to communicate with or even worship, the dead. In addition, given the enigmatic and mysterious nature of life and the world around us, the action of the elements were also a driving factor in human believing in forces beyond the natural, beyond human and beyond this world.

WE ARE NOT ANIMALS

Many animals have a rigid social order, especially some insects, some birds, fish, and mammals. Humans also follow a highly complex social structure; still we have individual ambitions, wills and whims that must be formed and managed inside this structure. We are capable of adjusting to a great variety of environmental and social changes. The ability to adapt to any geography, weather, and social norms is specifically a human trait. While other animals must become specialists in their ecological niche, human cognitive faculties and our ability to fashion the environment, enabled us to adjust and eventually inherit the whole planet. We have social and spiritual needs not evident in the animal kingdom. Although this makes the human social structure infinitely more complex, it also gives us immense adaptability. Built from so many individuals with conflicting interests and ambitions, our complex structure must be managed to avoid turning order into chaos. We have witnessed how chaos spreads quickly after natural disasters, and the social order momentarily weakens (people resort to looting, settling personal accounts and violence). The biblical story of Sodom and Gomorrah represents, not only a moral breakdown, but also chaos and social breakdown. A social order that lacks morality (as seen repeatedly throughout history), sometimes despite its religious component, will lose the necessary social bond and eventually not hold, with disastrous consequences. Social order that is based on militarism and Spartan brutality does not last either. Morality, a uniquely human feature, is a crucial building block for any society and morality seems to require belief in an authority from above, not only from within (the Kantian postulate). Many societies have built their own alternative religions, symbolism and even mythologies, to compete with our traditional past, such as Communism, Nazism, Fascism and the like. The results were often monstrous. Much critic has been leveled on the various churches in modernity, but they all preached morality and a social order that is based on a moral code and a justice system.

The early gods allowed the foundation of many mysteries, coalescence of groups, a certain solace and the creation of authority beyond us that helped establish the social order. The later introduction of a caring God (mostly through monotheistic religions), a God who is universal and watching us, caring about us and rewarding or punishing our ways, was a critical step in the cognitive evolution of religion. A certain purpose emerged, beyond the caprice of the older gods.

ORGANIZED RELIGION & MONOTHEISM

As communities and civilizations grew, the concepts of early pagan (polytheistic) religions - the many gods, each with its functions and responsibilities - made little sense. A single deity started to emerge. The God not only transformed from many to one, from tribal to universal, it also became abstract and vanishing. If God was accessible to early biblical figures, it later vanished (receded) into the mythology of scriptures and the abstract. Even many Icons, as the symbols of worship, receded toward abstraction. Later, for example, in the Jewish tradition, after the destruction of the 2nd Temple, any claim of contact with God was immediately suspect (the Jewish tradition says, *"since the destruction of the Temple, prophecy was given only to the demented"*). A certain distance and reverence had to be created between the unknown and the informal. Initially gods were local, material and physical icons; but in time a more abstract idea had to develop, placing them beyond reality, shifting them from the local to the universal, from iconic to cognitive forms.

Symbolism and abstraction are natural necessities for religion's eventual emergence; the object of worship must be both elusive and spiritual. Statues, fetishes and idols served visualization purposes from time immemorial (including icons today), while later symbolism and abstraction were always part of religion because the god(s) presented divine powers or authority that required imagination.

Along with the agricultural revolution and the formation of large societies, the evolution of organized religion ensued to serve the group's emotional, ritualistic and political needs. It was necessary to standardize the rituals and organize the social structure for more coherent, interpersonal worship. Various events (such as birth, death, harvest, and marriage) required individual rituals that made the process easier to follow and accept. Organized religion also carried (carries) political motives and mostly cooperated with the political leadership. The church emerged as a central and organized authority to: * Create a central religious authority that regulates religious rituals.

1. Designate central religious authority to decide on controversial issues and could be related to the political leadership and act in tandem with it to harmonize the relationship with the masses through the authority of a supreme being.

2. Become the authority and arbiter of a system of rules for correct (later moral) and moderate social behavior.

3. Provide a better mechanism for social adherence. Common gods absolutely help the cohesion of a community. Initially, the political leader was also the religious leader (like Moses), but the functions quickly separated. Over time the two authorities came to be competitive and sometimes antagonistic. The prophets assumed a moral authority that objected to the king's behavior, sometimes politics. Later, the power struggle of church (now with political ambitions) and Empire during the High Middle Ages is an illuminating example, to this day when religion is also political.

4. Help create a unique identity for the group, hence social unity. God was initially very much tribal and continued as such for a long time. Winning a battle meant the superiority of one god over the other. The universal God concept came much later.

After the commencement of the agricultural revolution, religion became the most powerful force in the social order and some rulers became divine or Gods, hence the head of the church. In ancient Egypt, the Pharaoh played the double role of both political and spiritual leader. In the Jewish tradition, Moses was the one. His followers (Joshua, Judges), with diminishing religious authority, continued the tradition, until the people (Samuel I, 8:5) demanded a King. Thereafter, a king was anointed by the messenger of God (the prophet) or the high priest. The King was a special man "chosen," blessed from birth by the God(s) and endowed by special gifts (such as healing, heroism, and dynastic immortality). The rulers had a vested interest in a unified, coherent religion, which simplified their system of authority or coercion and helped pacify the people. The church cooperated for the most part. Religion placed an undisputed divine authority over the social order; it was absolute and always right ("what is - is good"); the God is infinitely powerful, just and benevolent and this is the best possible world. Worship became a personal obligation, which contained promises at individual and communal levels. The community was promised to be God's favorite if they followed his commands.

In Judaism and later in Christianity, the relationship with God evolved from a social duty to a Covenant. Initially, a personal covenant was with the patriarch Abraham, then with the Jewish people on Mount Sinai, and later (during Christianity), as a universal relationship between Christ and Humanity. The people promised to obey God's commands and God's promises were for a better, just future. Initially, these promises concerned progeny and prosperity, later they became spiritual, cognitive by nature. A "contract" was established between the people and the divine. Because of life's inherent conflicts, some of the prophets questioned the "*prosperity of the wicked*" (Psalms 73) or the social injustice facing the social order. The allegorical case of Job is difficult to accept because a decent man was punished so horribly by the whims of God and his angels. However, the case is made for ultimate submission and faith in a just God, aided by the most magnificent poetry written in the Hebrew language. The position of God in this contract was not and could not be questioned. Job himself did not question God's justice and was later rewarded. The deity is/was always right, even if the people could not discern its actions; God's answer, in magnificent poetry, is about his greatness and our duty to obey; no answers about life's injustices can be provided.

Religion is also one of the few emotions capable of driving us into fanaticism. People were ready to sacrifice themselves or kill others in the name of their religion. Despite so many religions that have been roaming on earth, each sect is certain that they owned the only truth and that every other god was false. This led to forced conversion throughout history because the non-believers must be convinced, otherwise, they would be *"cast into outer darkness"* (Matthew 8:12).

CLASH OF CHURCH AND STATE

Today, the courts are the true shapers of our social order in free societies. The high- courts eventually decide also difficult, politically charged issues. In democracies, laws, not despots and not religious institutions govern us. This is a monumental concept that took long to shape. Although the early phases of society could combine political and spiritual leadership in one person, they separated quickly because of the natural conflict. Over time, the temporal and eternal pillars of the social order had to clash. Kings, too, aspired for spiritual authority and the church took steps to assert political muscle. The Catholic Church assumed an Empirical structure from early on and political maneuvers were not alien to church leaders. The Bible demonstrates the conflict between the moral person (prophet) and political (king), but places supremacy in the hands of the monarch. The prophets had no political agenda. The catholic leadership of the high middle-ages thought otherwise.

In the Jewish tradition, God chose the kings. Consequently, Saul's dynasty was deposed for disobedience, even if for a rather humane infraction (refusing to kill the Amalekite king and destroy their property). David, on the other hand, committed myriad crimes, but was still beloved by God. No doubt, the biblical writers preferred David (from the tribe of Judah) to Saul (from Benjamin). Poets and theologians took on the question: how can one be such a sinner - David committed every sin in the book - and still be most beloved by God? Judaism never dealt with the matter (God can have caprices too); Christianity found the solution in the concept of Predestination. David is a central figure in Christianity too, Jesus is from the house of David.

Constantine I (272-337CE), the first Christian emperor, was also the head of the church, but a schism quickly developed. Less than a century later, in a famous incident, St. Ambrose, bishop of Milan, humiliated emperor Theodosius by barring his entrance to the church, in retaliation of his infractions against Christians in Thessalonica (390CE)! It set precedence for the relative power of the church that was well remembered into endless future conflicts. During late antiquity and the early Middle Ages, as imperial authority declined, the empire broke into many small kingdoms. The one stable, universal organization remained the Catholic church, which then became the de-facto religion of the empire and quickly produced great personalities, among them: St. Ambrose, St. Augustine, St. Benedict and Pope Gregory the Great (540-604CE). Gradually the Church established a hierarchy and a canon. The prayer, liturgy and monastic order were formed, in tandem with the rise of the Pope as its central authority. The church also assumed growing political influence.

Although Charlemagne (742-814) was not the first King of the dynasty (his father, Peppin was anointed by a churchman), his coronation by a Pope in 800CE started a tradition that underpinned the church's claim of authority over the monarch. Many historians speculate that Pope Leo III actually outwitted Charlemagne by anointing him emperor (on Christmas day 800CE). We have reasons to suspect it was a more complicated process. Charlemagne and the Carolingians were usurpers; after two centuries of acquiring lands, they expanded their influence and developed bonds with other aristocratic families. By the middle of the 8th century, with the aristocracy's support and the Pope's consent, they deposed the Merovingian dynasty. The Pope crowning Charlemagne was another important layer in the Carolingians' establishment of the new dynastic authority and legality - the church recognized them. The coronation was more likely orchestrated between the King and the Pope, the temporal and eternal cooperated. But it was also helping the Pope in the struggle of hierarchy and relative powers. Kings sought alliances and incorporated bishops into their administrations as advisors. The Carolingians, who later built a large empire, understood the importance of cooperation with the church, which over time became the undisputed cultural center of communities, with libraries, monasteries, translators and copyists. Monasteries were known as the repositories of knowledge then. Knowledge authority was therefore gradually transferred to the church; the free study of the Greco-Roman era, in gymnasiums or schools, was redirected toward church dogma. This shift had significant effects on the development of the West until the rise of Humanism (14C). Medieval

Kings also tried to meddle in church affairs, which during the 11th century fomented the Investiture Controversy (a dispute between Emperor Henry IV and Pope Gregory VII). A power struggle ensued and the Emperor was humiliated in Canossa (1077CE). The political power of the church was rising until they became supreme, a specific apex achieved during the pontificate of Innocent III (1198-1216)[310]. A series of powerful Popes turned the tables on secular rulers, commanded the Crusades, earned political power and the church earned the upper hand, during the 12th to 14th centuries. Thereafter, a new era commenced with various reformers (like St. Francis) and heretics that shook the view on church political authority (from Arnold of Brescia to Marsilius of Padua[311]), until the Reformation split Rome. Then, the nation-state started to emerge (14 Century), the church was damaged from corruption and schism that led to the eventual decline of religious authority in politics. But this decline was gradual and the Pope continued to be a powerful political actor into the 16th century.

MONOTHEISM

From an intellectual standpoint, the step away from paganism toward monotheism was a monumental cognitive achievement. Instead the many gods for every detail, sometimes bickering and fighting one another, a single comprehensive God rose to integrate all the authority in one figure, one symbol. In time, humanity converged to Monotheism but it took long and remains unfinished to this day. Many of us are still "pagans" in certain ways. If God is almighty and omnipotent, how can there be another? The Abrahamic religions introduced many innovations beyond Monotheism, specifically pertaining the comprehensive code of living, social laws and the Sabbath. The Jewish God evolved to transcend time and place. When the Jews were exiled to Babylon, early in the 6th century BCE, their aristocracy did not take the common attitude of "the other Gods are stronger, we should join them." Rather, a new concept of an abstract God emerged, lacking any physical manifestation (land, temple, sacrifices), and allowed them, over the next twenty-five centuries, recreate a new relationship with their God. They continued their traditions, despite the loss of sovereignty, the destruction of the second Temple, and immense loss of believers (the exiled 10 tribes from the Kingdom of Israel, have disappeared forever) and later the immense loss of life (during the Bar-Kokhba uprising (130s CE), with an estimated 600,000 casualties and about 1,000 villages razed). In response, instead of picking another god as others used to do, the Jews converted their ritual from temple sacrifices (material) toward prayer (cognitive). The abstract allowed them to transform physical rituals to yearning and praying during various Diasporas that lasted some 2000 years! This monumental cognitive step was possible only within a fully cognitive, abstract God and system of belief. It was a historic achievement that enabled the people to continue to evolve their traditions with no icons, no sacrifices, no temple and no sovereign land. The God that had failed them was still the "One", in-spite of horrible hardship. Judaism was a large community in antiquity, there were an estimated 6-8M Jews before the great revolt (70CE); today it is a small minority, perhaps .2% of humanity. Regardless, their religion was the singular element that held the Jews together as a nation, even as the people were spread to the four corners of the world for almost two millennia - until the rise of the state of Israel. The Jewish God was tribal and strict, sometimes vengeful. The Christian God, on the other hand, was universal and of divine love and compassion; the fathers of the religion understood early the importance universality (by St. Paul) and welcomed any and every human soul willing to convert. Both Christianity and later Islam, acted forcefully to proselytize and actively convert - acts not pursued in Judaism and early Islam. Christianity acted on the universal plan and swiftly took over the Roman Empire, thus becoming the dominant religion in the west. Mass conversion of pagans happened initially in the areas surrounding the Roman Empire, then spread to the four corners of the European continent. Then, through the overseas empires, Christianity became the largest religion that spread all over the world. Conversion was one of the great successes of Christianity; by the 11th century, the whole of Europe was practically converted, including Scandinavia and Russia (Ukraine) then. The church learned quickly that conversion is first an act of compliance (not understanding) - first you obey, then you understand. The first priority was to quickly convert the leaders whose influence on the people was very effective. Once a core converted, they quickly sought to convert their family and friends, a religious zeal we observe even today. Then the whole community.

In Europe, the local monasteries helped convert the people and acted as the cultural centers of the area: Canterbury, York, Cluny or Aix-la-Chapelle (Aachen, Germany today). Pagan conversion spread to the far reaches of the continent (e.g., Scandinavia and Russia). Then in 1095CE, the Church turned the crusades into a religious-political movement; the first crusades were organized and facilitated by the church as a popular movement without the participation of monarchs! The political power of the church was in the ascent. The "golden age" of Christian church political authority started to abate after more than a thousand years, with the rise of the Humanists and coalescence of the nation state, especially in France. The conflict between Philip the Fair and Pope Boniface VIII, ending with a physical assault on the Pope's person (known as "Outrage at Anagni," 1303) is a watermark. Europe heard the outrage but nobody seems to have acted for the Pope!

By the Renaissance, clergy corruption had been legendary for centuries and was the object of the educated-class' many bitter jokes (see Boccaccio, Chaucer, Bracciolini and Leonardo, among many others); soon, Martin Luther appeared on the pages of history (1517CE); this was no joke. The authority of Rome was challenged within nations and communities thereafter. The Pope continued to wield political influence (Rome was a leader in the fight with the Ottomans over the Mediterranean, specifically Pope Pius V and his support, before the battle of Lepanto, 1572CE), but the church's political authority was checked and its influence was steadily declining.

When the ideas of the Enlightenment questioned the whole social structure, leading influential thinkers became Deists[304]. Napoleon crowned himself Emperor in 1804 to demonstrate his supreme command and the independence of the state over the church.

In modernity, the state asserted its superiority and sometimes separated from the church. Many western states support Freedom of worship, in many places this is a constitutional right (specifically in the U.S). Still, the church and specifically Rome wields a certain political influence.

During modernity, with the rise of the sciences and our ability to understand the universe better, religion may take different shades. While it adds content to daily life through rituals, traditions and communal services, it also evolved into a philosophy, aided by many religious philosophers; for examples: St. Augustine, Thomas Aquinas, Martin Buber, Baruch Spinoza, Blaise Pascal, Soren Kierkegaard and Abraham Heschel, among many others. Philosophers continue to develop very complex concepts about God and the relationship that humans might have with the deity, especially in regard to morality and social duties[292, 293]. Most of these theories are spiritual and complex, attempting to deal with the ineffable and our limited understanding when faced with the riddles of life's phenomena.

Despite these changes, we are witnessing a spiritual revival worldwide, characterized by a recurrence of fundamentalism in the Muslim world and Evangelism in the United States (aided by technology, especially radio and TV marketing), the rise of religion in the ex-Communist countries (Russia, China) as well as the spectacular religious-political zeal in the Muslim world.

20TH CENTURY & HOLOCAUST

The two World Wars of the 20th century and their savagery, brutality and the eventual inhumanity of mechanical mass killing, have shaken Western thought and religiosity. The technologies that enabled wholesale killing in the battlefield and mass murder in the concentration camps, could hardly be imagined before they occurred, nor are they easier to accept after the fact. Even before WWI, many expected that "war was impossible" because of the lethality of machine guns and heavy artillery. Technology gave us many advantages but also many curses.

Our history tells many calamities and atrocities but never before did we set up factories to mechanize murdering of the innocent in the hands of compliance by thousands. There was much evil in our history, western or otherwise, but nothing should ever be compared to the profound violence, inhumanity and cruelty perpetrated by the Nazis. The Holocaust was a religious disappointment for many, but for others, it was a religious catalyst. Indeed, the human soul is a great enigma if Heavens can be justified after such tragedy. No doubt, some of the survivors rejected their religion, but others embraced it! In the Jewish world, the issue of divine justice and the murder of innocent millions has not been addressed appropriately. It is a fundamental religious challenge because of the dimensions and monstrosity of the acts. However even many religious Jews could not accept the regular answers and prefer not to ask the questions. For this case, the usual "we cannot judge God's plans" does not seen sufficient.

The invention of nuclear devices fueled another illusion, that war would be impossible. Alas, Nukes have been used and their devastation and inhumanity horrified all. During the intervening 75 years, many wars (conventional so far) have ensued, but the threat of nuclear war increase with their proliferation. Even worse, the threat of terrorism using a nuclear device (not a bomb) is real! Moreover, life in a world of evolving technology has given rise to questions that science cannot address. Life is complex and confusing to many. Some have responded by returning to spiritualism, even delving into the occult, which is widely evident today. Great scientific advances notwithstanding, in matters of the soul, we are still quite ignorant. Rather than return to western religious tradition, various ideologies have taken up residence in the social order, to fill the void of the 20th century, among them Communism, Liberalism, Environmentalism and Capitalism. There are no Gods in these ideologies, but they have accrued many "true-believers." and their zeal is similar to the religious fanaticism we know.

Religion remains a powerful social and spiritual force. It has lost some of its political influence in various western, secular societies. But in Islam, the power of faith still dominates and affects politics. Some past Communist societies (in Russia, Eastern Europe and China) are currently experiencing a vast spiritual awakening. The Pope is still and will continue to be a powerful spiritual and political figure in world affairs. Religion will continue to play a central role in our lives as a spiritual and traditional resource. It is a stable age-old bastion in a world of change and rising complexity.

4.2 MYTHOLOGY

"Myths, so to say, are public dreams.
Truth sometimes must be concealed…myth contains eternal truth."

Joseph Campbell

Our personal memory is short and fragile but it allows the erection of monumental stories of the past, stories that help mitigate our personal, communal and national aspirations. Mythology, the stories people invent and tell to explain nature, history, or their origins, is a powerful and formative force that helps establish our identity, our contact with the past and the cohesion of the social order. It serves as the foundation of our religions, epics, our deep roots and origins. The main mythological players are Gods and Heroes, mostly through their accounts in the deep past. Throughout time, myth powerfully reflects humanities coalescent toward nationalism through art, music, poetry and symbolism. All religious origins are shrouded in mythology, yet myth constantly affects our lives and tradition as much as it affects religion.

Certain elements are central to myth, among them: the hero (a central element in Campbell's work), love, beauty, gods, heroism and fate. Typical mythological mottos include: bending or breaking natural law, the power of fate, superior characters, fate and warnings. For example, "but do not eat the apples," "but do not ask for the name," "all of the hero's body is protected but his back," or "but do not look back"...

In some mythologies, even the gods have limit, they are bound by certain regulations. In Nordic mythology, the gods are bound by their agreements (Wotan is bound by the contracts written on his spear). In the Bible, God says to Eve and Adam after they eat the forbidden apple: "Behold, the man has become like one of us...lest he takes also the tree of life, and eat, and live forever." Is the god bound by his own rules?

Many of the characteristic stories repeat across humanity in many civilizations' mythologies. Either from copying or from common forces that act on the human psyche. To quote Joseph Campbell, *"Life...sometimes requires life-supporting illusions."*

ON DEATH

Joseph Campbell, one of the "oracles" of contemporary myth theory, posited two foundational origins for the creation of myth - the riddle of death and the concept of time. Both are complex, evolving and unique to the human experience. Together with our yearning for the past (and the future), these origins are shrouded in deep mysteries and correlate with mythologies. We know the inevitability of our individual death, even if we cannot comprehend a universe without us, and yet we hope, for some semblance of eternal endurance through our progeny and nation (or tribe). Nobody can understand or comprehend true "nothingness", how can the world and reality be without oneself? To some, "We are starting to die when we are born," while for others "this life is but a corridor to the after-life." Still, for many, the birth-death cycle has a beginning and end, and no hope but the community. We cannot imagine what it means to be dead, to cease to exist in any possible way. Our personal universes vanish with us at our death, but we must cling to the belief that our lives must continue with our progeny and through the social order. We project that the world will continue after we are gone; this way we become a small part of a greater whole whose future is "eternal." Epicurus argued that we should be indifferent to death because death carries no pain or suffering; this is very stoic, but not how we naturally think. Religious folks create a relief mechanism in the afterworld, still, most believers found it difficult to exercise this confidence; most of us fear dying as much and perhaps more than we fear death. Campbell posited that the time component links us to the certainty that the social order existed long before we gained consciousness (our birth) and will endure long after we are individually gone. The fact of our finality - and we know well that every person who has ever existed has died (except in myth), is impossible to bear. How can we cope with this inevitability of marching time or with the attendant sense of uselessness and nihilism? Hence the after-life. Ancient burial sites reveal reverence for the dead and contain evidence of extensive preparations for the coming journey into the afterlife; such sited were stocked with food supplies, tools, jewelry, sacrificed animals and more. Although certain ritual occurs widely in the animal kingdom, the ritual that stems from mythological belief is unique to humans. Burial rites in all civilizations continue to be loaded to this day with symbols, mythological beliefs and traditions from the distant past.

Mythologies have other roots too. Life experience is riddled, rife with multiple enigmas, from the order of the universe we observe and the orderliness of the seasons and nature, to the mysteries of life and living matters' inherent "wisdom" in its spectacular variety. In modernity, we seem to be less sensitive because we have an illusion of "understanding" through our sciences. What do we really understand in the mysteries? Science after all seeks the orderliness of the physical laws, not why they are. For an ancient society that was not yet endowed with any of the scientific tools we enjoy today, these mysteries had to find an outlet in our imaginations, in our yearnings; some of this outlet was mythology, the invention of our imagination. Mythologies are not only a matter of the past, we continue to create them albeit in different fashions. Modern mythologies keep rising in religious communities or through artistic expressions.

NATIONAL/TRIBAL MYTH

In addition to the mysteries of life and death, we had to formulate other legends that helped the various social forces become a cohesive and functioning social order. The nation or tribe, themselves an illusion, require their own mythologies. We have a natural desire for worship and belief in something larger, deeper and older than ourselves, to anchor our origins and being and explain the social bond.

To resolve the "war of all on all," Thomas Hobbes (1588-1679) described the simplistic social order required contract. In return for giving up the right to do whatever one pleases (or alternatively, giving up some liberties), the social order's monopoly over force and authority, guarantees basic security to complying members. This was likely the original force that bonded larger human groups into early small communities to ensure all had food supply and protection. But membership in the prevailing social order demands more than merely following prescribed rules. It means becoming part of the order, becoming a committed partner, being involved in rituals and religious practices, inter-breeding and accepting the social make-beliefs that are always rooted in the deep past. One's acceptance of the rules yields a level of trusts and pride in the community and its leadership. Thus one becomes embroiled in the community's social life. A forced society will not prevail; the members must become loyal and believing in the life and rituals of the group. Initially tribal, once firmly established (with education or propaganda) these forces led to the movement we call Nationalism and the belief that we belong to a special and usually "better" group. This premise is mainly a make-believe construct and is based predominantly on myth (part of Nationalism is that ours is "better", hence the easy evolutionary emotions towards chauvinism and jingoism). We are made to believe in old origins, common ancestry and these have stories, legends. Such groups always share a legacy, a mythology, a fabricated common origin, with heroes and gods.

These days, we see the signs of a backlash from Globalization for similar reasons. People imagine themselves to be a part of a group, but not a part of the whole that is divided by history, language and myth. We imagine to be special, usually superior, while immigrants are "others," not part of our nation. Such self-determined divisions seem to be natural (for example, the recent "Make America Great"), even instinctive and under certain conditions, can alleviate the "nation" and create separation. If we are unique, we must be better. This eventually led to the state as the ultimate realization of the individual. Hence, should the state exist to serve the individuals or maybe we should sacrifice the individual on the altar of the state? Fascism made this its ultimate ideology; the state, the "Folk" is the supreme goal, individuals are made to be sacrificed on the altar of Nationalism.

Nation-states began to form as the High Middle-Ages waned, mostly in France, England and Portugal. These later evolved to their modern nations and nationalism became the raging fashion of the 19th century. Some national forces arise from the locality, language and common customs, while others align with an illusion of the nationalistic mythology (race, language, origins and religion). Many of today's nations coalesced only recently, often for no discernible purpose but geography, which led to difficulties that continue to this day (Basques, Catalans, Venetians or Kosovans are shining examples). Common myth requires common language. In the cases that do not share a history, language and a mythology (England & Scotland for example), the bond hardly holds. In the cases like the Basques, separate traditions and language (not even Indo-European) add to the difficulties.

ALTRUISM

Under certain conditions, an individual might prioritize the welfare of the community (or tribe, nation) over himself, out of altruism. Sometimes this leads to sharing, which is natural and prevalent and not only a human practice; it might also lead to self-sacrificing in extreme conditions. Our mythologies are loaded by numerous examples of heroic self-sacrifices, especially during crisis; these are well known and adored. Almost every nation has such mythology. For example, the Song of Roland describes a knight's heroic self-sacrifices in the days of King Charlemagne (it was written down only circa 1100CE). The epic poem is integral to the French tradition, definitely entered the pantheon of French historic mythology. Roland was the pride of French history at its zenith of fighting power and self-sacrifice. Such self-sacrifice and altruistic behavior that happens in almost every crisis or war, might be rooted in instinct or perhaps from such mythological epics that convince the individual to act contrary to his or her self-preservation instinct. What would otherwise make a young soldier, in a split-second decision, jump on a hand-grenade to save their platoon? Such Philanthropic acts also occur in the animal Kingdom and arise in a group context, when the individual is willing to give up everything for the benefit of family, tribe or nation. Sacrifice for family might be instinctive; for example, when a mother defends her cubs, but when the group is far wider, as in the military, the root concept must be different. The state's priority is elevated beyond the individual, even at the cost of one's life! This belief is part of our upbringing and the mythology of national heroes is integral to our identity, as part of our education and upbringing. These mythological heroes and sacrifices are ingrained in us at a young age and could, in a split-second decision, convince to sacrifice for the "greater good." Organized education and military training and indoctrination teach exactly these perceptions and aims, to turn the individual into an ultimately loyal member of the community. Boot-camp training is always exacting because its purpose is to "break" our individualism in favor of the group. It is well known that in battle, individuals make sacrifices for their fellows, actions stemming from inculcated group pressure and encouragement to fulfill the duties of courage and sacrifice, based on past examples and mythologies.

During the twentieth century, conditions that elevated the "nation" beyond the individual, proved the foundation of Fascism and Nationalism. Thus, the state, the nation, has a purpose worthy of personal sacrifices, the State above all - "*Deutschland uber alles*". If in democracy, the state exists to serve the individual, the Fascists turned the table on the concept and made the state supreme. Accordingly, Nazi Germany used both mythology and the mythological occult in its rituals to indoctrinate its youth. National rites, such as independence days or important dates for the party, were loaded with mythological symbols and a weighty degree of atavism (recalling ancestral times). Symbols of power, of marching together and past glories involved mythological symbols: flags, various coats of arms and theatrical use of rituals and fire (torches were especially effective, then and since), oaths and sworn allegiances. Many of our flags are mythological. The Austrian flag, for example, is based on the heroic deeds and blood spilling of the legendary crusader Duke Leopold V, hence the very red colors, the blood of the hero. One image, flag, tells a huge story and all of us can comprehend it by just one look. And still, the power that a flag wields is fantastic, practically over all of us.

Trends towards incessant militarism and parading are waning in democratic countries and used mostly for the purview of military and despotic regimes.

THE AFTERLIFE

The puzzles and fears of our own mortality found an outlet in religion, which forecast consolation and the notion of a "life in God." Eastern religions gave us the principle of reincarnation, the eternal life of the soul. In the Biblical narrative, we were created to live eternally, but disobeying God caused humans' expulsion from Eden and our eventual - since we ate from the tree of Wisdom and became responsible - condemnation to toil and death. The Jewish bible does not describe after-life, all rewards are promised in this world. Later among religious traditions, death was perceived as the end of one's life on earth. This life was interpreted as corridor towards eternity. By obeying God's laws, we learned, one can secure a life and its continuation to eternity. In Christianity, the concept of after-life was embraced immediately; an extensive monastic tradition (in both theory and lifestyle) developed over the generations as means to purify oneself before divine judgment. The after-life became a central proposition that required sacrifices on this earth; some religious ritual therefore requires sacrifices that are self-punishing in the extreme, as with Asceticism. Highly regimented and disciplined monastic life was physically and mentally difficult for most adherents, especially the ascetics who inflicted atrocities on their bodies (see for example St. Anthony (251-368CE) or St. Bernard (1090-1153) in pursuit of their spiritual bliss. Asceticism came early to Christianity, perhaps because the Christian Son of God suffered so badly; it also merged well with the concept of the "Kingdom of heaven."

Mythology is fundamental to every culture and embraces details unique to each civilization. The ancient Sumerian civilization has given us the epic of Gilgamesh, a hero of super-human strength and a great builder. The biblical Nimrod could be the residue of such an epic tale and demonstrates the influence of the local civilization (Babylon here) on the exiled leadership who wrote the Jewish bible much later. The ancient Greek gods were more humanized; mythologies surrounding their behavior and their illustrative tales are extensive, ultimately in our memories. In modern times, mythology captivated the artistic expression beyond the day-to-day, became the roots of various highly artistic expressions (for example, Wagner's Ring Cycle and the various other German operas based on mythological subjects). A great body of literature studies the stories and our attraction to the lavish productions.

Every civilization continuously builds its mythology to this day. Joseph Campbell taught, "*In the long view of the history of mankind, four essential functions of mythology can be discerned. The first and most distinctive - vitalizing all - is that of eliciting and supporting a sense of awe before the mystery of being. The second function of mythology is to render a cosmology, an image of the universe that will support and be supported by this sense of awe before the mystery of the presence and the presence of a mystery. A third function of mythology is to support the current social order, to integrate the individual organically with his group. The fourth function of mythology is to initiate the individual into the order of realities of his own psyche, guiding him or her toward their own spiritual enrichment and realization.*"

Today we enjoy a better understanding of nature and the universe, but this knowledge has added more complex levels of awe. The more we know, the more we stand in awe before our being, before the magnificence of a universe and the mysteries of life. Our awe before the symmetry nature's beauty and our ability to describe the processes in scientific terms or by following certain equations, some of them aesthetical in their simplicity or patterns, give rise to more questions. This is because physics describes how things might work, but not why. What are those if not mythologies? What is the hypothesis of the Big Bang? Does it posit a universe of immense dimensions being born from a singularity, before time, from nothingness? Is this not a modern mythology that most of us believe, mostly without understanding? We continue to create or evolve religious and secular mythologies based on people's visions; these take the form of meeting the past or past personalities; also as evident in the fruits of artists' imagination, for example the Arthurian tales - we had a White House we called Camelot; Tolkien's Lord of the Rings comprises entire Kingdoms based on ideas, faith, consequences and heroism. The ongoing saga of Star Wars (a futuristic mythology that quickly became ingrained in our culture and language) continues to expand our notion of worlds beyond our own and shrinking galactic distances in ways we can only dream of; these have become almost as real to us as our individual lives and their terminologies entered our language and life.

As we face a world of rising complexity, questions about the direction of future mythologies are standing before us. Although we still hear tales about a new shroud being discovered or encounters with old Saints (such as Fatima in Portugal or Knock in Ireland), certain mythologies have strung from our technologically oriented present. Sagas, such as Star Wars are fresh, employ new technology, expand visual imagination, scientific projections and the media's reach. These have contributed to mythologies that have entered our lexicon, language and world-view (George Lucas was Campbell's student and follower[306]). They have been wildly successful because, in addition to the genius of their creation, audiences are craving the next installment.

Publishing, movies and media technology create new tools for forming new mythologies. The art of storytelling is a bona fide revival of predominantly mythological themes (the various Rings, Harry Potter). Like all myths and legends, modern mythology engages from our sense of life's wonder, excitement, mystery, and fear of the unknown. We yearn for these fantastic stories that are full of good and bad characters, witches and sorcerers, and the triumph of justice and goodness. In addition, Redemption (usually by the death of the heroine; Wagner systematically destroys the poor, mostly innocent "pure-heroine" on the altar of some goodness, if sometimes too nationalistic) became central to the story and the music.

C. S. Lewis thought otherwise, writing that myth exist in our imagination because the God(s) implanted it, and thus, the human psyche becomes the realization of Gods' existence. Both Joseph Campbell and C.S. Lewis understood myth as a social force that reinforces cultural values. Over and above its influence on religion and identity formation, mythology has a fundamental effect on the creation of an implied character and national unity and craving for an imaginary past. We had better understand today symbols, 'rituals' and mythologies' power and influence on us and the hopes and threats they invoke. They have been proven to be awesome forces in the hands of charlatans and dangerous leaders. Such comprehension does not dilute the power that myth has on us and on the continuous foundation of our world and social orders.

In the end, we invent mythologies and religions to alleviate the fears and mysteries of life and the universe. Those must fit their times and reflect current world-view and the aspirations of civilization.

4.3 THE LAW, CONSTITUTIONS

"All life is structure.

In the biosphere, the more elaborate the structure, the higher the life form."

Joseph Campbell

The law is a system of rules that regulate our interaction and behavior in the social construct. The law evolved from very rudimentary and harsh beginnings more than 5,000 years ago, until today; its immense intricacy and complexity is one of the best examples of the rise of complexity in society. We should note that the Canon (religious) law continues to evolve and while eventually giving way to the Civil, it continues to be employed to this day (marriage, burial, baptism, family and religious matters).

Law and justice received various interpretations over time. For example, in the Middle Ages, specifically in France, the value of evidence could be made dependent on prowess in arms. According to medieval ideas, the stronger man in combat was right, or, to put it in the language of the time, divine justice was revealed through victory in personal combat[43]. So profound was this conviction that there was no difference of opinion among men that could not be settled in this way[324]. Otherwise, the law was the domain of the rulers and they sometimes wielded special justices (for example, confiscating property of adversaries). In modernity, Biblical and English laws combined with mostly the ideas of the Enlightenment, created constitutions like the US, whose famous preamble states, *"We the People of the United States, in Order to form a more perfect Union, establish Justice, insure domestic Tranquility, provide for the common defense, promote the general Welfare, and secure the Blessings of Liberty to ourselves and our Posterity…"* Thus, a principle was established that the law exists to serve and protect the people as a whole and not to regulate and serve the interests of a ruling minority. The law became the ultimate regulator of society. Democratic society declared a monumental principle: it will be regulated by laws, not by the whims of any person. In principle, every person in the social order is judged by same laws. This is quite new, just remember that the young Voltaire was thrown into jail, for indefinite amount of jail time, for just offending a nobleman, less than 300 years ago.

Every human society must have a system of law, a certain code of behavior, of interfacing with one another; even animals have one. Because conflict, disagreement, selfishness and incompatibility are fundamental elements of societies, regulating a social order can be maintained only by setting rules of behavior and by mechanisms that impose these rules or decide disputes before they become violent. Before the written law, a group's "Elders" sat in judgment or negotiated, probably as described in Exodus (18:14). They obviously followed prescribed social norms, based on traditions, common sense and locality. From those origins until today, the law evolved to encompass our civil rights, impose obligations, protect property and regulate the economy and our dealings with one another. In time, certain laws became "universal," like the **Ten Commandments**, and eventually transcended every code of law certified by moral societies. As the social order became more and more intricate, in tandem with the system of law, these codes became more detailed, more complex until today, a vast array of rules, regulations, constitutions, precedents and judgments. Our codes of law are some of the most intricate and complex systems we have erected and indeed, most of our lawmakers and politicians are lawyers - people who studied and applied the code of law, before they turned to politics. In principle, the law emerges from the moral code but is different because it depends on traditions and must be practical. Also, morality constitutes more of a personal guide for behavior while the law is a communal edict and property. Morality is eternal, but the Law changes in time. In a court of law, we frequently witness the difference between the law and justice. The law is a set of rules and regulations, a social formulation that is imposed while simultaneously attempting to be a practical manifestation of the moral code. This is one of the reasons that early laws were always from the "divine," which conferred reverence and authority beyond our authority.

A code of law "for the people and by the people" was an old Greek civilization concept; it was so unique that it was quickly aborted in favor of rule by monarchy and noble classes. The American Revolution that created the U.S. constitution, following the evolving English law, revitalized the concept, the notion of authority emerging from the people and that all the people deserve equality before the law, as revealed in the first seven words, "*We the People of the United States.*" The U.S. Constitution, an exemplary document, is a code of behavior written for the people, one that seeks "justice for all." It had become one of the great documents of western civilization and humanity.

ANCIENT ORIGINS

The earliest known formal code of law was Egyptian, some five millennia ago. No documents have survived, but we know that Pharaoh was the head of a system based on a local common-sense (most laws are) and community elders that managed ruling courts. Punishments were cruel by today's norms, and included fines, mutilation, enslavement, decapitation and exile. Hammurabi's laws (as discussed in the context of an earlier chapter), encoded about 3,800 years ago in Mesopotamia, was a comprehensive system that regulated social behavior and commerce, government, family relationships and rules for inheritance. This law demonstrated, albeit only rudimentarily, the origins of the concepts encapsulated in constitutions. It included government regulation (limited the power of one man) and initiated the concept of "*presumption of innocence,*" which later became the "golden thread" of western justice[294]. Hammurabi's system also included fashioned courts of law and used witnessed.

As commerce grew between and inside communities, new laws and regulations had to be imposed. Regulations always had few purposes: to smooth the procedures, encourage commerce and raise taxes for the rulers (government today). Standards were assigned, among them length or weight systems - fundamental measures that govern commerce and exchange of goods. The "true scale" was a challenge until modern standardization of units and measures. The law started its meandering path towards higher details, higher volume and rising complexity.

MOSAIC CODE OF LAW

A thousand years after Hammurabi, a revolutionary concept of law was introduced, the Mosaic code that was comprehensive, detailed for all facets of life and written within a theocracy - its authority was divine. Considered by many to be the supreme original manifestation of the law (as written in the Pentateuch, the first five books of the Bible), it comprehensively covered the ancient life; from religion to commerce, family to the socio-national, personal hygiene, diet, sex life, charity and social laws (it established the concept of the Sabbath, a rest day for all, even for slaves and animals). The Mosaic Law, through its adaptation by Christianity and Islam, has become almost universal and enjoyed vast influence on both Christian and Muslim communities around the world, now counting some 4 billion souls. Much of future western law was founded on this biblical canon too. Mosaic Law spans the following:

1. The pillars, the Ten Commandments, three of which deal with one's personal relationship with the one God, the others with fundamental social behavior.

2. Moral laws, concerning murder, theft, adultery, and economics.

3. Social laws, on property, inheritance, commerce, rights, marriage and divorce.

4. Dietary laws, on cooking, food storage and differentiating between clean and "unclean" foods for eating (e.g., Kosher laws).

5. Purity laws - relating to family, marriage and sex life, diseases and hygiene, birth and burial.

6. Religion - Holidays, sacrifice, priesthood, temple, agriculture, King and social order.

The code is so comprehensive that during the long Jewish Diaspora, orthodox communities continued to live by these rules, in some places to this day. Socially, the Mosaic Code is distinctly progressive, rejects the institution of slavery (slavery is legal but viewed very negatively) and supports a universal Sabbath - a magnificent social concept that demands a weekly rest-day for all. The code's great distinction was that it applied to *everybody*. Kings and nobles were not exempt since it is divine, according to tradition, through God's inspiration and authority.

CLASSICAL PERIOD (500BCE-500CE)

The evolution of the political order in ancient Greece, from Solon (590BCE) to Pericles (430BCE), has been a model for and a source of envy and inspiration for western civilizations for two and half millennia. Although Solon divided society according to degrees of individual wealth, Pericles was much more democratic and ready to pay for public services, thus ensuring that all can run for office. This non-differentiating principle is critical because it opened the door for far greater participation in leadership and thus, statistically improved the odds that the best citizens across the whole social order, reached leadership positions. Pericles did not finance candidates run, but compensated office holders; otherwise only the rich could hold office. We were not left with a systematic Greek law documents, but owe them so many social concepts, especially Democracy and the Meritorious society. Aristotle with his penetrating logic had already pointed out democracy's weaknesses and favored a particular version of Enlightened Oligarchy. His reasoning was simple; in democracy, the majority will eventually vote for benefiting itself (today termed "the dole") at levels not affordable otherwise; this will eventually bankrupt the state. Such reasoning already painfully operates across most of the western democracies today in the form of the welfare state. Some states went already bankrupt (Greek) for lavish working and pension conditions that the state cannot afford.

ROMAN LAW

This law first developed during the Roman Republic and later extended across the Empire and was codified throughout a millennium. Its legacy is a systematic written code of law, dating from the days of Justinian, in the middle of the 6th century CE. This codified law is also known as the *Corpus Juris Civilis* and was the official law of the Eastern Empire (Byzantine), which extended for a millennium, until the middle of the 15th century when Constantinople fell to the Ottoman Turks. The Roman codes were encyclopedic in scope and covered all aspects of law, such as commerce, family, inheritance, crime, litigation procedures, rules of court, and more. It was a civil law, secular, based on the authority of the empire. The Roman law became the foundation of many European nations' laws (clearly influencing English, French and U.S. common laws), many historians consider it the zenith of Roman achievements. After the Western Empire declined, the Eastern Empire continued to apply these laws for another thousand years. The German tribes that settled the Empire continued absorbing and evolving this law, as it became universally applied in the West. Jurisdictions still use its language, Latin, to this day.

OTHER LAWS

After the prophet Muhammad unified Arabia (in the 7th century), Arab tribes poured out of the peninsula; fired by their religious zeal they erected swiftly a vast Empire. From beyond Persia and India in the east to the Iberian Peninsula in the west, they accomplished the conquest within less than a century! Further advance into Europe was halted only after the famous Tours-Poitier battle, in 732CE (a Frankish victory under the leadership of Charles Martel). The Arab Empire subscribed to a newly formed religion that influenced its legal system. Sharia is the fundamental Islamic law and is based mainly on percepts in the Quran and the Hadith. Sharia law comprehensively deals with all aspects of Muslim life. Among its many facets: politics, economy, commerce, crime, personal relationships (both family and sexual), hygiene, diet, prayer and Muslim holidays. Sharia has somewhat evolved through the generations of lifestyle experiences - but never strayed from the specific religious commands of Islam. Some of the punishments prescribed in the Sharia seem archaic to westerners (as do many Mosaic laws), because they follow a literal interpretation of the ancient *"an eye for an eye."* Sharia is divine law written down as a discussion, rather than a list of imperatives. Judges—the Kadi— run the Muslim court without a jury system. Some fundamentals include:

1. Sharia is rooted in Islam.
2. The head of the family has dominion and represents the family before the law.
3. Women's position is subordinate to men.
4. Family honor stands above all.
5. Polygamy is allowed.
6. Sharia is not subject to political authority.

Sharia law separates leadership of state and religion. The Sultan is the head of state, while the Caliph is the head of religion. The Caliphate of Baghdad (the Abbasid Caliphate, founded in the 8th century) combined religious and state leadership and reached a zenith during the rule of Harun-al-Rashid, the fifth Caliph (786-809CE). His empire stretched from Arabia almost to the gates of Constantinople. Saladin (the 12th century hero of Islamic traditions) was already the head of a Sultanate and a political leader under Islamic law. When the Ottoman

Empire was established before the end of the 14th century, the Sultan already claimed Caliphal authority. Once the area known as Saudi Arabia was conquered (1517), the Ottoman ruler (not an Arab) could claim himself to be the protector of Islam's holy places.

During the rule of the Ottoman Empire, secular law existed side by side with the religious. This secular law - the Kanum law - was created after the conquest of Constantinople (1453CE) to deal with matters such as: taxation, administration, financials, real estate or penal law. This code served to integrate various groups under the empire. Today, the Muslim world is divided; Saudi Arabia still abides by Sharia law while others, like Turkey and Egypt, have moved on toward civil jurisdiction.

CRIME AND PUNISHMENT

Ancient systems exacted harsh penalties and specifically imprisonment conditions were horrific and cruel. The biblically derived *"an eye for an eye"* was harsh, exacted physical penalties like cutting hands or blinding the criminal. Prison conditions were traditionally appalling. Penalties included public executions (for example, the infamous *"drawn and quartered,"* a 13th century ritual that the British Empire still sometimes exercised in the middle of the 19th century[309]). Torture was an acceptable technique to extract confessions and exacting punishment, not merely during the Inquisition. Prisoners had no rights and were subject to starvation, no hygiene, physical abuse and exposure to disease.

During the late 18th century, the Italian jurist Cesare Beccaria's (1738-1784) influential book, *"On Crime and Punishment[160]"* became a milestone in modernizing the law, especially as its application to harsh punishments. Beccaria and his colleagues represented the more enlightened ideas of northern Italy and Austria. They called for the abolition of torture and discharge punishment that "fit the crime." They established a new concept that the punishment, in addition to the suffering, should also encourage rehabilitation rather than revenge and torture. Thus, with the exception of horrific crimes that demand life imprisonment, the punishment transformed from a revenge to a corrective procedure whose purpose is to also enable the punished criminal to reenter life corrected, after they pay for crimes.

In today's democracies, prisoners have rights and decent imprisonment conditions; torture has been outlawed and capital punishment is not exercised in most western societies.

THE AMERICAN VISION

The American Founding Fathers had a vision of a "perfect Republic" that had to be worked out through the law. The Constitution, the culmination of some 2,500 years of western law, was written by learned scholars (the founding fathers and local jurists, under the leadership of James Madison) and based on experience mostly of English law while drawing on the ideas of the Enlightenment.

Before they signed the constitution (in 1789) the states' representatives hotly debated the issues pertaining to the division of power and the relative power of the federal government and the states. They considered and criticized a few past models for a federation of previous states; for example, the ancient Greco-Roman republics, the Italian city-states of the Renaissance, Venice (once termed "the Serene Republic). British law and the writings of Montesquieu, together with the ideas of the Enlightenment were the guiding lights for a new constitution. They sought to realize their vision for a great and integrated nation, then composed of only some 2.5 million Americans who predominantly inhabited the eastern fringes of the continent. The tragic issue of slavery could not be resolved then and had to be fought for and amended some *"four score and seven years"* later. The hottest debate swirled around the authority of the central government. A compromise was achieved but the future, as we know now, witnessed the continuous encroaching power of DC with weakening of the states. We are witnessing the continuous ongoing rise of federal authority and decline in the power of the states while most Americans use state services and little of the federal. Perhaps this is eventually the result of DC and only DC's capacity to print money.

The U.S. Constitution was the first to guarantee freedom of speech and freedom of the press, stating, *"The people shall not be deprived or abridged of their right to speak, to write, or to publish their sentiments and the freedom of the press, as one of the great bulwarks of liberty, shall be inviolable."* In addition to the Bill of Rights, the Constitution called for the separation of state from the church, reflecting the heavy influence of the ideas of the Enlightenment. The concept of separation of power, fundamental to the U.S. system, had been debated since the days of Aristotle but was chiefly inspired by the writings of Montesquieu. US jurisprudence uses the jury system, a direct influence from English law. The law was comprehensive but evolving. It is open to revisions, amendments and the effects that modernity has on our lifestyle and world-view.

Any comparison between older and modern codes of law reveals the immense volume, scope and intricacy of modern law. It parallels the rise in scope and complexity of modern life and the intricate procedures and nuances that have been raised in every corner of the law and our lives. Attorneys must specialize in specific fields to achieve mastery and a sufficient level of expertise. In modern times, the law acquired an additional purpose - to protect the accused. Conservatives may say this is the indication of our decadence, liberals argue it is the outgrowth of progress. Whatever the reasons, the western legal system treats prisoners better than ever. Judicial principles we know today as *"the presumption of innocence,"* *"judgment before one's peers,"* or *"trial by jury,"* are by now traditional, handed over from the past. For example, 12th century King Henry II (Plantagenet) established a 12-person jury tradition as a tenet of English law; it emerged from old, tried traditions.

In modern law, protection of the accused was extended to include the "rights of the judged and the condemned" through amelioration of jail conditions and how the incarcerated are treated. Modern society was already engaged in the application of "humane" executions (the Guillotine was invented with this purpose in mind. Later electricity, poisoning and gas were tried, not very successfully). The more advanced societies continue to incarcerate law-breakers, but also pursue avenues to reform behavior and help criminals return to a normal, productive life. The fundamental questions of the purpose of punishment, revenge or reform, continue to linger but jails provide growing opportunities for education and the acquisition of tools that can be used (professions) post incarceration. With its deep traditions and complexities, the law is the pillar of the social-order. Not everyone can understand science, technology or the arts, but the law is commonly approachable because it affects everything we do in the day-to-day, and its application thoroughly affects our lives.

4.4 WORLD-ORDER AND DIPLOMACY

"The oppressed are allowed once every few years to decide which particular representatives of the oppressing class are to represent and repress them."

Karl Marx

"If voting made any difference they wouldn't let us do it."

Mark Twain

In the old traditional societies, it was natural to be ruled by a strict hierarchy dominated by a small elite of nobles. Relationships between neighbors depended on the whims of the ruler, personal relationships, dynasties inter-marriages or the interests of the King or Queen. From crusades to arbitrary conquests or suspicious inheritance claims, much of history was decided by the few and by the sword. It took almost all our civilization's force to realize the superior cognitive concept of "rule by law," not by men. The conviction that birthright conferred priority is an anachronism, a conundrum for sociologists rather than historians, but this illusion has not yet passed from the world!

The fundamental idea of "Natural Law," so prevalent in Enlightenment thinking and the basis of many modern constitutions, harks back to provenance as expressed by Aristotle. He posited the first political principle, *"government should govern for the good of the people, not for the good of those in power."* This Aristotelian principle has been interpreted throughout the ensuing centuries especially after the French and American revolutions. In addition to the law governing our social behavior, there was the issue of relationships between groups, later nations. These rules and international laws started to appear in the 17th century, at least in principle and are actually extending the above principles by regulating the relationships between groups and nations. As societies become more cognitive, the futility of most wars becomes evident and facilities are created to enable discourse. Wars that were so "popular" in the past have proven again and again that they benefitted nobody, that both sides were the losers. Consequently, international bodies were established to enable platforms for international discourse for the resolution of conflicts but also discuss planetary challenges and social problems that touch us all. A certain sense of responsibility has emerged, by the wealthier nations, to help regulate world affairs and try to solve disputes by moderation. Most conflicts, but not all, can be resolved by negotiations and deliberations, not only by the sword.

RULE BY THE SWORD

The concept of "world order," sometimes "new world order", is relatively recent. In the past, kings and despots were constantly involved in land-grabbing and wholesale robbery without regard for world order, a concept that entered the Cognitive-Cloud only much later. There was no concept of "planetary concern" or a sense of responsibility because one is stronger or wealthier, as is emerging in modernity. From early empires to the Middle Ages and beyond, the conquest of other populations was common practice. History is rife with accounts of the glories of Alexander, Caesar, Genghis Khan, Napoleon and many others. After the Age of Discovery in the 16th and 17th centuries, the various European powers positioned themselves to conquer and exploit entire continents and create vast empires. Later they preyed on one another in the high seas, sometimes monarchs (like Elizabeth I) investing in the pirates and sharing the loot. Sometimes these conquests were set up as private enterprises or planned by the mother country and its government. The level of exploitation in the colonies was horrendous and was later memorialized in our artistic expressions[33]. Ultimately, the sword decided everything. Losing a battle sometimes meant slavery (especially of women and children), the defeated population was treated as property in slave markets because their rulers lost a battle. The concept of human rights or human dignity did not yet register in the cognitive-cloud of tribal or empirical minds. Rivalries did not respect borders or civilizations and the strong devoured the weak and rulers lived by the primordial law of the jungle. The Bible indicates the horrific predicament of women from losing tribes, especially those who were already married (Numbers, chapter 31, 15-18). This was the spirit of the time. As central powers later rose to dominance with the waning of the Middle Ages and after the nation-states formed, certain rules began to arise. In England, ideas for the abolition of slavery (an institution that still exists) arose in the beginning of the 18th century. In Russia, Peter the Great made slavery illegal in the 1st quarter of the 18th century. Alas too late, but it was positive a cognitive shift; in the US, only the horrific Civil War settled the matter.

ORIGINS OF DIPLOMACY

Quite early in our history, a recognizable level of diplomacy, albeit not codified, was already in place and enabled a dialogue to take place before exchanging blows, in service of good will between neighbors. Messengers would sometimes be sent to exchange or clarify complaints and negotiate agreements before resorting to aggression.

The Bible chronicles that king David (~1000BCE) sent messengers to the King of Ammon to comfort the new King after his father's death "*So David sent by the hand of his servants to comfort him concerning his father...*" (Samuel II, 10:2). These neighbors most likely knew one another, endured a measure of conflict caused naturally by proximity and tried to negotiate; in this case, to show good will by comforting the new king on his father's death. Five hundred years later, communications between the Greek city-states and the Persian Empire were already well recorded. The process evolved slowly; ambassadors represented, and often spied on adjacent powers, as they do until today. Still, the Middle Ages spanned an epoch, a millennium of conquests, fighting, crusades and taking over territories quite arbitrarily. However, there were also communications between the rivals; for example, Saladin and Richard Lion-hearted used to exchange messengers, perhaps for mutual respect. Richard ravaged both Sicily and Cyprus willingly on the way to the crusade but Richard and Saladin even exchange gifts or medicine as a symbol of acknowledgment or respect. But the practice of raiding, kidnapping and subjugation were common even throughout the seventeenth century. The Ottoman Empire, then led by Suleyman the Magnificent, although perhaps the most advanced state during the sixteenth century, staffed its crack military units (the Janissaries) with kidnapped, converted Christian boys from the Balkan. Suleyman's beloved wife, Roxelana (1502-1558), was herself kidnapped from the Polish Kingdom, initially a concubine in the palace. But by then, the powers also used diplomats to communicate and regulate their relationships and disputes. For example, agreements between the king of France, Francis I (1494-1547) and Suleyman were already in force due to diplomatic arrangements (mostly in opposition to Emperor Charles V) even though the two leaders never met[211]. There was not yet a "world-order," but nation-states started to consolidate and better communications between them proved to be critical.

THE WESTPHALIAN SYSTEM (MID-17ᵀᴴ CENTURY)

The emergence of the post Thirty-Years war era (1618-1648) in central Europe and specifically the peace of Westphalia became a milestone in the development of such a concept of "world-order." At the end of this brutal conflict which tore central Europe apart and caused untold misery to millions, the various powers involved: France, Sweden, Spain, the Dutch Republic, various German states, and various states of the Holy Roman Empire, resolved to meet near Westphalia in 1648 and sign peace treaties. The outcome was much more than a peace settlement and an unprecedented event in the history of the west[106,143], by then already the dominating powers of the world. A "Westphalian System" emerged, based on principles of state sovereignty and equality that later led the evolution of a more modern world-order, specifically as it has unfolded during the 20th century. The foundational feature of the above system was that it confirmed states - not empires, dynasties, or religious orders - as the building blocks of the European order. It was a milestone in the evolution of state sovereignty, a cornerstone the development of the nation-state, and the ongoing relationships between them. Henry Kissinger wrote: *"The Westphalian peace reflected a practical accommodation to reality, not a unique moral insight. It relied on a system of independent states refraining from interference in each other's domestic affairs and checking each other's ambitions through a general equilibrium of power. No single claim to truth or universal rule had prevailed in Europe's contests. Instead, each state was assigned the attribute of sovereign power over its territory. Each would acknowledge the domestic structures and religious vocations of its fellow states and refrain from challenging their existence"*. Some of the basic tenets of the Westphalian system were:

1. The sovereignty of states, at this point only European states, were recognized (even Russia was not yet included in the agreement).

2. Legal equality between recognized states.

3. No higher authority stands above the state, except as the state voluntarily assents. This affirmed again the authority of the state over church.

The authoritative pope of the time (Pope Alexander VII) was naturally very displeased and raged about the agreement, *"null, void, invalid, iniquitous, unjust, damnable, reprobate, inane, empty of meaning and effect for all time."*

It is well to remember that the agreement was only for "recognized states" and that concept of the nation-state or nationality are rather new. It is not so long ago that persons were identified as: Saxons, Hessens, Gascons, Picards, Savoyards or Burgundians, rather than German or French. During the Middle Ages, one's loyalty was indeed to the feudal lord. This has changed toward loyalty to the nation only during modernity, with the rise of the nation-state and nationality becoming a fundamental driving force in our identification.

In Westphalia each nation-state won international, equal recognition and gave people the ability for self-definition as nations, despite concomitant geography and tradition. Some 170 years later, in the aftermath of the Napoleonic Wars, various leading nations, England, Russia, Prussia, France and Austria, met in the Congress of Vienna (1814-15CE), and thanks to the precedence of the Westphalian system, they had no need to establish rules of diplomacy and national order. As a result of this historic assembly, ambassadors (actually foreign ministers then) established national and geographic boundaries through negotiations and not by farther conflicts. All the involved powers convened, including the loser (this was a brilliant move that was forgotten 100 years later, when the victors met again in Versailles after WWI, but excluded Germany) and all were treated as respected participants. The Vienna Congress was blessed with three great diplomats - Metternich, Talleyrand (in particular, he managed to negotiate France's participation, which was not initially planned) and Castlereagh (1769-1822)[17]. They understood that the purpose of the Congress was in service of ensuring a lasting peace in the continent, not only to exact revenge. This world-order, at least among the European nations, withstood the rising tensions that occurred on the continent for about a century, until the catastrophic eruption of World War I.

It is impossible to ignore the role of the powerful British navy, specifically between the Battle of Trafalgar (1805) and WWI (1914-18); as the mightiest navy and the forefront of a great empire, it stood ready to intervene when others violated various agreements (or British interests). Naturally, the sword eventually matters, but only as a last resort. Wars erupted from time to time (such as the Crimean war (1853-1856), or the Franco-German war (1870-71)) and various conflicts erupted, either local or the instigation of the great powers, engaged in empire building during the 19th century . These conflicts were contained to locality (South Africa, Egypt/

Sudan) until the disaster of August 1914[48]. During this period (1870s - 1914), the German states united, initially under Bismarck, and fomented unsustainable imperial ambitions and tensions (especially after Bismarck's dismissal in 1890), which eventually, due to new considerations of modernity, technology and the challenge to the British Empire, could not be localized and deteriorated into the World Wars of the 20th century[303]. The war ended not with peace, rather with a cease-fire for 20 years, as Marshal Fosh forecasted. The victors of WWII seem to have learned the lesson and the new world order, after the horrific conflicts, were better organized for a modern world. It seems that in Western Europe, the age-old conflicts are now over and even unification, EU, has been pondered and implemented (to Russia's chagrin). The UN was established. There are certain preferences to the bigger countries (Security Council), but overall in the UN, equality rules (General Assembly). Since the establishment of the United Nations, no state has lost its status and participation continues to grow.

CONSTITUTIONS AND THE RIGHTS OF MAN

The concepts underpinning the "Rights of Man" are universal and absolutely modern. Ancient traditions respected, even sanctified human life, but the belief in unalienable rights for *every* person merely because of their humanity, is modern. The *Declaration of the Rights of Man and the Citizen* (a French Revolution document, 1789) confirmed ideas that seem thoroughly natural to westerners and democrats today but were revolutionary at their time:

- Men are born and remain free and with equal rights, as a universal law.
- The aim of all political association is to preserve the natural rights of man. These rights consist of liberty, property, security and resistance to oppression.
- In principle, all sovereignty resides essentially in the nation and its representative government.
- Liberty consists in the freedom to do anything that injures no one else.

Today, intellectuals are looking for adaptation of such enlightened principles beyond the self-interest of the nation-state. Modern democracies are acting to spread to democratic ideals of freedom around the world. A modern planet-wide interest, for the preservation of planet resources and health is still meeting opposition because our tribal nature and local interests. In-spite of local difficulties, these are eventually possible as we continually shrink distances by dint of sophisticated communications and transportation and assume responsibility for the planet. As we progress toward free press and greater integration of our economies, more and more of us are coming together to focus on the common interests that are everybody's concern, such as the climate, global warming (GW), resource control, water resources, pollution, trade regulations, health and diplomacy. In certain intellectual circles, discussions of "post-nationalism" are popular and with them the encouragement of immigration from other civilizations into the west, or the more affluent societies. The west is shrinking due to low birthrate, others are growing, immigration seems like a natural outcome. However, nationalistic emotions remain strong and volume immigration seems an increasingly major challenge for many western states.

THE UNITED NATIONS (UN)

After the debacle of WWI, various British and American leaders' initiatives led to conceiving and establishing the League of Nations (1920–1946), the first international organization ever formed to promote and maintain world peace through discourse and negotiations. The League's methods were similar to the United Nations' today, although the earlier body lacked any material authority and depended on the world's great powers among its members to drive issues to fruition. Japan and Germany's withdrawal during the 1930s sealed the fate of the League and led to the establishment of the United Nations (in 1945) after the end of WWII.

When U.S. President Franklin D. Roosevelt formulated the principles of the UN (in 1942-43), he was mindful of the lessons of the failed League of Nations, among them that both the United States and Russia, the two great powers after the end of WWII, were not League members. FDR had a monumental grasp of history and was a true republican in its purest sense. He objected to the Franco-English dream of renewed Empires after the war towards liberation of the various nations and establishing self-determination and democracies instead. He had both the authority and moral compass to ensure his dream of liberated nations, combined with the UN as the platform for world negotiations. Although the dream that included the "four powers"—the United States, Russia, China, and England - as the collective mediating authority, did not work out as he expected, it came close (the UN Security Council today consists of the four powers and France). China, then weak, was recognized and included due its geographical vastness, historic contribution and large population. The UN includes numerous bodies that operate beyond diplomacy and its activities extend into arts, culture, natural preservation, refugee support, human rights, peacekeeping and disaster relief. At this writing (in 2017), 193 nations are UN members and represent most of the countries of the world. The organization comprises a stage for the exchange of ideas and a platform to manage international issues, while the world continues to integrate and confront the myriad challenges and responsibilities that are common to all. These include the risk of terrorism, global climate change (GW, GCC), nuclear threats and health issues, among countless others. Technology enables instant communications between world leaders and rapid travel between member states contributes to the proactive and progressive international diplomacy.

There is also a growing body of law - the International Criminal Law (ICL), to regulate certain infractions, like genocide and war crimes. In addition, there are various universal conventions (like the Geneva convention, on which almost all countries have signed), for regulating behavior in war, towards prisoners of war and conquered territories, and various other tribunals. For example, the International Court of Justice (ICJ) for personal infractions, mostly war crimes and crimes against humanity.

In addition to the UN, the modern world consists of multiple international organizations and bodies whose purpose is to promote cooperation, economic progress, diplomacy, and peace. Among them are the World Bank, Unicef (UN Children Fund), the World Health Organization, and the World Economic Forum; there are also voluntary organizations, such as Doctors without Borders (Médecins Sans Frontières), and numerous other humanitarian organizations and non-governmental organizations, (or NGOs) that operate for the benefit of the whole planet and all people. Many such entities' initiatives are intended to help the weaker economies and poorer folks. They organize forums across the world to resolve tense relationships and promote cooperation, even fraternity.

During recent years, scores of the very wealthy have donated their fortunes to humanitarian causes, among them the spread of education, eradication of certain diseases, wildlife preservation, and such.

As mentioned in chapter 3, not all theorists are equally optimistic about forecasts for a new world order. Evidence shows the democratic systems ideology (Democracy, free market economy) undergoing a challenge (by China, for example), as well as questions how the system handles economy and power projection. "*It would be fair to suggest that the world is seemingly becoming more cosmopolitan but at the same time more parochial. Intricate patterns of transnational exchange compete with emotional ties of national identity. Nation-states are enmeshed in a complex network of transnational governance that includes corporations, banks, and intergovernmental and non-governmental organizations. In sum, the world today is being shaped by forces that challenge the Westphalian state-centric view of international politics[137].*"

Even in a Huntingtonian universe of cultural conflict fault lines, we can no longer deny globalization's growing force and influence. If conflict is inherent in human affairs, then Huntington made the point forcefully, but one hopes we can overcome ongoing discord, even on the basis of material and culture exchange alone. Globalization is a net-positive concept and the technology that supports it makes the world smaller, closer, and more integrated. The natural division of labor today, the wealthy countries gravitating to services while the others growing their middle class and consumption, make Globalization a natural force. This force also brings civilizational exchange and cross fertilization. Globalization however also erects challenges and the fear of work migrating to "other places" and competing with the local workers. Currently, the western and wealthy states seem to be steadily challenged, specifically because of economic forces, easy mobility, immigration, economies of scale, vast worldwide diversity, and the rise of ideas that demand better integration and resolutions. Transnational Corporations (TNCs) operate globally and sometimes violate the interests of a state and its people. Emerging titanic transnational corporations (Google, Facebook, Microsoft are few examples) accumulate vast fortunes and political muscle that might challenge the state. Checking such forces has proved difficult because their wealth provides political power and influence that is un-proportional. Still other organizations that act across borders and promote economic interests based on altruism and fairness are growing by the day. Concomitantly, we acknowledge the emerging need for cooperation to improve global security in the face of growing terrorism and web-security threats. Issues and threats of such magnitude cannot be contained within the borders of the nation-state. These foes, be it physical or in-cloud terrorism, operate across the globe and require cross-border cooperation to contain. Democracies have no choice but to unite their security considerations and activities. The resultant emerging world order will probably have to create new rules that incorporate post-Westphalian concepts. English is emerging as an "Lingua Franca - international language," a matter that could ease communications.

In 1942, FDR conceived a new world order for the post-WWII era. He was unwilling to accept subjecting the American people to the ordeals of WWII, only to resurrect the old Empires, a dream contained in the old countries' plan, specifically England (under Churchill) and France. FDR envisioned the liberation of world nations as self-governed and self-determined, and empires entirely dissolved. During the post-WWII era, many Southeast Asian nations were liberated, subsequently also Middle Eastern countries; later also in North Africa, South America, and elsewhere. After the end of WWII, the Russian Empire subjugated Eastern Europe, and the southern Asian zone of Russia was subsumed by the communist colossus. It collapsed after the fall of the Berlin wall (1989).

In the west, this new political reality, of sovereign nations without empires, has become known as the liberal world order, which has engendered both enthusiasm and debate during the past few decades. As the newly conceived order expanded, the nation-state weakens, especially in the European theater. The European Union (EU) with its open borders and lax immigration policies, has grown from the initial four members to around 20 countries today. The EU created a unified currency (the Euro) and enacted common policies that offend, sometimes, the notion and practice of national sovereignty, at least for some (see the Brexit debacle). Also, such lax immigration policies allowed large displaced populations to immigrate (current estimates are 50 to 60 million), especially from the Muslim countries - a direct consequence of the turmoil, particularly in the Arab and Muslim world, of the last few decades and the Arab-Spring. These events are causing national concerns and consequently intellectual and political debates. The results are revealing a marked degree of popular revulsion of globalism (also called "Populism") and a political chasm arising within nations, clearly expressed by Brexit, the election of Donald Trump in the United States and tensions in other places; among them Turkey, Eastern Europe, and the aspirations of schismatic groups like the Catalans. The loss of national identity coupled with the fear of very large migratory, alien populations that traditionally have very large families into the European theater with its collapsing Total Fertility Rate (TFR in countries like Spain or Italy is already below 1.5) is fomenting natural apprehension for many.

The questions pertinent to these issues also include critique of liberal ideology versus the conservative world-view. Liberals proclaim the value of immigrants and the collapsing European populations (German PM Angel Merkel recently opined that the demographic issue of western low birthrate can be solved only by immigration), while conservatives prefer to conserve the nation-state and national stability to stave off fast-changing and sometimes risky realities. The tension between the liberals and conservatives is so bitter they bear comparison to the Guelphs and Ghibellines of the Middle Ages. Unfortunately, the two factions do not converse; the liberal media speaks to its followers and conservative TV and podcasts preach to their base with little exchange. The issues are not only ideological, there are real threats to local labor markets with growing globalization. This situation is especially pressing as some politician point to the falling demographies of the west while others point to a future dominated by thinking machines and declining labor opportunities for all of us.

In his book *Diplomacy*[16] Henry Kissinger opined that in every century among the last few, there seems to emerge a country, a civilization with the power, the will, and intellectual impetus to shape the international system according to its own values. These powers - including, but not only the British Empire or the United States - fostered resentment for their domination and ability to force various issues arbitrarily. Perhaps this is lessening as the forces of globalization, technological advancements, and diplomats' and historians' political theories are leading to the emergence of a universal cognitive cloud that many share. We can project that the next generation's leaders, at least in the developed world, will be less selfish and more global in their view of the common good, the considerations of the planet, their citizens and others. The planet faces far too many global threats to ignore the issues brought on by globalization. Through cooperation and discourse, we have averted great military conflicts since the end of WWII. It is essential to be able to continue this tradition of negotiations, instead of exchanging blows (still going on in too many places from the Middle East to SE Asia and Africa) and expand its concepts so that the coming global challenges, which only intensify (like GW, over-population, terror, water resources and aquifers) can be mitigated and hopefully resolved through mutually respectful discourse.

THE UNITED STATES AND WORLD ORDER

The early U.S. developed its doctrine of Manifest Destiny even before it became a great power. Perhaps a certain arrogance or hubris convinced the young country's leaders of a territory so vast, isolated and protected, to be certain of their abilities; that they could affect world affairs as a dominant power. Indeed, the U.S. swiftly grew to become a great power with an overall highly positive influence, but its record in world affairs participation also leaves some to be desired (Vietnam, Iraq). The new country also quickly aspired to becoming an empire. Jefferson purchased the Louisiana Territory in 1804 and sent Louis and Clark to explore the American continent. In the meantime, settlers rushed toward the west, likely to fulfill their belief that such a push was justified and inevitable. Between 1846 and 1848, then-President Polk sent troops to acquire the southwest. His policies also were responsible for the annexation of Texas and the Oregon territory. A decade later, Secretary of State William Seward and the U.S. Senate ratified the purchase of the Alaska territory by treaty with Russia (in 1867), completing the integration of the continental United States (CONUS). A century after declaring its independence, the United States was already on the way to becoming the largest economy in the world.

The United States began its international influence earlier with the Monroe Doctrine (1823) and other smaller ventures in the Philippines and Cuba. President Jefferson already sent the navy to the Barbary Coast (1805) and Commodore Perry went to re-establish (actually force) trade with Japan in 1854, but the United States was more interested in expanding its sphere of influence than acquiring territories. President Theodore Roosevelt threatened the European powers not to intervene in South America in 1901 and received a Nobel Peace Prize for helping the negotiations between Russia and Japan (1906). However, the United States had a strong sense of isolation and withdrew even after the end of WWI. After the Japanese attack on Pearl Harbor (on December 7, 1941), the U.S. committed its resources to WWII and was thereafter continuously involved in world affairs as a dominant global superpower. After the war, the U.S. economy was world dominant for a while. US initiated many treaties and organizations that promoted peace and development, with constant support of the UN (funding 22% of its budget) as well as the North Atlantic Treaty Organization (NATO, formed in 1949, also at similar percentage). The United States suffered two embarrassing conflicts in Vietnam and Iraq. The current Trump administration is calling for U.S. withdrawal from many international commitments and cutting monetary support for the UN and NATO, while attempting to create a more equitable partnership with those organizations (traditionally the United States pays un-proportionally). The withdrawal from various conflict areas and the lowering of our commitments will have a significant effect on our influence and the world. At this point, our withdrawal creates a certain vacuum that other powers rush to fill (Russia, China) but they still do not have the US gravitas, wealth and clout. We have traditionally acted as a moderating force; our withdrawal will affect the world negatively (Syria, Afghanistan, etc.), weaken NATO and might even weaken the war on terror.

POST-WESTPHALIAN ORDER OF GLOBAL GOVERNANCE

Theoreticians have long discussed a post-Westphalian order. The process of globalization and the rise of non-governmental organizations, various multinational corporations, and global capital markets have introduced new forces and thinking; it also added complexity if, indeed, we are entering a new phase, characterized by a post-Westphalian global governance. Such an order is still a futuristic concept; nationalism remains a powerful force shared by practically all countries and people. Combining shared territory, history, culture, and language, constitute barriers that will be difficult to breach. We notice how difficult the integration of EU in Europe, where there is no common language and many nations come with long histories and traditions. This complexity has an additional component, stemming from the rise of technology and the constant improvement of communications. Beyond traditional media (radio, TV), individuals are now equipped with access to news and vast amounts of information immediately available on the web on mobile devices. Social networks enable personal communication across borders, civilizations, and languages. Messaging - itself a new technology - is developing as a new language, but primarily as a tool for easy access to an international audience on myriad social media services available today, these enable us to send texts, photo images, and videos around the world instantly. Academia, the modern repository of knowledge, is under pressure as its exclusive ownership of knowledge, learning and innovations are now being challenged. The most important R&D fields today, in critical areas like Computing, AI and Bio-genetics, are performed in private industry, by corporations whose financial capacity far outstrips academia, even government. And the academia is losing many of its bright stars who are attracted by the industry with a much better pay and research budgets!

The proposition of global governance, as a cooperative not mandated system, is new and its applicability is possible only in today's world. Karl Marx exhorted the workers to unite, but nationalism was a much more powerful concept - it still is. While the prospect of international cooperation is exciting, its complexity is immense. Local, national and geographical interests still take precedence. We have witnessed the extension of global trade, the division of labor across the planet (manufacturing has shifted from the west, to the developing world) coupled with rising cognition (considerations beyond borders, to encompass planetary responsibility) and much good will. Trade is forcing certain cooperation in-spite of borders. The possibility of bypassing local interests in favor of global interests - especially in matters of climate, pollution control, weapons, terror, or international law - signals another step forward in our cognitive phase. In the end, considerations that extend beyond national borders to central common issues benefit all and require that we broaden our horizons despite our shrinking planet.

There are positive signs in world affairs since the end of WWII. We (mostly the west) respect the independence of sovereign nations and their civilizations better than before. The domination of the Russian empire on eastern Europe and Asia has weakened but certain tensions and aggression in the Ukraine persist. China's growing power also points to more aggressive foreign policy and the conflict with Taiwan is kept alive, the Chinese can probably never swallow the separation while the US is committed to Taiwan's independence.

Technology shrinks distances and global commerce (inherent to globalization) leads to more than material integration. We share a common planet, same atmosphere and must take cooperative responsibility for the planet, our only home. It was only recently a catch-as-you-can world, but the age of colonialism came to an end during the 20th century. Since the end of WWII, this "jungle" has steadily progressed toward more organization and order, more international and corporal agreements (such as the 2015 Paris Agreement to combat climate change). The concept of world order, of established borders and states, could not have happened before the cognitive cloud - our modern mindset - was ready, when consolidation and better communications were possible and sufficient recognition of powers and rights was established to benefit recognized order.

In-spite of our vast progress, we are still facing major challenges. Despotic regimes keep rising, Nationalism and Isolation continues to be preached, even from the White House. The concept of Total War mostly constitutes risk to innocent population; so is the threat of nuclear war. And the evolving asymmetrical-war, by terror groups and rogue nations, is mostly threat to innocent population. Technology enable small groups to wield un-proportional risk to world community.

4.5 MONEY AND ECONOMY

"For the love of money is a root of all kinds of evil."

Timothy 6:10

"This is not from the benevolence of the butcher, the brewer or the baker that we expect our dinner, but from their regard to research their own interests. We do not rely on their humanity, but their selfishness."

Adam Smith

BEGINNINGS

World's economy meandered slowly across the generations, until about four centuries ago. Along the way, new technologies and inventions constantly arose, the population periodically grew (hindered sometimes by plagues and starvation), societies established better crop and field management; they devised better tools and commercial activity expanded, but overall progress was anemic. There were some financial innovations, but they were still mostly traditional. The common belief was that the economic pie was finite - the economy was believed to be a "zero-sum game." Financial innovations required significant maturation because they are all cognitive and sometimes complex, by nature. At the beginning of the 16th century and the acquisition of new empires, the western world's economic center shifted from the Mediterranean to the Atlantic. The volume of marine activity increased dramatically as well and included the Americas and the Far East. The world seemed to shrink, as the west acquired vast empires and globalization commenced. The industrial revolution, the mechanizing of labor and new economic theories about unlimited growth of wealth emerged. Science emerged as the center of natural knowledge and wealth creation.

We know of William of Orange (King William III of England), the Good queen Anne, or Marlborough, Sir John Churchill; but another great man of the era (beginning of the 18th century England) - Charles Montague, 1st Lord Halifax (1661-1715), was as critical in matters that helped create the British Empire; he was a financial innovator. At the time, England being almost a constitutional monarchy, the King/Queen could not raise taxes arbitrarily, they needed the consent of parliament, which was not very cooperative in the matter. But times were pressing, the Atlantic economy was in full swing, empires were erected, massive international commerce was evolving and England was a small nation, on a small island with very limited natural resources. To help alleviate the financial pressures, Halifax devised the Bank of England (established 1694) and then a genius financial-cognitive instrument - government bonds (IOU). These bonds paid a very fat interest (8%) but Halifax was careful to guarantee only the interest, not the principal! The trick works until this day - the US government can never pay its $20T+ debt but the bondholders care mainly about the interest, which the government pays very meticulously. The English loved these bonds and this borrowed money enabled the creation of a large army and navy that later guaranteed victories, trading routes, mastery of the ocean waves and eventually, a vast empire. This is not to discount the British genius for many other issues, but this rather simply cognitive act, most probably helped enable the empire and British world domination for two centuries. In addition, it also created a social disruption; a new rich, powerful and influential class was rising, the financiers; they were not land-owners, rather they dealt with currency, banking and finance, later with insurance too!

Concurrent with the industrial revolution, new economic theories about unlimited growth of wealth emerged. Science became a dominating force in the creation of wealth. With greater technology and mechanized labor, economic progress exploded and the worldwide growth rate accelerated from overwhelming poverty among the majority to a current planetary average gross domestic product (GDP) per capita of about $10K/year, and it is still growing swiftly. The great technological innovations fueled very high growth in productivity, machines mechanized work, automation made us productive and these required new financial instruments; those continued to evolve on a more liberating and complex nature to this day.

When our ancestors were still foraging, the tribe was usually small (no more than 150 to 200 people, including the children). Some sort of economy has always existed—but during these earliest times, the basic "household" was rather limited and means of exchange even more so. Humans' list of necessities was short, not very different from animals, and contained mostly food items; there was no personal property as humans were constantly moving. Historians have speculated that this early economic state constituted the most equal society because nobody had practically anything! Measurable property and wealth arose only when humans settled and became "civilized." When settled, people amassed material symbols quite early (for instance, jewelry, elaborate burial sites, prayer icons and other artifacts), and clothed themselves, not only for protection, but also to symbolize social status, for ritualistic, status or aesthetical reasons. The small communities of yore were self-sufficient; they hunted and gathered what they needed. When necessary or opportune, they could supplement their subsistence through barter because the exchange inventory and rate, although always in flux and sometimes limited, were sufficient. The currency was not invented yet and there were no standards for exchange. Tribes collected (foraged) or hunted for most of their food and enjoyed no luxuries, life was a struggle. The social structure was still somewhat loose and groups traded either by cooperating (during a hunt) or bartering to acquire missing items. There is strength in numbers and in organization; the Agricultural Revolution turned the original small-scale social structure into communities of thousands. Instead of foraging, communities settled into managed agriculture and animal husbandry. They also performed extra tasks that had to do with the structure of the social order: organization, social strata, defense, organized care and such.

People. Now settled, started to need "stuff," which later became the foundation of the consumer economy. Land became precious. Work had to be managed for any village to succeed, and most villagers labored in the fields or with their increasingly domesticated animals, in food supply and basic material such as leather, wool, and wood processing. To manage the various labor functions and resources, a ruling class emerged (tribal leaders who, in time, became land-owners). To set themselves apart, they garnered more luxurious accommodations, clothing and jewelry; those came to epitomize the status appropriate to property and wealth. Appearance was paramount (still is somewhat) and demanded the wealthy show off their luxuries. In time, the no-longer peripatetic community needed variously skilled artisans, warriors for protection (walls, soldiers) and a management team to support the leader or chief. The fighters later evolved into professional warriors, until the rise of the soldier-citizen status that started to solidify during the Greek polis. Such new stationary-community settlements required that some form of tax be levied to pay for communal infrastructure, including management and protection of the town (collected monies paid both soldiers and to maintain city walls) and later to glorify and the rulers (for example, by creating and erecting pyramids, palaces and decorative gardens). Large civilizations always showed an appetite for great structural projects.

Early human's overall trading scope was initially limited and bartering was still sufficient. Money came later - a seemingly simple concept that evolved into a highly complex commodity and means of exchange. Money works to the extent that it is a shared belief[4]. Only a few thousand years old, it is mostly a cognitive concept, the invention of our minds. The concept of *perceived* value is difficult to pin down because it is predicated on so many parameters, among them availability, affordability, desirability, competition, and market demand. Food and water were continuously the most critical resources for any structured community, hence the importance of land and labor. Precious metals gained value because of their rarity and later, due to leisure, class demand (jewelry) and coins. Physical labor, perhaps the most precious commodity of the past, had almost no perceived value in ancient times (labor was important, but the means of its utilization were cheap); the worker was subjugated to almost slavery and work conditions could be horrific. The tenements and living conditions of the working class, which deteriorated after the growth of the cities and the industrialization of labor, were shocking. It took a long history to correct these conditions and provide the worker with rights, fair wages and safety.

During the era in which writing was invented, cities continued to grow. The community's social structure became more formalized, it continued to grow. Communities of 20,000 to 50,000 souls must apply strict structure (organization, hierarchy) to prevent chaos and codes for behavior and social interactions (laws) must apply; hence the pressure to organize. Commerce was a central, communal function, mostly performed in the agora market, continued to evolve in scope. And the level of trading both inside and outside the community must have grown exponentially. For a group comprising several thousand, relying on the barter system must have proved increasingly cumbersome, especially when dealing with matters of exchange rate and tax collection; barter is clumsy. The great disadvantage of a barter system, a system that lacks a central, common instrument of value, is the need for willing and available partners. For example, if I have potatoes to trade and I would like to have your axe, unless you need my potatoes, we do not have a deal. Without a standard currency, exchange rates vary widely and are impossible to predict or regulate. How to set the exchange rate without an established record of communal standards setting the value of a cow, a horse, or a potato? Taxation was another challenge for any growing community. Everything was taxed, much like today, from livestock to cooking oil to burial services, as well as luxury goods or special products, which we term "excise taxes," exemplified today by taxes on cigarettes and alcohol. These earliest forms of tax records (written in cuneiform on clay tablets) must have also advanced the use of calculations, arithmetic. It is easy to imagine how burdensome collecting taxes would be when payments comprised produce or livestock. How does one store and value such "currency" and make practical use of such properties? Thus, the cognitive concept of money was born, probably more than 5000 years ago. Given these considerable daily challenges, it is surprising it took so long to invent coin money (some 1500 years after the initiation of taxes), the symbol that represents value, some 3,000 years ago (around 1000 BCE). A magnificent instrument was invented, the expression, the basic denominator of all material value has been established. Perhaps the long delay indicates the mammoth cognitive step required to accept money - a symbol that represents value. The concept is extremely difficult to grasp and requires a cognitive advance of the population, not just few. For success, the entire community must be trained in and be willing to accept the principle and the symbol. However, the advantages of a money system were so significant that once employed, it spread quickly. The same types of issues are in play today for the new forms of money, such as crypto-currency. The acceptance process is slow, difficult, and gradual, even though today's crypto-currency may not be as complex as the idea of money - a single instrument, by which to value everything, when it first evolved.

Initially, the "currency" of money consisted of common commodities such as grain or shells, but these proved impractical. Coined money quickly gained precedence. Coins were stable (they last) had a face value because it contained recognized metals that had value for their rarity and their market demand. The first coins on record are from about 2,700 years ago, in Lydia and China. Metals were used before for jewelry and art, but their greatest value and utility emerged as means for exchange, because such currency could buy any other commodity or service. The new concept simplified trade immensely; advanced economy is unthinkable without simple monetary instruments. Later, after money was well established, rulers quickly learned to dilute the precious metals from the coins and the value of the coin became more symbolic, abstract. Money gradually receded into the symbol, it established an exchange-value standard that was relatively easy to count and store. A coin became a simple instrument for measuring value and, as a means of exchange; currency drove economic flexibility and growth. Steadily, money became not only an exchange instrument but also a product, the ultimate product.

The invention of money was arguably one of humanity's great cognitive leaps. Money simplified the barter system but its initial use required a huge intellectual stretch, because money is a *symbol* of value and trust. Such a concept was challenging to grasp and perhaps still is to this day. Many of us still wonder, in times of crisis, how many commodities fall but currencies stay stable. By now we are well-conditioned, but imagine 3,000 years ago, convincing people to sell real estate or cattle for coins! It demanded a huge stretch of imagination and a totally new value system. The value of all material goods and services is thus expressed by a single value system: money. This genius concept changed everything! Even today, one can visit the store and for a $20 (materially worthless) bill, bring home a full load of fruits and vegetables, some of them flown from the edge of the planet - this is still striking. The food is real and the bill is just a symbol, a promise by authority (government) that we usually mistrust. The issue of money as coins, or minting, quickly became exclusive to the rulers. Trust is central to money's symbolic nature. Violation of these privileges (fake money) always carried heavy penalties. Banks or insurance companies, which arose during the High-Middle Ages, predominantly have been housed in large, imposing structures that symbolized power and security - hence trust. In the Italian republics of the Late Middle-Ages, banker families built impressive palazzos (e.g., in Milan, Florence, Mantua, Ferrara, and Urbino) for the same reason that modern banking and insurance buildings decorate our modern city skylines. These august, impressive structures convey the message to the people, the depositors: *your little deposit, here within our fortunes, is and will be safe*. In-spite of worldwide continuous attempts to build confidence in the monetary system, people are still suspicious, even today. A run-on-the-bank is always possible, as history has shown again and again, to demonstrate the centrality of trust in the money concept.

MARINE TRADING EMPIRES

After the decline of the Roman Empire, during the Middle Ages, most people in Europe lived in small communities (known as manors) and mobility was extremely limited for more than a thousand years. Without empirical authority roads were neglected, communications and commerce shrank to locality; the continent fractured into a thousand entities. Because cities were still small, most people lived their entire lives in and close by the area of their birth and the barter system was sufficient in these locales. The great empires - Byzantine, Carolingian, Muslim - struck coins, and the local barons sometimes set their own currencies, although their coverage was very much limited. Standards emerged for dividing the silver pound, for example, the Carolingian ratio of 1:12:20 (which later became penny: shilling: pound). The decimation of currency (1:10 ratios) took over only after the French Revolution. Great commercial changes occurred by the High Middle-Ages (11th to 14th centuries). The trading empires' (e.g., Venice, Genoa, and Pisa) commercial activity, particularly maritime, emerged in force. The Crusades fomented a marine economy that spread from North Africa to the Mediterranean and the Black Sea. These evolving economies became more complex and pointed toward the future of trade and exchange with evolving fiscal instruments. Travelers willing to risk long distances in dangerous waters could reap enormous rewards, and the substantial profits proved tempting despite the perils (they could encounter both pirates and their empire's foes, ready to rob them). Such ventures were rife with hazards that required a degree of protection - eventually leading to the insurance industry. To mitigate the risk, they created venture funds in liquid assets (that is, gold or silver), and the merchants were paid when they returned home safely and successfully (skillfully portrayed in Shakespeare's *The Merchant of Venice* play). These required the invention of new financial techniques. In time, it became evident that for many transactions, cash transactions were neither convenient nor safe. Gold can be robbed easily during raids or robberies (both merchants and Kings traveled with their treasury, and a lost battle could sometimes mean losing the "national treasure"). The 16 and 17th century Spanish fleet transported tons of gold and silver from the Americas that were frequently intercepted by private pirates or of other countries' navies (e.g., English, Dutch). Most sides of the exchange, the merchant and the folks who purchased his merchandise, borrowed from moneylenders, sometimes the same one. It became more convenient and safer to exchange funds by changing the ledger at the lender. This was again a great cognitive step of "money's changing hands" on the ledger, rather than by the trading sides. Because it was necessary to carry some cash to make purchases elsewhere and the risk associated with travel, insurance was born to ameliorate the risks of the various transactions at a reasonable cost. Insurance and credit were still in their infancy, but commercial pressures and maritime empires' needs, especially Venice's, required such services - and eventually led to the need to create banks with depositing and lending capacity. The first of these institutions were erected in Lombardy and the Veneto regions to serve Genoa and Venice. Commerce and finance developed more complex financial operations and methods for disaster protection. Slowly and steadily, like so many other symbols, transaction money took over and became the most popular symbol of value and instrument of commerce. In other words, large transactions happened on paper without gold changing hands. The concept of "double entry bookkeeping" started to apply, it was a revolutionary concept and one used to this day. Every transaction had 2 entries that had to balance (hence later the balance-sheet).

MONEY - A UNIT OF TRUST

Money is a unit of value and a fantastic instrument of exchange, but perhaps it is first also a unit of *trust!* In order to become the ultimate representative of value, the currency must enjoy the ultimate backing and safety. The U.S. dollar has high value and world-currency position today only because it is supported by the "full Faith and Credit" of the United States (as stated in the U.S. Constitution), the most trusted economical entity today. Specifically, the U.S. government declares its unconditional guarantee or commitment as a trusted entity to back the value, interest and principal of the country's debt and stands behind its currency. The English pound enjoyed a similar universal foundation when England ruled the waves. Since money is a symbol, it must have the backing of the most powerful, wealthy institution. The State, as the largest enterprise, guarantees (i.e., provides trust) its currency. Every U.S. currency note states on its face, "*This note is legal tender for all debts, public and private,*" and bears the signature of the Treasurer of the United States and Secretary of the Treasury. Every note issued is *a unit of debt* that the U.S. government promises to respect. The public and the world trust this promise because the United States is economically most powerful and rich country, trusted to honor its debt. Trust is therefore the essence of the currency. When this trust is violated - like the British pound was after WWII - the currency loses its premier value. In the United States today, or the British Empire in the recent past, the nation's economies, its reserves, and its history of payment provide the security and trust the market requires. While the US has already a vast national debt, practically all this debt is in US dollars; thus, the US practically cannot default on its debt because we print dollars. Obviously the above does not protect us from inflation (the cause of too much printing), but default is practically impossible. To accrue a similar foundation of trust, small countries can peg their currency on the other, larger and more stable economies. For example, many EU members forfeited their currency in favor of the Euro, which was backed mostly by the large and stable German and French economies. Obviously there is a price to doing so, the country loses some of its economical flexibility and authority.

The idea of currency that is trusted across borders is ancient. Common currency eased trade in early empires, be they the Roman, the Venetian, or even the Florentine empires. In some European countries the currency unit is the Florin even today, in memory of the trust placed on the Florentine gold coin. When the Renaissance waned and the power of the Italian peninsula declined, the center of commerce shifted from the Mediterranean to the Atlantic, while new empires (Spanish, English, Dutch) and currencies rose and the economy continued to grow across longer distances. Money evolved as a concept. New financial instruments and concepts arose in step with the maturity and evolution of markets. Money became the most universal make-belief. Not everybody is religious, but everybody believes in money.

CREDIT

People always had a need for loans and credit; but in antiquity, credit and debt were limited and alas, also the path to slavery. Most of the slavery laws of the Bible are indeed for people who lost their land because of their inability to pay back loans. As economic activity gained greater intensity and volume, credit became essential. Credit allows the use of money from large institutions to fire the economy and increase its activity and volume. Growing an enterprise requires more employees and tools, hence extra capital. Credit existed in simple forms, even before money, because people needed to borrow for reasons of subsistence or trade since time immemorial, but these were predominantly private transactions pertinent to locality and acquaintance. In time and with the growth of the economy, credit became one of its foundations. Before the modern age and the rise of the banking system whose profits accrue mainly through interest, many cultures regarded charging interest on loans to be sinful. Usury and any interest on loans were condemned in Judaism, Hinduism, Christianity and Islam. In German, the word *Schuld* means both debt and guilt. Among Christians during the Middle Ages, opposition to interest was a major commercial difficulty. The Bible condemned usury (see, for example, "*if you lend money to any of my people who are poor among you, you shall not be like a moneylender to him…*" Exodus 22:25). Even later, Martin Luther and other reformers voiced their objections to usury. However, the absolute necessity of credit was so powerful that soon various "remedies" were devised to overcome the obstacles of the old law (Hillel in Judaism, others in Christianity and Islam). A sustainable modern economy without loans and credit was unthinkable, and loans are not possible without charging interest on the debt.

Today, credit is the foundation of economic activity. The consumer economy is based on debt, credit, and interest payment. Debt, so loathed by previous generations is now the engine of economic activity, of growth.

Paper money, the total valueless symbol, was not entirely a new concept, but its practical application eventually took over the whole system of exchange in Europe only in the 17th to 18th centuries, fewer than three centuries ago. Modern-minted coins are only marginally better than paper in terms of their intrinsic value. U.S. coins (gold, silver, copper, and zinc) had some value once, but this metal is diluted now such that coins' values are also much depleted. For example, the U.S. quarter is 75% copper and 25% nickel and has an intrinsic value of about 3 cents. Paper money has practically no value. Only governmental bodies legally issue money and engaging in counterfeit remains a severely punishable federal crime that earns offenders up to 20 years jail. The next instrument of exchange, replacing the somewhat inconvenient cash, the credit card (CC), was conceived about 150 years ago, but manifested in its modern format, the coded plastic card, only in the 1950s. It acts like cash but usage cost (CC companies charge 1-2%) and owner payment is delayed, usually by few weeks. Today, it is the main payment instrument, especially for smaller accounts. Some credit card companies are gigantic—the Visa Company's market value is some $270 billion (2018) and its annual transaction volume is close to $7 trillion - such companies allegedly "declared war" on cash quite successfully. Credit cards are accepted almost everywhere in the world, and provide short-term credit convenience, some security, and payments must be made within four to six weeks. Technological changes, such as encoded chips onboard, keep improving security. Despite security measures, credit card fraud in the United States alone was reported at some $5 billion in 2017.

Modern economies are based on credit (or more correctly, debt), and credit required its own operational instruments. Businesses, consumers and governments must loan money, even in the short term, to run or grow their enterprises. The state regulates the rate that banks charge their customers through the rate the state charges the banks. However, such bank charges depend on risk and can deviate enormously from the official rate. Two important standards are the "prime rate" and the "discount rate," which is the rate the government charges the banks. In 2017, the U.S. prime rate was 2%, the inflation rate was 2%, home mortgages were below 4%—and yet banks and credit companies charged up to 20% on credit card loans! Credit enables enterprises to expand their businesses by taking on loans and planning a future with access to extra resources beyond the individual's or the business's capacity. Business expansion continues to rise along with increasing world population, growing consumer markets and the continuous advances in technology, international trade and transportation. Our productivity continues to advance; since the end of WWII, world GDP (adjusted for inflation) has risen by an order of magnitude!

The total modern consumer market is based on credit. Most Americans buy every high-priced product (e.g., home, car, appliances, and vacations) on credit, because otherwise it would not be affordable. Credit makes short-term debt into long term and allows to pay over a long time. Credit is the instrument that eventually liberated world economies to reach their full potential and enabled consumers to achieve the standard of living we enjoy.

In recent years funds transfer in the "cloud" has replaced the check (another cash instrument), the previous method for paying bills. The ever-widening trend forecasts the steady disappearance of checks, bank teller jobs, and eventually, perhaps, the physical institution of the bank as the bank-teller is steadily replaced by the ATM. Web access to financial institutions enables quick account activity, check identification, credit card account access, and is an excellent way to manage personal accounts. Web transactions also symbolize the "cognization" of modern society. Because all payments, bank accounts, and credit card transactions are available in the cloud, payment can occur between the credit card company and one's bank without the account holder writing or mailing payment orders. Simultaneously, the numerous facilities we once visited to pay bills (banks, utility, post-office) or take out loans, are already disappearing as more operations are performed in the cloud, obviating much interaction by people or facilities. As a case in point, when it comes to trading equities (investments), humans already have hardly any contact with Wall Street. Computers run the stock market (90% of the transactions are already managed by computers) and the pace of transactions is faster than we can fathom. One buys and sells stock, mutual funds or bonds from one's computer keyboard, soon to be replaced by voice-activated commands and discount companies make the trades almost charge free. Humans could not have physically supported the immense volume of trading that takes place today, estimated at more than 10 million operations in the United States alone (1 to 2 billion shares traded daily).

Money (bills, coins) is progressively disappearing from the real world and moving wholly into the cognitive sphere. Such economic activity requires that we simply trust the banks, the governments or the credit card companies, while we are capable of checking such accounts meticulously (the web absolutely improves financial transparency). They are all available on our computer screens at work or at home. The U.S. economy, with GDP of about $20 trillions, has an estimated total of just $1.5 trillion cash in circulation.

Interestingly - and this is part of the power of lending institutions - the trillions banks lend are never onsite because they lend the money continuously, always leveraging customers' deposits. Our money, in saving or checking accounts, is used by the banks to loan. If the savers or investors coordinated the withdrawal of these accounts simultaneously (because of a rumor or crisis), the fiscal system would collapse. The same would be true of the phone system; it would also crash if everyone tried to make a call at the same time. These systems run on estimated utilities (statistics) whose frequencies are known. Banks make their fortunes by borrowing the money they have "under management" from consumers (our deposits which pay almost no interest), financial institutions, or governments. Government regulations require banks to keep some reserves, but the number is very small, in the 5% range. Consequently, banks can leverage 20:1. Financial institutions count on government protection from "runs on the bank" or a too-quick deposit-and-withdrawal stampede.

In a recent visit to Zimbabwe, where the local currency has collapsed, no ATM was dispensing money! The banks and government were "broke" after president Mugabe retired; they have little money, which is used for purchasing critical materials (like oil). In such rare cases, when the local currency has collapsed, the official currency became the US dollar. It was indeed a unique experience to pay for every service with cash. Needless to say, it was very difficult to purchase dollars there; the tourist has to purchase everything in cash or, in certain places use foreign credit cards.

BONDS

The bond, IOU that carries fixed interest, was another significant monetary invention (about 300 years old), another debt and credit instrument for raising capital. The bond issuer promises to pay a set interest rate over a specific period of time. Once issued, this paper can be traded, particularly in modern times, because the worldwide bond market is immense - about $90 trillion - more than the planet's GDP. Initially, bond issues were available only from governments or extremely large financial institutions; it was an instrument to raise capital for public or private initiatives by promising a certain interest income. Later, large banks and businesses could raise debt by issuing bonds too. The bond market's basic mechanism is rather simple. A bond's value fluctuates in the market, especially with inflation, but also due to several other parameters, such as risk and market competition. For example, if the bond has a 3% coupon, but market interest has climbed to 4%, the value of the bond falls, because the market can get a better return. If the market's interest rate falls, the value of the bond rises. Such fluctuations usually span quite a small range, but in a highly volatile bond market, the value can swing by tens of percentages (when bank rate goes from 2% to 2.5%, its a 25% change!). Consequently, the bond market affects the official bond rate, which is influenced by government-set rates. In the United States, the Federal Reserve Board, supposed to be independent of the federal government, actually sets the interest it charges the banks and this ripples throughout the market (loan rates, rates banks pay to depositors) with an additional banking spread. In the past, only very large institutions could ensure the security and trust needed to issue bonds. Since the advance of the "junk bond," lesser issuers entered the market, whereby higher risk investors can participate by paying a higher interest rate. The greater confidence we have in the issuer, the lower interest they have to pay.

Today's immense bond market offers considerable bond variety: government, municipal, corporate, junk and more. Most governments are heavily in debt, but the service of the debt is mostly affordable. The United States' federal debt is close to $21 trillion (2018) because of its low-inflation environment over the last 20 years, the discount rate (the rate the feds charges banks) has been less than 1 percent hence low interest environment (cheap money). Consequently, the debt service (the interest the government has to pay) is about $350 billion annually, about 10 percent of the federal budget and about 2 percent of the GDP. This is a high number, but still manageable.

THE SPEED OF MONEY

The industrial revolution was an economic watershed. Because of the energy revolution, mechanization, industrial standards and manufacturing techniques, worker productivity grew by orders of magnitude. As a result, new standards were required to guide the exchange rate between currencies for various services: mail, banks, transportation, rail operations and asphalt roads. These accelerated both economic activity and the growth of wealth. A new class of financiers rose, with immense political, industrial and economical power. This influential class had no land holdings. When society was largely agricultural, young children had to help the family survive, sometimes enduring tough conditions but these mostly worked with the family. During the industrial revolution, these children worked in the mills and sweatshops, exploited and uneducated, sometimes 15-16 hours a day, 6 days a week. Some of the testimonials available today are rather horrific. As regulations expanded, jobs for children diminished in favor of education and eventually, the public-school system and mandatory education were established. This led to a more educated population and accelerated the rise of the working and middle classes. Social movements, garnering emerging political muscle, started to pressure governments for better working conditions, work-safety, and demanded higher pay rates. Socialism gained vast influence over world politics and economics, which continues to this day, giving birth to the 40-hour work week, five working days a week and retirement pay, all improved workers' conditions and lifestyle. As efficiency rose and machines started to perform the hard work, wealth and with it the institutions of finance grew and became more sophisticated. Still, investment in the stock market remained the lot of few until the recent few decades. A new paradigm of modernity is the simple observable fact that much of our wealth comes from investment, sometimes even more than from work! Government programs that provide tax advantages encourage people to invest and these investments become the resource for retirement. Today in the US, some 50% of us are invested. The US 401 programs are valued at $8-9T already (2018).

Another modern economy concept is the velocity of money, the rate at which money is exchanged in transactions and how much a unit of currency is used over a given period of time. The velocity of money is usually measured as a ratio of the GNP to a country's total supply of money. As a principle, economic activity and high velocity are healthy for the economy and businesses. John Stuart Mill, a British philosopher and economist, already understood the following famous equation 150 years ago:

$$M \times V = P \times T$$

Where M = money supply, V =velocity of money, P =average price level of goods, T = index of expenditures (such as the total number of economic transactions). A simple way to look at velocity: suppose you own a computer store. Imagine the difference in your business if you could turn your inventory 12 times a year (high velocity), rather than only three times a year. The velocity of money in the modern economy is one of the most influential parameters for growth and health of the economy. Indeed, the speed of money is an excellent indicator for economical activity.

WORLD DEBT

At this writing, it is estimated that world debt will reach about $300 trillion in 2017 (U.S. total debt is about $80 trillion), yet world GDP (Gross National Product) is only about $80 trillion. It is clear that such debt can never be paid back (unless there is very high inflation or a collapse)! Why are bankers and political leaders (and we, the people) not worried? Note, however, that except for government debt, commercial debt at about 75% of the total, should have collaterals. When we buy a house, or car with debt, it is protected by the value of the house. Thus, total debt considerations are more complicated than it initially looks. However, government debt, which constitutes about 25% of the total, has no collateral other than the good will and obligations of the states. There might be a few possible solutions to the conundrum. One fact involves the bond-holders (that is, us) who, as mentioned before, are more interested in the interest than the debt itself. So long as interest is paid, all is well - and in fact there continues to be huge demand for those government bonds because of their relative security. Another consideration is inflation. With ~3% compounded inflation; the money will lose some 50% of its value within the next 20 years! This seems to favor the borrower - or at least historically, the borrower has benefitted from the devaluation! Governments have always used inflation to fight debt, be it coin dilution in the past, or higher inflation today. Finally, another possibility for the resolution of the huge debt is, of course, an economic collapse and the re-evaluation of asset value sometime in the future. Nobody would choose such a solution, but it has happened many times before (for example, in Germany, during the Depression, when the value of the Mark collapsed). The media has circulated articles about such a "reset" for the U.S. but not many of us are worried. In the meantime, US federal debt is expected to rise to about $60T in mid-century and the interest on this debt is now estimated at 25-30% of the federal budget (it is now about 10%). Clearly something has to be done, but politicians continue to roll the ball forward…let another future president worry.

COMMODITY PRICES

Historically, the concept of money as an exchange instrument has not only evolved from physical items (commodities, foods, and coins) to the Cognitive sphere. The value of this "fantasy" relative to commodities has also improved astonishingly. Specifically in the last 400-500 years, with the rise of commerce and the integration of the world during the age of Discovery, and then the Industrial Revolution, the price of commodities has fallen precipitously in almost every case. As early as the 1500s, spices from India that used to come through the Silk-Road and exact high prices, could be purchased in Lisbon for 20% of their cost in Istanbul. The monopoly on spices from the east was broken by the age of discovery and Portuguese discoverers arrived in India already before 1500CE and started to bring goods[330] and lower their prices. With technology and transportation, we find ways to extract commodities from the bowels of the earth more efficiently (for example Shale oil). In-spite of the immense oil usage, proven oil reserves keep rising. We learn to recycle resources (alas not enough, especially worrying is our water waste) and our food productivity has improved even faster than the rapid growth of humanity. In-spite the above, inflation always exists in the economy. Apparently other elements are becoming more dominant than commodities and materials, mostly wage-inflation. Our productivity has improved astonishingly and so has wage compensation, which is now the main inflationary component. Thus, the cost of metals, grains and other natural resources has fallen precipitously when adjusted to inflation. The one exception to this "deflation" over time of commodities is gold. In the last 200 years, the price of gold has increased by approximately 24 times. During this period, inflation increased by approximately the same amount. Therefore, gold is one of the few commodities holding value rather well. As of this writing in 2017, when the U.S. federal debt alone stands at $21 trillion, metals and energy resources are again retreating and the price of oil has collapsed (2016) but recovering again. Part of the reason is our improved technologies of both mining and detection and ability to extract resources from the earth deeper and cheaper. Another trend is the rise in the value of services, instead of material, these are the new commodities; both Data and Ideas are emerging as the most valued commodities, competing with land and materials of the past— ***the mind is mightier***. The economy of the advanced nations is geared towards services, another sign of rising cognition. Especially when it comes to energy, we are gravitating towards renewable resources that are cleaner and eventually much more economic. Solar is making great advances, as is the technology of the electric home or car whose battery can be charged by the sun energy. Solar prices are already coming close to the price of conventional electricity and solar cells have a very long life, its efficiency is lost only at 1% annually. Eventually, we will have to fully convert to renewable energy; currently, solar and wind emerge as the leading technologies. In California (2017), some 600,000 folks are working in the solar industry, while the total employment in the U.S. coal extracting industry is less than 10% of that. Phasing out carbon will take time but it is already under way.

IT'S COMPLICATED

In modernity, money and its institutions assumed a position that is very different than just exchange instruments. Money and its management is the central tool for managing industry and economy, while money became a product (banks even have sales promotions), a means of exchange and a commodity. Money is simple to use but on the professional level, it is quite a complex tool because it is so much more than just an exchange instrument. The management of money can be a complex process, especially for bankers and the professionals that set up policies, rates, market liquidity and exchanges. Much is done in the background that is not transparent to the consumer. The financial service industry is one of the largest and still growing. The U.S. financial and insurance industries employed

6.2 million in 2016.

A process of supply and demand creates value, mostly by market forces and our perceptions. In modernity, value is driven not only by the "mysterious" hand; rather a confluence of forces, including the supply and demand pressures of the market, competitors and consumer behavior; also by psychology and the activities of trading agents or the market makers who connect buyers and sellers. Supply and demand are a complex concept, impacted by a variety of forces and decisions, including marketing strategies and even prestige. For example, wrist watches that cost $100K or Hermes-Birkin leather bags for even more. In its simplest manifestation, the value of almost everything is what the market shall bear.

World economies are mostly free-market capitalistic today. There are obvious exceptions even in the free markets. For example, governments will sometimes manipulate the price of critical food products like bread and milk, in the form of subsidies to help the poorer parts of the population and support critical industries. Another wild card impacting the effectiveness of the "invisible hand" is the exchange rate, which in free economies is floating. Governments can manipulate their currency for obvious purposes, making their products cheaper, and do so frequently. Manipulation of currency can have a vast economic effect, making products attractive or rejected, thus creating jobs and opportunities. This issue has been a matter of national dispute, especially now, as China is rising to compete with the United States for market dominance and control of the dominating currency (which some suggest, to use a basket of currencies rather than the US dollar). For example, if indeed the dollar was exchanged or supplements by other currencies (China and Russia already perform certain exchanges with their own currencies), the consequences to the US economy would be very serious, much more than most assume.

DIGITAL CURRENCY

Traditionally, the foundation of paper or modern money is trust in governmental institutions, from emperors to modern federal regimes. However, this trust is somewhat eroding among the population and it is perhaps time for a new foundation for a newer currency. The bases for such need are two-fold: the accumulation of vast debt by politicians who prefer to roll the responsibilities into the future and by the risks imposed by growing technologies that can disrupt markets and values. Everyone knows the amount of resources that government, businesses and banks invest to improve our confidence in their products and to fight the immense level of fraud. These means keep growing and complicating our access because the various institutions now require more and more identification tools to protect the accounts. There is also the fear of terror manipulations or cloud-wars with foes.

The foundation of new digital currencies may very well be math and technology. As skepticism and distrust of governments and large financial institutions continues (credit card fraud is already in the $5-6B/year and growing), digital currency such as the Bitcoin is waiting for the cognitive evolution that will revolutionize the monetary system. These are very new concepts that are currently used for trading, but their utility continues growing and popularization will most likely occur rather soon. In essence, digital currency is a shared, trusted, public ledger that everyone can inspect, but that no single user controls. Simply put, Blockchain, in this case a digital currency, is a mechanism for creating **trust** through very complex Encryption. The mechanism of implementing Blockchain is complex, but the promise of such a procedure is significant. Note that most of us do not understand how the financial markets are regulated, but the usage of money is rather simple. We need not be experts in Blockchain procedures as long as the tools to use them are simple and safe. Some of digital currency (Bitcoin) fundamentals:

Advantages:

1. Every user that signs in is visible to the whole network but stayed anonymous (privacy).

2. Paying with Bitcoin is like paying cash. There are NO 3rd party (banks, CC, feds) and they therefore can't charge for the transaction. Service is very cheap in comparison.

3. No real records to the government, especially for taxation.

4. Very powerful crypto protects the integrity of the system, the element of **trust** (technology), so fundamental to money.

5. The currency is universal, no currency conversion issues and fees. Universal pricing.

Disadvantages:

1. The privacy of the network invites criminality.

2. Government and banks dislike Bitcoin and will fight it. Banks and CC companies will lose significant revenues when it happens. Various banking operations are very much discounted compared to their cost today.

3. Still not popular, not many agree to be paid with this digital currency (2019).

4. Bitcoin has no management center, like central banks. Management is democratic. Democracies are wonderful for freedoms but are otherwise "clumsy".

Certain modifications will occur, perhaps to alleviate the difficulties; Bitcoin and Blockchain are here to stay but they are speculative, especially in the trading market at this point.

Blockchain *is a distributed database* **that maintains a continuously growing list of data records that are hardened against tampering and revision, even by operators of the data store›s** *nodes. The most widely known application of a Blockchain is the public ledger of transactions for crypto-currencies used in "https:// en.wikipedia.org/wiki/Bitcoin". This record is enforced cryptographically and hosted on machines running the software.*

One can imagine the added efficiency of an almost personal currency, without the constant brokering and heavy cost of financial institutions. In addition, transactions are registered in more than one place. Most of the services that institutions currently provide, like transfer of funds, are cumbersome and expensive, mostly producing significant profits for the bank, not the economy. Block-chain has been described as a liberation process from some of the larger bodies that are controlling our lives. This is a further democratization of the concept of currency and its management. Others call Blockchain the next evolutionary step for the Internet, as means of exchange of information and value on individual value, without the trust provided so far by governments or other powerful central bodies.

In summary, the element of trust, so fundamental to currency, has been transformed for digital currency. Instead of the size or the credibility of the institution - a sovereign or a central bank, providing the trust by size, authority and muscle - the new digital money delivers security through technology and crypto-math - a new monetary cognitive foundation. It will take time to accept such trust, but it may happen rather soon. We are probably waiting for one of the large retailers to accept Bitcoin, or similar digital currency, to make it happen.

Since Bitcoin is using the most complex Crypto we have, the data centers that run Bitcoin must have very high processing power, more than the Google data centers! The energy demands of such centers are so high that some of these facilities have been relocated from the big cities, where financial centers reside, to rural areas where energy costs are much lower than in civic centers.

When implemented, the possibility of bypassing the banks, with their extra cost - sometimes for simple transactions, which lowers economic efficiency - becomes possible and desirable. But more important than bypassing institutions' fees, the new types of currencies enable trust to be distributed across the network, rather than centralized. In the past, centralized systems have been reliable and steady, but they are less so today.

Terror and cloud-warfare are complicating the equations.

Obviously, banks and financial institutions dislike digital- currency, which will not only shift business away but will also hurt profits. These struggles happen in the cyber space all the time, where negative messages are implanted against what seems to be the inevitable.

CONCLUSIONS

The economy and financial management have become very complex in modernity. At the end of the Middle Ages, world economy was agrarian and economic theory hardly existed. With the break of the industrial revolution, certain theories started to emerge. Adam Smith was optimistic, he thought that the "invisible hand" of the free market economy would raise all. Malthus predicted demographic gloom and David Ricardo already predicted the freezing of wages to the subsistence level because he thought that, otherwise, population growth (Malthus) would eventually destroy the working population. Rousseau and the Romantic poets (Shelley for example) thought industrialization to be evil altogether because it destroys nature and with it, the souls of men and the social structure. Then came the early Utopian socialists, like Saint Simon (1760-1825) or Robert Owen who, unlike Adam Smith, thought that Laissez-Faire capitalism was evil and inefficient - everyone only cares about their own interests. It took modern experience and models to show they were actually wrong, but their point about the nature of capitalism and its corruptive effects, especially as we watch the Gap grow, struck a chord and emerges as a significant social force. Hegel followed with a more historical analysis (the Utopians were quite ad-hoc theorists) of the evolution of the Geist, and then Marx turned Hegel on his head and focused on the economic theory of history and his Marxist interpretation. Many other theories were working, but the world continued to industrialize and continue developing the economic theories of the socialists and the conservatives. Communism and Capitalism became the battleground of super-powers after WWII, based on ideology but exercised as living viewpoints. Today, China is challenging the west on matters of Democracy and free economy, especially with their brand of capitalism. They claim that their model of managed economy "from the top" has been even more successful, maybe more efficient than classical capitalism and their growth numbers are convincing many. Within a century, Economy as a science that did not exist before mid-18th century became a huge amalgam of theories, some historical, some mathematical, some social, and of huge variety and complex models.

Money is a very complex concept, one we all understand, but only to a certain level. We have learned the concept of trust and the importance of the quality of the guarantor, the baseline of value, and that money is eventually the ultimate product.

The concept of money and financial instruments continues to evolve. Instead of the traditional cash and land, the modern economy is based on credit and debt, money transfers, credit cards and web payments. Consequently cash-money has practically vanished from the market; we pay with credit cards or web file transactions. Who uses cash for serious payments anymore?

Money management becomes more complex as time goes by. Understanding the fundamentals of money and investing is critical to our personal well-being. It starts to be clear that wealth is influenced very much investing, sometimes more than by work! Not investing is not an option as money in savings accounts or CDs is stagnating with inflation; not investing means loss of value to inflation - even a low inflation rate of 2% annually, accumulates to 55% loss after 40 years career. Even if one decides to use a financial consultant, one had better understand what they are doing!

Matters will only grow to be more complicated and while the consumer needs not be an expert, a fundamental understanding is a must these days. Perhaps even teaching the fundamentals in school.

We know debt keeps rising as hundreds of millions in Asia, especially China and India, keep joining the middle class; these and the consuming west will therefore draw even more credit. Is the growth of debt a risk or an opportunity? The debate between growth and debt continues to rage among economists. Should we allow more debt as investment in future growth, or will the mounting debt eventually cause a calamity?

In comparison to metals or land of the past, today the most precious commodities are DATA and IDEAs. In other words, cognitive concepts have become the most precious properties! Knowledge and understanding are critical to our material success.

5. THE SOCIAL ORDER

5.1 COGNITIVE PROGRESS

"We know what we are but know not what we may become."

Hamlet, Shakespeare

If we accept the concepts that Individualism, Civil Rights, Civil Freedom, Critical Thinking, Free Press, Democracy, Diversity and the emergence of Humanism is progress, that the abolition of Slavery and the struggle with Racism and Misogyny and for Meritocracy mean "progress," then the evolution of our society in the last 6,000 years and specifically in the last 500-600 years must be the sign of progress. It is also the indication of rising Cognition in the social order, resulting hopefully in a tendency away from violence and towards humanity. There are an equal number of reasons to be pessimist, mostly stemming from our inability to learn from the past.

From almost slavery, to oligarchy and then to human rights, free press and instruments of criticism, the social order had evolved mightily. No other species has achieved the level of dominance we have over the planet, even if the future might belong to "ants and termites". This is absolutely due to our brain, intelligence, language and ability to abstract and model, plan for the future and comprehend increasingly complex concepts. Our brainpower made the difference within a social context because our power is in our ability to act as a very large, diverse group, a group that can propagate and disseminate information. Indeed, humanity keeps gravitating towards higher "networking" (or Globalization) and our hierarchical systems, while providing much freedom, are also becoming more intricate and complex. In addition, our world-view, sciences, art, technology, knowledge base and politics have grown so vast, abstract, and complex that the "Renaissance man" of the past is no more. Nobody can hold all of today's information in his or her heads anymore, not even that of a single discipline, as our total knowledge base multiplies every few years. This path towards "progress" was not linear, nor was it steady; there were difficult cultural retractions, step-backs, periods of dark history and barbarism, even in our recent past, but the overall trend indicates, for good or bad, the rise of both Cognition and complexity. We do not know what drives accelerations or stagnations, but they come and go in history.

The signs are evident all around us. Art, Science, Technology, Music, the Economy and practically all we do, has grown increasingly complex; so have the models, either thought process, imagination or computer models we've created for the environment, weather, human behavior, art and the universe. We have taken dominion over the earth and we are reaching for the stars; human colonization of other celestial bodies now seems inevitable. Our basic physical needs - of food, clothing and shelter - are mostly available quite abundantly, for most people. A small percentage still lack basic needs, this is usually due to corrupt regimes and local chieftains, not because of material want. We manufacture more food and goods than the world needs, but also waste immensely; and we live much longer and healthier. We have conquered many diseases and we will conquer even more. Our cultural, economic and agricultural achievements are phenomenal as are our technologies and sciences that provide us with more accurate, if more complex view of the universe and ourselves.

DIALECTICS

Our nature is built on dialectics, on contradictions and sometimes on conflicted disputes. We must guard this progress constantly because as humans, we have not changed as positively as technology or knowledge. The question of evil still remains in today's political, social and religious realities, and technology adds new risks, as the world is moving from reality to cyber; due to technology, destructive forces can operate from small centers - there is no need for large militaries and facilities today to cause much damage in a world managed by cognitive means.

Social injustice is not new, we must be aware of civilizational differences and the dangers that nationalism and religious fanaticism still pose. And we must guard against the worst angels of our nature. A fast-changing world is not favored by many, nor do many desire it and the rate of change scares practically all of us. The powers of our emotions and conflicts are still around us. There are some 500 militant groups in the U.S. alone, bent on destroying our democracy, towards some imaginary new order, mostly forms of Anarchism or Racism. The rise of cognitive capacity and better communications should enable us to find compromises, moderate the emotions and lower tensions, caused by certain political leaders and national or religious conflicts. Better communication, technology and organizations do alleviate the pressures of the past, but dangers still linger. Technology, while very beneficial, actually increases the capacity of the frustrated, the fanatic or the demented, to cause more damage (cyber-terror) than ever before; these can come from really small groups today, that can cause power disruption, terror and fear-mongering by terrorist and ideology groups.

The progress of the cognitive ladder is evolutionary by nature, most likely not Darwinian. It is cumulative and driven by cognitive forces, thus directed. This progress, unlike Darwinism, is biased and constantly points to higher understanding and knowledge, since the "material struggle for survival" for humanity has been practically mitigated. The number of hungry people is now (2017) estimated at about 800 million, about 10% of humanity. As mentioned already, most of these are due to corrupt governments and localities, not material want. For very many of us, this is the best life humanity ever had, at least materially. FDR articulated his 4 freedoms (of speech, religion, from want, from fear) only few decades back; they were mostly cognitive and they are still, for too many, only a hope. Too much of the world still lives in fear and political oppression. Eleanor Roosevelt's dream was "a glass of milk for every child" and this dream is coming true. In modernity, while too many are still hungry, obesity has evolved into a major medical and social problem; in the US, obesity has developed into a national crisis for it hurts the young (almost 20% children and adolescents), while specifically in the west, enormous amounts of food are going to waste. Same is true for clothing and other fundamental material needs that plagued the past.

Humanity is made of complex individuals, societies and civilizations, loaded with traditions, mythologies and religions that are pulling us in various directions. We are learning to respect them all. We have shown that human affairs are not always driven by reason and that even the most "scientific" disciplines are affected by emotions, ambitions and tradition. From the evolutionary standpoint, we have been a great success (see figure below). Consequently, we have "evicted" the other inhabitants and Nature starts to be restricted to few areas where wild-life can roam freely, mostly to satisfy our touristic appetite. We have subdued the planet, but her forces are still awesome as are her mysteries. And we are not owning our responsibilities to the earth, those are vastly violated.

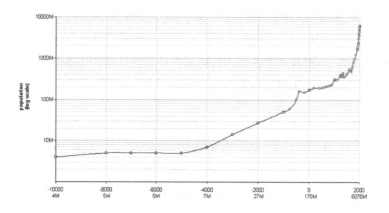

Figure 4: Growth of human population

We are not yet within a humanity that universally shares progressive opinions, but at least in the west, and specifically in the last few hundred years, the central ideas of the Enlightenment gained political and social influence. Among them: human centrality, reasoning, human rights, free press, democracy and the right for dignity. Our curiosity and wish for understanding, and our ability to self-develop with rising cognitive faculties, have been recognized as the path to a certain progress.

Western dominance has influenced other nations and the planet in the last half millennium. This grip is now loosening. Nations like India or Japan have subscribed to the western democracy styles, without losing their unique national traditions. We came to realize that our science and reasoning run ahead of our understanding of our nature, the 20th century taught us that with great pain. We started to develop institutions, some outside of governments (like NGOs) that work for the common good and for the environment. We have tried hard to unshackle many of the old social norms of classes, birth privileges, race, gender and superstitions; we wish to arrive at the attitude expressed in the words "*we hold these truths to be self evident...*" and to agree that there are certain "***unalienable rights,***" part of our wonderful make-believes, among them human dignity. The

West is far from being innocent when it comes to many social and racial issues. Western influence has been dominant in the last few centuries and our attitudes and wars for domination, sometimes enslavement (especially in colonies), affected the whole planet. Still, there is a genuine attempt to make progress and sometimes try to repair the errors of the past. In modernity, diversity, the meritorious society and issues related to wealth distribution and women liberation have become paramount for world leadership and the press.

In-spite of our criticism, the world is more meritorious today than ever before, while striving to better equality and opportunities. It took a long history of struggle to arrive at these liberal views and realities. The future is still uncertain because there is still so much conflict and strife and iniquity. And our future cannot be predicted, especially when the change is so immense, at neck-break pace. There are still many destructive, coercive forces that try to bring us back, perhaps to an illusionary past world of religious dreams and ideals. What thinkers, like August Comte (1798-1857), thought as the first "theological age" is now emerging as a new ideal for large religious communities who are despairing of modernity and its integration with their traditions.

In-spite of the many conflicts, the world today is well connected and is sharing many principles. Because of technology and transportation, the world is also very open and information exchange is only improving. In-spite of the differences, we actually share in many ways, a common civilization. On the surface, most of the world behaves and lives similarly. North Korea calls itself "the Democratic People's Republic of Korea;" even despotic regimes wish to be, or thought of as republics, democracies.

The drive for scientific and technological excellence, the rise of the working class and the economies of the world are very similar in their fashion, direction and goals. While under critic or even assault, Globalization evolves mostly as positive force in the cultural, political and economic domains. And the world is relatively peaceful.

Cognition, the way we define it - specifically abstraction, logical thinking, planning, reasoning and communication - is not possible without a highly developed language. The whole animal Kingdom behaved for hundreds of millions (and billions) of years by the "wisdom of their body," by memory and instinct and sheer bodily chemistry, not by much Cognition (although, animals have a powerful memory for certain aspects of survival, such as location and navigation), definitely in comparison to ours. Our intelligence allowed us to adapt uniquely to places and climates, and eventually to subjugate the environment to our will and convenience. A form of "mobility," the consequence of unique cognitive capacity for adaptation, allowed us to spread across the earth; sometimes we spread overseas and across straights, because of our ability to adapt and build sophisticated tools, boats, housing, hunting and social organizations. The machines we built help us not only overcome material difficulty but also enable the extension of our knowledge and our senses (scientific instruments). The microscope, the telescope and the Spectrometer allow us to see far and deep, much beyond our senses. Our machine-tool usage is much more than a lever, they become cognitive.

Our ability to cooperate in large groups depended on a sophisticated language, the main tool of complex communications. The study of Language, its origins and capacity, perhaps among our "final frontiers," is a science still in its infancy, in-spite of much progress in the last few decades. Language will not be fully understood before we know much more about our brains, our "final, ultimate frontier." Our language is the instrument our brain uses to interpret the world. Otherwise, what is thinking, but speaking with ourselves?

COGNITIVE SHARED BELIEFS

The mechanism that allowed the rise of the ordered social structure, mostly our cognitive shared beliefs, continued to evolve over time, to encompass the totality of our lives, economy, customs and world-view. Today, we are embedded in these shared beliefs and in time, our world has become more abstract and more dependent on them, our language and our abstract mind. Modern society is so complex, so cognitive that the issues that control our attention are mostly in the cognitive space, much more than the material world. Our economy, our arts and sciences, our behavior, entertainment and beliefs, our nationalism and rituals, these are all receding realities towards a certain make-believe world and abstractions.

Our arts are now absolutely symbolic, our currency, our mythologies and national aspirations, our world-view and religions, all make-belief. These make-beliefs, so central to our being, are also the reason that different nationalities cause so much differentiation, sometime hostility. We are born with little instinct, at least in comparison to other mammals; we are groomed into these beliefs and they become part of our universe. Nationalistic leaders and various despots always knew to harp on these beliefs and focus the attention of the people to these characteristics. Again and again, we notice attempts to foster unity, nationalism (we are one and we are better), loyalty and hostility to others, mostly via historical mythologies, propaganda and the occult. Moments of historical crisis always draw the people towards the mystical, super-natural and make-beliefs.

The shared beliefs, the hyper-realities that exist only in our mind, are usually shared only within our community, the group sharing language, religion, customs and kinship; later it evolved towards nationality, our "bigger family". The world, in other words, is becoming more virtual, more dependent on our cognition and minds. That Virtual Reality (VR) and Augmented Reality (AG) are technologies of high interest is not a surprise. Virtual Reality is already present in modern life and both VR and AG will undoubtedly impact our future.

Among the most important components of this "hyper reality" that we invent perpetually, is the social structure itself, the social order, tribe, or nation; the result of our adherence to certain social shared beliefs, religion, mythology, past, and the recognized position we hold within the whole social construct. The struggle for this position has gradually become the driving force in the social struggle for respect and recognition. Humans are the only animals whose social construct can involve many millions. The intricacy of this social order is complex, requiring lingual nuances, conventions, modes of behavior and even rituals that frequently, if not continuously, affirm the structure. In addition, authority figures - from monarchs, nobility and priests, to the political leaders of today, have developed extensive rituals and myths that affirm our cohesion as a tribe, nation and their centrality in the structure. In time, as the monarchs specifically became more and more symbol, these rituals became more significant, as these symbolic leaders lost all their executive privileges. Thus, crowning processions, as well as, military or historic-ritualistic parades, act to foster the social order. They provide cohesion and security through the ritualistic past.

The social structure erects a system of coercion to force the law, instill conformity, provide protocols for trade and behavior and deal with those who commit infractions. Anarchy and lawlessness are part of our nature, too. Thus, our social behavior is built on mainly two pillars: a. system of belief or make-believe, learned as part of our upbringing, education or conditioning, affirming that operating within the Law is beneficial to us and the group, and b. a strict code of punishment for violators.

Additional consideration for the authority of the law is, of course, our moral code and the cultural vestiges from our heritage. Some believe that the divine inspires our morality; others believe morality is an evolutionary force. The origin of this moral code is an internal force from within; most of us are moral, even without the coercive power of the law. This powerful force is probably the result of evolutionary, behavior condition, emerging from the social pressures that make us work within the community. This internal force, telling us right or wrong, is a fundamental human trait and a subject that interested many philosophers. Religious or Evolutionary and behavioral, perhaps the most important function of the gods (or God) in modern religion and philosophy is to become the guardians, the foundation of our morality.

The real world, whatever our interpretations, is part of our culture, our emotions and our language, interpreted via our shared-beliefs, while forming our social contract and world-view. Understanding that our "reality" is not absolute, rather the product of our perceptions and beliefs and changing in time, will go a long way towards helping us understand one another better and hopefully resolve many of our existing and future conflicts. In the end, concepts of nationality, race, color, and gender *are mostly in our mind*. The histories of civilizations have been loaded with nationalism or tribalism, racism and misogyny, but civilizations do not have to succumb to prejudice or conflict forever. The post-WWII history of Western Europe demonstrates the futility of war and the power of alternative cooperative solutions and diplomacy. That being said, the verdict is still out on whether humans have learned their lessons. Nationalism and tribalism are powerful forces that can be exploited by dangerous leaders, as we notice the rise of Populism and the instability of old alliances.

The character and features of political leaders have changed little since the days of David or Agamemnon. With all the progress we made, a combination of natural leadership skills coupled with ambition and cunning is still the staple of such leadership. The other important leadership skill, especially in modernity, is the focus on the Word, specifically the spoken Word. Who does not remember Churchill's speeches during "*the Darkest Hour?*" A leader's words will move, encourage and inspire confidence in the face of calamity. With the evolution of mass communication technologies, the spoken word reigns supreme. In the past, kings or other leaders had to speak to the masses in assembly. Later candidates had to travel to speak to the masses, from platforms or trains. Today it is via radio, TV or Internet (social media), instantly to millions. The propagation of this information via paper is in serious decline, as electronic media is faster and more efficient. No matter where we are, we can watch speeches, news or messages on mobile devices.

MERITOCRACY

Meritocracy is rather a modern concept. Most societies until 200 years ago were managed by a tiny elite, meritocracy was not yet in the cognitive-cloud of the time. Meritocracy is not only the "right thing to do", it is socially beneficial from almost any angle. Specifically:

1. Without the participation of the majority, the economy could not have advanced the way it has. Large markets allow economy, tooling, pricing and affordability.

2. Meritocracy brought forward better leadership, the need for welfare and interest considerations of the majority - better schools, welfare.

3. Majority participation allows the talents of the whole social order to advance, to provide opportunity for all to participate according to skill, ambition and personality.

4. Helps mitigate social tensions.

Meritocracy, no doubt has also brought a certain level of mediocrity, a price we are ready to pay. It has become a burning issue in modern media because of the concept and the growing economical (and educational) Gap. The social order might gravitate to stratification, but the opportunities must be open to all. The worry of the growing Gap are factually justified; parents with affordability will provide better education, hence opportunity; this will not change. Today, we are also observing certain individuals and titan corporations that have become too powerful; perhaps "too big to fail". And they use their power and influence for advancing their own interests. Among them many technologists that are practically defying the interests of the state, for profit. The current "fight" between Senator Elizabeth Warren and FB founder, Mark Zuckerberg, is just one example.

CHALLENGES

Historically, the horrific events and wholesale murder of WWI shook western thought to its core. The death, sometimes in horrific industrial methods, of a whole generation, was contrary to the expectations of the west at the end of the 19th century. After the war and as a consequence of the frustrations it generated, a new era ensued (1930-40s), in which dictators thought they could resolve national problems by being Spartan, militant and by conquest (Hitler, Mussolini, Tojo). The west has never recovered from the shock caused by WWI, WWII and the following histories of decadence and corruption were consequences of these frustrations. After the end of WWII, a new world order emerged, this time with the US and Russia battling a cold war that managed to avoid nuclear cataclysm but left us with new challenges. What are citizens to think when governments invest fortunes in weapons everybody knows can't be used? And old, local disputes, aided by despotic regimes continue to wreak havoc on their populations and eventually spill out to the rest of the world. The naive dreams of the Enlightenment have been checked by a cold reality, life cannot be reasoned alone, other forces are at work!

We are again facing debate and a fork in the road. The immense migration waves we witnessed in the last few decades, from many of the recent war-torn or corrupt government countries, are another result of despotism and fanatic religious movements.

Frustrations in the west are giving rise to nationalism and other bestial emotions that sow fear and terror cause.

EDUCATION

The continuation and evolution of progressive societies depends on improving education and spreading the rise of Cognition across the majority. Our civilization is basically "one-generation deep," we depend on the next generations for progress in a fast-changing world. In addition, the "Gap" between the educated and the not so educated, will indeed spread for lack of quality education. A cognitive society - the US economy today is already more than 70% services - provides advantages to the educated and this advantage is highly leveraged in economic terms. With the advent of automation, globalization and the rise of the machine (AI), manufacturing is leaving western societies. Many new professions and services keep emerging, but most of them require an educated, trained, updated workforce.

Globalization has benefitted most, but the masses of working folks are anxious, witnessing their jobs migrating to other countries without government regulation.

Our progress is now very swift. Most of our politicians are the children of the late industrial revolution. They are facing a new world in which, the next 15-20 years are a technological mystery - definitely for the older generation. Some are trying to join the flow, while others prefer to go back to an imaginary glorious past. We are facing, at least in the west, a crisis of leadership and our confidence in the path they are choosing. The academia and educational system also face major challenges as its exclusive ownership of knowledge, science and innovation is dissipating while titan companied compete successfully and new techniques for passing information continue to evolve. Large corporations have their own R&D and education capacity and large corporations also attract young "stars" from the academia, for they offer much better compensation. Education is therefore a huge challenge from any angle, in an era of explosive information and very many that are not ready for this new era. The education we provide to the next generation is more critical than ever.

DISCUSSION

The evolution of the Cognitive-Cloud is a great mystery; we do not know the mechanisms that moves forward our abstract thinking, comprehension and creative processes. Imagine the Cloud to be the surface of a sphere with our ideas, inventions, arts, innovations and brains defining its surface. Every time a new idea, invention, innovation or art surfaces, the sphere swells. A small invention will have a small effect, a big one much bigger, but the process is similar. Because of our language, every invention can easily propagate from one, few, and to many. The sphere hardly shrinks and there is hardly any attrition. To shrink, every person and every record of an idea must disappear, for even if only a few have the knowledge, it can propagate again. Such forgetfulness happened in history, but rarely. We definitely lost much in antiquity, for example much of Aristotle was lost, some literature and much plastic ancient art, painting, statues that did not survive the long years. Luckily, when the west lost appetite for the work of the "pagans", Islam picked it up. Since the middle of the 8th century, enormity of Greek work was translated to Arabic and commented on, especially in Baghdad of the late 8th century. We miss some 17th century music (Monteverdi operas for example, many pieces by J S Bach as well), and many others, which (hopefully) might still be found in obscure North Italian, French or German libraries. However, very much of the science and math has survived antiquity, as did most philosophy, holy books, mythologies and rituals. In the big picture, we are missing only a minority because these are cumulative process and the language allows us to efficiently propagate and store information. Even during the epoch we consider stagnant, the Dark Ages, which apparently were not so dark, most of the information was preserved. Information might have migrated to other civilizations, Islam in this case, developed there and then came back to the west and eventually preserved. Thus, the allegorical sphere continues to grow and specifically with almost no loss, more so since the invention of the print. In modernity, when knowledge doubles every few years, there is practically NO loss of information, our recording and storing technologies are excellent. And it seems that the volume of the sphere is now accelerating! We acquire knowledge at an accelerating rate.

5.2 LANGUAGE

"Speech is 95 percent plus of what lifts man above animal!"

Tom Wolfe

"Speech is so essential to our concept of intelligence that its possession is virtually equated with being human. Animals who talk are human, because what sets us apart from other animals is the "gift" of speech."

Philip Liebermann

Without speech, there is no humanity. While we use gesture, pointing or facials in our communications, speech and writing are of the fundamental tools of our cognition. They are the means of our communication, expression, interaction and thought. In fact, science and math are not possible without writing, our capacity to remember math operations and tables are limited.

The nature of human language is abstraction. Language is all symbols, the bizarre dictionary of our cognition and one unique to every language in existence. Language is a mysterious trait, an enigmatic human capacity. There is mostly no correlation between the word and its meaning (there are exceptions, called Onomatopoeia, like: mom, cuckoo, miaow, etc.). There is something innate and magical in language, not only by the speed babies acquire it. We manage to communicate and to bridge across immense ambiguities with little effort and we can easily convey abstract thought, emotions, and imagination. There is no doubt much ambiguity in our lingual expressions and they are a source of much misunderstanding, yet our communication capacity is still fantastic. Is language a vast instinct? It might be (ref. 73), but we really do not know yet. Language enables us to convey, even implant our ideas, visions, and beliefs in others' minds! Everyone with language is already connected to our genuine worldwide information highway and the cognitive-cloud. The advantages language brings to the evolutionary process are clear, we can learn from others without having the experience and we can cooperate like no other species. Mama bear can show the cubs where and how to fish for salmon; we can convey a thousand times more. We can convey imaginary worlds, tell mythologies and imaginary tales about glorious past and future, nations and Gods, heroes and villains, mostly from our imagination. And we somehow know that a table - a four-legged article that comes in a million shapes and forms - is a table.

Thus, the 1st instrument of our cognition is the means for our invention of our world and the foundation of our social order: religions, mythologies, relationships and so many illusions of our being. Without these abstractions, there is no humanity and language is a social phenomenon, created, shaped and shared by all.

Earlier scientific attempt at Language (beyond the many literary geniuses we developed over the last 3000 years) origins was with BF Skinner. Skinner tried to emulate Darwinism, fashion the nature of language as an evolutionary behavioral process. During a well-known encounter between Skinner and the philosopher Whitehead (1934), the philosopher immediately invented a bizarre sentence and charged Skinner that this cannot have been the result of behavioral acquisition[337]. In the mid 1950s, Chomsky, who believes that speech has genetic origins, passed severe critic on the behavioral nature of language acquisition. Chomsky quickly became the authority on language matters in the last 50-60 years. It seems that language is an integral part of our being; the genetic assumption made a lot of sense, even if lately it has been somewhat rejected by others, towards a more evolutionary interpretation. Others speculate that the origin of our language was initially in mime with arbitrary words or signs added later. Some even speculate that the accelerated growth of our brain, relatively 3X that of the other great apes, had to do with its supporting a growing vocabulary, reaching numbers in the tens of thousands of words and the complex grammatical-structural mechanism. As if language and brain size support one another.

If the origin of our language is indeed in mime, then much can be learned from sign- language. Why and when did we switch from mime to speech? Mime or gesture can be extremely detailed and expressive, but speech took over because it is much more. However, sign language is well and alive, it follows speech and every language has its own sign language. And signs are also part of our language anyways, we are still using much gesture, facials and pointing, or expressing with our hands or faces.

Speech is obviously very complex; it is mechanically and mentally difficult to project a world of four dimensions into the single dimension of speech. Consider the capacity of sound to express the details of everything from function, to emotion and the fantastic artistic expressions and the enormous achievements that speech (and later writing) evolution gave us. While gestures and mime lack grammar, our high language must have a certain structure specific for each language; we learn this structure during the first few years of our being. Language must be regenerative, we can create infinite sentences that make sense. We easily create and understand sentences and recursive sentences, no matter how complex, that we have never heard or uttered before. Thinking is mostly talking to ourselves; we practically live in the language, as much as we live in the world, as we think with words. Some 6,000 languages and dialects are spoken worldwide, a huge variety. There were probably tens of thousands of languages in human history, as languages evolved and declined quickly. Language changes constantly and swiftly. The investment Evolution made in the creation of languages is immense, most probably brain size, but it paid off very nicely. Here we are, taken dominion of the planet mostly because of our lingual capacity and our ability to communicate within very large groups.

Human language is recursive, a built-in complexity that we have no problem to grasp. To the best of our knowledge "*even the peoples with least complex cultures have highly sophisticated languages, with complex grammar and large vocabularies, capable of naming and discussing anything that occurs in the sphere occupied by their speakers. The oldest language that can be reconstructed is already complex, sophisticated, complete from an evolutionary point of view and…by the age of six, the average child has learned to use and understand about 13,000 words; by eighteen it will have a working vocabulary of 60,000 words.*[217]"

Language is a fundamental human trait; all humans talk and most read and write; world illiteracy is now down to 10%. Other humanoids, like Neanderthal or Cro-Magnon, certainly had a language, but we do not know much about its nature. We know that the Neanderthals could not produce the wealth of sounds we can because of the structural differences in their Larynx and tongue. Theirs was more like Chimpanzee's sounds, lacking our diversity. This brings about an interesting question: is there something innate that is different in our brain (Neanderthals had a bigger brain), its structure and organization or is it just a matter of sheer brain size and our ability to process information in a much higher level than any other species?

Much has been written about the evolution of the Larynx[218,219,220], an organ located in our neck and involved in breathing, sound production and protection against food asphyxiation. Much has been speculated about the evolution of this organ because its shape is so unique to humans among other apes [212,217]. At about the age of one year old, the Larynx changes shape and sinks lower in the throat; it is initially higher to enable babies simultaneous suckling and breathing; also it enables more freedom in the generation of various sounds at the cost of increased suffocation risk. Lieberman (reference 102) indicates that in the U.S., food asphyxiation is the #4 cause of death in adults. Consequently, biologists concluded that speech received high priority in the evolutionary process, even above the risk of asphyxiation. Human capacity for producing distinct sounds, especially vowels that are critical for conveying meaning and word intricacies, obviously significantly more sophisticated than other apes[220]. The tiny differentiations between certain words (especially in the syllables that contain high frequency, like: s, h, th, sh, etc...) is critical later, when with age we lose some hearing and find it difficult to distinguish between them (comprehension). Certain animals can be taught to imitate a few words, sometimes many words; parrots and crows are known as good imitators but they do not have language. Animals might obey our spoken command and even "talk" to us, but they never try to "chat" with one another.

Language is first about speech. About 95% of the languages used today have no writing at all. Writing is a refined mode of language but lacks the capacity of spoken intonation or gesture. Reading is, of course a highly complex cognitive feature. For example, in Hebrew, among other languages, the vowels are not used like in English for indication, hence the letters "pt" can be read as pit, pet, pot, put or pat. Reading a Hebrew sentence is therefore a continuous process of guessing and manipulation because only through the complete sentence are the exact words revealed. Even in the ease of our Roman vowels, reading in every language is a very complex procedure - many words have many meanings - a task our brains perform so easily.

The print, a later technological manifestation of writing, that is not yet 600 years old, was another crucial evolutionary process because copying became so easy. Due to printing and its mass production, the price of the book quickly collapsed and allowed the spreading of reading to the many, rather than it being the domain of small elite. Books existed much earlier but required manual copying; printing made books easy to produce in large volumes. Some historians speculate that both the Reformation and later the Enlightenment, were impossible without the print (books, pamphlets). This is most likely, but we should note that the age of Enlightenment saw also enormity of letters, the writing instrument that was more personal. Until today, the term "*man of letters*" has a certain attraction. And most writing is still personal and never copied, our endless correspondences, letters, messages, tweets or emails.

Every language has syntax that gives it a unique structure, even if some are more complex or intricate than others. Such syntax is mostly carried in our memory as every language has its unique structure. Language allows much flexibility, sometimes called "generation," but still the syntax forces a structure and was probably a later manifestation of lingual evolution. Languages also have different rhymes; most music for songs or opera are written for a language and almost all composers compose in their mother language. There have been very few exceptions here.

Languages have various unique traits, among them cursing, jokes, humor, etc.... There has never been a spoken language without cursing (sometimes swearing, profanity)! Cursing helps us express: fear, anguish, relief, various emotions, pain and sometimes do it in humor. Absolutely unique to humanity. No animal curses, even if they have reasons, but some parrots were trained to do so.

Literary expressions, especially by the great writers, have also gone through the path of rising cognition. Story-telling and the centrality of the tale (Decameron, Canterbury Tales, for example) have been replaced by writing for a purpose with little storyline. Modern writing is much more about the personalities, the relationship and critic over social behavior (Balzac, Camus, Bellow, Dostoevsky, Boll, Flaubert among many others). Flaubert's dream was to write a literary piece "about nothing". The tale is then more about the personalities, their inter-relationships, position in the society and thoughts.

CHOMSKY

Most linguists accept that our "higher-language," dawned or matured some seventy to one hundred thousand years ago. Chomsky, one of the towering figures in 20th century linguistics, postulated that language dawned on us swiftly, a kind of "step-function" from the primitive to the advance; perhaps by a gene mutation - obviously after a long evolution of our species towards such cognitive capacity. His school has much data to rely on, among their considerations:

1. Language is innate; we seem to be born with the skill.

2. We learn the language so quickly.

3. Babies have the capacity to distinguish some 150 sounds; individual languages use 1/3 of such number.

4. Language seems natural, almost an organ - like a hand or a tongue, it manifests certain genetic traits.

5. It seems like a feature as much as a learned skill. We can and do invent new sentences we never heard before.

The postulation of the swift genetic process, later termed "Language Big Bang," assumes that we are born with a faculty, like a computer operating system and as we grow up, the language is simply downloaded into the mind somehow. Chomsky's linguistic theory postulates the structure of language as biologically determined, hence genetically transmitted. If the language Software is in-born, then there must be a Universal Grammar (UG), which Chomsky also postulated, perhaps a Speech Organ in the brain, and the Recursive character of human language. The special skill of human language is therefore the ability of our finite brains to produce infinite sentences with the correct grammar. The Chomsky postulate has a significant implication even if by inference. If language, the instrument of our thought, has a genetic component, then so is our thought process! It follows that we are not born "Tabula Rasa" as many have assumed before (initiated by John Locke).

The Chomsky school is facing severe opposition in recent decades. The alternative schools are ready to view language only in the light of Evolutionary theory, hence a gradual, million years with many starts, long-term process that evolved to provide survival advantages of sort, a process that matured about seventy thousand years back. People obviously communicated earlier; the Homo Erectus, 1.4M years ago knew how to manufacture stone tools (various knives), an indication for high cognitive capacity and cooperate in groups; but these early "languages" were poor in comparison, nothing like the later wealth of words, expressions. Speech indeed does not reside in a small area of the brain, rather all over the place and there are doubts about the Universal Grammar; the various grammars of thousands of languages are too diverse. These postulates, so influential by the authoritative Chomsky and the "Chomsky brigade" - the many loyal followers who defended his theses fanatically - have made a commanding influence in the last half century, but recently come into question (see ref. 190, 220). Chomsky's commanding contribution and supreme intelligence is never disputed; he is a giant in the field and a genius mind.

Speculations, like mime as origin or especially the discovery of the Piraha Amazon tribe language, used by a small tribe of few hundred persons, lacking numbers, past or future tense - everything is in the present - and without some of the very common characteristics of other languages, have emerged as contrarians to mainstream theories. Was the large brain the cause of the appearance of a high language? Was language a trigger in the reorganization of our brain? These questions are still being pondered. We still know little about the origins of this wonder. "*Of course, holes still remain in our knowledge, in particular, at what stage did language leap from being something new which humans discovered to being something which every newborn human is scheduled to acquire? This is still a puzzle.*" What many linguists agree on is that "*the origin of human languages can be discerned - but most probably not strictly via the theory of evolution.*[p.12]".

Darwin struggled with language in his "*Descent of Man*" and speculated its Evolutionary nature. He dedicated 10 pages to language evolution and speculated wisely about its corollary with other creature's language (specifically song-birds) and the evolutionary process of grasping concepts. He also speculated on brain growth being instigated by language.

Speech must have changed our biology very fundamentally, "*Looking more closely, we will discover that a radical re-engineering of the whole brain has taken place, and on a scale that is unprecedented. In order to speak a word that has been read, information is obtained from the eyes and travels to the visual cortex. From the primary visual cortex, information is transmitted to the posterior speech area (which includes Wernicke's area). From there, information travels to Broca's area, and then to the primary motor cortex to provide the necessary muscle contractions to produce the sound*[217]." How did all this occur in just a few tens of thousands of years? Are we raising the speculation of a human brain with capacity to change much faster than we can imagine? Thus, the opposite interpretation, evolutionary in style, is that it took millions of years in a slow, gradual evolutionary process rather than a "Big Bang." On the other hand, nobody can explain, especially without genetic component, how a baby of four can acquire a few thousand words and then when she/he reaches eighteen, the number jumps to tens of thousands, without some preconditioning. The rate of absorption and then, the quick acquisition of grammar are just too astonishing.

LANGUAGE EVOLUTION

Languages change very quickly and evolve constantly. Languages change radically across rather short time spans. Folks who speak Hebrew can easily read most of the Hebrew Bible, written almost twenty-five centuries ago. This unique situation is due to the "petrification" of this language - it was frozen for more than two thousand years. Rather than being a living language, the exiled Jews used Hebrew mostly for prayers, but otherwise used the languages of their Diaspora, or their dialects (Yiddish, Ladino). Since the language was resurrected a century ago in Israel and spoken regularly, it already suffered swift changes and evolution. Many words, idioms and street-terms have been added after the two millennia freeze. On the other hand, Shakespeare wrote only four hundred years ago, but in a living, actively evolving language. Just four hundred years have passed and the language is already very different. Most of us can read Shakespeare, with difficulty, but English has changed mightily and its vocabulary has swollen immensely too. If we stretch the period from 400 to 600 years, we arrive at Chaucer; the Chaucer we read today is already translated. Six hundred years is only some 25 generations!

Looking at a bit longer span, Latin was the language of a great Empire less than 2,000 years ago, the official language of the Mediterranean basin in an Empire that consisted of some 60-70M souls. Today, Latin is practically "under wraps," used by some scholars, the church, in old music or by certain snobs. Instead, we have French, Italian, Spanish, Portuguese and Rumanian with their many dialects. In less than 2,000 years, about seventy generations, the mother-language changed so much that a Spaniard could not be understood in the streets of Paris, and none of them understands Latin. The language is a living, cognitively evolving "being," but probably not on the Darwinian path. It evolves with our cognition and the new universes our cognition invents in social, scientific, technical and artistic fashion and therefore, is a swift process. Today we are witnessing an accelerated evolutionary lingual rate because the many cognitive fields that are born and require new terminology and new communication technologies. Also, Twitter and Text-Messaging are creating new versions of the languages. These are extremely concise lingual versions, messaging was even termed as "speech writing" (McWorther[189], he also termed them "emergent complexity"). These are new languages, evolving quickly, specifically with their shortcuts, abbreviations and acronyms. Some speculate these might be dominant languages of the future in the day-to-day electronic exchange. Total estimated world messages volume is in the 120-150 billion a day!

New disciplines, study objects and the world-view we constantly invent, require new terminology, hence the vast evolution of languages in modernity. Between the times of Dr. Johnson (1709-1784CE), the author of the first great English Dictionary and the present day, some 250 years of separation or about 10 generations, English grew in volume about ten times! The latest Oxford dictionary contains more than 500 thousand entries. The language today must facilitate a much more intricate and complex world than the Doctor's.

Languages fill niches and usually adapts to the speakers' needs in mysterious ways. If the language serves an advanced, evolving civilization, then the language is rich and growing. If it serves a hunter-gatherer group, then it changes slowly because its needs hardly change. Still, the language is peculiar to every group, perhaps as a means of survival, in term of privacy and intimacy. Languages over-grow their practical needs (some languages are extremely rich in nuance) and their evolution was never explained in Darwinian terms. They might not follow any path of "survival," even if their invention was a first-class survival instrument, but the outgrowth of a language - more complex syntax and wealth of vocabulary, reflect something else in our cognitive evolution. After all, nobody has a vocabulary of hundreds of thousands of words, which the English language contains.

Mixing languages, like mixing people, causes mutual influences; when people immigrate to new area they influence the local spoken language, as well as being influenced by locality. Places that witness many invasions or migrations in their history, like England or USA, develop languages that are heavily influenced by others; the Latin, French and Saxon influence on English is clear. And it is not only a matter of new words copied from other languages; even the grammar is changing under the influence of new vernacular introduced into the vocabulary market.

Speech process is an absolute enigma. The words are coming out so automatically and quick, as if there is not enough time to prepare. When exactly do we form that order and flow? Speaking comes so naturally that it feels as forming without thinking, sometimes regrettably. Therefore, it is a cognitive process in our mind that somehow converts to the spoken word, with its intricately complex muscle system, including tongue, lips, cheeks and Larynx. Speech feels easy, almost automatic, as if without tight control. However, there are signs that the process is very complex and a certain delay in our speech indicates the measure of thinking-processing it obviously takes. Orators have a fantastic skill in this matter; rhetoric can be somewhat learned but only to a limit. Great orators are born, not brought up, in-spite of the legends about Demosthenes.

If languages are like species, then there has to be a certain corollary in their evolution or extinction. We seem to be on the precipice of a great lingual extinction. Scientists have counted more than six thousand languages in use today, but due to our technology, urbanization and mobility, their numbers are shrinking swiftly. It is expected that thousands of languages will go extinct in the next century.

From the genealogical standpoint, language is only about one generation deep. While adults mainly perpetuate its development, lingual maintenance depends on passing it on to the younger generation because language is one of the certain characteristics we acquire from our parents and family. My grandmother, who never learned Hebrew, was the reason I understand Yiddish, it was her only language. This singular person was sufficient to make me very fluent in the language. However, if only one generation fails, the language will be driven close to extinction. Refugees and immigrants watch their offspring lose the language in a generation. Yiddish specifically, used by communities in the millions in the Eastern Europe of yore, is now in the usage of a very small minority and universities. Many other communities, immigrating to new lands, especially for the ease of mobility in modernity, witness their offspring losing the old language. This process is very prevalent today as mobility improved. Humanity has ballooned to more than seven billion, and demographers expect the number to grow to eleven billion before it starts to fall. With urbanization, the number of languages can be expected to fall precipitously. Imagine the transformation of some 500M Indians (a country with many languages), moving from villages to large cities in the next 35 years. In the city, the indigenous languages have less utility. The children are educated in public schools, where a more common language is taught, the television or their mobile devices come in the "dominant" languages. Even if the parents continue to support the older language or dialect, the chances of survival are slim; especially if the language has no written component. There is also social pressure on the kids to "convert." Because of this mobility, experts expect that within the next century, the numbers of spoken languages will collapse to but few percentages of today's number.

Languages can be resurrected, but this is a very unusual process. The best example is the already mentioned Hebrew, a language that was petrified for almost two millennia, used mainly in prayers and then, totally resurrected in modern Israel. In-spite of this viability, it is probable that the Israeli/Jewish example is unique. Many indigenous languages of the world today are in a different situation and are probably passing from the world rather quickly. Many of them might not be rich in written heritage, thus only depending on speech. This process of lingual attrition due to urbanization does not bode well for the many thousands of indigenous languages in use today, to the chagrin of many scholars.

The search for a universal language (like Esperanto) never really caught. Perhaps our language is too personal, too intimate for us. On the other hand, imagine a world that could be communicated with or traveled without worrying about translation. Technology might interfere here too, with translation devices, as voice interface is now quickly maturing. Today about 95% of us command some 20-25 big languages (like Chinese, English, Spanish). Some of us command more than one language and this trend is growing because of globalization.

ALPHABET

There are vast differences between the spoken and written language, which is richer, subtler and usually better organized. Speech is the "mother" and written language is its refined manifestation, but only a few thousand years old. The written language has an intricate evolution as well. It appeared first with the cuneiform (wedge) lettering in Sumer more than five thousand years ago. They were mostly pictograms, written on soft clay plates. During the old Kingdom in ancient Egypt, the hieroglyphic writing system developed as a combination of artistic expression and alphabet. Early writing was pictorial and required too many letters. While in principle our memory has no problem dealing with thousands of letters, some languages still use them, a better method had to be invented for simplification and to enable the many to read and write. The phonetic alphabet, using concise, flexible writing technology and just a few letters, was discovered some two thousand years later, just some thirty-five centuries back. The latest research speculates that people who served the Egyptian civilization invented phonetic writing in the Sinai Peninsula of Egypt. Today, some three-quarters of world population excluding certain southeastern-Asia nations use a variation of the original Phoenician lettering, the first comprehensive phonetic alphabet. The shape of the letters itself has a fascinating history. The order of the alphabet and even the letters' shape can easily be traced back to the Phoenician.

There is much tradition and fascinating history in the lettering systems. For example, in English we really need only K, but the Phoenicians needed K, C and Q, thus, bequeathing us the three letters. All letters were capital until the Middle Ages. Part of the 8-9th century "Carolingian Renaissance" was the invention of their minuscule, more rounded lettering. They also introduced the space between words, which made reading easier. Beforehand, writing was continuous without word separation.

The initial clay written tablets were heavy and difficult to store. The Egyptians then discovered the Papyrus plant as a medium. Writing on papyrus scrolls was cheaper, lighter, mobile and easier to store. It proved to be durable and spread through the Mediterranean and Mesopotamia. Ink was made from various natural pigments that were processed, consisting of mostly dark or red colors. The Papyrus, after invention, forced the evolution of a new, modified lettering system that fit the new medium better. In China, writing on bamboo shoots that were treated for paper-medium, used a similar medium technology then.

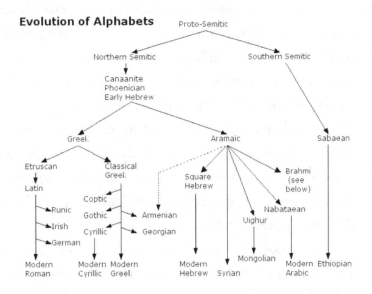

Figure 5: Evolution of the alphabet

Following shortages of papyrus in Europe after the Arab conquest of North Africa (7th century), ubiquitous usage of vellum (calfskin) and parchment followed, especially in the west during the middle ages. The conquest of Egypt by the Muslims caused a certain economic separation with the west (see ref. 13) and the growing popularity of vellum in Europe, but it was never a cheap, economical medium. As long as books were hand copied, the medium served its purpose. In modernity, vellum is still used for special applications, like symbolic, traditional or holy-documents.

The print-press is considered by many historians to be the real harbinger of modernity and one of our greatest inventions. This writing, printing technology had an incalculable effect on our knowledge because books became easy and cheap to produce and distribute. Suddenly, every family could have affordable books. In addition, the pamphlet, then the newspaper and journal were born, had immense influence in modernity. With the revolutionary invention of the press (circa 1453CE, Gutenberg), a much cheaper and lighter print material was needed. Paper was invented earlier in China but achieved mass production and enormity of volume only in modernity. The paper-book became the lasting technology of economic printing for hundreds of years. Paper is a useful and cost-effective medium, even if its production and manufacturing is offending certain modern environmental challenges: logging, transportation and manufacturing process. The dawn of the 21st century brings another revolution in print – electronic books (e-book), and paper, might be losing its primacy. The electronic book and electronic documents are so advantageous that one simply cannot find a reason to use paper books, beyond habit - "liking the feel of the book" is the current excuse for paper-books. The same reasoning is true for documents, especially with our growing ability to sign them on electronic media. Electronic media is clean, easy to control and purchase, and does not require material resources, like pulp or wood, or transportation, that use energy and pollutes. A typical book size requires about 4-5M byte of memory. Even 16-32 Gb tablets easily contain hundreds and thousands of e-books. The e-book is also advantageous in management and reading. It is easier to control font, font-size, background light or page format on an e-book. Also marking and notes are much easier than in paper book. No doubt the e-book is superior in every respect and environmentally friendly. With the aging population, font size is easy to adjust on electronic format. One travels easily today with hundreds of books, all contained on a tiny tablet. Many books are published nowadays only in e-book format. And of course, eliminating paper books goes a long way to create a cleaner industry without the pulp, the logging of forests for the wood, or hauling materials and storing books.

In the end, books are still the main instruments of learning, more than anything else out there, but technology is now offering alternatives in video or audio seminars on electronic media. Books will continue to populate libraries, especially older books, but even today, one can almost do all research in the comfort of one's office or home without visiting a library. It will not take long to store all our sources on electronic files and make them available worldwide. Some of the larger tech companies, like Project Gutenberg or Google Books (some 30M books digitized already), have already started digitizing enormous numbers of classical books making them available to the public. Books copyright is usually 75 years; hence most of the classic work, until modernity is practically available free on e-books. Whatever the medium, the influence of the book on our learning and artistic expressions is immense and not going to change anytime soon. In-spite of the popularity of the book, video teaching and MOOC (Massive Open Online Course) technology are advancing.

Technology will enable new methods for teaching, but the book, in any format will probably be the instrument of learning for long. Let us not forget that study can be fun, not always for practical purpose. The origin of the word school is the Latin *Schola* = leisure! Indeed, being in school or at home following a MOOC is leisure in comparison to herding the sheep or building the city wall.

The development of computers and the origins of what we call Artificial Intelligence (AI) started after WWII. The study of languages was quickly coupled with AI since our attempt has been to create artificial machines that "think like us." AI researchers were immediately drawn to the mechanism that enables children to learn language. Initially, the Chomskian genetic paradigm ruled, but some opined that perhaps the best way for the machine is not to focus on our genetic capacity or perhaps a "universal grammar" (not available to any machine) and instead, look for neural-networks model and its nodal and inter-connections properties. Even if this path was practically aborted for a long time to be replaced by other methods, it resurrected in the early 2000s, changed the name from "*neural-network*" into "*deep learning*," and is the leading path for the future development of AI. Perhaps such machines and algorithms, as have been devised by Deep Mind (now part of Google), an English company led by pioneers Demis Hassabis and Mustafa Suleyman, can later shed light on the way we learn to speak. Today, training (data examples) and parallel processing dominate AI. Within just a decade of the breakthrough, many companies already offer consumer products that understand our commands (Alexa, Siri, Google), seem to understand our language well enough and enable translation between many languages. Many machines already accept voice-command as voice-interface is the most natural for us. And computers have been able to correct our spelling mistakes, style and even syntax errors for long. A real dream comes true, the ability to travel the world and be able to communicate via the machine. Products are already available in the market (Google translation ear-buds).

5.3 MONARCHY & NOBLE BIRTH

*"Are you aware that Alexandra has the smallest head ever seen? I dread that -
with Bertie's small empty brain – for future children..."*

Queen Victoria on her first born and his wife

"In England, a King hath little more to do than to make war and give away palaces...of more worth is one honest man to society and in the sight of God, than all the crowned ruffians that ever lived."

Thomas Paine

Notwithstanding Plato's philosopher-king[338], most of them were not. When Thomas Payne published his pamphlet ***Common Sense***, it was a scathing attack on the institution of monarchy, old and new. Not much can be added to the document after almost two-and-a-half centuries. What reason is there to anoint an untested person, just for his or her birthright for life, or being the emblem of a whole people, while making the position hereditary?

And still, most European nations chose monarchies or despots until late in our history! There were many traditional and social reasons that folks, for thousands of years did not question. It was a traditional regime when the power of the state or tribe was held by a small minority, those blessed by "noble birth".

The king of yore however, the supreme commander and leader, was no doubt a force for unification, a symbol of the people, the person at the top of the social order. The king or queen became the "father of the nation", the "absolute authority that never errs" and the "God chosen" leader of the people. Their authority was total, their word and interest, absolute. As modernity dawned, many of these titles disappeared and the monarchs became mostly a symbol. We continue to accept one person at the head of the pyramid (President or Prime minister) but those are chosen frequently; the position is not hereditary. Consequently, depending on one's taste, much of the monarchies has become ritual, symbol, sometimes circus; but many of us are still attracted to the pomp, the ritual, the symbol and the "show". For many, the monarchy, maybe more than the monarch, is a symbol of the state; an apolitical position of tradition, continuity and respect. The English, for example, adore their monarchs, so traditional and lasting. They imagine monarchy with political independence; the monarch becomes a-political with mostly symbolic status, thus, representing the whole nation, unlike republics with their politically biased leaders. The monarch becomes the traditional symbolic head of state, devoid of authority - its head of ceremonies, a unifying force and sometimes a source for solace. Since they have no executive power, one notices the opulence, wealth, waste, circus, the scandals and yellow-journalism surrounding those families.

When in late 1494 (Pope Borgia ruled in Rome and Michelangelo was 19 years old) the young, unattractive, delusional and deformed king of France, Charles VIII decided to invade Italy and restore his "rights" over the Kingdom of Naples (then under Spanish influence), it was a personal, rather than national decision. Italian princes were looking for alliances with the French, Spanish and English monarchies, who quickly developed territorial appetites, like those of Charles. French princes had a certain perceived ownership of southern Italy since the days of Charles Anjou (1227-1285) who managed to destroy the house of Hohenstaufen in the south but lost his chances after the famous Sicilian Vespers (1282CE). Charles VIII and his court were certain without a shadow of a doubt, that the Kingdom of Naples was his right; he had some dubious claims on Naples through his paternal grandmother. The land and the kingdoms were treated as the private property of monarchs and nobles. Consequently, the resources of his kingdom were committed to the task. The King was the State, even though it took another three centuries to express it (*"l'etat c'est Moi"* - Louis XIV). It is hard to imagine such world-order, one in which leaders, mostly of noble birth, decide to march on other lands arbitrarily, commit the resources of their state and take them over based on dubious claims.

The practice of invading other lands was common in the past. Kings, sometimes on a whim, would conquer and enslave populations and rob their wealth, vitality and in some cases, their identity. Selling prisoners in the slave markets was common. These adventures usually cost their own people dearly because wars were rarely profitable.

Military adventures would bring glory, but not much profit. Heavy borrowing funded many of these pursuits. Indeed, a hundred years earlier, Edward III, at the beginning of the Hundred Years War, owed so much money to Italian banks that he had to default on part of the loan, causing serious agitations in the northern Italian banking system (indeed the Peruzzi and Bardi banks were knocked out). The military mostly consisted of mercenaries that had to be paid well and on time; default was not an option for them. This phenomenon of territorial expansion is not limited to the times of yore. Later European nations and, in many cases, private enterprise supported by monarchy, embarked on creating Empires in far-away lands and exploited their population, until the 20th century.

Charles' claim on Naples was doubtful indeed, but this did not prevent him, when the political scenario aligned, with the Borgia Pope's support, from entering Italy with a vast army. He brought some twenty-five thousand troops, among them thousands of Swiss mercenaries and new war machinery never seen before in Italy. After the long march, with visits to Lombardy, Florence and Rome, the Duke of Milan - Ludovico Sforza duke of Milan, known as "Il Moro" - emerged as an ally. Alexander VI, the Borgia Pope, had a complex relationship with the king, but hosted him in Rome and let him pass. This large army took Naples easily. The Italian peninsula was shaken with consternations. The Italian city-states were accustomed to small armies led by the mercenary leaders, the Condotierri. Their battles were described more as a "dance" (tactical positioning) than brutal fighting. Their hired armies were too frugal to allow the loss of too many soldiers. The French army was too powerful for them, its prospects too scary for the local princes. Such was the lot and behavior of absolute monarchy.

There was much symbolism in the foundation and support of the institutions of the monarchy, but it was also a natural consequence of power play. The origin of our social order has been in the family. There is power in numbers and families had to eventually combine into tribes. Then tribes had to further combine when bigger threats appeared, into "nations" with a single commander at the top, the King. He (it was mostly a male then) symbolized the tribe, but also provided the military and political leadership that is necessary to keep the social order safe and from chaos. In time, the king's wisdom was more important than his heroism. The first biblical king, Saul, the "tallest" and probably most powerfully built, did not read the political map correctly and continued to fight the Philistines, while a much more powerful foe was forming in the north, the Kingdom of Aram. David read the political map much better and came to an agreement with the Philistines to combine forces and fight the bigger threat to both.

The figure of the leader, the one who is powerful and smart, has been steeped in our consciousness from time immemorial. The king also ruled "by the grace of God," (Ramesses = the son of Rah, the sun god) with the church mostly by his side. Monarchs were considered divine; their command came from God, their touch could cure ("Le roi te touche, Dieu te guérit" – the King touches and God cures)[290]! As long as the authority of the king and the rights of the people resided together compatibly, the balance was maintained. It was Louis XVI who said, "C'est legal, parce que je le veux (it is legal because I want it)." Not for long.

Since the monarch is a symbol, the courts were magnificent and affluent, wasteful with grandeur. The magnificence of the King had to be demonstrated and since the institution is symbolic by its nature, what is more natural than a stunning court and palace, rich attires and rituals, some of which we observe to this day? For an American, abhorrent of the monarchic institution, the visit to certain European countries steeped in old monarchic traditions, is sometimes stunning, even disturbing, considering the reverence still shown for those institutions. Inspite of the lack of any real authority, the symbolic circus they sometimes produce is continuously in force. The circus, the ritual, is a part of our traditions and lifestyle. No doubt, most of the people in these countries adore their monarchs and dynasties, which are the focus of so much gossip, journalism and controversy. However, even in conservative England, there are constantly voices (a minority) calling for the abolition of the institution even when the monarch is still drowning in the nation's adoration.

There is no doubt that early societies chose leadership based on personal heroism, both courage and fighting prowess, and on leadership characteristics. The ability to manage, negotiate and rule is often coupled with the person's ambitions and charisma. However, charisma and leadership are not hereditary while leaders wished naturally to create dynasties. This was another reason to separate the ruling class from the majority, so that a small elite group could make decisions in close form. As the ruling classes solidified early, they required their own social structure and leaders that were elevated to the pinnacle of the system, eventually becoming divine, thus kings. The king had a cadre of deputies from which they arose. Records show that this social layer coagulated quickly into a noble class managing the people: workers, bureaucrats and soldiers. The ancient political order is well described in Plato's Republic, with the later addition of "those who prayed." The rulers needed the priests and a complementary relationship to quickly evolve. We know of early leaders like Sargon – a dynastic figure or Gilgamesh, who rose from the bottom and soon ruled Empires. They were the ambitious, the powerful, those at the top of the pyramid, creators of dynasties, initially war lords. Sargon had already commanded a standing army. These historical and mythical characters, demi-gods in their civilizations, were therefore military leaders, perhaps great warriors, ruling some 4200-4500 years ago. They formed larger social orders and, via conquests, erected Empires by absorbing new domains by force and subjugation.

The ruling order, especially kings, had to separate from the crowd; the more removed, the better grows the reverence and respect for the mythological king. Based in the misty past, the first Jewish kings - revered biblical figures, are no exception; we know historically almost nothing about king David or Saul. The blessing of the God, by his messenger (prophet), in the case of the early Jewish kings, was critical. Indeed, God quickly rejected king Saul, who emerged from a small tribe, and his dynasty was extinguished by a new dynasty based on the dominant tribe, Judah. And if the king was divine, does it not follow that his blood is also special? Thus rose the dynasties, which could never guarantee a smart, courageous heir.

The Kingdom was always driven by complex forces[261,262]: geography, economy, political competition, ambition, culture, traditions and later by technological advances. The complex organization had to develop a chain of command with a singular person at its head. This has not changed; the modern state or corporation, are still commanded by one person at its head (president, prime minister). In many cases, the commoners could not approach the king at all, such distance adding more adulation and respect. Interestingly enough, in the early Ottoman Empire, touching the Sultan by a commoner was unthinkable and resulted in harsh punishment, sometimes death, even if the purpose was to help him in difficulty; the monarch body was "sacred". If the early kings were still accessible, later the nobility became separated, elevated, sometimes assumed of having exceptional powers. In Europe, monarchs still bestow "nobility" status (knighthood in the form of Sir or Dame) in certain countries.

Political disturbances sometimes caused replacement of monarchs, but the social order suffered no changes, it just went through a short upheaval and then settled back to its origins. If Charles I (or Louis XVI) were beheaded, they were soon replaced by another monarch, a family member or a son. The social order was still not ready for self-ruling; the king was still revered. Just remember, Alexander Hamilton, a sworn federalist and one of the supreme political geniuses of the age, suggested during the Constitutional Convention that a president (Washington in this case) should be elected for life!

The relationship between the people and the leader has always been complex; in-spite of certain natural disdain for authority, it seems that most people are searching for a figure to obey, trust and follow. The monarchs are role models and more, they are revered, admired. When the authority is emerging from a long history, like dynasties, mystified in the glory of the past, this emotion and symbolism are stronger even if the performance of their past is mediocre. The concept of king/queen, as part of the monarchy, never dies; they virtually own "two bodies,[24]" the corporeal and the dynastic. "*The King is dead, long live the King*" or in the French origin, "*Le roi est mort, vive le roi!,*" indicating both the continuity of the monarchy and the divine role of the monarchic symbol, being more than a mortal. The monarch is a person, man or woman, and there is the dynasty; the dynasty is an entity meant never to perish.

Whether coercion or adulation, fear or admiration, the support of the people was critical for the position - a monarch's power always emerges from the bottom. A wise Frenchman once said "*you can do many things with bayonets, but sitting on them is very inconvenient*"[210]; the best way to control the people is mostly by consent. Consequently, the most despotic regimes, those who apply the worst terror, engage in the richest propaganda. When Stalin died, millions lamented the monstrous dictator; he was the "father" figure for many. The monarchs, in most cases, viewed themselves as the "father (or mother) of the nation" and parents always mean well. Rituals and magnificent pageantry in all monarchic traditions were created to honor the monarch, to elevate them above mortals, all part of a vast organization to dignify their names and position and create the aura of superiority.

MONUMENTS TO LEADERSHIP

The large construction projects, initially monuments to the leaders, palaces and temples and the pyramids or gardens, also demonstrate the immense ancient authority, the organization of material and labor on very large scale. Building a pyramid required an estimated 40,000-100,000 laborers, perhaps more than 5%

of the total adult male population of the upper Nile then. Such projects required a very well organized and disciplined community, in addition to intricate design and control of labor, material and food supply. All for the glory of the leader King. Design skills and labor organization of very high sophistication were needed as we can assume that the worker was ignorant and illiterate, therefore required tight control. As detailed graphic design techniques for construction surfaced only much later; hard to imagine how this was done earlier (see ref. 325). Such projects required a very rigid, authoritative order. A united noble class is critical to stability of the structure, as supporting the head in the various functions required to manage and control the social order. The pyramids were the monuments to the divine Kings, themselves a marvel of architecture, building technology and reverence. The workers could be well organized and disciplined, or coerced, by a small elite for reasons that work until today; we are mostly disciplined and obeying authority. In some of these organizations, the social structure is held by terror, in others by adulation and reverence for the ruler. Coercion was required when the adulations are not sufficient:

1. Most people are subservient; rising up against authority is not natural. The lesser educated are usually easier to control. We know that modern uprising leadership (say Communist Russia or China), for which we have more detailed information, is never from the bottom; the leadership is mostly educated.

2. While the force available to the ruler is always small in comparison, this force is organized and disciplined. Such force is designed to control local disturbances because the authorities can usually muster significant local superiority. The authority is always much better organized than the mob.

3. Anointed, nominated, represented, elected people command a certain respect. Authority is naturally respected; consider the person lecturing before us or standing up on a stage preaching - they immediately become experts, leaders. Politics, religion or teaching, commands immediate respect; it is part of our "herd mentality."

4. Education, propaganda, opulence and ritual instill the "superiority" of the leader above the people.

The leader's charisma is fundamental to his or her ascent. Charisma was defined by Max Weber as "*A certain quality of an individual personality, by virtue of which he is set apart from ordinary men and treated as endowed with supernatural, superhuman, or at least specifically exceptional powers or qualities. These are such as are not accessible to the ordinary person, but are regarded as of divine origin or as exemplary, and on the basis of them the individual concerned is treated as a leader…*[151]" Powerful leadership always comes with ambition, dominant personalities and a certain charisma that attracts the followers and provides the lubricant for accepting authority under certain mystical powers. Alas, charisma is not inherited and most dynasties, even when blessed by a charismatic originator, rule without it. The sons/daughters of the originator were already "blessed by birth," even without charisma; and then there is the ruling organization, the apparatus that supported them. Nobility in the past, party apparatus in modernity.

THE CHOSEN HERO

The Bible objects to monarchy; God preferred the Judges that were local, of limited influence and not hereditary. The twelve judges of the bible were leaders that rose to deal with local challenges until the people demanded a king (Samuel 1, 12). Both Homer and the Bible ascribe to the King more than just physical prowess. David, perhaps with Moses the most admired person in the Jewish Bible, is already a "chosen man," a natural leader with infinite luck, charisma and personality. God chose him when he was still young and not yet worthy, is on his side and speaks to him through the prophets. David, the young legendary hero with infinite courage, rules his warriors and is so dominating that later, he does not even participate in battles that are managed by the generals, while he stays in Jerusalem. The Bible boldly portrays David, the warrior, poet, natural leader, also as a most immoral person yet still favored by God (the house of David begets the Messiah)! Much has been written about the interpretation of such phenomena, because of its contradictory nature. David committed almost every crime in the book; he not only coveted his general's wife, but also sent him to certain death in battle. What can be more vain, immoral and wrong? And still he is the chosen one, beloved by God; from him will come the Messiah, also chosen to represent the ancestry of the Christian Son-of-God. This concept of pre-destination, of the few chosen by God with no correlation to their deeds, later became one of the fundamental beliefs in Calvinism and a life driver in their communities - "*damnation of the damned is caused by their sin, but the salvation of the saved is solely caused by God."*

At about the same time, in Homer's Iliad (circa 750BCE), Agamemnon is not divine, a man fraught with human weaknesses, ambitions and contradictions. He is the most powerful King, but also driven and eventually falling, by personal affront. His power lies in his boundless ambitions, political acumen and a certain uncontested leadership. During the war with Troy, Achilles is the hero of the story. When Agamemnon demands the maid Briseis from Achilles, even Achilles the hero of the Greek military does not dare challenge his authority. Physical prowess has already given precedence to established leadership, character, cunning and even dynastic privileges.

Early Kings had to prove their superiority by deeds, mainly via conquest and heroism, but also through large projects and wisdom, Solomon the wise judge being the supreme example. The king outwardly also relied on various instruments to awe, whether weapons, palaces, monuments or robes, the symbolism was always critical. In the early Byzantine Empire, artists would devise magic mechanical devices or chairs to dazzle visitors by the Emperor's "magic," superior powers, as part of the marvels and riches of the palaces having similar purpose.

In the battlefield, the king would be recognized and well guarded, a symbol of encouragement, but also danger. In many battles the king's death or injury was catastrophic - for example, in Hastings (1066CE) or King Saul by the Philistines, or Emperor Valens by the Goths (378CE) - his injury or death delivered ultimate victory to the opponents.

The Bible chronicles certain custom of early Kingdoms' military conquest style. The Assyrian and Babylonian conquests consisted of subjugation and exile of the ruling classes. The nobility, the more educated leadership was eliminated, murdered or exiled from the conquered land; it helped to control the worker-population, which was necessary to continue to work the land, feed the soldiers and pay tribute to the Empire. Some of the local conquered land provided slaves for various construction projects within the Empire or utilized slaves for the nobility's personal purposes. Nebuchadnezzar (634-562BCE) controlled a large Empire containing today's Iraq, Jordan, Israel, Syria and part of Arabia and Sinai. The Empire commanded 8-10M souls and Nebuchadnezzar, himself born a prince, was already a great warrior, conqueror and builder. The walls of Babylon and the famous "Hanging Gardens," as well as many of the temples were built or restored during his reign. Nebuchadnezzar, in addition to being a warrior was also a diplomat, some of his political moves, including marriage, proved to be beneficial to his Empirical growth without further fighting. Political or diplomatic considerations started to emerge and with them the understanding of a wider political order than the state or its close environment. Brute force started to be supplemented by certain political exercise and sometimes clemency towards foes.

It took only a short time until Cyrus II, the Great, in mid-6th century BCE, who built a vast Empire, including all of Asia Minor and Iran of today, demonstrated political wisdom beyond brutality. Cyrus was probably the first ruler to recognize the various civilizations of his Empire and respected their unique character. He seems to have understood that his civilization could not be imposed arbitrarily and that ruling would be easier with recognition and a certain respect for locality. Cyrus allowed some of the exiled conquered to return to their original lands and even helped finance the erection of their monuments. He was also a great builder, but sanctioned various religious freedom. In Babylon, the emperor was head of the religious institutions, but the high priests had certain separate spiritual authorities.

Because of the uniqueness of the king's position, it was difficult to acquire the title if the ruler had no "mythical" past and was not part of an existing dynasty. In the west, the crowning authority was relegated to the Popes and they were very stingy with the title. When the Normans took over southern Italy, starting in the middle of the 11th century, they could quickly achieve the positions of Count or Duke, but Kingship was a completely different challenge[145]. The first Norman King in the south, Roger II (1098-1154CE) was already the ruler of a large and immensely wealthy Empire. When his mother (Adelaide de Vasto, 1075-1118) was sent to marry the crusader King of Jerusalem (Baldwin I, 1060-1118), she came with untold riches that stunned the crusaders in the holy land. Roger was the ruler of the kingdom but the monarchic title was elusive for this ambitious man. He was also shrewd, wily (both his father, Roger I and famous uncle, Robert Guiscard, were astute politicians in addition to warriors) and exploited a papal conflict to acquire his title from an anti-Pope, Anacletus II. He was invested in 1130CE and even then, many nobles and the church considered him a usurper and his dynasty did not last long.

The "divination" of the monarch had to be established by many rituals, one of them being the anointment by prophet or Pope with holy oil, allegedly from the original temple. In France, the legend of the oil came with the "Holy Ampulla," a vial that descended from the heavens and was originally used to anoint Clovis I, the 1st Frank King (466-511CE). It was traditionally used during the coronation of French Kings. The English used an eagle-shaped Ampula for their coronations. The Germans also used holy oil for coronation, Chrism or Myrrh, a special resin used for the celebration. The coronation was a process loaded with symbols, from the location (usually a religious center or great cathedral) to the dressings and the various rituals, mostly based on historical preferences of locality.

The relationship between the monarch and the nobility was always complex. In England, the power of the King was checked rather early. William the Conqueror subjugated the land by alliances, the sword and exile. But his great-grandson, the weak King John (1166-1216), lost too much property in France, especially after the failed battle of Bouvines (1214); this resulted in the discontent of his nobles, many of them being themselves French. Consequently, he had to sign Magna Carta (1215CE); it acquired monumental symbolism but it was mostly an agreement between the king and the barons. The document has very significant historical importance, one that subjugated the King to the law of the land. The English king could not arbitrarily confiscate property without due process as easily, as was the case in the continent. The right to property became a cornerstone in the English Law and US constitution.

A certain distribution of authority started to appear later in history. In the 15-16th centuries, education in schools and universities spread throughout the land, mostly consisting of "common" students, not part of the nobility (See table below).

Students	England	Continent
Nobility	7%	14%
Gentry	7%	38%
Bourgeois	79%	43%
Lower	7%	5%

17th century higher education classes

In time and with the rise of the republics, the position of the monarch weakened and the executive authority passed to elected or nominated deputies. The English Bill of Rights (1689CE) became a baseline for a constitutional monarchy; it curbed the power of the authority, declaring the rights and liberty of the people and establishing the concepts of free speech and Habeas Corpus (1679CE). These, among other freedoms, would eventually be emulated in the US constitution and then in all Western Europe and many other places that inherited the western tradition. Soon, hereditary monarchy came under serious criticism[36].

Since the formation of the nation-states, the monarch was gradually transformed to be symbolic, above political position and became the symbol of the nation and its traditions. As the political apparatus developed into opposing ideologies and parties, the monarch stayed above and represented the total integrated nation. Thus, a national symbol of unity emerged, representing the traditional nation, rather than ideological parties, the institute that represents the whole nation, beyond politics. The King quickly became a cognitive symbol, a person and institution - the dynasty. This complex position has been highlighted by Kantorowicz who dedicated a book to the complex personality of the King, "The King's Two Bodies[24]," that of the mortal person and that of the dynastic immortal institution.

Unfortunately, in some locations today, even the institute of absolute-monarchy still exists. These are mostly corrupt regimes that use the tradition of the institution for subjugation and exploitation, not much different from despotic regimes.

REBELLION

"There are no bridges in folk songs because the peasants died building them."

Eugene Chadbourne

There are many reasons that drive people to open revolt and disruption of the social-order, among them are political upheaval, economic difficulties, extreme taxes, religious tensions and war. Later in history, some of these toppled the monarchy and executed the monarch: England (1649), French (1793) or Russian (1918) are noted in modernity, but these were extremes. Earlier, other rebellions still had awe before the monarch and their ambitions more modest, mostly wishing to demonstrate displeasure, take revenge on deputies and demand changes.

Late in the 14th century, in the difficult period after the first breakout of the Plague in Europe - the Black Death, a series of peasant revolts erupted: the Jacquerie in France (1358CE), the Ciompi in Italy (1378, laborers in the silk industry of Florence), the "Wat Tyler rebellion" in England (1381) and others. These revolts erupted for economical or tax difficulties but were not necessarily against the monarch. The people accused the administration, sometimes the nobility, but the king was mostly above the fray. Later in Germany, a large peasant Revolt (1524-25) erupted; these revolts were suppressed again and again, ever more cruelly; in Germany some 100-300K were slaughtered during these uprisings. These horrific events found expression in works of literature and later re-used for the American scene[146, 177]. While initially successful they eventually failed, snuffed out by the rulers and the aristocracy who were better organized, disciplined and armed. Times were not yet ready for such social changes and the power and authority of the large, but badly led mob could be checked by well-organized ruling classes. It was a beginning of a social movement that initiated objection and despise for the ruling classes, the tax system and overall work conditions, as well as the awkward distribution of wealth and endless wars that rewarded only a few. But conditions have not changed until late in the 19th century, when the Industrial Revolution created the "working class" and the socialist movements that change the political face of the west.

5.4 FANATICISM AND "WORKING TOWARDS HITLER"

"If you took the most ardent revolutionary, vested him in absolute power, within a year he would be worse than the Tsar himself."

Mikhail Bakunin

"Propaganda does not deceive people; it merely helps them to deceive themselves."

Eric Hopper

"A fanatic is one who can't change his mind and won't change the subject."

Churchill

It is a tragic judgment of history that during the 20th century, when there was so much hope for betterment and the triumph of science, that horrific regimes rose, based on racist and murderous ideologies that defied every civilized idea and all that had been achieved during previous progress and the Enlightenment. This horror goes on in our days and sometimes with new vengeance. ISIS has not only spread terror and hell in the areas it captured, it also demonstrated horrific savagery and destroyed monuments of the greatest important to our civilization, like in Palmyra in Syria where ancient artifacts have been ruined in few hours and to what purpose? It seems that most of us can't comprehend the zeal and madness of the fanatic. We study history continuously and diligently but somehow fail to learn its lessons. The west, horrified and confused after WWI - a conflict that swept away the old regimes and brought technological innovations to the war machine - faced even greater evil when the essence of these regimes, especially the Nazi regime, exploded into history. The 19th century naive dreams of human-brotherhood were brutally violated and national leaders turned again to nationalism, racism, conquest and subjugation.

In the 1920s-30s, new regimes rose that called themselves Fascism (from Latin Fascio - the symbol of the civic magistrate authority in ancient Rome). The prophet of 20th century Fascism was actually Benito Mussolini (1883-1945). Hitler was a later follower that quickly became the dominant partner of this unholy alliance. Mussolini grew up in poverty and was a defiant and violent youth. By the power of his written and spoken word, he became the sole ruler of Italy in the fateful era, 1922-1943. The country was poor, not really united; social pressures brewed under the surface while the king and the ministers were blinded, stuck in their old world and class politics. Mussolini's method was both common and revolutionary, leveraging on the modern technological tools of communication and the power of the word he established the methods of the Fascist state:

1. Violence and traumatizing the population.

2. Acting within the democratic institutions and exploiting their weakness.

3. Develop an ideology of national superiority. A promise for national and historic renewal and power.

4. Indoctrination and propaganda; special focus given to the youth and children. Develop the personality cult.

5.   Creating an enemy - within, then without.

6.   Very large, monumental public programs. These usually act to magnify the dictator but also create work and economic activity.

7.   Extensive usage of radio and papers (later TV and social-media).

8.   Eventual wars of subjugation and conflict to cover the weakness of the state.

For such programs, the people must be conditioned to accept the horrific messages. Italy of the 1920s was in no condition for conquests when Mussolini, as part of empirical dreams, committed vast national resources to the futile conquest of Ethiopia. The economy was in bad shape and the military antiquated. Still, the demagogue managed to sweep the nation after his delusions that cost thousands of casualties in Italy and hundreds of thousands in Ethiopia. For what purpose?

Eric Hopper published his famous book "*The True Believer[116]*" after WWII (1951); it is a thesis on the nature of mass movements and fanaticism, a monster that raised its ugly head so devilishly many times in history and particularly during the 20th century.

Hopper used the short work to demonstrate and explain the phenomena of what he termed the "true believer," in politics, religion or social behavior - a form of fanaticism that drove the 20th century to the worst excesses in our long history. Fanaticism became a popular political phenomenon, its activity adored by many politicians and intellectuals all over the world. There was certain admiration for the ruthlessness and efficiency of such ideologies until later, the details were exposed. Apocalyptic prophecies have driven many believers from the past to the present day, whether propagated by charlatans or believers. ISIS might very well be such a movement, drawing many young from Christian backgrounds who might not even be religious or Muslims. These believers are motivated by deep emotions, hatred and fanaticism to an idea and community. The results are sometimes murderous and horrific. In the name of ideals or religions, the most atrocious acts are leveled, mostly on innocent populations. The fanatic phenomena are as old as humanity, but Hopper published his interpretations because he saw them in a new light and the horror was so evident in the 20th century; a century of technological modernity that enabled, with technology aid, the mass propagation of ideas and worst deeds.

There is no doubt that modern communications, first the radio, then TV and now the Web, have aided in the ability of demagogues to propagate their visions across a vast audience in a manner not possible before. Initially in sound, then using images and today's fantastic graphics tools and social media, these powerful instruments are double-edged swords. We are only now starting to realize the power of social media in politics and subversion of the social order. As the world turns cognitive, these become the first instruments of communications and sometimes the instruments of the evil.

Perhaps this was Hopper's attempt (the book was published in the early 50s), at an explanation to "How could Nazism have happened?" or "How could Stalin have happened?", questions that do plague the western mind. As we study history and watch the radio and TV orations of the Nazis, we keep asking the same questions. Today, many of these leaders look ridiculous, theatrical, sometimes comic figures with insane dreams, but there was nothing comic about the havoc they rained on us and the catastrophe they caused to humanity.

Hopper's thesis was that all forms of fanaticism, be it Nazism, fundamental Islam or the Crusades, have similar human characteristics and can be explained together as a singular human phenomenon. Hopper thought the "believer" is a special case of persons and conditions that convert to "belief" by certain social conditions that create opportunities for a mass movement. He opined that such movements require special leaders, charismatic men or women, fanatic in their own beliefs, ready and willing to lead the mob towards fanaticism and the most virulent actions.

Mass movements begin with "men of words" or "fault-finding intellectuals," the theorists of the movement. These can be clerics, journalists, academics, dreamers and students who condemn the established social order (for example, Gandhi, Trotsky, Bakunin). Many of these dreamers are peaceful, human-loving folks who would never dream of resorting to violence. These "men of words" sometimes feel unjustly excluded from or mocked and oppressed by, the existing powers in society and relentlessly criticize or denigrate present-day institutions. While invariably speaking out in the name of disadvantaged commoners, they are also motivated by deep personal grievances. The charismatic man of words relentlessly attempts to "discredit the prevailing creeds" and creates a "hunger for faith," which is then fed by "doctrine and slogans of the new faith." A cadre of devotees gradually develops around the man of words, helping to spread the word and adulation. Eventually, the fanatic "man of action" takes over leadership of the mass movement from the man of words. There are cases where these personalities materialize in the same person (for example Hitler). While the "creative man of words" finds satisfaction is his literature, philosophy or art, the man of action feels unrecognized or stifled and thus, veers into extremism against the social order. Although the man of words and the fanatic share a discontent with the world, the fanatic is distinguished by his viciousness and urge to hurt, to destroy. The fanatic feels fulfilled only in a perpetual struggle for power and change. As the movement moves towards the "man of action," they are more practical and more realistic and will use coercion, propaganda or proselytization. On the receiving side, the following masses of the true believers suffer a loss of confidence in the existing traditions and social order and are hungry for promise, for hope and a charismatic leader who can leverage this hunger for "self-renunciation."

These, according to Hopper, are mostly coming from the "new poor," industrial workers, social and religious minorities and various "misfits" - people who feel emptiness and a life without purpose. Such mass movements must not believe in God but must believe in the Devil and the rituals of the occult! There is inherent violent trait in the movement but a fanatic will never admit to being one.

The leader is the symbol of a change that acts forcibly in the mind of the believer with expectations that are much higher than the leader has ever promised. In the end, the masses adore the leader and will follow him to the end of the world. Most of these leaders are charismatic and driven by ideology, be it religious, social or racial. Some of them are driven by hatred, the consequence of personal experiences and grievances. The movement is fed with hate and the creation of enemies who threaten the social order. The "enemy," sometimes the fictional creation of the leader, is a very effective instrument in the movement, be it the bourgeoisie, the foreigner, the "Jews" or the "Other." The result is a social and sometimes ideological revolution and social fire that leads to extreme, mostly violent acts.

Hopper opines that true believers are insecure, that belonging to the movement gives purpose to their lives. These emotional substitutes, like national pride, self-confidence or memberships in a collective that promise much, are coming from above, instead of true understanding. Therefore, they find purpose, sometimes in the most horrific ideologies of race and hatred.

As mentioned before, the fanatic leader and the man-of-action sometimes incarnate in the same person. *"Hitler (both the dreamer and man of action), who had a clear vision of the whole course of a movement even while he was nursing his infant National Socialism, warned that a movement retains its vigor only so long as it can offer nothing in the present…but much in the future. The movement, after establishment still concerns itself with the frustrated--not to harness their discontent in a deadly struggle with the present, but to reconcile them with it; to make them patient and meek[18]."* One of the leader's challenges is to keep the revolutionary fire going. Hitler had a vision of an endless revolution (war being a process of struggle and purification, of purging the weak) and continuous struggle, an endless social Darwinism incarnate.

As the movement matures, focus shifts from immediate demands for revolution to establishing the mass movement as a social institution where the ambitious can find influence and fame. *"Leadership uses an eclectic bricolage of ideological scraps to reinforce the Doctrine, borrowing from whatever source is successful in holding the attention of true believers. For example, proto-Christians were fanatics, predicting the end of the world (Apocalypse), condemning idolatry, demanding celibacy and sowing discontent between family members. Yet, from these roots grew Roman Catholicism which mimicked the elaborate bureaucratic structure of the Roman Empire, canonized early Christians as saints, and borrowed pagan holidays and rites."* As for the established new order, the dogma, the propaganda must be supplemented by terror, as Goebbels noted, *"A sharp sword must always stand behind propaganda if it is to be really effective."* There it was, the devil incarnate!

In the absence of a practical man of action, the mass movement often withers and dies with the fanatic. For example, Nazism died as a viable mass movement with Hitler's death.

People were always obedient, especially to a charismatic leader but the fanatics, fired by propaganda and mass media are a new breed. The Nazi and SS soldiers that went out to conquer and subjugate, were more motivated, more fired up than the opponents. They were such a good military because they deeply believed in the cause, a cause that was horribly monstrous. We see similar motivation in Al-Queda or ISIS fighters today. The zeal of belief in a dream that involves horrific ideologies and murder of the innocent. In the 21st century we are witnessing fanaticism rising and threatening world-order by terror attacks on the population, as well as on the Cloud: financial institutions, military targets, infrastructure, and the threat of disturbing our lives by people whose fanaticism we do not understand. WWII is only 70 years old but our progeny, in-spite of education, museums and art, hardly remember the atrocities. Hopper did not focus his work on the lever that new technologies and means of mass-information propagation afford; such techniques are available today via mass media and social media - new phenomena in modernity. These technologies are making such movements more powerful. The use of the web in modern terror, both propaganda and disruption, is well known and amplifies the threat many times in comparison to the past when acts of terror were sporadic and mostly performed by desperate or fanatic individuals[49]. The modern fanatic leaders have graver ambitions in regards to destruction - see 9/11 or terrorist threat of nuclear devices, not necessarily bombs - in civic centers. There is no doubt that the technology that gave us so much and created so much promise, is also a double-edged sword.

The situation is aggravated in modernity because of the fantastic communications technologies we developed. Modern politics and propaganda can and are advanced by using the electronic media, both for raising supportive funds and for spreading information or propaganda.

WORKING TOWARDS HITLER

An excellent example of Hopper's thesis has been demonstrated by Ian Kershaw[23] in the concept he called "*working towards Hitler.*" The general idea is that the fanatic adulation for the leader is so complete that the fanatics will "work towards" what they perceive as the will of the leader. Kershaw quotes a Nazi admirer, "*Everyone who has the opportunity to observe it knows that the Fuhrer can hardly dictate from above everything which he intends to realize sooner or later. On the contrary, up till now everyone with a post in the new Germany has worked best when he has, so to speak, worked towards the Fuhrer. Very often and in many spheres it has been the case—in previous years as well—that individuals have simply waited for orders and instructions. Unfortunately, the same will be true in the future; but in fact it is the duty of everybody to try to work towards the Fuhrer along the lines he would wish. Anyone who makes mistakes will notice it soon enough. But anyone who really works towards the Fuhrer along his lines and towards his goal will certainly both now and in the future one day have the finest reward in the form of the sudden legal confirmation of his work."*

In the specific case of Hitler, who was a rather lazy dictator, his domination over the true believers was to sketch general principles and spew the poison. His deputies and believers continued with the details, from neutralizing political foes all the way to the fabrication of factories to destroy humans. Such a position is carefully nurtured by relentlessly building the public-image of the leader, crafting them up towards a super- human even messianic capacity; they become the one that knows better than us and deserves following, blind following. Such adulation eventually creates a mythological character, one that is at once remote, but also supreme and one that will take the group or the nation to the "Promised Land". *"Once Hitler was in power, his public persona as the Führer of the German people encouraged both government officials and other Germans to take initiative on their own to help the nation realize the goals he expressed. In fact, he left it to others to figure out how to carry out policies and govern Germany. In a 1934 speech, a government official from the ministry of food, explained: Hitler stated goals and provided guidelines, and then, he either appointed specific individuals to ensure that his goals were realized, or he let government bureaucrats and Nazi Party officials figure it out themselves[23]."*

Therefore, while the fanatic leader is the mover, the movement is ultimately caused by a large apparatus that is left to imagine and execute the perceived wishes of the leader. Such movements do not happen in a vacuum, it is always based on historical or social background that produces the opportunities for the instigators. Note in the case of Nazi Germany, the educated class mostly signed up for the Nazi program. The judicial system, the economists, the intellectuals bought into the vision, the promise and the lies. There was little opposition and the social compliance is an indication of the power of such a movement once a sense of criticism is lost.

Apparently, many are capable of subjugating themselves to ideas or to personalities in the most extreme fashion and to be possessed, even to the point of self-sacrifice, pursuing such symbols to the bitter end.

Today, we notice again rising social and political tensions. Some of it from our improved communications, some from frustrations caused by the vast inequality that emerges in many democracies (and despotic regimes) and from the poor education that many receive, lacking the historical lessons and the edge of nihilism. Quality education might eventually be our greatest challenge.

5.5 ANARCHISM

"The liberty of man consists solely in this, that he obeys the laws of nature because he has himself recognized them as such, and not because they have been imposed upon him externally by any foreign will whatsoever, human or divine, collective or individual."

Mikhail Bakunin

Anarchism was never a large or popular movement; few believers, the prophets of the movement, were mostly the core that held it together. People were dreaming for long about an idealistic regime based on our benevolence and good will without authority, but during the 19th century, when societies started to liberate, the bases for the philosophy of Anarchism developed with the concept of "natural law." Most of us like the idea of political freedom, especially the young, but instinctively reject the possibility of a social order devoid of authority. Even if we think that government is a "necessary evil", the focus is on necessary. A society will not run without a structure, without a certain management and imposed order. Depending solely on our benevolence is naïve and always erroneous.

Anarchism as a movement was born in the middle of the 19th century, a splinter movement away from Socialism and worth mentioning, for the idea of anarchism seems so attractive, if somewhat impractical. Unlike the fanatics that were led mostly by leaders saturated by hatred and frustrations, the Anarchist prognosticators were interesting, educated, idealistic characters, sometimes human-lovers: Proudhon, Bakunin, Kropotkin, Malatesta, Emma Goldman among others. These saw goodness and fraternity as the possible force of the social order – people will live peacefully together without any authority to command them. Endowed by natural law, morality, kindness and fraternity, these will rein the social order. With fraternity and liberty, also comes equality, the hallmark of the French revolution and Anarchism. Instead, their ideas, so attractive to the many poor and destitute, have sawn murder and mayhem, assassinations, hatred and bombs in theaters. It was a movement that preached idealism, Utopia, goodwill, humanity and the ultimate political freedom, but yielded terror and murder. The fiery speeches and pamphlets, promising fraternity and equality, trickled to the bottom, where the desperate, the wretched, heard only the voice of despair and went to demand justice and revenge, mostly through violence and terror.

Anarchist and Anarchism[47,58,59] imagined a society built on total personal freedom, unshackled from social inhibitions; no government at all. Political freedom was mixed with personal, social and sometimes sexual liberties, towards fraternity, sometimes the elimination of property and lawful authority. A beautiful dream, but how can this work? Here was an ideal state built on good will, on fraternity and justice without central authority, based on natural kindness; self-governing coupled with voluntary institutions and good will without a guiding hand. The Frenchman Proudhon (1809-1865CE) founded the movement mainly on despise and disgust for central authority, "...*to be governed is to be watched, inspected, spied upon, directed, law-driven, numbered, regulated...indoctrinated, taxed...authorized, admonished...mocked, ridiculed, squeezed, extorted...outraged, dishonored...That is Government, that is its justice, that is its morality[148].*" A social order without authority must be based on equality, thus Proudhon expounded on the matter of his hatred to Property, "*Property is theft, Property is Despotism, and Property is impossible (ibid).*"

Desperate people were listening. The industrial revolution caused migration of millions to cities, be exploited, live in horrible conditions, became dispossessed, hopeless and vengeful. The echo of the agitators fell on fertile ground as people lived in horrible squalor, filth and disease. During its heyday, Anarchists managed to assassinate heads of states, including: Tsar Alexander II in 1881 and French president Sadi Carnot in 1894. Bismarck was shot but survived in 1866. President McKinley was assassinated by an anarchist, 1901, as was later Italy's former prime minister, Aldo Moro, murdered by the "Red Brigades" in 1978.

Anarchism could never organize as a force; its own ideology, which rejected any system of organized authority, prevented organizing! There was a paradox in its reasoning. Marx understood that Anarchism could not work, but the anarchist Bakunin had the historical foresight to see that if the Marxists take over, they will simply replace the "ruling classes." Indeed, Che (Ernesto Guevara, 1928-1967) the idealistic and charismatic folk hero might have been a perpetual revolutionary but his erstwhile and more practical partner Fidel Castro was eventually proven to be a tyrant, as were Lenin, Mao and so many other revolutionaries. The anarchists managed to create terror in the population, as they do today in the guise of political, nationalistic or religious frustrations. The majority victims were always the innocents, especially when bombs were thrown into the crowd.

While originating in Europe, the idea also propagated to the US and few of its cases became infamous. The Haymarket Affair in Chicago (1886) is perhaps the most famous US anarchist affair; it started as an orderly labor demonstration and ended with bomb throwing at the police. The other famous event was the failed attempted assassination of Henry Frick of the Carnegie Corporation by Emma Goldman and her lover Alexander Berkman (1892). This event has been chronicled not only by historians but also by literature - the author Doctorow did not disguise the modeling of his more modern story (Ragtime[146]) on Michael Kolhaas[43] by Heinrich Kleist, which tells an episode from the peasant revolt in Germany of the middle 16th century. Emma Goldman, one of the more known anarchist leader and theorist, a naturalized US citizen (immigrated from Russia), was eventually deported from the US (1920). Goldman was a woman of infinite personal courage and conviction, she did live as an anarchist and liberated woman (as a professional nurse). After deportation, she was quickly disillusioned in Russia but could not return to the US. She died in Toronto but later allowed to be interned in Chicago.

In modernity, Anarchism has become associated with terror, a new political instrument in the hand of small splinter groups, expressing political, sometimes religious dissension: Ireland, Basque, Kurds, etc. and various religious terrorists that have emerged in the figure of Al-Qaeda, ISIS, Boko-Haram and others. Modern technology, both weapons and communications, give leveraged power in the hands of terrorists, just see the crime of 9/11 and others perpetrate all over the world. The possibility of WMD in the hands of terror groups is a major headache everywhere and a serious threat to all. The asymmetrical war is complex and challenging, especially for the western world, when small groups can cause large damage and biological and nuclear weapons are always a scare.

The Anarchist idea has never died - will never die. It resurrects again and again in different forms and ideologies and eventually became political-historical power to reckon with.

5.6 RISK - COGNITIVE COERCION

"Anti-intellectualism has been a constant thread winding its way through our political and cultural life, nurtured by the false notion that democracy means that 'my ignorance is just as good as your knowledge.'"

Isaac Asimov

"When enough people understand reality, tyrants can literally be ignored out of existence. They can't ever be voted out of existence."

Larken Rose

"To force oneself to believe and to accept a thing without understanding is political, and not spiritual or intellectual."

Siddhārtha Gautama

Science and study provide us with knowledge about the behavior of the world; much of this knowledge is unintuitive, as if hidden and needs to be explored. Just consider the motion of our body, within the complex motion of the Earth, the sun and the galaxy, something we hardly notice; the whole phenomena - the earth is not steady nor is it the center of the universe as assumed by antiquity - was revealed, explained and reasoned only a few hundreds of years ago.

Most advances of modern science were based on old observations or philosophies (even Copernicus was inspired by an old Greek) but are the result of later cognitive achievements; first came philosophies that formulated the nature of knowledge, Bacon-Descartes for example; then, by breakthrough thinking (Galileo, Kepler) and what was later called the "thought experiment." Einstein is the best-known thought experimenter, but so were Newton and many others. On earth, there are no motions like Newton idealistically described (there is friction, air resistance, surface tensions, etc...) but he could imagine bodies moving in empty space, in ideal settings. Or, imagine conceiving the law of gravity to be universal - the force that attracts the apple is the same phenomena like the force that attracts the moon to earth and earth to the sun!

The early modern natural-philosophers (later called scientists) created a great revolution of thought towards experimentation and seeking knowledge in Nature's behavior. These early modern scientists were deeply religious: Newton, Kepler, Brahe, Galileo, etc... but also dedicated to the acquisition of knowledge in an open, critical and inquiring manner. The axiom *"within the scientific discipline, look only for natural causes"*, has been already established in the 12th century. Since then, our progress at unlocking the secrets of nature, have been astonishing and scientific progress has been the source of our trust in future progress, growing comfort and wealth. The progress has been so astounding that most of us started to believe that all progress comes from scientific inquiry and its technological applications and governments started to invest public fortunes in scientific and technological innovations. This has proven to be not accurate and even science proved to be a double-edged sword. We must continue to aspire for progress in the many artistic and humanity studies as well and indeed, many technical schools started to pay attention[339]. As the influence of science and technology grows, as the large technology giants become more powerful and influential in politics and the social order, technologies should be trained in the humanities too, and even in ethics; it is necessary to bring humane purpose to their studies, voice their opinions in the application of the technology and become part of the symbols and traditions of our being. We can no more tolerate scientists who develop the technology and then "leaving it to the politicians". This has proven itself a big mistake.

The philosophy of science, specifically in the matter of questioning what is science, has gone through a similar revolution, specifically in the 20th century (Popper, Kuhn). However, our science today is already very complex, not accessible to the popular audience as it was up to about a century back. Before the 20th century, educated people comprehended the scientific horizons, be it Newton physics, optics, Thermodynamics or even Cosmology – the universe was the Milky Way then. They were absolutely comprehensive to the learned minds, on the level of high-school today. The 20th century brought a great change and most of us can't approach the limits of science today, most of it too complex. Still, we ask the majority to agree, to support and fund the science and technology we mostly do not understand because of the successes and progress of the past.

Modern science, mainly Quantum theory and its various variants, Cosmology, Molecular Biology, Biotechnology and AI (Artificial Intelligence) are scientific and technological disciplines not well understood, even in their fundamentals, by most. Quantum and Cosmology are difficult due to the complex math and the abstractions they utilize, while Biology and AI because of their intricate details and immense variety. In addition, many new sciences have been developing in the last 50 years, of global and statistical nature, among them Earth sciences, Climatology and the almost universal interest in issues like Global Climate Change (GCC or GW), which are currently on the headlines of mass media on a daily basis. Still, how many of us understand, comprehend how a quantum event (the Big Bang) could have produced a universe from nothingness, with some 100 billion galaxies and estimated mass of some 10^{55}Kg? Or the meaning of General Relativity and its Tensor equations! Or that receding galaxies are an illusion, that what expands is the whole universe! How did the universe begin from nothingness and expand? Expand into what? What are the equations and patterns that govern earth climate, why are there so many models for GW (56 now and growing with expected temperature rise of 2-8F by the end of the century)? Is such range of possibilities, 2-8F even a scientific number?

A large industry of popular books has been created to simplify the concepts. Anybody who read these books knows that in the end, while we get some of the useful details and gossip - scientists wars, jealousy and hubris - we are still left as puzzled as in the beginning. The models of these theories, from General Relativity (Cosmology) or Quantum to GW use math tools that are simply beyond the level of even college graduates, even those in engineering or the sciences. In addition, modern science has turned from the classical "deterministic" models into statistics. Most of our modern scientific theories, either climate modeling, particle physics, polling (for elections, consumption) or cosmology, are statistical by nature, hence with another level of difficulty and possibilities of interpretations.

Those of us who read the above literature know how enjoyable but feeble their explanations, how frustrating to read many of the popular books only to realize that we do not really understand more. There is apparently no easy path; to understand the various theories one must make the effort and really dig into the details, hence the math and its interpretations. Let us hope many are ready to make the effort, otherwise such knowledge will continue to stay with a tiny minority.

Early scientist were curious individuals that were seeking the truth about nature's behavior and the world. It was a personal endeavor, a natural human curiosity, our inherent need to know. However, in the last 150 years, science became mostly the domain of the experts and the state, seen as an instrument to advance our wealth and well-being. Scientific teams grew is scope and size, can count in the hundreds even if in the end, one is awarded a Nobel or similar awards. And the budgets we dedicate to scientific research are immense, as is our belief in the advantages science brings. Fact is that the majority of the practical progress we made in the last 1.5 centuries were mostly by engineers, in applied sciences or engineering. Some of them had no formal education or math, among them James Watt, Faraday, Edison or Tesla - people with genius intuition for the working of nature, without equations. Modern science depends on immense budgets and with these, come people whose talent is mostly in organization and fund raising or PR, not always in science. Science became also political because raising such budgets require more than math skills.

A new trend developed recently by the Maga-Tech corporations, to fund their own R&D (mostly applied sciences) that does not depend on government funds. And these corporations now compete even with the Universities in knowledge and smarts. Many of the inventions are patented and their purpose is mostly for profit, not necessarily in the enlightenment of humanity for knowledge.

Old habits die hard and criticism is central to the scientific method which is today so huge that political and social considerations apply to the motives too.

For example, the recent Global Climate Change (GCC, GW) paradigm has become a popular scare for the general population, probably rightfully so. Since the 1970s, the temperature of the earth has continued to rise in every coming decade. Consequently, GW has become a media panic. Scientists and most of us are not doubting the warming data and seriousness of the environmental threat; rather the imminence of the threat, quality of our current models in face of the immense complexity of earth's weather patterns, our contribution, sun's influence and the enormity of the various parameters that control it. GW should be treated as a serious threat that demands our attention, but is it, as claimed by few, an apocalyptical process[320] about to happen tomorrow? But then, if you question anything, even the apocalyptic predictions, some by academics ("not a single human will survive in 10 years!" [320]), other by politicians, you immediately become a "Climate Denier"; are we back at the witch-hunting of the past? There is no shame in asking questions, or even being a skeptic and try to investigate and learn the data, mostly delivered by reporters whose knowledge in science is very feeble anyways.

The phenomena are disturbing, especially when so much angst is created, in many cases, without real data, without scientific background and sometimes for the support of ideologies that could be social or political and not in the scientific discipline. Our ignorance is a threat and will be used against us by scrupulous operators. And yet, many try to make the effort and the difference. To be involved and try to be heard. For example, during the Ford presidency (1974-1977), the administration decided to cut off the budget for the Hubble telescope. Hundreds and thousands of letters went to Congresspersons, Senator and the White House. The administration yielded and eventually renewed the project. Hubble has been a great blessing in our quest of knowledge and understanding of the universe.

Progress depends on critique, on constantly evaluating our hypothesis. Developing a blind belief in science is not necessarily a good habit in-spite of the great successes of the past. Science and technology have also made and make numerous promises that never happened. Because of the inherent complexity of scientific issues and modern science/technology as a whole, perhaps only one in a thousand of us understand modern physics or math, beyond the fundamentals. And few in a million can comprehend quantum principles and its math. It was the great teacher and scientist Richard Feynman who predicted that the quantum effects, and even their most fundamental description, the double-slit experiment, (see http://en.wikipedia.org/wiki/Double-slit_experiment), could never be intuitive.

Now, when it comes to modern math (thank God, math requires no budgets), imagine the abstraction and complexity level of the recent proof of Fermat's Last

Theorem, that "$a^n+b^n=c^n$ has a solution only for n=1,2" the most famous math conjecture, with an all-time record of false proofs of the last three centuries (proven in 1995). For this level of complexity there are maybe 1 in a billion of us, just few in total humanity of some 7.5B, who comprehend the subtlety of such complex mathematical proof spun over hundreds of pages. Is our science starting to assume the position of a religion, requiring a certain blind belief? Have we become too depended on these beliefs?

The character of science has changed as well. Careers and huge budgets are on the line. In modernity we are called to make contributions in the billions to farther advance our knowledge. Newton requested no support for formulating the law of Gravitation or Calculus. Today, the investments made by nations count in the hundreds of billions per year. Science had shown its benefits, we are happy to fund the work of course. Our quest for knowledge is always justified and mostly leads us to better understanding or better exploitation of the forces of nature, but how does it compare to other needs? How do we decide what is worth investing for when using tax money? Needless to say, the reverence we have for science - one might add, the justified-reverence - has never allowed us to question the process. We never ask for the meaning of these commanding disciplines and their effect on the social order when only a few understand them. And today, with the growth of the titan tech companies whose wealth and influence start to challenge the power of the government and traditions of academia, their purpose is only to provide more wealth to the stock-holders and influence, prestige of the owners-managers! We should start to question the benefits of our invested tax dollars.

Humanity makes progress by the genius of few but these few need the social structure to support their "reaching to the stars." No genius works in a vacuum, the Cognitive-Cloud advances only when the social structure advances. Beethoven, Newton or Michelangelo emerged in an environment and expressed their times after all. There is no Newton or Michelangelo without their times; we all have a stake in progress, in history. Social political pressure starts to demand, justifiably, for more equity now.

We are gaining on understanding the fundamentals of life's chemistry and starting to make inroads into the human brain - our greatest riddle, the final frontier. However, as we move forward, we are leaving too many of us behind and we are losing our independent thinking and the ability to critique. Science and technology start to assume a different position. It was about the search for knowledge; today it is also cloaked in ideology, wealth, influence and politics.

We have discovered that knowledge is power and wealth, and that knowledge in the hands of few can be dangerous to the well-being of the social order. Technology enabled the swift propagation of information to the whole human community, all that within fractions of seconds via a vast network of mobile communications and the web. We already have most of the information we need under the tips of our fingers and soon, all human knowledge that is advancing at an immense rate will be available to all. We are on the verge of making machines that can design themselves to operate better and imitate our thinking process, and in many cases faster and more accurately than we do. We are on the verge of understanding our genetic makeup and being able to improve it via genetic manipulations in ways that were unfathomable only a generation ago. We are also improving life expectancy and quality at a pace that estimates millions of centenarians within a very short time. We are now on a quest to eradicate various diseases that plagued humanity from time immemorial - the 14th century plague reduced the population of western Europe by 35 -50% within a few years and kept coming, until modernity. The discovery of germs, hygiene, later anti-biotics and the fast rise of non-invasive operations, revolutionize medicine.

The rise of our scientific and medical progress in the last few centuries is simply meteoric. In the US alone, the federal government invests some $60B annually in scientific R&D (total R&D funding in the US is estimated at close to $600B). Science has proven to be critically beneficial for our economy, health, wealth, standard of living and security.

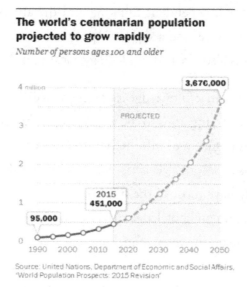

The world's centenarian population projected to grow rapidly

Number of persons ages 100 and older

Figure 6: Projected number of centenarians world-wide

But science is a double-edged sword. With all the above, we have also invented and use methods and technologies to pollute the earth and specifically the oceans, to endanger and eliminate numerous species and to actually risk the viability of life on the planet from threats like GW, pollution or depletion of water resources. Our actions are not as nimble as they used to be, we seem to act on levels that are "planetary" and risk the delicate balance that the planet holds and maintains. Dangers lurk amid the fantastic progress. A measure of critique is fundamental to our continued well-being. We have become the stewards of the earth; it comes with responsibilities. These responsibilities require critical knowledge and educated population that will not be coerced by ignorant leadership or unethical avaricious industrial leaders driven by vanity. The earth requires our attention, we are violating it too much so the attention to its "health" is justified.

Our Cognitive Sciences are actually very young. Our understanding of the mind, the way our brains operate and the nature of consciousness are still at the starting point. In fact, when it comes to the very fundamental issue of mind-body, we are absolutely ignorant. To quote Thomas Nagel[98], "*The physical sciences and evolutionary biology cannot be kept insulated from it and I believe a true appreciation of the difficulty of the problem (mind-matter) must eventually change our conception of the place of the physical sciences in describing the natural order.*"

Our quest is ongoing; one can expect a modified Physics in 50 years and definitely a new biology. We expect all the sciences to change radically in the coming century. Let us democratize the sciences as much as we can and try to make them accessible to many. In addition to the books, a new education tool is rising in the figure of the MOOC - Massive Open Online Course. The best courses of the best teachers are massively available online, at the leisure of our home or other convenient environment. These are either free or very affordable; enormity of knowledge by the best teachers, on so many topics. In the meantime, all of us are called on to participate (our tax money) in the investment and funding of advanced science, which is now very expensive and requires resources on the national level. The following table from UNESCO (2010) demonstrates the national investments and commitments we make in % of GDP.

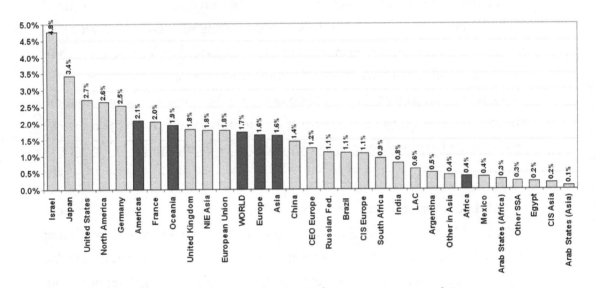

Figure 6.1: National investment in R&D as a percentage of GDP.

The issue is fundamental to our democracy. What is the meaning of knowledge in the hands of few to Democracy or meritocracy, if only a small minority is involved? What happens if this process continues to intensify because of lack in interest or limited intellectual capacity? What are the risks of dissemination, both knowledge and its benefits, only to a minority? Or otherwise, how do we act to disseminate the knowledge better, to make our population more interested in the acquisition of knowledge? These questions are not just theoretical, definitely not while Mega-corporations and awesomely wealthy individuals control some of the most important resources. Can government regulate the ambitions of such corporations for the good of all?

If knowledge is advancing so fast that the most important decisions are made in corporate boards of information technology corporations and not in political democratic cabinets, what is the future of democracy and egalitarianism? Or otherwise, what is the meaning of the political and financial power that the vast techno-corporations are assuming (some of them with market valuation now surpassing the $1T) via lobbying and the political influence they wield, that comes with the immense wealth they are creating? What is their capacity to influence our opinions and politics (view the ongoing Facebook political saga and our disappointments with their behavior).

It is true that many of the wealthiest have shown interest to invest their fortunes in charity enterprises, but history tells us that trusting such good will can be ill-advised. It is much better to plan on a more balanced social-order, one in which all have a stake and vested interest. And of course, there are many other tycoons who do not follow this path of charity and do not make their appropriate contribution. We have marched a long history towards regimes run by laws, not by persons. We will be well advised to continue this style and not descend towards Oligarchy of sort.

In addition, as we are marching forward in the Cognitive sciences, other social and ethical issues are rising. Are we going to replace manpower with machines? Will an elite minority dominate our future via technology? Is technology capable of eliminating massive labor sources (driving, assembly, teaching, janitorial) and the effect on society. Is it possible that already, technocrats do the most important decisions today within powerful corporations and not via the democratic process? How do we control such process democratically, rather than by corporate greed? How do we mitigate the effect of technology on the democratic elective process? We already have alarming experiences.

The future is knocking on our door and it is…COMPLEX.

6. COGNITION, COMPLEXITY AND THE ARTS

"If our brains were simple enough for us to understand them, we'd be so simple that we couldn't."

Ian Steward

"Let us tenderly and kindly cherish, therefore, the means of knowledge. Let us dare to read, think, speak, and write."

John Adams

6.1 COGNITIVE PROGRESS

Do not believe anything only because it is said by an authority

Buddah

By three methods we may learn wisdom: First, by reflection, which is noblest; Second, by imitation, which is easiest; and third by experience, which is the bitterest.

Confucius

RISE OF LIFE

There is no doubt that the phenomenon of life is based on information and living matter process information constantly. The interface with the environment, the energy drawn from foods or the environment and the management of the numerous bodily functions are all information based. Extremely complex organizing, self-sustaining processes are mostly performed by the "wisdom of the body" - the natural intelligence of adapting and sustaining bodily functions by very complex and intricate chemical and electro-chemical processes - are all information based. The DNA molecule is information based, written in the chemical alphabet of protein production. The origin of the DNA molecule, still a fundamental mystery, produced the vast molecule (most DNA are composed of millions and billions of letters) with immense diversity potential. It enabled variety and evolution from single cell micro-organisms to the elephant or thirty-meter long blue whale; the DNA is life's blueprint, it codes our being, behavior, nature, body's chemistry and adaptation while enabling a copying process by division - the double helix. There are numerous bodily processes (breathing, kidney, liver, digesting, heartbeat, etc…) that operate continuously as automata, without our consciousness and they are adaptive and magnificently flexible; they continuously regulate the lives of all creatures. The body's ability to cure (our auto-immune system is still the best), to regulate and to function in various environments and its adaptation are still a great mystery. Yet, with the exception of higher animals cognitive thinking, most of these processes do not yet demonstrate or require intelligence. Our bodies operate like automata of wonderful self-learning, growth control, adaptation and immune capacity of the highest intricacy. More than 90% of living matter has no brain at all yet their lives, adaptation to the environment and breeding mechanisms are fantastically complex and functional. They fit the environment well because they emerged from the environment; this dualism is wondrous but also natural, we are the product, the outcome of the world. What are the forces that drive towards our "will to live" and the immense complexity that takes life from a single cell to multi-cellular, to the development of the various organs and eventually to bodies of living matter? Is this the nature of certain physical laws, the character of living matter, features of the DNA or just a speculation in the mind of one species? We simply do not know.

The evolution of living matter, from inanimate to living and from simple life forms, into the complex variety we observe now is a demonstration of the relentless drive to higher complexity in a universe driven to chaos. Many Darwinist will deny any force or direction or the "superiority" of higher organisms, still there is no doubt that factually, we observe such drive in all of nature. Not only the intricate of order in living matter, but also in the inanimate, from the structure of storms, to planets and galaxies, as if driving by ordering processes. Evolution takes very long time and within our short lifespan we can hardly observe any of the Darwinian mechanisms, especially on the higher animals. Still, this drive to "higher, more complex" organisms can hardly be denied. This order, this "life force," eventually created intelligence in the animal kingdom, and then human intelligence. Certain lower species, like birds (parrots, crows) and even fish, also demonstrate impressive tool making, as well as imitation capacities and behavioral intelligence. Since we do not know how electrical processes in the brain create consciousness, emotions, or thought, we do not know the quantitative value of such relationships - brain size and cognition. Even the small-brained creatures possess unique and amazing power for emotion, sustainability, memory, navigation - animal migration is astounding, birds cross thousands of kilometers of tough navigation challenges, fish, mammals and turtles can even navigate in water. It seems that the development of a high language and consciousness of human level required a larger, very complex brain, which as mentioned already is drawing some 20% of our total body's energy needs. We have no way to quantify this phenomena, but the fact is that the process drove to create humans, who took dominion and are the only species capable of inventing complex concepts like time, high languages, religion, adaptation to almost any environment on earth and probably hyper-consciousness - to be conscious about our consciousness. The superior power of our cognition alone, we are feeble creatures after all, is clear; we took over the planet.

For those who do not believe in biological course, the concept of "progress" would be anathema (mentioned above) because it points to a certain "direction" or perhaps even "purpose" for living matter. We have never been capable of defining such direction or progress, the mysterious forces of life propel us to survival and procreation, we know not why. And yet, without these forces, there is no life.

Some 3.7-4 billion years ago, oceans covered the planet and the atmosphere was saturated with carbon dioxide and some other, sometimes poisonous, gases. Living organisms emerged in water first, and from this primitive form, capable of sustaining, duplicating and evolving, the photosynthesis process was "discovered" (some 3.4B years back); it converts carbon dioxide and sun photons in the water environment into carbohydrate - energy to fuel itself, and oxygen as a by-product.

This is the basic chemical process that sustains life on earth.

$$6CO_2 \text{ (Carbon dioxide)} + 6H_2O \text{ (Water)} \xrightarrow{\text{Light}} C_6H_{12}O_6 \text{ (Sugar)} + 6O_2 \text{ (Oxygen)}$$

In time, the atmosphere built up significant amount of oxygen that replaced many of the other gases. For about 2 billion years the process continued until the atmosphere was "cleaned up" and contained enough oxygen to support life on land. The continents started to emerge by their relative motion of plate-tectonics forces and bigger, more complex organisms started to emerge. Initially, these were multi-cellular creatures that about 1200 million years ago "discovered" the sexual reproduction process. This process enabled much more diversity as the product of their mating carried the genetic material of both, hence more variety. Slowly and steadily fish emerged, with a skull and skeleton structure and life spread across the oceans. At about 600 million years ago, the ozone layer was sufficiently formed to protect life on land and some sea creatures started to migrate into land with its plentiful resources and easy mobility. Life found a way to "liberate" itself from water, so long as it could carry enough water within its body - we are still 70% water, carrying the "pool" with us and requiring a constant water supply. Some 550 million years ago the Cambrian Explosion happened when the vast diversity of life appeared within some 20-25M years. 200 million years ago, very large land creatures, the dinosaurs, already roamed the earth and eventually commanded it. Mammals appeared at about the same time frame. Some 67 million years ago a great extinction event happened, most likely by a huge meteorite strike. The dinosaurs mostly disappeared and mammals had a Darwinian opportunity, which eventually led to the evolution of apes, then humans; the genus Homo appeared some 2M years ago and then the Sapiens, 200K years ago. Sapiens developed their high language some 70K years ago. Then, the road to taking over the planet commenced some 30,000 years back when most other humanoids perished.

The above process was also blessed by an immense rise of complexity, from the fundamental life building blocks all the way to the human brain. It was not a linear, progressive process and the possibility of "a long series of lucky events" is highly probable. Life constantly faced very serious headwinds; beyond the complexity of living matter, there were catastrophic planetary, atmospheric and out-of-space events. These caused atmospheric disruptions, radiation and extinctions; still life held, continued its march into the unknown; it also demonstrates a tendency for increased complexity. One could assume that the complexity of life made it very susceptible, but this was not the case. Life seems to be stable, able to take hold everywhere, withstand extreme temperatures, starvation, even radiation.

And the high complexity gave it the capacity to adapt, thus we note the awesome adaptations of Migration, Hibernation, Transformation – fertilized egg to baby, worm to butterfly, etc. A month-old tiny hummingbird with a grain of rice size brain makes its way from Canada to Mexico, some 3000 miles, navigating perfectly! Similarly, many birds, butterflies, fish and mammals return in paths they never navigated before!

While the DNA molecule is itself immensely complex, it has the ability to evolve into complex structures and eventually, the emergence of cognition. Our brain is obviously the product of the evolution of such vast molecule.

What can one make of this immense and unrelenting line, lasting some 4 billion years (a very significant number, even in the cosmic calendar), with an endless drive towards what seems to be higher and more complex creatures and structures? Indeed the evolution of species endowed with immensely complex bodily functions and then, the marvel of our brains and, cognitive genius and consciousness!

No doubt, progress is a matter of cultural definitions. It is clear that from complexity and consciousness viewpoint, we have made immense progress in the evolution of the human brain, modeling, understanding and language - our highest cognitive manifestation. And we continue to march into the cognitive domain in force with new sciences and models. In addition, we have learned to invent and use machines that help us penetrate the secret of the universe and our body much beyond our senses.

SCIENTIFIC PERCEPTIONS

If the universe seems to evolve into more disorder (rising Entropy), how come living matter allowed the continuous evolution of higher and higher complexity, creatures that eventually could develop the consciousness we possess? Obviously, life does not violate the laws of nature since local decrease in Entropy is possible. As we investigate and know more about the behavior of the world, the nature of our knowledge is being studied by philosophers and scientists. It has been hotly debated in the last century. Are we in search of an ultimate truth or are our sciences theories that evolve in time and subject to our perceptions, world-view or even language?

Plato, in his Sophist[236], posited the "Gods" (Plato's opinion) against the "Earth Giants" (the Sophists) in an intellectual discourse that has not left us. Plato (and Aristotle after him) took the position of an ultimate knowledge and truth that are eternal, absolute, objective and universal. While these two giants developed a different way to look at the world, they both believed that there is a "truth" out there. This was a western position until very recently; but later in the 20th century, the arguments towards the Earth Giants (the Sophists) are surging. Is human knowledge objective, universal? Can we reach the ultimate "truth"? Or is our knowledge relative, historic? Thinkers like Kuhn[29, 327], Shepler, Polanyi[94] and others started to hack at the Platonic monolith (see chapter 6.3 below). Is knowledge, which we know is evolving in time and change, sometimes radically, universal or is it even "socially constructed[76]?" Are we embedded in our Cognitive-Cloud so absolutely that we can never be objective? Foucault and Derida[237] went even farther. The details of these philosophical thoughts are less important than the principle...are we prisoners in our Cognitive-Cloud, each in its civilization, biases and world-view?

We must recognize that our bodies, nervous system and mind are the product of the world, of Nature out there. We are mysteriously coupled to this world, mostly by our language, but also by chemistry, intuition and spirituality. Also, our senses operate on the phenomena of the world, what else? Only our mind can free itself to dream of the outer-worldly. Since we have developed a capacity to describe the world, these expressions are manifested in many ways: Newtonian Physics, Quantum Mechanics, Renaissance Art, Beethoven's music or Impressionism, all relevant system of description of a world and world-view. We should consider that each of these is a new language and usually one that builds on the past not negating it. But our world-view is relative to our civilization and is never absolute. The absolute reality, the Platonic "truth," has turned somewhat fuzzy. We have become cognitive enough to realize that much of what we do and imagine is the invention of our mind. Indeed, the language is becoming central to our attempt to understand knowledge. In the end, everything is text! Even words like Tiger, or the Moon, are eventually text of a form of text. Therefore language affects everything and during the 20th century became central to philosophy. The Cognitive Sciences are eventually of lingual character. Also, there is a certain "relativism", as the secular westerner, the religious fanatic or the New-Zealander Maori live in very different worlds. These different realities absolutely exist in the minds of women and men all over the places and affect the way we see the physical world too. The Sun meant something very different before we started to understand the source of its energy, its structure and its position in the universe, actually only half a century ago. It used to be this bright ball in the sky that burns and warms; it is now a much more complex object. And we start to recognize, to understand these differences and even try to accommodate them because of the tensions, misunderstanding and animosity these differences, between civilizations or religions, created all over history (see Huntington, chapter 3.13).

The knowledge, the progress we made in the last twenty-five centuries and then, more recently, during the last five centuries, is so immense that some of our modern writing, or thinking, can be suspected of arrogance, even if they are only allegorical. We seem to trust scientific forecasts, based on the fantastic achievements of the scientific method, as if they are "truth". But science is more about the behavior of the world than what it is. We have good models for the behavior of matter, but what exactly is it? Titles like "The Mind of God" or "How the Mind Works," or "Defeating Intelligence," even if not taken literally, demonstrates how far we think we have come. However, we also know how little we know and how far is the road ahead, mostly in the cognitive spheres and the matters of the mind. Some of our limitations lie in the fundamental limits of our knowledge, others already in the limitation of our language. And if the promises of Deep Learning (AI) are to be believed, we might cross to a new form of "thinking" that is not biological and not hindered by our physiology, rather by the ever-increasing speed, algorithms and memory capacity of our machines.

The concept of progress is itself modern. In the past, we believed that *"One generation passes away and another generation comes but the earth abides forever... the sun also rises and the sun goes down, and hastens to the place where it arose..."* (Ecclesiastes 1:4-5). In other words, the more things chance, the more they stay the same. The Cognitive-Cloud of the past was about a static humanity, its classes, wealth (zero-sum game), conditions and an immutable, steady world-order. This also meant socially to accept one's position in the social order. This has changed in modernity, we are breaking the limits of classes and promise every child that they can go as far as they are able to.

The Cognitive Sciences are rather young, emerged seriously only in the middle of the 20th century. These multi-disciplinary or rather inter-disciplinary academic and industrial disciplines stand at the intersection of many fields, among them: ***psychology, neuroscience, computer sciences, robotics, linguistics, anthropology, AI and philosophy***[69]. The word Cognition dates back to the 15th century, meaning "thinking and awareness." The encyclopedia offers few newer definitions, frankly too confusing because it is difficult to pin down their exact meanings. Among them are, mental processing that includes sensory input, memory, language, comprehension, abstraction; specifically abstract symbolic reasoning, intuition, decision making, perception, judgment and problem-solving. Cognition touches so many fields because it involves complex abstract phenomena that are not yet fully understood. Many of the cognitive fields came lately into focus, as we understand better brain function: consciousness, language, abstraction and the nature of the interface between our thought and the physical world, a central element in the philosophy of science.

6.2 COGNITIVE SCIENCES & LANGUAGE

"The limits of my Language are the limits of my world."

Ludwig Wittgenstein

Every process that occurs in the world is the result of certain information processing. To understand any information process we have to understand its language; we have learned that generally, the language of the universe is in Quantum as the material universe is the product of these phenomena. There are however many cognitive disciplines that command our understanding, among them our cognitive thinking and human psychology; they also require a language. The study of language already started with the Humanists but philosophizing about its potential and capacity came later. Flaubert, for example, dreamed about a novel that will be about nothing, its purpose would be aesthetics, to exercise the beauty of language and style; language in the service of language. He believed that eventually, we will find redemption in language. Dostoyevsky, who despaired the promises of science, also saw lingual expressions as a path to understanding our soul, which he considered our fundamental intellectual challenge.

We know that languages evolve and change quickly and we know that today thousands of spoken languages are being used. There seems to be a tight correlation between the language and the folks that use it. It is natural since the language defines us. Doesn't German reflect a tendency for craft and structure; Italian for aesthetics and leisure; English for cerebral utility; French for refinements?

ORIGINS AND DIVERSITY

There was a vision for a common language, perhaps English, for an integrated world, especially in a mobile and shrinking planet; but even in Europe, English is not yet prolific, except for the central cities. The whole of southeastern Europe or Asia with its vast populations, except for India, does not use English or any other common language. A Chinese dialect might become a dominant one and many young are already training in this language as China's position in the world is rising quickly. Technology might come to the rescue, products, either cell-phone applications or special devices that translate speech in real time, are already starting to emerge (2017, see the Google translate app, (*https://www.cnbc.com/2017/10/04/ google-translation-earbuds-google-pixel-buds-launched.html*). Technology is also racing towards voice interface, which is the most natural for us. Devices like Amazon's Echo, Google Home, or Apple Siri are already impressive, economic and prevalent. These are the first steps…we are already close to voice translation interface.

When the Internet was introduced, it seemed that English would dominate its language. Today, some 35 years later, web-English is less than 50% worldwide and people are not giving up on their language so easily. Language is so central to our being that we prefer to do much to continue to use our mother-language, even on the web. People therefore continue to produce programs, movies or seminars in their language even if English produces a much larger potential audience.

It is possibility that all languages sprang from one, the "mother" language, but this is not likely because language dawned too late, when we were already spread all over the places. It seems that the bodily hardware: throat structure, larynx, brainpower and cognitive capacity, were ready, maybe earlier than speech broke. We know that the Indo-European languages mostly used in the west: Germanic, Latin, Turkish, Russian, Celtic, Slavic, Hellenic, etc. (see ref. 73) evolved from a single language, probably originating in the area of the southern Russian steppes. It was only recently discovered that central Asian tribes invaded Europe some 5000 years ago and influenced language mightily. It is speculated that Lactose resistance made them more competitive, physically bigger, hence dominant[110]. Still, all this happened only 5000 years ago, some 250 generations. Today, more than 3 billion folks (half of humanity) use these languages, which originated not so long ago! We also notice that Latin, the mother language of Europe and the west, has been "replaced" while evolving into many other languages: French, Spanish, Italian, Rumanian, Portuguese and their various dialects – all happening within just two thousand years, or seventy generations. This gives an idea of the swiftness of lingual evolution and the pace of change. Since language is so central to our cognition, perhaps it is also an indication of the fast rate of our cognitive evolutional changes.

If speech is the fundamental, natural instrument of language, then writing is perhaps the crowning achievement of the language and print, only some 500 years old, one of the greatest technological revolutions we ever conceived. Written language achieved magnificent expressive capacity, even before antiquity - who can compare the descriptive and poetic powers of Homer, the book of Job, Ecclesiastes, Plato or Cicero, among many others? This is a great mystery indeed, because these masterpieces were created early after the invention of the phonetic lettering. Writing then followed a long tradition of the spoken word; these great classical works were conceived from mythological traditions. Still, their symbolic and expressive value stays as the zenith of our achievements. A new expression technology usually takes time; in this case, the transformation to writing greatness was very swift.

The 14th century Humanists already understood the centrality of language to our being; they quickly developed the scientific discipline we call Philology; first among them Francisco Petrarch. Language became their first passion. In their search for better style and expressive power, they were looking for inspiration in ancient models, to use them for study, to copy and hopefully surpass their quality. The adoration of the past drove them to search for forgotten or lost ancient manuscripts in monasteries and private libraries. Soon, famous Renaissance personalities like Pogo Bracciolini (1380-1452), were surveying the northern countries in search for such treasures in churches and monasteries where, for centuries, books were collected and copied in their Scriptorum - the copy room. It was Pogo who uncovered the orations of Cicero, Vitruvius' ancient architecture books and Lucretius, the famous Epicurean follower[154]. When print started to arrive in Italy, printers did not hesitate to copy Pogo's magnificent handwriting into the font we call *Italics* today.

Soon the science of Philology was advancing to give language a theoretical foundation. Its scientific methods were put into immediate use - to survey and search the authenticity of ancient documents, sometimes with a political bias towards the church; the state and church struggle reached a zenith then. Lorenzo Valla (1407-1457CE) analyzed the Donation of Constantine, the famously fraudulent document that "promised" the western Empire to the Church and specifically the Papal States - and proved that it could not have been written in the 4th century by Constantine I. Valla worked in a court of a prince that opposed the church's ambitions on his territory. Beyond the politics, this analysis, published in a book, is admirable for its professional quality and resulted in identifying the real age of the document that was forged in the 8th century. There were many similar cases, as the study of language became a science. A bit later, even the Bible was treated as a document worth of historical investigations with vast implications on the way we view the historical Bible today.

Excluding the arts, which in many cases use their own languages of aesthetics or musical expressions, our brains constantly use two language types. One is common to all living matter, the mysterious language of the body, written in electro-chemical code, part of the DNA software that regulates our being; it is the continuous information flow necessary to maintain and sustain us through the day by day myriad of chemical reactions happening mostly unconsciously. All living forms use an enormous flow of unconscious electro-chemical information that is necessary to run our organs and sustain our being's flow. This is part of the "automata" of life, what Bergson called *"Elan Vital"* and others called "life force," or in the words of the poet, *"the maleficent power, which acts relaxingly upon us by the fluid circulating through our nerves..."* (Balzac). Our body is very much an *autonomous* program, we are unaware of the bodily activity that is going on continually in all living creatures and starts at the miraculous moment of conception. Our lives are therefore mostly autonomous, the body must overcome constant threats, diseases and encounter situations it has never seen – all done successfully and functions brilliantly; there is no immune system like our bodies. This miraculous "wisdom" is completely decoupled from our conscious knowledge and flow and still commands most of our lives. Every microbe "knows" how to draw energy from the environment and use the continuous flow of sensory data, and how to process this energy, efficiently if not consciously. Animals "know" how, where and when to hunt, migrate or mate, but the process of developing a fetus, a cocoon, a worm or a chick from an egg is still a total mystery. Our bodies perform thousands of functions every day, growing the right tissues at the right time, at the right pace and draw resources - materials or energy, without us ever knowing it. From an egg and a sperm cell, a complete complex organism emerges without any need of knowledge by the parents. No surprise that we consider every baby born to be a miracle. Our understanding of chemistry has progressed immensely but is still short of deciphering the full action of the DNA. We still know very little about this language of the coded electro-chemical instructions commanding the regulation of our body and mind. Even today, the best cancer cure methods are instigating the body's chemistry to fight, rather than applying direct medicine or methods. However, we have started to make inroads into this language as well and our understanding of genetics is starting to be supplemented by deciphering the various mechanisms around its application. For example, the recent CRISPR gene-editing procedure for the sterilization of the Anopheles-Gambiae mosquito, in the fight against Malaria, (see ref. 328). In addition, we have developed the second unique cognitive language, the product of human evolution, brain and intelligence, one that is so rich, powerful and intricate that it allows us to express our emotions, convey very detailed information to ourselves and to others, consciously. And the language enables us to convince others, to draw them towards our opinions or will and to teach.

This language is the one giving us access to the mind, to reasoning, emotions, actions. As mentioned already, the language is our key to the accessing and comprehending the world. While the first language is natural, inherent, and universal and requires bodily instincts rather than cognitive intellect, the spoken language is especially human and defines our Cognition. While we can't survive a minute without the first, we can't be human without the second, the one that defines our mental being, intelligence, ambitions, social structure and world-view. While the first has been developing over millions and billions of years and evolved as the complexity of life forms did, the second is relatively young and is the one now racing forward. It seems that our intellectual quest runs towards integrating these separate languages as the complexity of our consciousness is hastening to match instinct. While the first language assumes the Darwinian paradigm, the slow and meticulous evolution caused by the random-outbursts nature of life and genetic mutations, the second is the creation of our still mysterious and directed mental capacities. Its pace of advance is accelerating as it is directed.

While many other animals have certain hyper languages, the means to convey information by smell, body jest, sound or motion, human language is unique in its richness and flexibility. We are able to convey, to exchange the most intricate information in the finest details such that it eventually enables not only description of the physical world, but also our imaginations, mythologies, past & future. And we can express our emotions in great details too. This is a critical point; our language enables the exchange of cognitive ideas beyond reality, in the past or future, in the real or imaginative; we can communicate on the mythical, religious and abstract plains. Even more, we can impress our minds on others. This helped us foster the formation and adhesion of large social structures with interest beyond the local, the now and beyond personal acquaintances. Our high language has enabled us to develop writing and extend our memory capacity outside of our body. We can use metaphors and symbols, concepts that hold the social structure. Our language enabled the learning process; we learn from the experience and wisdom of others in a way that only humans can.

The metaphor is central to our language and intellect, has elevated the language to a status of an "organ of perception" and more – the creator of our realities. Early in the 20th century, Gottlob Frege (1848—1925) and Ludwig Wittgenstein (1889-1951) have turned Philosophy on its head by redefining its central questions. Specifically, they turned the eternal question "What can we say about the world," since all we can say must be expressed by our language, into "What is the relationship between our language and the world." Language became central to philosophy. For a time, Philosophy turned into the study of language and its relationship to reality.

For Wittgenstein - one of the originators of 20th century philosophy of language - the universe, reality and language shared a similar structure, making language the creator of our world and our perceptions. Soon thereafter, the cognitive sciences were founded - Turing, von Neumann and Chomsky being its leaders.

The mechanics of our acquiring language is also a great mystery, specifically our command of it at such a young age. The parents and the family have the greatest influence on the matter, but in modernity, certain technological devices, like the TV or Smartphone have an effect too. After some 24 months, a baby already commands her language pretty well, we seem to be born with an innate language skill. Indeed, we are able to acquire and imitate the sounds of new languages accurately, but only up to a certain age. After the ages of 12-14, most of us develop a speech accent no matter how long we live in the new language. Why do we lose such skills? There seems to be a sharp cut-off after which, the acquisition of a flawless accent is rarely possible. Our cognitive faculties continue to rise after young adulthood, but not in the matter of language acquisition. One of the explanations has been that grammar is stigmatized, while accent is not.

ORIGINS

Some have speculated that the origin of language was actually in gesture (sign language), which might be more natural. If so, why did we make the "switch" to sound? There are obviously many comparisons and differentiations between mime and speech, among them:

- Sign language is rich. Today there are complete academic programs in sign language, but speech is much richer.
- Sign can be communicated over long, sometimes very long distances.
- Sign is performed in silence. The beasts are usually hunting by smell and sound, so sign language could provide some protection.
- Sign requires no evolutionary bodily modification as speech required because our hands were completely evolved when language started to be used.
- Speech requires no line-of-sight, like behind a bush or in the other room;

it is a very efficient communication method, especially for a group.

- Speech propagates well over objects, unlike sign it covers a great volume.

- Speech is heard in the dark.

- Speech frees the hands in comparison to signing.

- Speech is a much richer, more abstract form of communication.

- Speech also required significant evolutionary modifications in our vocal chords and jaw structure, the parts of our bodies that are very busy, like breathing and eating.

Thus, speech, the richer form that enables to express much more nuance and became the dominant means of human communication. Yet, we often use mime; our facial expressions, finger pointing and body language are powerful resources in our communications repertoire.

Why is it that we have developed so many lingual expressions, that every community developed its own dialect if not a language? Was there an evolutionary advantage or is it simply the outcome of the underlying unique character of every tribe or group? Does the language "code" provide a certain protection from foreigners? Is it helping group identity? Is it natural to expect the individual diversity of so many groups? Was the unique language a mechanism of protection, separation or identity? We naturally show more sympathy to those who speak our language and even more so if they speak with our accent. Is language a code for group identity? Are the languages representing the diversity inherent in human society or is it a selective Darwinian process?

Of course, the language has its limitations in descriptive power, communications and cognitive expression. Perhaps Wittgenstein expressed this limitation best when he concluded his masterpiece Tractate by noting: "*Whereof we cannot speak about, Thereof we must pass over in silence.*"

Interestingly, the Biblical prophet also exclaimed Godliness in silence, "*Now there was a great wind, so strong that it was splitting mountains and breaking rocks in pieces before the Lord, but the Lord was not in the wind. And after the wind an earthquake, but the Lord was not in the earthquake; and after the earthquake a fire, but the Lord was not in the fire; and after the fire a sound of sheer silence. When Elijah heard it, he wrapped his face in his mantle and went out and stood at the entrance of the cave…"* (Kings I, 19,11-13). Thus, the prophet thought the God was sometimes revealed in silence! Indeed, prophets and saints communicate in vision, in dreams; not directly, not by words. But Gods revelation on Mount Sinai, before the whole nation, was anything but silent!

Our lingual historical evolution, as best understood today, also led to the growth of our bigger brain; learning a new language points to increase brain capacity. The functions of our larynx and the shape of our tongue are of critical importance for the evolution of language. The cognitive process was followed or adjusted by physiological changes that were necessary to accommodate speech. While our species, Sapiens, have emerged some two-hundred thousand years back, our evolutionary branching started some 7 million years earlier with the split with Chimpanzee lineage. The Homo Habilis - smart man, started to use stone tools 1.5-2.5M years back. Our upright gait (Homo Erectus, starting some 1.5M years back) freed the hands and, while we lost speed and muscle-power, we gained brainpower[102]. Then bipedal gait freed the rhythm of breathing from walking and might have helped us towards speech and gesture. The ability to use fire for protection, lighting and clearing the steppes, separated the humanoids from every other creature. With fire came cooking, which enabled "pre-digesting" of the food, thus shortening of the digestive tract, of digesting time and providing more time for other activities. Animals spend their lives seeking food and digesting but we found a way to shorten the path. Aristotle would have said that this left us more time for reflections. This could have had a fundamental effect on our biology because using fewer bodily resources for digestion might have enabled a growing brain, an organ that draws immense energy relative to its size. There was also shrinkage in the size of teeth, which could have helped in the shaping of our jaw for speech. The vocal expressive range of human speech is very wide in comparison to other animals, specifically because of the structure and location of our larynx and tongue. Note that in Evolution, many traits evolve for a purpose but then being used for another; for example, consider the evolution of the wing or the lung. There seems to have occurred various evolutionary changes that helped speech when it became necessary or mentally possible. We believe that various evolutionary pressures, some physical and some behavioral or mental, contributed to the rise of our ability to communicate so richly via speech.

The Homo Erectus era of our evolution lasted, until about 150-200 thousand years ago. This genus already lived and hunted cooperatively, which by its nature requires more social interaction, thus behavioral pressures. The growing practices of hunting and eating more meat enabled faster brain growth. About 170 thousand years ago humans started to use clothing. Losing the fur is speculated to have helped heat body regulation, specifically in the brain area. Soon language of sort starts to progress, certain words and then the ability to string them together. The timeline for the evolution of our syntax is still elusive. In the end, Sapiens through superior cognition, became so powerful that they destroyed all other humanoids, most likely by competition over food resources - the competition mostly starved, rather than murdered. About thirty thousand years ago, while we destroyed the Neanderthal, we invented painting and simple musical tools for emotional expression. Some speculate that the introduction of arts is a sign of cultural complexity that must indicate an already highly developed brain and language.

Our Genetic sciences are still young[181], but we already know certain genes affect speech directly. One such gene, the FOXP2, residing in chromosome 7, has been shown to affect not only human speech but other species as well: songbirds, mice.

Is it possible that another species will learn to speak? Not likely. We have no understanding as to the drivers for such evolutionary forces because the language is still a great mystery. Also, as we have taken dominion over the earth, it is doubtful that we will ever let that happen. Most animals we control today have been subjugated to our will and serve a purpose, mostly not cognitive. But we are already training our man-made pets, the thinking machines, and they start to talk!

Without knowing the vocabulary of the civilizations that advanced forward some 6,000 years ago, writing emerged as part of the language, perhaps part of a second cognitive revolution because the effects of writing were enormous. Writing might not be as fundamental as speech, but it is impossible to imagine our progress without it. The writing revolution was fundamental because writing enabled recording and memorizing outside of the brain and therefore extended our ability to learn and spread knowledge. Writing also sharpened our poetic expressions via genius writers and poets. Writing is by nature, more calculated, planned, careful and refined. Writing quickly acquired an artistic fashion and was used for more than practical purposes and therefore, artistic expressions emerged! We know already the revolution that the print has allowed in our social discourse and the influence the print, another form of writing, had on our civilization.

ALPHABET AGAIN

The Phoenician Alphabet is considered the "mother" of most world Alphabets (excluding south-east Asia, one-third of the world population today). It consisted of 22-23 letters. Since the Phoenicians were the masters of antiquity's seafaring, others probably copied from their merchants that traveled all over the Mediterranean. The lettering system has gone through significant modifications, but the order and the sound is almost universal today. Thus, the Hebrew looks and sounds different from the Latin "a" or the Greek α, but they are all the 1st letter of their alphabet and fundamentally sound the "a." The order of the sound (a, b, c, d, etc.) is similar in so many languages. Initially, letters assumed the shape of articles that start with the letter (for example, bet – 2nd letter for beit = home, or gimel = 3rd letter for gamal = camel, etc...). Later letters evolved in the various areas it spread to, hence the different lettering and nuanced pronunciation that must emerge from the local spoken language.

Mediterranean languages have a different usage of vowels than European. Various languages have certain specific sounds too. There is no "h" sound in Russian, "ch" in Hebrew or "r without rolling the tongue" in English (like the hard "r"). Every language uses specific sounds; usually we own about 40 (per language) of the possible 150 available in human languages.

The growth of our language in volume, intricacy and complexity and its ability to express abstract concepts and the complexity of modernity is evident in our ability to deal with a world of growing complexity, itself the outcome of our evolving cognition. The latest issue of the Oxford dictionary contains more than half a million entries. Half a millennium ago the lingual volume was only a small percentage of this number, which now continues to grow quickly. The scientific-technocratic revolution of the last few centuries alone has created a new view of the universe and our position in it, much more complex than the previous religious-traditional paradigms. Our progress in the natural sciences and understanding of the natural world has improved so much that new lingual terminologies are constantly expanding as necessary to describe these new views. We are witnessing the introduction of new terminologies all the time and new disciplines always require constantly their own.

The print was invented in China much earlier than Gutenberg, but it probably did not spread because of the number of letters (in the thousands). Universal literacy of the social order is a modern phenomenon, but earlier, even if 5-10% of the population started to read made a significant difference in the efficiency of society in comparison to just a few literate. Our progress always depended on the spread of the cognitive capacities to the many, not just the elite few. Books and later, the print, were part of the instruments that allowed us modern propagation and progress.

There is no doubt that the evolution of literature is following a path of increasing abstraction, just compare Proust, Bellow, Marquez, Joyce or Becket to the old writers. Is the structure of the language itself growing in complexity? There are no agreeable scientific methods for assessing the complexity of our languages. Syntax, dictionary-wealth, hierarchy, and abstraction can measure complexity. Some research has been initiated in the field, which is still lacking. Other possible criteria for complexity include abstractions used for the metaphor, simile, allegory, symbolism or euphemism and the complexity level of the issues; these are mostly in the nature of human relationship and in respect to the social order. Metaphor specifically seems to be a feature of human speech; our language is so rich in metaphor, simile, and allegories. There is no doubt that the issues we challenge today, whether in science, technology, psychology or artistic expressions, are much more complex than before and this complexity and higher level of abstraction shows in all-modern artistic endeavors, which turned more to the abstract. Beyond the metaphor, the language is the means of expression for our intellect, artistic taste, emotions and personal world within the Cognitive-Cloud of the era. A language must evolve within a social structure, which it helps to create. Because we think in language, people tend "to live in their mind," in the realm of their language[67].

The study of the origins of language is particularly exciting not only because of its importance; it constitutes one of our greatest intellectual challenge. Also because the traditional fossil record - not much help for the evolution of language, this work starts to be supplemented now by the advance science of Genetics. It helps that the field is not totally dominated today by one personality or school (Chomsky in the past). Here is a quote from reference 220 about a debate that was taking place in the late 80s (Chomsky-Gould vs. Pinker-Blum): "*Chomsky is the smartest guy in the world and the dominant figure in linguistics, and Gould (Stephen Jay Gould) is this lay saint, this wonderful writer and brilliant synthesizer. And they're both telling you the same thing—that language didn't evolve as a result of natural selection.*" etc. More diversity in cognitive sciences is always beneficial The issues are very complex and our evidences still lacking.

Our language continues to evolve quickly; shorter languages emerge due to technological advancements, like messaging. We are making progress in the cognitive sciences but many fundamental challenges remain, as our understanding of the working of the brain is limited.

CYBER

One of the rising cognitive disciplines, still ignored or unknown to most of us, is the Cyber and "Cyber-operators" and the effects they have already on our language, economy, art, democratic institutions and electoral results. Social networks specifically added a tool into this menacing discipline as we learn recently. Many of us already live in the web and enable computers to analyze what we read, for how long (did she just look at the headline or did she read the whole thing?), our responses, our friends and family, our purchases, travel routines and more. All this enables corporations to analyze our political and economic tendencies and later help them design messages for us (never forget that anything we get on the web free, actually comes with a price, specifically social-networks and search engines) to sway our opinions and purchases. In addition, the data enables, in the hands of foes (terror, other countries), to foster the social tensions that exist already. These are already known to have been used effectively not only in political debates (Brexit, US presidential elections 2016), but also instigating social tensions (racial, immigration), especially targeting the west. These are tools to create division and social mayhem, and sway political opinions. Programs devised to such effect are continuously written and have significant influence on our social behavior and politics.

In addition to the economic angle, not a single political campaign today has any chances of success without the aid of these emerging cognitive technologies that are possible because of the proliferation of cyber usage and our vast computing power acting on Big Data files. It is unfortunate these have become a threat to our democratic institutions and that they enable serious public-opinion manipulations.

6.3 KNOWLEDGE AND SCIENCE

"Even if the open windows of science at first make us shiver...in the end, the fresh air brings vigor, and the great spaces have a splendor of their own."

Bertrand Russell

The evolution of scientific knowledge and our interpretation of this knowledge are on the path of higher Cognition and becoming increasingly complex. To quote writer Paul Davis: *"...Sometimes during the 20ᵗʰ century, a major transition was made. The theory of Relativity undermined the notion of absolute time and the shared reality of the entire universe. Quantum mechanics then demolished the concept of eternal state of reality in which all meaningful physical variables could be assigned well-defined values at all time...the ground of reality first became transferred to the laws of physics and their mathematical surrogates, Lagrangians, Hamiltonians, Hilbert spaces, etc [227]."* Reality and our perception of it, has become for some a cognitive, statistical, abstract phenomena, sometimes a lingual, historical and even relative phenomena. To others, even a Socially-Constructed one.

The investigation into the nature of knowledge, Epistemology, is at least two and half millennia old. Plato originated this path with Idealism; with his marvelous intuition he already sensed and reasoned that the world as we see it is the product of our mind's interpretation rather than its real nature, whatever this nature might be. Plato always shines but as mentioned, his "absolutes" are challenged by Protagoras (the Sophist). We are realizing that the absolute is not the measure, but rather *"**man is the measure**."* For most of the elapsed time, western civilization sided with Plato's Idealism and the sophists went into a deep slumber. This meant that there is an absolute Truth about the world (or history) that we can, at least in principle, reason and know. But with the birth of a modern philosophy of science, just a few centuries back, the Sophists have awoken and their view of knowledge or science, being only "in context," have gained interest and some of the philosophers of science have taken us to new places. The fundamental question has not changed: is science about revealing the true nature of the world or is it a convenient process to summarize our experience into a consistent, workable method? Francis Bacon already preached for empiricism – study nature meticulously and the results will come out (genius need not apply), while Descartes thought otherwise, that science is in our minds. Others evolved to think that the nature of science is about investigations of terms and concepts invented by scientists. The history of the philosophy of science is fascinating if one has the patience for this kind of philosophical mind-bending, but the issues are real[237]. In the end, **science works!** This must be the undisputed consequence of the last 400 years of immense success in science-technology, whatever the philosophical implications of knowledge.

Thinkers like Popper and Kuhn[29], later also Foucault-Deridda[237] with many others, opined that science and knowledge are also influenced by social forces or the Cognitive-Cloud - the contemporary world-view, civilization and even language. The question is not about the real world being there, which is undisputed (see Bishop Berkeley), but rather what is it and what is the nature of our understanding of reality and how our mind is part of this reality's presentation. Physics eventually seeks to explore how nature behaves rather than what nature is. The shift from Newtonian to Einsteinian world-view is not only a matter of accuracy (most space programs still use Newtonian mechanics for navigation of space vehicles), rather a whole different world-view: space and time are not absolute (rather relative), the geometry of the universe is not Euclidian, the universe is not static. Observations (the Microwave background noise, expanding universe) lead us to think that there must have been a "moment-of-creation;" time is changing in the presence of gravitational fields and other phenomena not intuitive to our thinking. The world is different and much more complex than we are intuitively trained (or innately conditioned) to think it is. These issues of real vs. imaginary have not been decided, maybe they can never be decided, but both sides of the argument have good claims for their interpretations of the nature of knowledge and the relationship between the natural sciences and reality. In the end, we can never see an electron of for that matter, a black-hole; we can only measure their influence and infer how they effect their environment. We might never know what the electron is but we have good models for its behavior.

We realize that scientific knowledge changes in time with our rising understanding, experiences and ability to formulate and measure. The data we collect is changing; the instruments we use are changing, and so are our theories. As we invent new instruments, instruments that were designed to find specific phenomena, we can measure the world more accurately and this by itself gives rise to new phenomena. Such advances extend beyond their field. For example, the threat of GW has expedited our ocean sciences towards a much better understanding of currents, their heat flow and heat absorption, all rather new sciences. Our knowledge of the world is inductive by nature; we find patterns that seem to repeat our experiences consistently, until we feel confident enough to write a law, sometimes a universal law that must be obeyed at least in very close proximity, we call some laws "universal," but how do we know? Experience is not a proof after all, remember that Europeans believed for millennia that all swans are white. We observe the universe mostly from immense distances. Does the scientific method influence the way we view the world? And let us realize that every language, every science uses its own terminologies. The language of Cosmology presents a set of equations and particle physics has another set. The language of biology is the language of chemistry and the language of psychology another altogether. Science is not "democratic", if you wish to engage in the debate, in the development, you must to be able to speak the specific language, to accept the tenets and terminologies. If you are too far off, if you don't speak the language, you will be rejected and not accepted for publication. And like our language, such relationship leads to a certain equivalence and influence. The paradigms lead in every science, until they are replaced. As long as they hold, one has to within the paradigm or not too far to participate. Science advances by finding small deviations from or interpretations from the paradigm until they accumulate to a level sufficient to consider a new paradigm. Science is therefore an ongoing historical process that acts like "improved illumination" on ordinary vision. Our direct experience has proven to be inaccurate – the sky is not rotating around earth, rather we are rotating around the earth's axis and nothing is steady, all is moving. Slowly and steadily we are building a more and more accurate picture of the world and specifically the way it behaves. Alas, as we progress, our understanding improves, but also becomes more complex. There is no doubt that today, while we know more, our perception of what the world is (matter, time, motion, systems) are more complex and more mysterious than in the past. When Newton wrote his 2nd Law that force is the time derivative of momentum, $F=d(m*v)/dt \sim m*a$, nobody imagined that mass can change with time or relative motion. A bit later, as our understanding of the world improved, we started to see better and made the corrections via the theory of Relativity. Relativity is much more complex, its principles and math not intuitive like Newton's (Euclidian, absolute universe). Relativity made certain predictions that took many years to test and verify[239]. Even in 1921, Einstein was awarded the Nobel for other work, Relativity was still too speculative 15 years after its first publication. Other parts of general Relativity are still debated and the means for measuring an accelerating Universe (ref. 240) are immensely complex and speculative, even doubted by few academics. It is so complex that practically very few of us understand the concepts or the measurements.

And politics have entered the sciences, especially when sciences demand such mammoth budgets. Let us hope that only scientists decide on the sciences. And one can only hope that the attitude of the past, "we will do science and leave the rest to politicians," will be reconsidered. Scientists must be involved in the political consequences of their work!

Science is also predicated on certain a-priori assumptions or axioms, based on civilization, language and systems of beliefs. We must consider seriously that even Science is somewhat of a cultural phenomenon to a degree. If alien creatures were to visit us, their concept or perception of reality must be very different than ours. Will their physics be different too? What would be their universe like if their senses were different, if they saw in X-rays, if they were deaf? What if their innate geometry was hyperbolic, not Euclidian?

And science is a cultural phenomena, especially in modernity. As the sciences become more complex and more remote from the majority, our perception of what science is and public involvement in the pseudo-sciences confuse an issue that is already complicated. Some philosophers observed, *the person sees, not the eye.*

6.4 VISUAL ARTS

"All Art is quite useless.
Art is the most intense mode of individualism that the world has known."

Oscar Wilde

A sense of aesthetics, beauty and their expression in painting and sculpturing must have dawned early in our history as so many caves and artifacts show, those that withstood time spans of tens of thousands of years. The mere idea, concept of representing the world (figures, landscape, artifacts) or the self (hand marks, figures) must be considered an immense cognitive revolution as is the capacity to project reality on another medium. Every projection, even a map, is the creation of a new reality (a 1:1 map after all is not practical or possible) and requires a significant cognitive advance in both concept and execution. What a concept we have developed, of projecting reality on a 2-dimension surface, one which we have signs already some 100K years back! The quality of the hand and mind that painted these horses or bulls, or carved goddesses was already amazing and most exquisite. Indeed, the ancient artist invented a new "language" to express, to describe and relate to the world and to convey them to his or her tribe.

Notwithstanding Wilde's brilliant aphorism about the "uselessness" of art, fact is that beauty, aesthetics and art are a fundamental feature of the human affair and has been so long before we became civilized. We adore and value beauty, art and artists more than anything else in the professional sphere. More than few scientists and thinkers have searched for a Darwinian "survival advantage" for our attraction to aesthetics, music and the arts. And still, we believe that beauty is a value in itself and we have admiration for beautiful people, art, monuments or nature. It was always a fundamental part of the human affair and today, with the centrality of visualization in our media we came to the point of "***pixel everywhere.***" Technology enables visualization everywhere and picture taking is instant and prevalent for personal, artistic and safety satisfaction (a billion public camera usage is now predicted for major cities worldwide).

There is no doubt that aesthetics plays a role in the matter of sexual-selection but it is also hard to argue that natural selection acts to beautify. If it did, we would all be Venuses or Adonis; alas, we are not. And yet, nature gave certain species colors and magnificence that does act in the process of sexual selection, sometimes very indirectly. Darwin opined that selection was done based on attraction – alas, aesthetic attraction is not the whole story. Seinfeld even joked that so many of us match or marry because "of Alcohol". Fitness and physical prowess, not aesthetics seem to be the main driver in animal female selection, as we see in nature again and again. As if they choose to be endowed by the "best genes", or at least this is how we interpret the various rut-rituals exercised by bulls, or other males, in the process of dominating but also selecting.

However, art is specific to humans; the creation of aesthetic expressions for the purpose of beauty, meaning and appreciation is unique to our emotional and physical needs.

Arts, the way we express our impressions and emotions of the world and self, are another life mystery and depend very much on the artist's imagination and hand. And the arts use their own languages, be it in color, sound, harmonics or shape, all according to their various rules of aesthetics that we created and that change in time. These are also mysterious and individually appealing with varying sensitivities. We seem to share an appreciation of beauty in certain landscapes, color combinations, shapes, structures, of excellence in motion; we seem to adore excellence across the board and excellence is not easy to define but beauty is part of it. It seems that the sense of beauty, beyond the aesthetical part, which is hard to define (what is beauty?) is also affected by cognitive considerations. Fine workmanship, abstraction, even the preternatural, always attracted our senses and thought. People started to create beauty in the old caves paintings and artists were always admired for high aesthetic skills and workmanship. Indeed, in modernity, as we liberated our thinking from dogma, the arts have expanded their reach beyond the just "beautiful." The beautiful melody or artistic detail of the painter must be supplemented by thought, contents, structure, symbol. Art assumed social-cognitive messages and values beyond just the aesthetics.

Of course, a certain sense of aesthetic attraction exists throughout the animal kingdom too, from flowers attracting insects with magnificent colors for pollination all the way to animal mating choices and sometimes spectacular male displays to attract females, mostly by power and physique. But in humans, art has a certain "uselessness" characteristics, we adore art without any utility but our pleasure, appreciation and the enrichment of our soul.

The concept of evolutionary art has been introduced already by Giorgio Vasari (1511-1574CE), the father of art theory. Vasari, himself a painter at the tail-end of the Renaissance and the author of "*The Lives of Most excellent Painters, Sculptors and Architects*" imagined art evolving from the first light that dawned on the universe, until the culmination of its "divinity" with Michelangelo – "***El Divino.***" Michelangelo, the creator of legendary work left us immense beauty, but even he, later in his career, left many unfinished works, grasping the magic of art that allows an "open end", to imagine where it can go and of endless abstract possibilities.

Our view on art has changed in time, especially in modernity; it is drawing on the past, but we also associate art with a cognitive-aesthetic sense, one evolving in time; art has evolved towards cognitive quality together with aesthetic. There is a clear evolution from the simple, transparent towards the abstract, symbolic, which focuses on the cognitive angle of the art and its implied meaning beyond just beauty. As arts progressed over the generations, more and more tools became available to the artist (perspective for example, paint material, expanding world-view) and these made the art richer in contents. To enjoy such art genres, better understanding and learning is necessary together with a wider background of the history and evolution of the art form. Art always used symbols and metaphors, but they are more abstract as time marches forward. And the effect art has on us is individual, depending on our sensitivities and taste. Most modern art cannot be appreciated on the aesthetic level alone; there are cognitive demands in modern art, imposed by artists and the new more complex world. We expect the artist to leave much to our imagination, our thinking and eventually to our social values. Modern artists are challenging us, forcing to study and analyze the art and its meaning, not only by impressions. It is not always easy and requires study and understanding.

There is no doubt that art is also a product of the "plenty", both time and resources.

We can imagine professional art emerging from the material plenty that was created when human communities started to emerge and create excess wealth in villages, beyond survival needs. Personal talent in few always existed, but art requires patrons, those who had the taste for beauty and who funded the creative genius. The ruling elite, those enjoying the plenty, having sufficient supply of the material necessities of life and the time to enjoy the extra leisure, were naturally searching for a new outlet and for new pleasures. They supported aesthetical and intellectual talents to exercise arts. We witness the emergence of magnificent art in early civilizations, in museums like the Pergamon - Berlin or The British Museum - London. Rulers and aristocracy basked in magnificent gardens and palaces adorned by artists. Hence the emergence of the poet or the professional artist, serving the ruling few who defined taste and beauty, both affected by civilization or geography or certain natural traits.

Monuments were erected to glorify the ruler and the state, palaces and large projects, like the Hanging Gardens of Babel, the Pyramids, various temples, etc. Some historians go so far by defining civilization's origins by social-structure, writing, use of metal tools and the erection of great structures. Some of these structures of antiquity, as old as 5,000 years ago can be found in the Mediterranean, Malta, Ireland and others.

Monuments are indeed a common trait of advanced civilizations.

There is no cultural activity below 500 calories consumption a day; such conditions of starvation attract all our attention towards survival. But as we became more bountiful, as the social order became more civilized, started to create extra food and extra time, even if only for a minority, we create other needs that are not material; some in the intellectual sphere - poetry, philosophy, and some in the aesthetics. Periods of great creativity like Athens or the Italian Renaissance demonstrate how far the process can affect the social order. The Renaissance city-state has been modeled as a work of art - Florence especially, human relationship imagined by harmony and cordiality (Castiglione[127]). Even battles have been fashioned more on strategy then bloodshed, during the reign of the Renaissance states - Federico Montefeltro was a famous Condotierro of this fashion. In modernity, we notice the inexorable march from "stuff" to the abstract and the rising value of art which is now decorating the homes of the middle class, not only these of the "mighty".

Consequently, art expression reached a zenith during the Italian Renaissance when the city-states defined their successes in aesthetics and architecture was elevated to an art form. The whole city was envisioned as a piece of art, especially Florence. In books, the Urbino Bible is but one example of their possible magnificence, with paintings, illustrations and beautiful handwriting. Sculptures, carpet-tapestry, buildings, architecture, music - all were fashioned for their glorious appearance; human beauty was related to the divine. Art reached an apex, but new styles and new expressions were always in store as artistic expressions and human world-view were changing towards modernity. If the previous Byzantine art fashioned express-less characters, mostly of Biblical contents, the Renaissance artists added expression, livelihood and cognitive meaning, and departed from painting only saints and Madonna. The portrait became prominent and subjects from the classic or Roman times became popular in addition to ideas and occasions (for example Botticelli's Primavera). Even pagan scenes were allowed as the grip of the church loosened.

Tastes have changed not only across geography, but also in time - thus, the many artistic styles of the many centuries. Renaissance artist that we adore strove to replicate reality very meticulously; some of them look like exquisite photography with the fine detail of every figure, article or landscape. Such style required very long time of planning and working with meticulous technique and attention to details; this was later evolving to different priorities that were constantly found to be mostly progressing on a path to higher abstraction, thought, and symbolism, leaving details for the observer; the trend demonstrates rising complexity, either in the intricacy of the art (for example Byzantine to Renaissance) or in its expressive means and metaphor. Soon, the arts became a symbol of social status with clear artistic preferences that were defined by the aristocracy and later by the professional mavens.

Later, the steadfast patrons of the arts, once the aristocracy and now the wealthy, have been supplemented by the professional experts, who are the true arbiters of art quality as this taste changes in time. The command that this sometimes-small group (critics, academics) holds on the many, who wish in modernity to join or follow the elite group, is sometimes unbelievable. Taste and style are absolutely commanded by the experts today, critics or academics. Eventually, only time is the arbiter of taste and quality.

In modernity, after the middle of the 19th century, at about the rise of Impressionism (1870s-1880s), the middle class is participating in the collecting and promotion of art - be it in museum visits, concert going or purchasing art for homes and offices. Impressionism like any art genre, is just another way to look at the world and describe it. If until the middle of the 19th century, painters of the various genres tried to express the object of their painting as accurately as they could, the Impressionists found another method. It was more cognitive, less detailed, somewhat more fuzzy and abstract. We loved it! Art stores, galleries, even public auctions are promoting the affordable artifacts - some original, some reproductions - for the general public. Art auctions can be found even on luxury cruises and art decorates most homes today! Indeed, Impressionist artists had an opportunity of a fast-growing market, they could not spend months on a single painting (Leonardo is said to have spent 16 years before he was pleased with the Mona Lisa). The preferences and mentality of the higher social strata (the Leisure Class, so many of us), their taste and needs have been well described by Thorstein Veblen and[128] others. The consequences of these fashions can be sometimes bizarre and shocking if studied objectively, but they seem to fashion our changing tastes and vanity.

In the days of yore, a minority held the total resources of the social order and were the small minority that required such luxuries as art. They also had the time and energy to enjoy either palaces or concerts and art artifacts, new and old. Art was created for their sometimes delicate taste. However, in the last two centuries, with the rise of a substantial middle class constituting the most-significant percent of the total population, the market for arts increased many folds. Not only museums and art institutions, but also a desire to own art pieces has created a vast market. Art style and production had to change to accommodate such growing markets and styles. Impressionist artists already changed the subjects and style of painting which became more fuzzy, more abstract. Some of these could complete 2-3 scenery pieces during an afternoon. Many of them became affordable, at least in their times. Even today, some of the prints coming from their shops - Toulouse-Lautrec, Degas, and even the later Picasso or Matisse, are priced quite affordably.

Picasso is said to have produced some forty-thousand pieces of art. Leonardo did not produce even twenty color paintings. Artists were always respected for their genius, but this was not followed by material wealth, just watch the lives of the many great Renaissance artists, Rembrandt going broke or musicians of the 18th century. Many of them were poor like the "village organist" – the way Wagner described Bach's life in poverty. They acted under the thumb of Popes, princes or other wealthy patrons, their purpose to please such patrons. The workload of Haydn in the Esterhazy estate, where he labored for some 30 years, is shocking. Social pressures and attitudes (especially artists like Beethoven) started to change this reality. The knowledge or expertise in arts became a symbol of social sophistication of joining "the higher ranks." In time, artists' status in society rose, until today; they are practically at the top of the pyramid. This provided the artists with much-needed freedom to develop their art and a certain disregard to the popular taste. Also, the arts have become much more intellectual, rather than just aesthetic; we are looking for contents as well as beauty. Just watch modern music, literature, sculptures or painting, sometimes completely misunderstood and miscomprehended by many. The artists mostly working to satisfy their taste or sometimes their circle, be it artists or critics. The popular taste matters less as long as the "mavens" continue to support the artist, while our tastes mature - or not. Progress involves complexity, abstraction, experience and those not in the professional field must be given time to adapt. Progress also involves social participation and many artists are driven by social conditions, social pressures, social injustices. Sometimes art is socially or politically driven - the Guernica is a shining example of a political, humane outrage expressed by artistic means.

ART & QUALITY

What makes great art? We do not know and the process of determining such quality usually takes time to sort out. It also depends greatly on the experts, art critics and academics. Part of the nature of art and its magic is in the fact that its quality cannot be quantified and its attraction is individual and time-dependent. What most of us know or believe is that a genuine piece of art is exciting, both to the senses and the intellect, and that genuine great art is almost universally adored. However, taste is also a matter of civilization, education, adaptation and time; Van Gogh could not sell a single picture in his lifetime!

Not everybody will adore modern art, even if some of it is now a century old. Art is indeed in the eye, or ear, of the beholder. Still, great art, of all civilizations, is mostly recognized and holds value over time. There is a certain eternal quality in great art. Is there such a thing as universal beauty? Certain people or objects and art are admired all around for their beauty, no matter what geography or social order. What exactly it is, we find impossible to define. Beauty, like quality, is something inherent we know or feel without the ability to explain. And there is a sense of the universality in great art. Nobody stands indifferent, unmoved in front of Michelangelo's David, the Pieta, Mozart's Figaro or Beethoven's 5th.

And yet, artistic taste is not objective and changes in time. Salieri and Meyerbeer were great composers in their time – *Sic Transit Gloria Mundi*! They are not heard much today even though their contribution is acknowledged. Piero Della Francesca is the opposite example; not being from the Florentine "school," even if influenced by Florentine masters, but mostly working in other places, he was not much appreciated until the last century. Today he resides with the greatest. An added component to his late emergence is his intellectual component, sometimes cryptic, leaving us pondering its meaning and expression beyond the fantastic quality of his detailed art. The below is considered by some to be "the greatest little picture (23"x32")."

Figure 7: Pierro della Francesca - The Flagellation (circa 1455CE)

Art seems to express that basic human need so difficult to explain or express in word. The ancient Greeks associated beauty with harmony, symmetry, unity and perhaps a touch with the absolute. The Renaissance Humanists associated beauty with the ideals of the past, with decency and the nobility of the soul. With the introduction of perspective (Renaissance), the artists added the capacity to project reality in a two-dimensional manner and use intricacies of color by inventing new coloring materials. The element of light and later, projected light - Velasquez, Rembrandt, and the intellectual elements of the scene - Velasquez, Goya, added an intellectual dimension to their art. In the meantime, Photography was invented in the mid-19th century and painting to describe accurately the world lost its centrality.

Early 19th century Romanticism revolutionized the way we look at art. During the Middle Ages and the Renaissance art was serving only the mighty, be it the church, the pope or the leaders of society, be it the Medici, the Gonzaga or such. Romanticism thought otherwise and the subjects of art started to democratize. Art started to liberate from its classical subjects and patrons. Towards the end of the 19th century, painting took a big turn with the introduction of Impressionism, a fundamental break from the past. The ideal of a detailed, accurate description of reality was replaced by the artist's impression, towards a more abstract, cognitive art form. The colors, light and expressions changed as the artist had to show more than the surface, its purpose to penetrate the emotions, the desires and the changing world via their art. At the beginning of the 20th century, artists under the influence of Impressionism, post-Impressionism and Expressionism still struggled to present a visual art that was, albeit not linear or detailed, still natural. However, the shift was made as the ideal of the natural was breached with the idea that art should express more than exact reality and that the artist's viewpoint, social perception or even ideology is more central. Since the Romantics, the artist became the center of art. Sometimes a hero, sometimes a viewer or even reformer, art assumed more and more cognitive values. Painting started to take an intellectual angle together with the aesthetical. As art became more complex to absorb, the experts gained importance, as interpreters of the arts and to the public.

While the new modern movements originated mostly in France, others contributed as well. Specifically in Vienna, the Secession movement found its characteristic expressions especially demonstrated with the work of Klimt and Egon Schiele. Klimt created a body of work that was aesthetical, but also intensely original and complex. Schiele, a genius that tragically left us at age twenty-eight, invented a new painting language, one that is both complex and imaginative. It was Schiele (1890-1918) who in a letter to one of his patrons wrote *"for me, painting from nature is worthless; I must paint from my imagination!"* What a concept! And the figures he created, mostly people, are the product of his fertile imagination. Schiele's unique expression of modernism is part of the drive to abstraction and cognition in modern art.

Figure 8: Egon Schiele, self-portrait

In the 20th century and later after the horrors of WWI much changed. The west was shocked after a century of so much hope. Humanity demonstrated its bestiality in a way nobody could fashion. War and killing became mechanized and the carnage beyond description. Art took another turn towards more abstraction and the fashion of Impressionism, ex-Impressionism and Expressionism took the next steps into abstraction. The modern artists were looking for new ways to describe reality or their imagination and gravitated towards more abstraction and complexity. The figures or objects become less distinct and less easily identified and distinguished. The modernists - Picasso, Matisse, Braque, Miro, started to tinker with more abstract forms towards Cubism and cognitive abstract painting. Soon, the world of art would be treated to Picasso's *Les Mademoiselles d'Avignon* (1907), an expression of brutal, violent, raw looking prostitutes, with marked, rather unattractive faces that remind tribal features, to usher a new artistic style. And then, his Guernica (1937), the horror of a cruel humanity expressed by suffering of both humans and animals, the whole of nature has been violated via a brutal expression of violence and disgust. Thus, Cubism was born – to present objects from various points of view, simultaneously.

Jackson Pollock (1912-1956) altogether flattened the canvass, on the floor, rather than upright and used his "drip technique" for his abstract paintings. To many of us they seem marvelous, to others of no sense. This no doubt is art that affects our aesthetics because it is featureless, still immense beauty of form, otherwise known as Abstract Expressionism. Interestingly enough, many of the modern pieces, both in painting or music, are better accessible to the young who have not yet been "corrupted" by our traditional taste.

Figure 8.1: Jackson Pollock, "drip painting"

In comparison to previous periods, the 20th century has been blessed by a myriad of artistic styles and terminology, another sign of increased intellectual activity.

Certain "clarity" would somewhat return in the middle of the century, especially by American artists now using visual technology - Lichtenstein and Warhol. One knew again the figure and what they meant to be (which is sometimes hidden in modern paintings). However, the attraction of abstract art was already too tempting for artists and the tools available to the artist only growing; abstraction no doubt provide more flexibility and dimension. Young artists wish to use all the tools available to them and the new abstraction techniques could not be denied. And art was affected by modern technology, especially when mixing photography or manipulating photographs or painting using computer programs.

While the Cognitive-Cloud supported the advanced cognitive component of art, very much like in music or science, modern art became sometimes less accessible. It was no more just the genius of the artist hand and imagination; enjoying the intellectual art requires knowledge, background and understanding when styles like Pointillism, Cubism, and Surrealism or Drip paintings appeared. These required more imagination and artistic intellectual background.

Figure 9: Mattise – Le Bonheur de Vivre, 1905

Not everybody is ready to make the effort and try to understand Rothko or Pollock, a style that requires background and certain understanding. Not surprising, children seem to be more open to modern art than adults are. Anybody attending adult-education art classes has met the many willing individuals, somewhat older, complaining about modern art. Time will sort out the great artists from the mediocre; there is more artistic activity today, than ever before and we do not lack talent and genius, they are just of different style and technologies. But modern art also opens the gate to charlatans

There is no doubt that modern art is a progression, the continuation of artistic expressions over the millennia. Modernity offers more expressive tools, better technology and the capacity to view and enjoy the art, either via electronic media or by visiting as travel has become so affordable. Also, our world-view and the trend of rising cognition and complexity are demonstrated by art, music and architecture, perhaps the highest expressions of our civilization.

6.5 CONCERT MUSIC & OPERA

"Music expresses that which cannot be put into words and that which cannot remain silent."

Victor Hugo

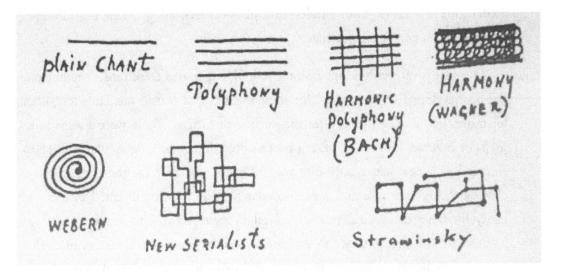

Figure 10: Igor Stravinsky's evolution of music, circa 1000-1920[121].

Delving into the history of what is called classical music, concert music, program music, or serious music, reveals a fascinating journey into the minds of our brightest geniuses and our most intricate and abstract artistic expressions. We are born with an innate attraction to sound, to music, whose style and expressive power continue to evolve. Music is a combination of aesthetics and intelligence in art without a clearly delineated border because music is abstraction, the most abstract artistic expression. The effect music has on us stems from its inherent magic and mystery. For many of us, music is central to our being.

This chapter focuses on concert music, its most abstract art form, and the single musical genre of the last millennium that has evolved along with western style and world-view, not merely for ritualistic purposes.

All told, what is music? Is music the sound in time? Is it the sweet melody? Or musical structure, rhythm, tradition, tempo and development? Perhaps it is about the magic of abstraction? Music is one of the highest languages of expression that humans have developed. We can manipulate it, become absorbed and emotional, and yet not fully understand its effect on us, because it is too complex and abstract. Serious music as a genre deserves scrutiny because its history has already spanned millennia and stood the test of time, compared to such modern genres as jazz, pop or rock (mentioned briefly below). Many popular musical genres developed only during the past century, when music distribution exploded through electronic media; this is done via both wireless and physical technology, such as audiotape, compact discs, and electronic files.

Originally, music developed along folk and religious traditions. The ancient Greeks developed secular music for their theater; this music was later forgotten for more than a millennium after the decline of Athens. There were always folk-songs or lullabies but in the west, a professional branch among secular musicians emerged as a new genre only 600 to 700 years ago, first for the consumption of the nobility and later as a more popular form of entertainment. Most of the many branches of classical music evolved in style, form, and scope, as well as intellectualism, complexity, abstraction, tonality, and chord structure. This evolution included counterpoint, explored dissonance, instrumental tone quality, sound processing and manipulation, and then, atonality (known also as extended tonality). During the 20th century, distribution and music reproduction saw a commercial revolution with the rise of digital, recording technology and mass online distribution. Classical music in the last two centuries, since Beethoven's mature period, has focused increasingly on the intellectual, the abstract and the expression of the artist's emotions and art. Modern concert music has transcended the melodic beauty and even its harmonic contents in favor of structure, development, and introspection. "Contemporary" (modern) music is, therefore, different and sometimes sounds alien to our ears, at least for many of us.

Not long ago, live music, opera and theater were the main forms of entertainment without the electronics we have today - delivered anywhere, anytime, at our convenience. Popular demand and listening styles have changed concomitantly during these last few centuries and changed the music too. Once music evolved to a professional and popular level, audiences demanded new compositions and became actively involved in the presentations. Our listening style has changed over the past century. In the past, a concert was not the passive experience so pervasive today, when audience members expect to sit dead silent and hardly move during a classical performance (when Horowitz was asked about coughing during the concert, his response was "they should die before they cough"). In contrast, in popular music concerts, we are expected to participate, sing-along, or shout encouragement or approbation. These musical styles attract almost opposite experiences; pop events often draw huge, participatory, and sometimes deafening crowds, while concert hall audiences are very quiet and attendance is inexorably slowing. Demand for concert and opera is in serious decline (except in the Germanic countries).

Contemporary classical music has become so complex, intellectual, and demanding that as recently as 200 years ago, a critic commented after hearing Beethoven's *Eroica* premiere, "*music could quickly come to this point that everyone who is not precisely familiar with the rules and difficulties of the art would find absolutely no enjoyment in it.*" Even if this response seems exaggerated, imagine this man's possible impressions were he exposed to today's modern music, which has lost a taste for melody, focus on atonality and concentrates on harmony and abstract integration of musical styles, fashions and instrumentation from all over the world.

MUSICAL EXPRESSIONS

Musical and sound expression has been integral to every human society since time immemorial. For some, music is solace, for others entertainment, leisure or a window into the divine. It must have developed in step with our evolution, perhaps even before language, because music is a natural expression of mental conditions, emotions or moods. Some sounds are related to bodily functions, such as pain, ecstasy, and dance, some to personal and social emotions. Early music must have emerged to express emotions or the opportunity to show affinity to or anger among family members or friends and some of these emotions are inexpressible in words. Over time, music has formalized and evolved as a hyper-language, and western musical notation is now quite universal. Today, music is the most abstract method of communication and artistry and makes use of sophisticated instruments, tuning techniques, and vigorously trained performers. Related technology enables recording, intricate post-processing and mass distribution. Music has been codified and standardized for almost a millennium in the West. In-spite of advanced recording techniques and accurate reconstruction technologies - even single tone of an instrument in the orchestra can be edited and some recordings employ dozens of microphones - many of us still believe that live musical performance is superior and remains one of the only places to achieve catharsis by "making contact with the infinite" and accessing the emotions through magnificently created and manipulated sound. From the quiet halls of ancient monarchs to slaves' horrific tenements, in the stadium together with many thousands of other participating fans shouting themselves into ecstasy, or admiring the masters silently in the concert hall and opera house, music provides the ultimate hyperconscious cognitive moment, the vanishing point for a perfectly spiritual experience beyond words.

It is natural for mothers to produce musical sounds for a baby's lullaby, and many animals make sounds in the face of danger, threat, alarm, or moans during mating - sounds that express emotions, sometimes transcending words. As early human communities evolved, they expressed their emotions in the community as singing, with or without dance, during religious or social rituals. We seem to be "hard-wired" for singing and rhythm - mothers, artists and shower-singers will attest to this, as will so many music aficionados. Sing-along were regularly included in performances, whether in religious or popular venues, except in the modern classical concert hall, and group singing still persists in certain forms of popular genres (choir, barbershop also known as *a cappella* singing). Various ranges of vocal expressions or utterances and rhythms are also common in mammals and other species (particularly in marine mammals). It is reasonable to speculate that humans' musical evolution correlated with the development of language, as vocal chords adjusted to expressing our growing lingual vocabulary, as well as a bit later for rituals, religious and ceremonial events that started early in our socio-cognitive evolution.

Our earliest-known song is about four thousand years old. Historians found very little notated music from Mesopotamia but learned enough to know that music was somehow formalized. Musical expression and performance, whether in rituals or as curative practices against depression or mental suffering, acted like endorphins. For example, David played for King Saul some 3,000 years ago to alleviate his depression, "*Now the distressing spirit from God came upon Saul ...and David was playing music with his hand ...*"(Samuel I, 19:9). The ancient Greeks employed music and a chorus in their early theaters, either to accompany the actors as a singing character or narrator intoning for the Gods, Fate, etc. These secular expressions of the theatrical experience later served as the model for opera that emerged early in the 17th century. The Greek model, or how we imagine it, was subsequently emulated in musical expressions, first by the Humanists in the 14th and 15th centuries and then by early opera composers; initially as the originators in the late 16th century when opera was invented and again in the 19th century. Richard Wagner specifically sought to emulate this musical form in his operas and eventually turned them into a certain "cult-religion" for many of us.

MUSIC IN ANTIQUITY

The prevalence of music making represented on ancient Greek clay pots, clearly communicates the importance of music in that society. Music records from around 2,500 years ago, some discovered only recently, show that the Greeks were using letters, lines and dots to indicate musical pitch and note duration. Some of these records have been deciphered and converted for modern performances. It is difficult to speculate the aesthetic value or complexity of such early music in our time; but we know how significant music was by the attention it received from contemporary philosophers, like Plato, specifically in his *The Republic*[208] (380 BCE), and Aristotle in his discourses about education; many others gave it similar credence. A comprehensive musical language and theory began with the ancient

Greeks as well. The school of Pythagoras, in the 6th century BCE, had discovered important relationships between the length of a string and its pitch, the frequency of vibration. The Pythagoreans realized that pitch produces a lower frequency as the string gets longer, and that relationship is exact: $F \sim K/L$, where F is frequency, L is string length and K is a constant. The second important discovery, credited to Pythagoras himself, was the realization that strings generate harmonics, not only individual tones. Thus when a string is plucked, it vibrates at the fundamental frequency but also at the harmonics, x2, x3, x4, etc…When two strings of length L and L/2 were plucked, their pitches merged, producing consonant tones; the Octave was born. From this observed phenomenon, the octave became a universal musical element in all civilizations. The full mathematical solution to the "wave equation" that describes the complete vibration of a plucked string and its harmonics arose some two millennia later. The relationship between the fundamental tone and its harmonics, always exact multiplications of the fundamental frequency, is a basic property of all musical instruments. The difference between a middle C on the violin and the piano is their relative harmonic contents; the frequency of both is the same but the relative power of their harmonics is different and this is what creates the different, specific timbre of all instruments. Every instrument has a clear "harmonic signature" that produces their special sound, one we can easily distinguish. The octave was divided differently in various places (into 5 – the pentatonic scale, or 7 – the heptatonic scale and eventually to 12), but the 2:1 frequency ratio. The modern piano spans seven to eight octaves of fundamental tones, practically the whole range of human hearing. Because the shorter string (L/2) generated a tone that was double the frequency of the original, the Pythagoreans tried, for more resolution, other divisions by changing string-length ratios and by comparing the consonant or dissonant ratios that emerged from their lengths' product. The next great development in tonality occurred when they observed that round rational length ratios (such as 3/2, 4/3 or 5/3), also created merging, consonant tones. Specifically, what we term a 5th today (seven semitones' separation, a fundamental harmonic relationship in western music) was used for centuries and drove, a millennium later, the division of the western chromatic scale into 12 semitones, which remains the worldwide standard. The Pythagorian system however proved problematic and other divisions were tried. Even if the ratios are not exactly rational (expressed by a ratio p/q, p, q being natural numbers) in the

equal-tempered modern tuning system, this division (a process that evolved over many hundreds of years) has proven to be a magnificent construct of mathematical and harmonic near-perfection. Thus the frequency separation of a semitone (any semitone), say C and C#, is $2^{1/12}$ or about 1.059 (a semitone separation is ~5.9%). For an equal semi-tonal separation between consecutive tones, the western well-tempered tuning, the product of interval 7 (the Fifth), $2^{7/12}$ (or $(\sqrt[12]{2})^7$) is close enough to 1.5 (3:2 ratio) or exactly 1.4983. We call this ratio "the fifth," the ratio at 5 tones (or 7 semitones) apart from a fundamental. The complete scale system is based on the "circle of fifths," rotating clockwise or anti-clockwise to produce all 30 major and minor keys of western music. Note that in this system, the semitone separation is not equal frequency difference but a fix percentage. The various civilizations developed a myriad of scales, some very different from the western. But the octave and the fifth are fundamental to practically all. Interestingly, the Pythagoreans intuited that correct number ratios separate noise (chaos) from order, hence the conception of math being the language of nature, the "harmony of the stars" etc...which later became the realization, in modernity, that the laws of nature are indeed written in math equations.

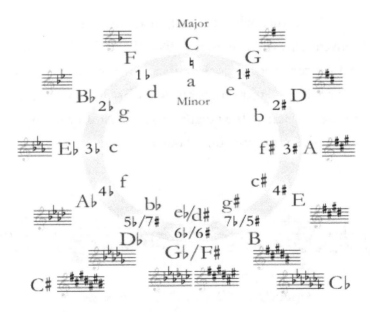

Figure 11: Circle of Fifths (major keys)

Music was among the seven liberal arts of the Middle Ages. Since science and music were driven by philosophy and religion at that time, their progress, or rate of change in the next millennium (3rd to 4th century to the High-Middle-Ages) was painstakingly slow. Early Christianity borrowed from many, including ancient Jewish traditions, as well as various local European pagan and Roman rites. These quickly evolved into a liturgical canon that became part of the monastic and prayer traditions. St. Benedict (480–547 CE), included chanting as part of his monastic code of behavior, and Pope Gregory the Great, 540–604 CE, a Benedictine monk himself, soon codified these chants. They became the standard liturgy of the Roman Catholic Church. The chants' format was formalized two centuries later, but Gregory's revision and inclusion of the Catholic liturgy was acknowledged as part of a vast body of music, composed over more than a millennium and known as Gregorian chants. Most of these chants, with their monotonous tone and lack of meter, served not only the church and the daily ritual, but inspired future composers. Around the 9th century, musical notation termed neumes appeared[331]. It used a four-line staff and was practiced as a method to mostly recall the melodic chanting of the various Gregorian compositions. The resulting music was monophonic; square shapes (later circles) on the staff identified the pitches, to this day.

By the 10-11th century, when musical notations started to evolve in the West (specifically invented by Guido of Arezzo, 991-1033CE), a large body of Gregorian chants existed and continued to grow. Musical notation was still crude, comprising mainly symbols above the text - probably as a reminder of the melody rather than for sight-reading or singing. The notation had no bar division, no measures, and no meter or key. The music was continuous and rather monotonic.

Figure 11.1 : "Dies Irea" chant in modern notation

Gregorian chants were (are) monophonic, unaccompanied vocal expressions of religious devotion, submission and repentance, sung by monks who knew the tunes. The monophonic style (consisting of a single musical line) is the simplest form of music. Gregorian chants were mostly written in what today are termed minor or darker modes. They did not use the scales we recognize today, because musical theory based on the twelve-tone system developed later. Chants were part of the disciplined life in the monastery. The musical notation style that already existed in the 10th and 11th centuries was still simple but included more details after the neumes. A representative example from the 13th century, the famous *Dies Irae* (later frequently used by many composers, including the Symphonie Fantastique), the "Day of Wrath," can be heard at the link below: *http://www.youtube.com/watch?v=Dlr90NLDp-0.*

Famous composers of these chants included Odo of Arezzo, Peter Abelard—the famous (or infamous) Scholastic philosopher, Hildegard of Bingen (whose music and writing have gained popularity in modern times); Leonin, and Perotin - the more advanced among those who came later. Guido d'Arezzo also invented his "Guidonian Hand[322]," a graphics tool that helped musicians read the manuscript and sight-sing (hand solfege is still used today, see ref. 188). Tempo notation was introduced much later in the 14th century. Dynamics, such as volume, indicated by terms like *piano, forte* and *pianissimo,* arose only in the 16th century, and were attributed to the Italian musician Giovanni Gabrieli. The metronome, a mechanical timekeeper, was invented early in the 19th century, and was necessitated when composers marked tempo in their scores. The machine was famously mocked in Beethoven's eighth symphony (2nd movement). Beethoven loved the metronome and metered many of his pieces, some even retroactively.

MUSIC IN THE LATE MIDDLE-AGES (1050-1600)

With the arrival of the High Middle Ages (1000-1350), a secular musical style emerged that we have come to categorize as troubadour or minstrel songs. In southern France, troubadour music - based on ancient myth or the ideal courtly love - bloomed in royal courts like Eleanor of Aquitaine's (1122–1204 CE) and quickly spread to Italy and the rest of southwestern Europe. The troubadours were wandering artists, composers, and singers who developed the art of chivalrous singing made up of many expressive forms including songs, dances, and laments. Eleanor's court boasted famous schools of troubadours in the middle of the 12th century; their songs could be sung for every occasion, but focused chiefly on chivalry and courtly love. The words were witty, sensitive, poetic, and sometimes humorous, even bawdy, in comparison to sacred music texts. Some of them started to use the vernacular, not Latin. The court of King Arthur and his Knights of the Round Table (in remote Cornwall, England) were popular subjects, as were love songs, crusader songs, and pastorals, comprising metaphysical, allegorical, intellectual, and prosaic themes. Being secular, they also included humorous or vulgar (and sometimes sexual) satires. *Canso* was the most popular style among the famous genres of the time. Singers could be either male or female. For examples, see: http://www.youtube.com/watch?v=ijqNBpOU5Vs. The new troubadour musical genre was more complex than plain chanting. It evolved into homophonic styles in which more than one voice harmonized, was also accompanied as instruments were added, and as the genre grew, both the music and lyrics were significantly less restrictive. The songs' themes were not biblical and could be jolly or even bawdy. If the initial accompanying voices sang an octave or a fifth apart (for example, C and G), the harmonies subsequently evolved into a full homophony of higher complexity and sophistication.

The French musician Leonin (1150 to 1201 CE) shifted musical complexity to a higher level; he composed in polyphony and harmonized two or more melodies. Along with accompanying instruments, such harmonization increased musical color and Leonin's expansive style widened the mode of expression and range available to musicians still struggling to accommodate the supremacy of the word. Words predominated compositions because certain textual content was required in music, until the development of instrumental music, specifically the concerto, in the 17th century.

Another significant musical and linguistic step, both in style and notation, happened during the 14th to 16th centuries as the **madrigal** gained maturity; this song-form was a precursor of opera and its arias. The madrigal featured two to eight voices and sometimes was accompanied by sophisticated orchestration (by Monteverdi and Gesualdo, among many others), signaling the beginning of a form of counterpoint. Gesualdo (1566–1613), the Prince of Vanosa near Naples - who later became infamous for the gruesome murder of his young unfaithful wife and her lover - was composing music with tonal complexity that was matched only centuries later. He used chromatic combinations, chords and chord progressions that achieved a degree of complexity, even beyond some of the classics. These madrigals peaked before Monteverdi turned his attention to the opera, but he too continued to publish them late in his career.

By the 15th century, the seven-pitch octave was replaced by the 12-tone (by adding five semitones). The musical expressive power of seven (the Pythagorean scale) proved insufficient to support the improved musical experience, and musicians and theorists requested more tonal resolution and refinements. The number 12 has been a practical compromise between the ever-growing need for tone resolution and the practical matter of performing the music (with five or 10 fingers on the keyboard or strings). The system of "well-tempered" tuning ("Well tempered" meant that the twelve notes per octave of the standard keyboard were tuned as explained before, replacing the various tuning systems before and fitting well to play music in all major or minor keys that are commonly in use), was originated simultaneously in China (by Zhu Zaiyu) and Europe (by Simon Stevin) before the end of the 16th century - a brilliant mathematical insight into a complex musical problem. After the expansion of the octave, composers could improve the level of intricacy that the 12-tone octave offers. Other civilizations embraced other octave divisions, but the 12-tone became, voluntarily, the international standard, due to its magnificent tonal, tuning, and theoretical completeness.

Sixteenth-century musical notations were already similar to the system we use today. The musical language was practically complete by this time, even if a variety of genres (symphony, quartet), styles, and additions (such as meter) were added later. J. S. Bach and Mozart could not meter their pieces due to lack of standards, but added tempo markings (for example, *allegro, andante*). By this time, music was a complete, complex language and was written on a five-line staff. Pitch (denoting tone frequency, A4 or C#4 for example) is indicated where notes are placed on the staff, sometimes modified by "accidentals" (additional sharps [#] and flats [*b*] not in the key signature). Notes' duration and pauses between them were indicated by their own specific symbols. Other referent symbols developed later and signified volume or tempo. The various notations indicate break (silence), duration, key signature (e.g., C# minor), clef (most music is written on 3 just clefs) and meter. The 12-tone resolution was sufficient until modernity. Many instruments can produce finer resolution but only few modern composers use it.

The extensive musical language comprised an intellectual platform for musicians that, as early as the end of the 14th century, allowed them to syncopate compositions to a high level of complexity, greater than anything yet developed then. The modern music sheet, already mature in J. S. Bach's times at the end of the Baroque Period, contains a wealth of instructions for a performer or sight-reader. Intellectual in its nature, music progressed to attain professional status, which meant it came with teachers, theorists, and critics. Art criticism became central to performance and evaluation. A critic of the time hypothesized that Brahms (1833–1897) inaugurated *"the academic age by designing works more for scholars than for popular enjoyment."* Whether we dispute the statement or not it is clear that the transformation to an intellectual dimension was complete, even before Brahms. Music had gone cognitive, specifically when words were omitted (as in a concerto or symphony). Enjoying the music involved more than following the heavenly melody. Musical complexity and structure complement but sometimes defeat a melodious progression, at least for some listeners. This simultaneously artistic and cognitive trend evolved continuously and the resulting changes might define the fundamental shift into modernity that occurred in all arts. What did Beethoven mean to say in his Fifth Symphony (which, in a significant historical detail, was included on the Voyager spacecraft "Golden Record"), especially in the symphony's first movement that lacks a melodious theme? The answer is personal, abstract, and universal, because practically every person is as deeply affected by this piece as they might be before Michelangelo's David sculpture or other equally monumental works of art. If one is ready to listen carefully to a great piece of music, the experience becomes personal. No one can tell what it is, but the listener and his inner self. Are the four tones the sound of Fate calling the symbol of the struggling artist? Is it the symbol of Victory (as interpreted by the allies during WWII)? Each interpretation is distinctly personal.

As musical styles continued to evolve, the melody's centrality, fundamental to the classic genre, gradually gave way to harmony, to form, to structure, to working the theme, meta-morphing, modulating, counter-point and integration. Later complex musical formats developed, composers explored dissonance and then atonality, which aborted melody sometimes and follows the laws of structure, rhythm, aesthetics and harmonics or even the artist's whim. Music has become the supreme abstract art form. It's no surprise that a movie like "Close Encounters of the Third Kind" suggests musical contact between alien species, as a common language. Even the hand signals used in the movie are derived from musical exercises. Music is indeed a language, perhaps the most abstract one we have invented.

BAROQUE MUSIC

Early Baroque composers (officially 1600-1750), such as Gabrieli (1554-1612) and Palestrina, some of whom composed mainly for the church, continued to expand polyphony techniques in sacred music, found in such forms as the Motet, Cantata, the Mass and the Magnificat. These composers brought these genres to high states that found their musical and intellectual zenith in the genius of Georg Friedrich Handel and specifically J.S. Bach, a master, a titanic genius of style and the intricacies of counterpoint and harmony. Melodic voices related harmonically, but not necessarily in polyphonic rhythm, became its founding structure during the Baroque and classical periods, when lines of music that sound independent come harmoniously together. These added another layer of beauty and richness to the music's counterpoint. Counterpoint multiplied the complexity of the tonal experience and allowed each independent voice its music contours. The high practitioners of counterpoint (chiefly Bach and Handel) perfected the form at a peak of musical complexity. Counterpoint (the integration of voices which are harmonically interdependent yet independent in rhythm and contour) is subject to strict structural and tonal rules that result in music of intense beauty and originality and require mastery of the theory of harmony.

The opera was born around 1600CE and would become the foundation of all musical genres that followed. The Florentine Camerata, in which Galileo's father partook as a theoretician before the end of the 16th century, intended to emulate ancient Greek theater. The gathered group engaged in intense intellectual discussions and analyzed the role of music in this dramatic new musical format, which gave rise to the aria after the madrigal and the recitative forms. The opera represented an evolutionary leap in the history of music, due to its showiness, secular subject matter, and ability to integrate all existing art forms. Written in

1600, "Eurydice" by Jacopo Peri (1561–1633) was the first opera to survive to modern times. Its lyrics were introduced during the recitative over the basso-continuo (harpsichord or viola da-Gamba). Monteverdi's genius, inspired by Peri, quickly elaborated the genre into a giant musical production. The genre had great potential - a grand show of music, theater, lyrics, and decoration (sets) was now possible. Soon it developed outlets in the *opera buffa*, the comic style that became widely popular entertainment venues, especially in Italy's Baroque era.

The opera was not born in Venice, but opera received the greatest attention and development in Venice of the 17th and 18th century. The city was past its empirical glory and had become a tourist attraction where visitors craved entertainment. Claudio Monteverdi (1567-1643), employed initially by the Gonzaga family in the court of Mantua and later in San Marco, Venice, was one of the first and greatest opera composers and innovators. With him, the opera catapulted to the top of the musical world as he introduced innovations (opera was just formed then and its format of overture, recitative, aria and the melismatic fashion (singing few notes per one syllable) continued to develop during the next 1.5 centuries) and wrote for an unusually large orchestra and chorus. Monteverdi, who started with sacred music and madrigals, quickly realized the much greater potential of the opera. His 1607 "L'Orfeo" (performed first when Monteverdi was still in Mantua, working for the Gonzaga court) is one of the first operas whose score has been fully preserved and is still performed. It is a great piece, full of many innovations that were adapted by opera writers long afterward. L'Orfeo was scored for a large orchestra then (40 instruments, unusually large for the time) and a large ensemble of singers. It signified a revolution that early composers of the opera undertook, both in breadth and depth of orchestration. The opera promised vast expanses of musical and emotional expression before a willing audience who required ever-higher levels of entertainment. The opera story was mostly told by the recitative and the aria—when time stops and the characters talk about their emotions, plans, feelings and reflections. Monteverdi, sometimes considered the transitional figure between medieval and baroque style, spent the last 30 years of his life as musical director of San Marco in Venice, where he composed up to another 20 opera scores, of which only a handful survived. Opera, really the supreme art form, served as the lever that lifted western music beyond the sacred, continued to celebrate secular subjects. With opera, orchestras grew, new instruments were added, their musical range expanded, and tonal range and quality peaked for a few stringed instruments. The great Cremonese stringed instrument-makers of northern Italy - the Amati family (1507 to 1740C), Guarneri (1626 to 1744CE), and specifically Antonio of the Stradivarius family (1644 to 1737CE) - created the most marvelous stringed instruments of all time. Only some modern stringed instruments, designed with elaborate scientific tools and simulation models, may compete[332] in clarity, sound quality and robustness (musical instruments are sensitive to temperature and humidity, require constant tuning).

Bartolomeo Cristofori (1655–1731), inventor of the pianoforte, paved the way from the harpsichord, which had a fixed volume plucking mechanism, to the piano and its complex hammer action that allowed good control of dynamics (from *piano* to *forte*). His "*gravi-cembalo col piano e forte*" appeared around 1700CE, but the grand piano had to wait another century. Musical expression expanded by dint of the breadth of the instruments and their tonal capacity, even as technology and materials advanced.

The opera, so large in scope for both singers and orchestra, provided a worthy backdrop for intricate compositions and vocal performance prowess. Its popularity soared and eventually reached a certain degree of vulgarity because, by the beginning of the 18th century, it had become a big business, replete with trade secrets and storylines based on history and myth, known as *opera seria*. Singers became superstars and were demanding both music style that enhances their performance and pay. Composers tailored arias to their stars' vocal demands. The Castrati rose in Italy, the modern counter-tenor. Famous *castrati*, such as Farinelli or Marchesini, were huge stars. The great sopranos of the day (the prima-donna) were as temperamental as musical history has described them and earned financial fortunes. The opera Seria (serious) genre was exhausted (Mestastasio, 1698–1782, its great lyricist) and eventually replaced by the *opera buffa*, or comic opera. Gluck (1714-1787) was a major force in the transition - his heavenly melodies and orchestrations paved the way for Mozart. Salieri was a trailblazer and a serious and respected artist in his time; he recently earned an undeserved bad reputation due to his characterization in the film *Amadeus*. Salieri and Mozart were actually on cordial, respectful relationship; the saga of the rivalry started actually with Pushkin (*Mozart and Salieri* poem-play, 1830) because the rumors and gossip caused by

Mozart's early death. In Venice alone, more than 800 operas were produced during the 18th century. Given its popularization, the orchestra had to grow; commercial success allowed for expansion and innovation because the market demanded bigger and better performances. The opera took music to a higher level because of the other dimensions it incorporated and now, being secular entertainment, for its ability to express the breadth and depth of human emotion.

Inevitably, the prima donna was born! Capricious stories of the magnificent singers have filled history books, scandal sheets and gossip columns. A story worth telling (on the over-the-top embellishments of the Belle-Canto era): Prima-donna singer to old Rossini after the performance of his opera: "Maestro, what did you think?" Rossini: "very beautiful, but who is the composer?" Indeed, the magnificent singers were (still are) the stars of the opera (the composers are the gods), some of them with amazing vocal quality and control. Classical singers are much more than just the voice. Voice is an instrument and the singers are about very tight attention to this instrument, hard work (imagine singing for hours on stage, while acting and paying attention to the conductor and orchestra, not to miss a single beat – many in the audience know the music all too well), sacrifices (many singers, especially women, gave up family life because of the frequent need to travel and attention), persistence, great memory, acting and constant pressure. They deserve our adulation.

In the meantime, a different style from the Italian was developing in France, initiated by Jean-Baptiste Lully (1632–1687 CE), the court composer of Louis XIV. This opera genre had to deviate from the Italian because French language prosody and rhythm are different. This market also requested that opera provide ballet, which became a fixture in French opera and overall was a better fit for French culture and temperament. The centrality of 19th century Paris added ballet to many other operas (Verdi, Wagner). With Lully's refinements, opera became an even more integrative art form and included music, lyrics, acting, dancing, singing, decoration and production. New instruments were continuously incorporated into the musical ensemble to enable the more complex forms and expressions demanded, by both the artists and the audiences.

By the 1680s, music took another major cognitive step. The concerto had arrived, a mature musical form devoid of human voice and story line. The genre was mostly developed in Italy and more specifically in Bologna (Corelli) and Venice. The concerto was an extension of the opera form: instrumental soloists emulated singers' arias and recitatives (see Stradella, Torelli, and the divine Corelli, fathers of the concerto). Concerto composers were liberated from the yoke of the spoken word and could explore the abstract, although sometimes still burdened with the need to introduce a "musical story" into each composition (Vivaldi's The Seasons). Previously, music was based on the primacy of language and the voice, whether religious or secular. Early operas were considered "words in music" or "voice melodies." Music had to illuminate the story, while remaining subservient to the lyrics, and later to the whims of divas. In stark contrast, the concerto liberated these composers. Free from structuring music around words, music quickly evolved into total abstraction, and program music was soon to follow. Starting with the middle Baroque period, many composers favored instrumental music even as they grappled with the new genre. Listening to early concert masters (Torelli and Stradella among them), one identifies their difficulty with the new form, which sometimes sounds repetitive or flat to modern ears. The next development of the form fell to the following generation, which included Vivaldi, Telemann, Scarlatti, and Handel (1685–1759). Soon Baroque music would approach perfection with the arrival of one of music's luminaries, Johann Sebastian Bach (1685–1750), who composed such complex, intricate, and intellectual music that he transcended his era. Contemporaries could not appreciate the material that was adored by later professionals (Mozart and Beethoven included). It took a long time for his compositions' revival in the beginning of the 19th century (credited to Mendelssohn). Bach brought musical form and counterpoint to a level that has never been matched. He commanded perfectly what we refer to as musical theory and contributed to the establishment of the "tempered scale". His music is a marvel of construction, his command of musical theory unmatched. He also was a "numbers person," interested in numerology (the number 14—the value of B-A-C-H in numbers—and 41, its reverse, figures ubiquitously in his compositions), signaling another cognitive element. Under his hand, the concerto, cantata, suite, partita (a collection of dances), and keyboard music reached new levels of complexity, structure, melodic beauty and harmonic perfection. He wrote many vocal pieces but no opera. Bach was too complicated for his time, and considered mainly as a great keyboard performer rather than a giant composer. He lacked self-promotional skills and preferred to work for a small community (unlike Handel) and confined his life to a small territory in central Germany. He was a product of the Baroque, too humble before his noble masters, some of whom are remembered today only because of him. Bach, not sufficiently appreciated although well known as a fantastic keyboard performer, was mostly forgotten late in the 18th century. Felix Mendelssohn who operated in Leipzig too, resurrected Bach in the late 1820s and performed Bach's works, some of which had never been performed during the master's career. From then on, Bach's position in the musical pantheon continues to grow. Doubtless many musicians knew his compositions, including Haydn, Mozart, and Beethoven, and drew from his resources. Some of Bach's work has been lost; his score papers were used for purposes too embarrassing to enumerate. He charted a path for musicians and influenced later generations of both classical and popular music. The great keyboard works (for example, partitas, chaconne, passacaglia, variations, offerings, etc.) and sacred music demonstrate immense creative power, imagination, command of the instruments and orchestration that took advantage of their timbre. Bach's music is endowed by marvelous structure that can be described as mathematical. His harmonic command and the counterpoint have reached a zenith of aesthetics and intellectual contents.

During the late Baroque period, music started to formalize. Although many of the pieces were still left up to performers' interpretation (especially in the basso-continuo part, which was mostly shown only as chords and left for player interpretation), standards were set nonetheless. Musical notation was based on standards and tempo indications (for example, *andante, allegro, presto*) became commonplace. Baroque meter was left to the performer or sometimes indicated by the genre. For example, the various dances that constitute a partita had established tempi while other parameters followed tradition.

CLASSICAL PERIOD

By the end of the Baroque era (1600–1750 CE) and definitely during the classical, the social structure of the west changed and musicians steadily broadened their reach, composing and playing for larger audiences. Bach wrote for the glory of God and the contentment of his masters. Even the young Haydn told his Esterhazy boss, *"I write music to please your highness."* The classical era was the product of the Enlightenment, and musical artists paid attention to the growing middle class. These audiences were perhaps less sophisticated than the educated nobility and music initially turned back toward structural simplicity to appease the growing audience. Simplicity was an Enlightenment concept for expanding the listening space, but this era's sound was much richer and its expression more powerful because of the growing orchestra, refinement of the instruments and the new instrumental genres (for instance, trio, quartet, and symphony); also the natural rise in the cognitive element of the music and the "working of the theme" so central to Beethoven's art, started to affect music. Instead of counterpoint, composers preferred the homophonic style - a central theme supported by the orchestra, with variations, although with a much richer canvas of sound and expression. Melodic simplicity did not mean overall simplification; however, as the classical evolved from the Baroque's single-thematic (fugue) into a multi-thematic movement (usually two); the music assumed a certain format: introduction, development and eventually the summary, or "recapitulation", as the conclusion. The "sonata-allegro's" development sections were formalized musical structure for the next 150 years, a staple of the classical genre.

Just as the concert emulated the opera and a solo instrument the singer, the classical period saw the maturation of the symphony into a fully liberated musical genre without human voice. Instrumental music stood on its own and conveyed the total artistic impressions, without words. The later classical period of Haydn - the great innovator of musical form (such as symphony, quartet, sonata-allegro forms), originated the mature, four movement symphony and string quartet; he and Mozart catered to a growing middle class, mainly burghers who had the time, the means and the appetite for music and artistic refinement. Haydn spent much of his career employed by the Esterhazy estate (a wealthy family in Eisenstadt, Austria, some 20 miles south of Vienna). In the early 1790s, he was released from his duties and went to London for a substantial contract and adoring crowds. When he returned to Vienna, he wrote, now as a famous and successful composer, as a freelance artist. At this time he became the most revered musician of his time in Vienna, known as the father of classical music, "Papa Haydn." Haydn perfected the sonata and gave us the symphony, now written for a large ensemble, a form he refined by composing as many as 140 symphonic works, some of which are now lost. He practically invented the string quartet, other chamber music forms, and the piano sonata.

Mozart, a follower and admirer of Haydn, elevated the opera, chamber music and the piano concerto to a zenith. His genius for both melody and harmony are simply unmatched. Mozart considered himself an opera composer who wrote concertos for a living and chamber music for friends, but he was really the "ultimate package" in the history of music. He also expanded the string quartet and quintet, together with a variety of other concerti, lighter compositions, and sacred music. Mozart was a unique historical phenomenon, a genius of the highest degree with a unique sense of drama and unmatched musical knowledge and talent. He grasped the work even before it was committed to paper and left us an unmatched legacy. Mozart sought to write for a patron, but eventually created his masterworks as a freelance artist and wrote for the public. Whether concerti or opera (or his Singspiel, a form of operetta or opera Buffa for the populace) he achieved a rare melodic and harmonic beauty, never to be surpassed. With Mozart (1756 - 1791) a new era of musical genius dawned. No one before or after has written more sublime music that begs to be sung, seems so natural and easy, yet is still so complex. According to Rossini, a great master himself, Mozart united the Italian genius for melody and the German genius for harmony. Rossini quipped, *"Mozart was an inspiration in my youth, desperation in my maturity, but then consolation when I aged."*

Opera existed long before Mozart, but Mozart truly established the grand opera, the most magnificent form of musical presentation. His mature operas (such as Figaro, The Magic Flute, Don Giovanni and Cosi fan Tutte) stand at the pinnacle of this art form, unparalleled in their beauty, dramatic perfection, comic situations, and orchestral/melodious genius. His piano concerti and other musical genres seem to have been created effortlessly, even if much of his work does show virtuosic planning, sketching, and resorting to previous masters. His counterpoint and dissonant, chromatic combinations are a marvel of compositional beauty. He was and remains the "*Golden Boy*" of music forever. It might be cruel to say but thank God for the Viennese's endless demands. Mozart left behind both an unmatched legacy and great volume of works. He seems to have possessed an endless fountain of the most beautiful melodies and the ability to orchestrate them perfectly. And if you need a good cry, try the d-minor quartet or g-minor quintet, perhaps his most personal and greatest chamber music expressions.

Initially, early classic composers inspired by the Enlightenment thought the Baroque style too elitist, too adorned, and unsuited to middle-class listeners. Rather, they sought a level of simplification to address public audiences that were evolving. Music started to be written for amateur performers and a growing market developed for ensemble players, of both concerts and scores. Counterpoint and the musical complexity inherited from Bach, with its harmonic acrobatics, would not be developed further; perhaps Bach took it to the ultimate apex. In the meantime, better instrument technology improved musicians' ability to tune a large orchestra and its sound. Classical period composers further developed the symphony and the sonata forms, new experimental chords, and more complex and growing orchestrations. Dissonant passages were tampered with while compositional focus remained on melody, lyricism, and orchestral timbre. The classics, even if their structure was simplified, shifted music onto a higher intellectual plane because of the extra richness, the new color of the music and the use of dissonances in counterpoint. The maturation of form, perfection in beauty, the development of the simple theme to a complex whole and the expansion of harmonics and overall musical scope elevated musical content.

BEETHOVEN

"Music is a higher revelation than all wisdom and philosophy."

Ludwig van Beethoven

Ludwig Van Beethoven was born in 1770, twenty years after Bach's passing and when Mozart was only fourteen. With him shone perhaps the brightest light of the cognitive musical sky and music fully embraced structure, program, intellect, development, and cognition. Beethoven absolutely operated within the classical paradigm but broke through and expanded the various genres. Every tool was investigated and examined, and even rhythm could become a motif; Beethoven was the most rhythmically audacious composer. He was a revolutionary artist in his compositions and the way he saw his position, the artist in society. A colossal personality — a very great if difficult and tragic man - he changed our attitude toward art and the artist. The poor Baroque composers had to compose enormity of quantity (Bach at the time composed a Cantata for every Sunday; not easy to be original with such schedule); nobody would dictate schedule to Beethoven.

He had a tragic childhood, suffered illnesses and a disastrous love-life, but times changed and he became a proud master, fully realizing his value and greatness. If we consider Mozart and Bach as the great lights of the past, one with a singular genius for melody and harmony and the other with a mastery of harmonic-acrobatics and counterpoint, it was Beethoven that turned music into the intellectual realm. Although he could write tunes as beautiful as anyone, this was not what he was searching for when he matured as a composer. After Beethoven arrived on the scene, everything changed in a way we understand, appreciate and interpret music, and maybe art. Beautiful tunes were integrated or gave way to the magnificent edifice of musical architecture; form and structure took over. He focused on what he could do with the simplest musical elements. His music (for example, the Third, Fifth, Sixth, Seventh, and Ninth symphonies) comprises a structural marvel. His art concentrated on the intellectual, the structural perfection of musical inquiry and the art of analyzing, studying, digging deep, and creating variations. He was absolutely dedicated to the quality and integrity of his art and the ability to develop the simplest motif into a grand structure. His music appeals to our intellect and as he aged, his focus on the intellect grew especially via the quartet genre. While Monteverdi, Bach, and even Mozart composed to please their masters, Beethoven wrote to satisfy his standards and his art. He was a true romantic revolutionary; he had many patrons but no master. Being a rebel, he could not be subdued and kept evolving to the end, even when his hearing was totally lost. In the fashion of a hero of romanticism, he struggled with his own demons to compose expressive and always revolutionary art. He adopted simple motifs, sometimes almost no motifs, yet fashioned them into a magnificent construct. Haydn and Mozart inspired the younger Beethoven, while Bach and his immense musical complexity influenced the later. Maybe he understood that Mozart had already taken melody to its ultimate zenith. Maybe the power of Beethoven's intellect conceived that music's evolutionary path was contained in its cognitive value and rising complexity. Are the *Große Fuge* (op. 133) or the C# quartet (op. 131) beautiful or are they simply monuments to the art of structure and "working the theme?" At a relatively young age (1807-08), in the second movement of the String quartet #7 (Razumovsky, op. 59 #1), Beethoven took the quartet beyond anything that was before. The 2nd movement is actually devoid of a melody; it starts with a cello playing the same tone (B-flat) 15 times and this becomes the baseline for the entire 10-minute movement. It is a rhythm, rather than a tune and constitutes perhaps one of the greatest pieces of chamber music because of what he could do with the material; the making "something from nothing" became the artistic challenge. Just four tones form the totality of the first movement of his Fifth Symphony (a structure that later obsessed musicians), but they are spun up magnificently and mined to high heaven. And then, when the listener is exhausted after the first movement, the four tones reprise again and again in later movements, transformed or disguised. The four-tone device was a Beethoven specialty, evidenced also in the violin concerto, the piano concerto #4 and other masterpieces. The Fifth Symphony demonstrates what can be achieved by weaving, modulation, and variation, coupled with an immensely creative imagination. It is vintage Beethoven; it is the character of his music. He seems to have challenged himself: what can I do with the simplest material, bringing it almost to an absurdity by the spare and elegant construction using the orchestra's timbre and structural mining? He advanced the art of constructing an edifice made of simple, elementary tunes, constituting not even a melody (especially in the late quartets - the apex of Beethoven's creativity). Libraries have been written to explain his pieces, but for our purposes, suffice it to say that this music transcends words. ETA Hoffman, who changed his third name from Wilhelm to Amadeus out of awe of Mozart, opined that Beethoven's music sets in motion the machinery of awe, fear, terror, and pain, awakening infinite yearning that is the essence of romanticism. It expresses the emotion of purely instrumental work, opening the realm of the monstrous and immeasurable. Note that Hoffman never used the word "beauty." And there is no doubt that Beethoven's art possess infinite beauty but sometimes of a different flavor. This Beethovenian form haunted future musicians, notably in Brahms' attitude of working in the shadow of a giant, or the beginning of Mahler's fifth symphony. The whole Romantic genre stands in awe before his work.

Beethoven did not invent the symphony or string quartet genres - he was no form innovator. Rather, he summed up all that came before him by elevating complexity, by working the material, by developing the concept of "never forget the thema," all to perfection. The techniques of mining the material, including variations (for which he had a special genius), and thoroughly working a theme, often following composers who preceded him. Bach's Goldberg variations, the Chaconne, Pasacaglia (in A), or so many Haydn and Mozart pieces corroborate this fact. The intellectual challenge became planning, investigating, and mining the material. This is not a style of spontaneous genius, rather one of working and editing hard. It might have been demonstrated chiefly in his fifth symphony, but his later pieces are repeated testimony. In the Diabelli variations (1823), he turned what he called "stupid little waltz," into the zenith of variation, managed to convolute the theme so magnificently among 33 variations that he transformed the "stupid waltz" into the greatest existing set of variations (together with Bach's Goldberg variations). The level of musical complexity was raised another step as Beethoven transformed this art form into an intellectual practice that became the musical composition standard. He set the direction of the future of music, and the following generation - the Romantics - were his dedicated followers; his shadow looms on all future music. One can imagine the frustrations of composers studying his awe- inspiring scores.

Toward the end of his career, now totally deaf, Beethoven turned almost exclusively to writing string quartets and composed music that was exquisitely personal, intimate, and already resembling modern compositions - in particular, the A minor (#15), B-flat (#13), and C# minor (#14) quartets, among the towering achievement of his art. From the beginning of the C# quartet (his favorite), the music is introverted, somber, personal and deep. This orchestration required intimate knowledge not only to compose, but also to understand its effect on listeners. In his Opus 130 (the B-flat quartet), the last part was so difficult (intellectually) that the publisher convinced him to separate it into a new opus, known today as the *Grosse Fugue* (opus 133). To fully enjoy it, one must understand what goes on beyond the aesthetics. Such music was not previously conceived. Himself an innovator of the first degree, Stravinsky called the late quartets, "*an absolutely contemporary piece of music that will be contemporary forever.*" As expected, this music was not understood well at the time and many musicians dismissed it as the work of a deaf old man; the fact is that Beethoven was almost a century ahead of his time. The intellect required to comprehend the pieces was modern. Beethoven was constantly changing and never stood still. The sixteen quartets he wrote - each a miracle of chamber music - passed through an evolutionary cognitive process. The first six, the Op. 18, albeit already Beethovenian, were still heavily influenced by classical Haydn-Mozart style and structure. However, the next three, the op. 59 (Razumovsky), already broke the mold. These were very personal means of expression. The four instruments expressed individual personalities, the level of orchestration, and the short themes' development, now Beethoven's staple, were unsurpassed. The quartet form became the supreme artistic instrument to convey the artist's most intimate emotions. The music itself is complex, hard. It is well known that when these quartets were first presented to the Schupanzigh quartet in 1807 (who premiered many of his quartets), the players complained about the technical difficulty, to which Beethoven responded in a legendary retort *"you think that I care about your difficulties when the muse talks to me?"* Beethoven's late quartets, specifically op. 130, 131, and 132 brought the genre to its pinnacle.

Beethoven did not change the classical form, however, he changed the quality and projection of musical expression forever. Some of his revolutionary elements follow:

1. Employed the simplest motif and sometimes none at all.

2. Worked the motif endlessly to create a large edifice, sometimes termed "musical pointillism."[289]

3. Utilized unusual improvisational style.

4. Made music a tool of self-expression.

5. Turned to the abstract, intellectual, and focused on structure.

6. Extensive musical architecture expanded the scope of the musical forms. He conceived the work as an integrated whole by interlocking motifs across a grand design.

7. Was committed to an evolutionary process, in Beethoven's words, *"Art demands that we continuously improve."*

Although a small-statured man, Beethoven had a giant personality, one of the greatest men of his time, beyond being a great artist. A natural rebel and independent thinker, he changed the position of the artist in society and helped transform the Humanist attitude of "placing Man at the center" into the modern concept of "placing the Self at the center." He helped dispense with "creating art to please your Highness," instead, the artist moved to the head of the social hierarchy, ever loyal to his art and to no other master. This revolutionary way of thinking signaled the passing from the Classical to the Romantic. The artist became the "hero" who no longer created to please the Gods, the nobility or, for that matter, anybody except one's artistic standards. Beethoven wrote, in a letter to his great patron, Prince Lichnovski, "… *What you are, you are by accident of birth; what I am, I am by myself. There are and will be a thousand princes; there is only one Beethoven.*"

How far did he see? Some musicologists suggest that the *Grosse Fugue* (Op. 133) is the first assault on the diatonic tonal system (if you take the view that music is the evolution of the dissonance, then this piece is a great example); it took two more generations of musicians to temper seriously with the form, after the emergence of the second Viennese school (Schönberg) and Impressionism. Altogether, Beethoven was a force that changed the projection and scope of musical expression and shifted it toward abstraction, complexity, and atonality.

ROMANTICS AND BEYOND

Many years and geniuses passed before anyone could seriously challenge any of Beethoven's genres again, such as piano sonatas, symphonies or quartets. The Romantics tried to cope with his forms (for instance, Mendelssohn, Schumann, and Brahms), composing in his shadow. Others, later tried to move on (such as Mahler, Schonberg) and new genres emerged, especially on the piano (Chopin, Liszt, Schumann) and symphonic/tone poems (Liszt, Richard Strauss). In the end, composers pursued other avenues (as evidenced by works by Wagner, Richard Strauss, Stravinsky, and Schoenberg) although symphonies and quartets continued to be attempted. The shadow Beethoven cast on the future of music was so great that Schubert asked to hear the C# minor quartet played repeatedly on his deathbed and to be buried close to Beethoven. Composing music must have been mortifying for some of the musicians who came after him, so they resorted to new genres instead. These included songs (lieders), shorter piano pieces (Chopin, Schumann, Liszt), different chamber combinations (e.g., piano quintet, sextet, octet) and symphonic poems.

Program music, intended to evoke images or render an extra-musical narrative, became a central genre for composers, especially in the wake of Berlioz's "Symphonie Fantastique," and perhaps heralded the beginning of modern ideas in music. Such music existed before, like Beethoven's Pastorale symphony or The Seasons by Vivaldi but it took a different shade for the Romantics, more Impressionistic in style. Berlioz and Chopin were rebels; Chopin (and the young Liszt) aborted the classical style altogether, invented a new musical language and composed mostly short piano pieces that deliberately did not follow classical structure. Berlioz published his Fantastique in 1830, just three years after Beethoven's death. The symphony was revolutionary in myriad ways, he wrote it for a massive orchestra, used an "idée-fixe" theme and the level of orchestration and sophistication were fresh. The five movements, the story of an artist in desperate-love, were not named for their tempo anymore (e.g., allegro, andante, presto), but communicated the program of this Impressionistic piece: Reverie, Ball, Fields, Scaffold March, and Witches Sabbath; such titling was unheard of before. Then came the various Symphonic-Poems, by Liszt and later Richard Straus. Nonetheless, early Romantic German composers remained under Beethoven's sway for a long time. Johannes Brahms composed his first symphony at almost 50, and Mendelssohn and Liszt, among other piano greats, hardly touched the sonata, even though Liszt eventually produced a B-minor masterpiece in Beethoven's style. Brahms constantly complained about walking in the "Beethovenian shadow." Even the quartets were relatively subdued, until the arrival of works by moderns like Bartok and Shostakovich.

The Italians and French took their cue from other sources. The Italians continued to write *opera buffa* (Rossini used to joke that he can write an opera for a laundry list), which flourished in Italy during the beginning of the 19th century mostly as *"Bel Canto"* style. Donizetti, Rossini, and Bellini, who dominated the genre, left us a marvelous legacy of beautiful arias, written more for the heart than the intellect. The genre allowed singers' embellishments, but perhaps encouraged this too much? It was partly a matter of style (Italians will sacrifice anything for the beautiful melody, for which they have infinite talent) and partly due to singers' and audiences' demands. In Italy, music is entertainment, forever. In the late 1830s, a new giant emerged - Giuseppe Verdi. He had a very long and fruitful career that started as a Bel-Canto master (from his first great success "Nabucco" to "La Traviata" and then "Aida" and "Falstaff", when he was already legendary in Italy). Verdi possessed a virtuosic sense of drama and was an endless wellspring of beautiful and dramatic melodies, but his compositions eventually evolved to become the complex, chromatic style evident in his greatest pieces, "Don Carlo" and "Otello." Specifically, Otello is a mature grand opera whose large orchestration is as central as the singer, perhaps in the "Wagnerian style" (continuous music, grand orchestration). Verdi eventually composed 28 operas and at least a dozen of them are constantly in the repertoire. In France, the grand opera took stage specifically through Meyerbeer (1791–1864). He merged the German with the French style and created immense productions, very long pieces that included ballet and the latest, most lavish stage technology.

In central Europe, music continued along Beethoven's creative arc. With the advent of the romantic style, few innovations materialized. Following the rise of nationalism, some composers embraced a nationalist style (such as Glinka, Grieg, Mussorgsky, and later Bartok, Stravinsky, Smetana, and Dvorak, among others). Mikhail Glinka (1804-1857) specifically burst into the national and international scene with his Ruslan and Ludmila (1842) opera - so many Russian operas are based on Pushkin poems - which was a break from the German influence, into a traditional Russian folk story and music. The Russian style later influenced the "mighty Five" (Rimsky-Korsakov, Borodin, Mussorgsky, Cui and Balakirev).

The piano's tonal scope and quality grew from the early four octaves into the grand forte-piano (Liszt's contribution is immeasurable). It had by then (mid-19th century), an enormously complex hammer mechanism and keys spanned seven or eight octaves - the modern grand piano. It became the chosen mode of expression for the "artist hero" of the romantic genre. The orchestra grew to comprise sometimes more than 100 players (for example, Mahler would compose the "symphony of a thousand" and Berlioz requested an orchestra of a thousand). The artist as superstar was born in the person of Franz Liszt with all the signature mannerisms. As the superstar performer, Liszt developed a new style; fainting on stage, playing with body motion, women throwing jewelry and sometimes more intimate articles... sometimes a sort of a sexual Bacchanalia, at least visually, not to mention the endless lovers he collected. As a composer he was a reformer, the symphonic poems were compositions to illustrate an extra-musical poetic scheme derived from a play, poem, painting, or element of nature (somewhat *Impressionistic*). Among the many "Impressionist" pieces are the remarkable "Au Bord d'une Source," "Le Jeux d'Eau a la Villa d'Este," (indeed played constantly in the Villa d'Este in Tivoli; water flow serving inspiration to many composers later) and "What One Hears on Top of a Mountain" - titles that sound almost Impressionistic. Debussy (1862-1918) was the true expression of Impressionism in music and his extensive use of other scales, among them pentatonic and far-eastern; Debussy on art *We must agree that the beauty of a work of art will always remain a mystery [...] we can never be absolutely sure "how it's made." We must at all costs preserve this magic which is peculiar to music and to which music, by its nature, is of all the arts the most receptive."* His "symphonic sketches," the result of his opinion that "since Beethoven, symphonic work has become formulaic, repetitive..." is a marvel of impression and abstraction, like "La Mer" or the opera "Pelleas and Melisande." He wrote no symphony.

RICHARD WAGNER

Toward the end of the romantic era, Richard Wagner (1813–83) practically exhausted the limits of tonal music and chromatics. Wagner, another musical titan, left behind a new concept, new musical and artistic styles and potent operas. He invented a new musical language, which he termed *Gesamtkunstwerk* (integrated art form), his ideal work of art, somewhat after the Hellenic concept. While Verdi and the 19th century Italian-French operas presented stories about real people and real-life events, Wagner's music was inspired by symbolism, almost all of it drawn from mythology. His works were about events and characters from the world of "no place, no time," eternal and symbolic, and based on much Germanic mythology (his Ring Cycle especially). Wagner's music - an attempt to emulate the Greek ancient theater - eliminated the aria and flowed across an entire act, which in his compositions could last up to two hours. He called his operas musical-dramas and brought the opera to a zenith of structural complexities, both in scope and style. His orchestration, texture, harmonics, and leitmotifs - musical phrases that represent ideas, characters, or physical objects - ushered musical complexity into a new peak and opened a new highway in the development of modern music. Wagner's complex orchestration makes him Beethoven's true heir, given the immense increase in scope and sound-richment he delivered. Indeed Wagner considered Beethoven and Carl Maria von Weber his great influencers and specifically in opera, Weber's "der Freischutz". Without Wagner it is impossible to imagine the next generation of innovators: Mahler, Richard Strauss, and Stravinsky. He seems to have exhausted the edge of chromaticism and tested tonality; he coupled it with his genius to compose for the human voice and bring orchestration to an apex of richness and tonal expression. This music, which achieved a pinnacle of lyricism and chord structure in "Parsifal" and "Tristan and Isolde" (the Tristan-chord may be the most famous in all of music), is a marvel of structure and architecture. Tristan, perhaps another milestone of atonal music (the Tristan-chord is dissonant), is written as a musical flow structure that never resolves, until the last chord (5 hours later). The musical sentences continue their irresolution to the end, perhaps symbolizing the roman between him and Mathilde Wosendonk, a passionate roman that was probably never consummated. Also, its rhythm is sometimes difficult to resolve (for example, in the overture). The piece is a great mystery from beginning to end, both key signature (a-minor) and rhythm (6/8) somewhat disguised, fuzzy, specifically unresolved. Wagner wrote his own lyrics and his racist ideology made him a most controversial, sometimes revolting historical personality. His music however is really a Beethovenian extension of a climax of structure, complexity, and intellectualism. If one can separate the vile personality from the man's art, a performance of Tristan or Parsifal can be the most cathartic musical experience and absolutely the greatest music out there. Wagner's works became a new cult-religion of sorts, and many of us still travel to the ends of the world (and Bayreuth, where he built a temple of music) to attend the marvels he created.

Thereafter, while the Germanic music center continued to strive in Vienna, musicians turned increasingly toward atonality, and music entered modernity. The contemporary age of complexity developed under Wagner's sway demonstrated exploration and abstraction of the chord, timbre (represented in the music of Mahler, Debussy, Schoenberg, Stravinsky, and later Bartok or Poulenc), with elements of new tonality. As mentioned before, the more modern musical style was another way at describing the world, with less inhibitions and better potential. If the previous classics focused on the melody and stayed loyal to the harmonic path, the newer looked for a certain liberation, a new way to describe the world and the world of sound. It was more cognitive, less restrictive and we loved some of it. Stravinsky specifically focused his music on rhythm; his orchestrations very rich and making the rhythm their central theme, especially in the ballets that catapulted him to international stardom. Schoenberg embraced the dissonance and formulated a motif without a central underlying melody and successfully extended the allegedly opposing styles of Brahms and Wagner, which fomented much fury (opposing camps fighting, promoting and criticizing the other hero, one Eduard Hanslick very well known, possibly the model for Wagner's Beckmesser in Meistersingers) in the Viennese musical society of the late 19th century. Schoenberg's innovations personified structure in atonality, specifically in developing the twelve-tone technique, a method that manipulated an ordered series of all twelve notes in a chromatic scale. The music was composed without a traditional central scale. Musicians have experimented with other scales beyond the Ionian and Dorian. New instruments were added to the orchestra, such as Stravinsky's expanded percussion section that borrowed from African music.

20TH CENTURY

The 20th century brought a new group of revolutionary composers, their music sounded different, mostly more difficult and strange to our ears. Musicians decided to unshackle their compositions from the limitations of the past, harmony, melody, rhythm and key. Proponents were Schönberg (whose name alone scares many of us; his purpose was artistic expression and aesthetics had a lesser importance), Prokofiev, Stravinsky, Shostakovich and Bartók and their followers. Stravinsky was a revolutionary that introduced much rhythm, heavy orchestration and rich percussion across a long career. Béla Bartók gave us a taste of eastern music (incorporating elements from Turkey, Bulgaria, and Rumania) and integrated such rhythms into western modes. He is specifically known for his many piano, opera, and instrumental compositions and the marvelous "Concerto for Orchestra," a magnificent piece worthy of our effort.

During the world wars and other horrors that occurred during the 20th century, musicians sought new expressive modes. Life had become too taxing, too terrifying; humanity has shown a new monstrous face, it was not possible to continue composing in the traditional genres, which in some ways may have also been exhausted. The oppression of despotic governments, the realization of what people could do to each other by dint of racial ideologies, concentration camps, death marches, and gulags necessitated new modes of expression. As the West faced a new historical crisis, especially after WWI (see reference 113), music had to climb another level of abstraction to describe an even more complex world that could not have been imagined before. The flower of youth in Europe and the colonies were gassed and murdered in the trenches on the western front. Intense atonality had to develop, from early Schoenberg and Stravinsky to composers of the generation of Olivier Messiaen's "Quartet for the End of Times" - composed in 1941 when he was a prisoner of war - to express depths of feeling and desperation that no one could have imagined before and dwarfed visions of the apocalypse that had been expressed so brutally by painters of the Renaissance. The 20th century, when technology was mobilized to destroy millions of innocent human beings, naturally triggered new artistic expressions.

Music is always emblematic of expressing and representing the spirit of the current time. After the Bolshevik revolution, Lenin's party decisively subjugated composers to the proletariat political dogma. Many of the most gifted Russian composers left the country and settled in Europe or America (Prokofiev, Rachmaninoff and Glazunov among them). Many decided to stay (such as Shostakovich and Khachaturian) and suffered the party's high-handedness. For example, during the early 1920s, Glazunov complained that he was running out of paper, while Shostakovich - the brightest star in the Russian modern musical firmament - suffered condemnation, humiliation, and terror. The Bolshevik leadership recognized the influence of music on the totality of life and how deeply Russians took it; through political dogma they tried to force their beliefs on artistic expressions. This still occurs today; music has come to be considered a social force, even an ideological one, beyond mere entertainment.

After the 1950s and 1960s, with the passing of the older modern greats, music entered a "contemporary" period. Composers wrestled with another fundamental issue that was already 50 years old; why continue to create within the strait-jacket of the classical genre format or even the strict rules of harmonics, specifically of the 12-tone chromatic scale? Romantic composers had stretched these concepts to a limit; why not go all the way? Expressive methods could embrace dissonant and atonal structures. It is difficult to gauge the influence of newer music from the likes of Ligeti, Crumb, Stockhausen, Cage, Esa-Pekka Salonen, Jack Haggie or John C. Adams, considering that our vantage point is recent and therefore, unclear. The music is sometimes difficult for listeners, and many have leveled criticism at the composers or on the other hand, at conservative orchestras that, to attract a wider patronage, do not dare to stray from the traditional musical canon. The difficulty and complexity inherent in the contemporary modern genres are evident in the music and help make the point that this is *modern*; orchestras sometimes have to cater to their loyal but more conservative customers. Such music is challenging to enjoy, for many, without a deep understanding of its underlying theory and a willingness to embrace complete artistic openness. In some cases, the experience might be too cognitively enigmatic. Even Schönberg did not expect his music to be pleasing the first time around. Composers are striving to create - they must try, despite it not being easy - new venues and departures from the melodic past to develop a complex, intellectual future music. Is this music cerebral instead of visceral? If so, are these not the ultimate symbols of cognition? Not easy to judge when so many of us have no understanding of this artistic expression and are turned away.

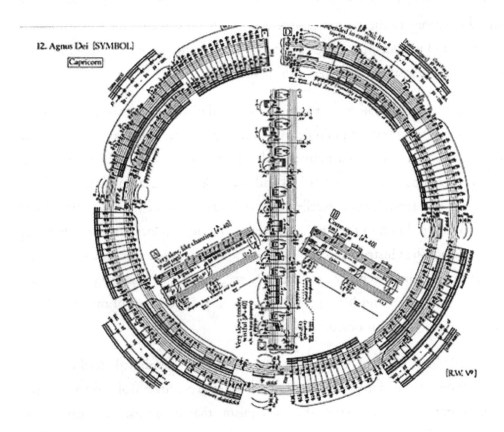

Figure 12: Roger Crumb, graphic score

We might not comprehend art like this, but still support the search for new pathways in musical expression. Just listen to John Cage's piece, 4'33" of silence, during which the audience is exposed only to ambient sounds.

Contemporary opera seems to be moving toward a "total production" that makes music a part of an integrated show (the "production"), exemplified by "Moby Dick" by Jake Heggie or "Rappaccini's Daughter" by Daniel Catan (Mexican composer). The opera genre has been aided by technological advances, among them lighting, laser projections, video, and 3-D presentations. Stage directors have become centrally important in opera and other theatrical productions. These comprise signs of the artistic integration of musical and visually aesthetic experiences. Postmodern music has employed new technologies for sound processing and presentation, among them electronics (used by Stockhausen, among others), sound recordings (including animal sounds), specialization (such as 3-D components), unusual timbres and further tonal exploration. It is the nature of art to explore, change, and add dimensions to the artistic experience. Artists must search for new expressive avenues, and it seems that cerebral experience is a major theme in modern music, more than the aesthetic experience for many ears.

Modern sound quality, the richness of musical diversity and vast content of the past four centuries - a variety of styles and forms, and our recording and reproduction capabilities - have achieved marvelous levels and quality; superior instrumental sound (live concerts, the concert hall and opera do not use amplification) and in recording and reproduction excellence. If only the old masters could have had an opportunity to listen to their music played by modern orchestras on finely tuned and well-polished instruments. Our current access to music is instantaneous. Just imagine that a mere century ago, the only access to music was live performance. Today, every phone and MP3 player contains hours and hours of music and web access ensures variety is practically infinite.

Music has perennially been an art form that combined aesthetics and abstraction - it aimed to please our senses within the confines of absolutely abstract expressions. We may not know the mechanisms that act on us, but music has an immense effect on our soul and mood. People are ready to go to the end of the world to listen to an ear-deafening Rolling Stones concert or, on the other hand to a Verdi opera where absolute silence is expected. Over the past three or four centuries, music entered a highly cerebral or cognitive era. Standards have been established; we follow musical and harmonic rules, traverse increasingly complex harmonics and, in modern forms, aspire total abstraction. This amalgamation has allowed combining emotional expression with musical architecture that explores scale combinations, musical tonality, harmonization, melodic structure, and a wealth of instrumental timbres. Musicians have continually aspired to create better emotional and cognitive expression in their compositions. Currently, in postmodernism, when new sounds are explored, it is difficult to forecast the directions music may turn. We must expect change, and farther exploration even if some musicians are turning back to tonality. Perhaps we can expect an integration of genres and styles as the world comes together and gravitates toward increased complexity and intellectual content, subject to shrinking distances and better communications between civilizations.

Like all historical trends, music does not evolve linearly, nor at a constant rate of change. Music has seen periods of great change and periods of digestion, consolidation, and sometimes digression, during the overall evolutionary process. Musicians' station in society, until the classical era was quite low, and the effect of nobility's taste and religion's dominion over music was almost total. Western music after the Greco-Roman period stagnated or may even be said to have stepped back from its abstraction as religious forms took control. The effect of the social order combined with the church's natural conservatism is unmistakable. This could be interpreted as a step back; we are never guaranteed that each step takes us forward! The earliest religious music took place during times of aversion to change due to the nature of the conservative authority that held sway. However secular music re-emerged (13-14th century) and led to great innovations over the past millennium, as evidenced in musical theory, new genres, advanced instruments and tuning, and the rise of harmonic complexity and composition. When the yoke of the church loosened, specifically during the last 500 years, musical disciplines manifested clear developments in every way, including higher-quality instruments, improved timbre, tuning accuracy, and a great increase in the complexity of the structure, chords, orchestration and musical form itself. Tuning accuracy challenges throughout the Eurasian continent found a marvelous solution in the tempered-tuning system of the 12-tone scale, but the tuning frequency standards (such as establishing middle A4 = 440Hz) were formalized only toward the end of the 19th century. And they keep creeping up (A4 used to be 432Hz).

In 1802, Beethoven wrote to a friend that he was on a "new path." It took a couple of years to clear that path, but it led to the "Eroica" (No. 3), the 5th, and the "Pastorale" (No. 6), which changed western music forever. His Symphony No. 5 (in C minor) became the symbol of victory (the letter V in Morse code is ●●●–); its structure broke with musical traditions. It lacked a clear melody, perhaps signifying not only the struggle of the individual, the hero artist against a hostile world, but also hope. Later, Debussy, Stravinsky, and Schönberg ventured beyond established classical forms altogether. Their music and what followed cannot be fully comprehended without their intellectual components that span beyond musical theory. Today, like most other art forms of the last two centuries, music has reached a "mindful," intellectual phase. Many of the modern pieces are not "easy to digest." Modern music must be analyzed, understood to be enjoyed. E.T.A. Hoffman wrote some 150 years ago, "What if music difficulty is with you and not the composer?" Is contemporary music facing the same questions and an ever-increasing complexity and structure, or are modern artists seeking a new path that can be better understood and appreciated by popular audiences? Current audiences' verdicts are not good; sad to say, classical music and opera are in serious decline except in the Germanic countries.

Classical music could not compete in popularity or funding with more accessible forms of dramatic music like jazz, pop, or rock, and therefore, it was inexorably pushed into the minority, even though recently the Met HD (Metropolitan opera High Definition opera in movie theaters) boasted an audience of millions for its broadcasts. Today more than ever, *musica-seria*, the so-called "classical music" and its critics are shaped by professionals and a declining number, but perhaps more educated, eager to follow audience. The art form struggles to be relevant and to advance. In a nod to good music not having actual boundaries, many of the most skilled popular bands, particularly in jazz, movies and instrumental groups constantly borrow from the classics.

Jazz was born as an African-Caribbean-American art form, forged on classical, African, and Creole music and rhythms. Jazz is a bright comet among our artistic genres. Developed by natural musical geniuses (Louis Armstrong, Charlie Parker and many others) without intervention by the established musical community of the United States, it evolved quickly in the first half of the 20th century. The greats include, Louis Armstrong, Sidney Bechet, Duke Ellington, Charlie Parker, Miles Davis and others were the trailblazers who charted this new genre. Swing was music to soothe the soul. Charlie Parker continued in mid-century to push the envelope through his incidental interpretation of tempo changing, interpolation, rapid chord progressions, and complex melodic lines, which represented an altogether new musical form. The style he developed had never been heard before; his career encompassed a true moment of artistic magic. The next generation of jazz greats, led by Miles Davis and John Coltrane, focused on the sheer tonality of their instruments. They were key figures in jazz's evolution, spectacular not only for their innovations, but also for their unusual control over the sound and for developing free jazz in the 1960s. In modern times, jazz seems to be merging into the classical thread and many younger performers have a very strong classical education. By the 1970s, musicians like pianist Bill Evans produced sound and tonality very similar to modern classical. During the century since jazz's inception, the art form has transformed from Armstrong's amazingly clear and magnificent pieces, through Parker's transformation, to Miles Davis' introspections. Jazz has become more complex, more convoluted, and not as easy to listen to and absorb, paralleling classical music and all of art.

Our listening method has also undergone a revolution. The modern concert hall etiquette rejects crowd participation, a controversial issue in some circles. Such concerts also command a very high-ticket price, especially for opera performances. Perhaps this stems from the rise of the superstar, lavish productions, competition with other musical genres, or maybe the recording industry. The paying crowd has become more conservative and more selective, while a new generation of conductors and managers is forcing the issue and introducing new modern pieces. This is not exclusively the purview of current conductors and managers; new music has always had its champions throughout musical history. We acknowledge that atonal music might never feel like "second nature," but neither will the math nor concepts of quantum mechanics. The next generations maybe smarter and more adaptable when they are exposed to the new, richer tools available to composers. The true revolution in listening has come with technology that gives us an opportunity to listen to any music, any time!

Thomas Mann's Adrian Leverkühn (from his novel *Doctor Faustus*) was wrong; music does not have to emerge from the cold darkness. It can and does emerge through thought, abstraction, and cognition in the hands of musical geniuses with a special sense of aesthetics and artistic expression. Music has a magical influence over our soul, not necessarily by the "devil" as some have opined. Today, the digitization of music enables endless distribution. Music files representing every genre and every period are available cheaply on the web or in music stores. Very high-quality recording technology, coupled with popular distribution networks and compression techniques, make music very affordable for the home, in the car, or multiple other mobile applications. Voice reproduction technology is excellent and ubiquitous. It is a vast market the old masters could not begin to have imagined. Music is available in so many interpretations by countless artists that can be studied, compared, and analyzed.

The quality and durability of artistic expressions are only tested over time. We must wait for future generations to judge music's modern expressions. In the meantime, composers will further explore classical music, perhaps making it still harder to grasp or understand, and critics may accurately describe some composers as "musical thinkers" or "music intellectuals." Let us hope that is this a compliment.

6.6 COMMUNICATION AND ENTROPY

The fundamental problem of communication is that of reproducing at one point either exactly or approximately a message selected at another point.

Claude Shannon

While animals and humans started to communicate from time immemorial, the formulation of a theory of communications and information is a very modern concept, the product of the 20th century scientific revolution.

Communications of any type requires a language and Alphabet. Earlier, various symbols of longer distance communications included: flags (Semaphore), colors or positions, fire and such. Great progress towards a system that obeys the laws of modern communications, mostly by intuition and common sense, was devised by Samuel Morse (1836) and others; the system was based on genius intuition and one that is popular until this day. Morse and his colleagues developed the Telegraph (sending electrical current on long electrical lines) and decided on an alphabet that will be practically binary, it included only 2 letters, ON-OFF or the dash and the dot. The great step that was taken next was a statistical analysis to determine the occurrence of the various letters for the Morse code for maximizing transmission efficiency - how to minimize the message size for the most efficient transmission. Thus, the common letters are short, for example E, has the shortest symbol (just one dot). This was done intuitively with some statistics from the used language (many letters have marginal use, they were the longer), without the mathematical rigor of information theory that came later, but the intuition and common sense has proven to be quite optimal.

International Morse code for Latin letters and numerals

A	·—	J	·———	S	···	1	·————
B	—···	K	—·—	T	—	2	··———
C	—·—·	L	·—··	U	··—	3	···——
D	—··	M	——	V	···—	4	····—
E	·	N	—·	W	·——	5	·····
F	··—·	O	———	X	—··—	6	—····
G	——·	P	·——·	Y	—·——	7	——···
H	····	Q	——·—	Z	——··	8	———··
I	··	R	·—·	0	—————	9	————·

Figure 13: Morse Code

The development of systematic information theory started only in the beginning of the 20th century (Nyquist, Hartley, Wiener) and received its mature mathematical formulation in 1948 when Claude Shannon published his seminal work on the nature of information. Before Shannon, much work has been done as radio transmission increased its popularity in an exponential manner. Various modulation techniques have been devised for the transmission of sound, data or video, first analog and then digital. The representation of an analog signal by digital encoding became theoretically very well known if not yet popular in the 1960s. The advantages of digitization (storage, data manipulation) became clearer in time.

Shannon developed a comprehensive mathematical model for the nature of information and the transfer of information from a source to a destination efficiently.

Communications technology face two fundamental challenges: A. Information sources usually contain much "redundancy." Efficient communication should remove as much as possible of the redundancy (Morse code is doing it well, in modernity we use MP3 for sound coding and others for video, with reasonably (little) cost in quality). This process is called Source Coding. B. Communications is usually done within a noisy environment (who does not remember the "Whisper" game when we were young). Methods should be developed to optimize transmission and reception (**modulation and demodulation**) and correct errors that might occur during the transmission (or recording, like magnetic tape or even solid-state memory). This procedure is called Error Correction (in digital).

Shannon correlated his information measure with Entropy. In the previous century, much work was done on the theory of Thermodynamics and the concept of Entropy was born (Clausius - 1860s, Boltzmann – 1870s). Entropy was devised to describe excess heat generated in thermodynamic processes and was later correlated with a measure of disorder. Shannon realized that the transfer of Information bears similarities to Entropy. When information is transferred from location to location its fidelity can only be destroyed. If the scientists of Thermodynamics proved that when energy is transferred from one form to another, it must be at the cost of some extra wasted heat (rise of Entropy); in the case of Information, Shannon formulated transfer in noisy channels and the measure of the information contents in the source. Such errors are the measure of disorder that happens in the process of transmitting information from a source (radio station) to the destination (a car driver some 10Km away). Shannon went to define the Entropy of an information source with alphabet xi, with a probability of occurrence p(xi), by $E=-\sum p(xi) \log(p(xi))$. This term has a maximum value for p(xi)=.5, or when the probability of 0 or 1 are equal at .5. This is rather intuitive because the information contents of uneven probabilities diminishes and goes practically to zero when the probabilities are heavily skewed (if the source generates 99 "1" for every 100 data bits, it is easy to guess the next one, hence little information). The extension of the theory enables to measure the capacity of channels to transfer information with good fidelity.

The theory of communications is well developed and matured today, with numerous standards for both source coding (Hoffman, LPEG, MPEG for images, sound) and error correction. Source coding allows us to eliminate redundancies, hence "compress" the bit stream that comes out from the source.

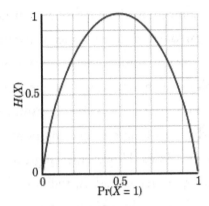

Figure 14: Information contents of a binary source with varying p(x)

Consequently, much work was done in error correction codes and the various techniques necessary to process them, to lower errors on the communication channel.

RADIO

The science of the Electromagnetic waves started in earnest towards the end of the 18th century (Ohm, Cavendish) and later by physicians like Oersted, Ampere and tinkerers like Faraday who contributed mightily to the development and applications of magnetic flux and its effect on coils that carry electrical current and eventually – electrical engines. These early devices enabled the development of simple apparatus for the telegraph, but the integration of the Electrical and Magnetism into a unified theory happened only late in the 19th century when Clerk Maxwell (1831-1879) postulated one of the most universal laws in physics, the Maxwell Equations (later evolving to quantum Electro-dynamic). These set of differential or integral equations (4 today) are mathematically beautiful (for those who love that kind of simplicity and symmetry) and believed to describe the complete behavior of the Electromagnetic phenomena. Maxwell, one of the titans of Physics demonstrated that his equations formulate a wave that propagates in space at the speed of light and that the equations are correct for the whole

Electromagnetic spectrum – from radio to light and beyond. Based on Maxwell's equations' predictions of "radio waves" (circa 1865CE), Hertz followed with experiments that proved their existence (1887CE) and their propagative properties. A giant revolution was in the offing, wireless communications - first terrestrial radio and then via satellites. Communications across large distances became possible and practical. Thereafter, Marconi and other pioneers invented the radio and enabled true distribution of information across very large distances (early 1900s), on mobile devices. Radio technology for military and commercial usage developed quickly. The technology of HF radio band (2-30MHz transmission, still used by Amateur radio operators) was the very long-distance solution, until the development of satellite technology in the 1960s. However, even greater revolution started in the early 20th century with commercial radios, then only recently with the merging of computer, wireless and web technology into mobile communications that have revolutionized life in modernity. We are practically connected to the "Cloud" all the time and anywhere, mostly wirelessly, and therefore, in communication with the world and information sources all the time. These tiny devices, the cell-phone, are a marvel of technology, sophisticated platforms that keep developing quickly and find new applications on a daily bases.

The evolution of the complexity of both the modulation schemes and the Internet networks is immense and continues to evolve and grow. Wired solutions use both cable and fiber technology capable of delivering terabyte/second information on a single fiber and this technology is migrating towards optical interface, while the challenge of density in the wireless systems was resolved by the concept of "cellular," which enables spectrum re-usage.

The challenge of serving millions of users on a relatively narrow spectral bandwidth, which has to be allocated by the FCC, drove to the brilliant cellular solution and the development of the mathematics of Queuing Theory that deals with various protocols that optimize the capacity of a network, see ref. 271.

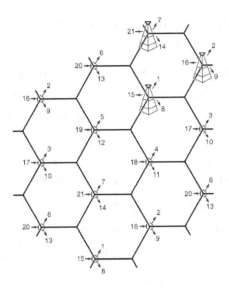

Figure 15: cellular network frequency reuse

PC + WEB

After WWII and with the invention of the transistor and later, the integrated circuit, electronics entered a very fast evolutionary process. Usage of electronic circuits in so many applications gave rise to a historical technological boom that continues to accelerate. Digital circuits started to store immense chunks of data, a technology still growing quite quickly. Memory "sticks" containing 256GB are now (2016) common and double in size every year. Soon, digital circuits that performed basic arithmetic and logic functions were born and with them the computing machine. Thereafter, computers grew in size and scope, until the Personal Computer was born, only 35 years ago (1980s). While the computer serves so many purposes, the need to communicate started the evolution of computer networking (Queuing) theory and with it the fast spread of the World Wide Web. The world had turned digital and it was a vast revolution in technology, life and thinking. Technology took over almost everything, from work to leisure, from research to advancing the arts. Digitization of our technology and computing machines has turned our presentations into numbers, numbers that can be processed and manipulated. It was obviously a great Cognitive revolution and our ability to model almost everything improved immensely. Storing and manipulating numbers is much easier than doing so to analog signals; in-spite of the analog nature of the world, we have quickly found that digitization brings immensity of advantages.

Once images were digitized, a new industry of image processing has been emerging for both entertainment and science. Many sensors were developed to sense the environment and provide data: sound to flow, vibration, temperature and the many sensors that are being developed for monitoring nature, the environment and our body. Soon, these sensors will communicate with our cell-phones towards a new medical technology.

The Web, or the Internet, a vast system of interconnecting computer networks started circa 1990 and is now the central means for storing, distributing and processing information. Interestingly enough, though instigated by military and security, the network developed as an entrepreneurial private system with numerous contributors. For all practical purposes, all of humanity is already connected via the web, even if not every person has access or mobility yet. As of 2010, the web enjoyed >2B users and we are already seven years later. There are already more than 2B cell-phone users in the world. The capacity of the Hibernia Atlantic cable system alone is in the order of 8Tb/s (or 8×10^{12}bits/sec), and growing. The Internet of tomorrow is planning delivery speed of up to 100Gb/s to the home! In the meantime, the cell-phone and smart phone (2000s) were born, together with wireless radio protocols that allow mobile connectivity from almost anywhere. They constitute today a vast system of hundreds of millions of such nodes (the cellphone) that improve speed and quality constantly. Such vast networks can only be managed by computers for the very high complexity of the network. Remote areas can use satellite access. All this is done with extreme economic efficiency, while many protocols and services (like WiFi) are free.

The computer, being a computing machine operating extremely fast on arithmetic and logical functionality is beginning to manage most of our daily routines. Artificial Intelligence (AI) already enables the machine to read, speak, respond to voice command (products like Echo or Home are already economical to the consumer and have on board excellent speech comprehension), analyze images and of course store and manage vast amount of data. In the developed world, most of the "hard labor" is either being exported or soon to be performed by machines. Technology application and penetration in agriculture, manufacturing and service is already threatening the "labor markets." The developed world has already transformed into a "service economy." Even weapon systems become automated and guided by electronics and sophisticated machines that can collect and process data much faster than we can. Missile systems defend against missiles or bombs are already operational!

Muscle is quickly giving way to Cognition!

THE "CLOUD"

With the introduction of Satellite communications (1960s) and later the cellular network, the advantages of digital communication became evident; the age of computing arrived (for the consumer, in the 1980s) and the same scientific theories, both of coding an information source and correcting erroneous data, has been applied (Cellphones, mobile devices, Computers). Currently, this connectivity that enables storage, processing and communications has been delegated to a vast network that is "remote" and has recently been termed "the Cloud." This technology, of quick emerging utility (all the tech giants are racing to increase serviceability as life moves from the real to the Cloud) has revolutionized life and the attention or occupation we have with the electronic media; cellphones, tablets or laptops have basically taken over our lives. Cloud personal computers rely on cellular-connectivity and come with a limited local memory (today usually 16-256GB) that is sufficient for only local purposes, the rest is assumed to be residing in the Cloud, the practical residue of human knowledge on computer servers and other storage media. The Cloud, also known as Cloud Computing, a technology, which is just forming and maturing, is not only the repository of human knowledge and data, not just a huge memory bank. It is rather a vast distributed system of knowledge, communication and information processing of a gigantic, unprecedented scale. With the application of Artificial Intelligence (AI) as a means to manage, communicate and process its information, the Cloud is a vast network of nodes that is almost independent of human activity (managed by computers) and capable of processing and delivering information at a rate completely inconceivable to our brain. And the Cloud capacity and utility are growing exponentially, by the day; soon 5G wireless will be introduced with x100 the capacity of 4G! Steadily, our total data and knowledge and its access are moving into the Cloud, as is the communications between the nodes. On the evolutionary path, many communications and processing technologies have been devised (and continue to do so as the process is still at its infancy). Communities with the best infrastructure to optimize the Cloud and its functionality will be the leaders of the near future and political leaders all over the world understand this and make efforts to participate. Soon, the Cloud (or Clouds because there are currently many Clouds) will be a vast network that connects all humanity, enabling cooperation for all our intellectual activities, as well as disruptions (there are already cyber attacks, which have the potential to cripple financial institutions, industries and military projects). The Cloud is already assuming the nature of the social structure with its human characteristics, local identities, conflicts and progress. Beyond this point, especially with the evolution of AI and the gigantic size of such networks with their vast memory capacity and computing power, we can only speculate its future, but we can already be certain its influence on our lives and evolution will be significant. The information and distribution value of the Cloud for industry, entertainment, learning or finance cannot be denied already. It is already the repository of the largest database of knowledge, art, music and education. Soon, our health will be monitored and adjusted on such networks using bio-sensors and reporting systems. We as individuals already have under our fingertips access to vast information sources that could only be imagined a generation ago. Not only bank accounts or national statistics, but with the help of social networks and large service companies, our personal data and even the day by day are deposited in the Cloud and managed by distributed computing systems.

Only a few thousand years ago, our total information capacity, including the aggregate social memory, was stored in our brains alone. The collective memory of humanity then consisted of the sum of the individual experiences, traditions or mythologies and of course the knowledge contained in our bodies or genetic material, mostly unknown to us until this day. Our bodies contain vast knowledge that has been collected over millions of years and most of it, specifically in the chemistry of the genetic code, is still in the process of being deciphered.

Then, writing was invented. While the written language started to evolve beyond the practical into art, literature and history, the book was not yet available beyond libraries, mainly for scholars. The print was invented only half a millennium ago and the book became affordable and popular only recently. The ease and affordability of the book created a vast revolution and changed human history forever. Even today, there are billions out there who grew up without a single book at home and if there was one book it was the Bible. However, literacy rate has been growing magnificently and the collective Cognition therefore continues to rise. The book, which has been the main source of learning and knowledge in the last millennium, is going through a transformation into electronic media. This makes the book much more affordable, in terms of natural resources, distribution and storage. While our reading capacity is very limited (even an avid reader reads no more than 6,000 books in a lifetime), books are being converted to digital form at an immense rate. Millions of books are already available on the Cloud, mostly free (project Gutenberg, already 42,000 books strong; **book.google.com** claims millions of books and there are so many others coming). Already today, but few years after the invention of the electronic book, which enables downloading all of the classics practically for free (copyright on books is not long, 50-70 years), one can easily travel anywhere with a very small, light package (tablet) that contains hundreds and thousands of book for a small fraction of the cost of paper books. This makes the book and overall knowledge distribution, extremely ubiquitous.

Works of art, music and even a vast inventory of educational courses in every discipline are available, mostly for free on the Cloud.

The utility of the Cloud in everyday or for study and research is just starting to become clear. The Cloud is becoming the space we occupy and live in very quickly. The vast variety of applications, from financial to entertainment, from eBooks to medical sensors, from music to the arts is changing our lives towards the more cognitive experiences.

Obviously, certain risks arise from the technology. Beyond the capacity to destroy and disrupt national services by small, smart groups (terrorists) we are also finding that the technology has vast applications in military domain and even more so in the loss of our privacy. Our privacy has been invaded without the possibility for repair and we are learning every day how bad it is. Suddenly, we are tracked, spied on and exploited not by the government! We have discovered that the many "free" networks, be it search engines or social-networks, have been collecting vast amounts of data about us. These data files have to do with our interests, movement, politics and hobbies, spending habit and practically all we do. If the KGB or others failed because it was impossible to file manually the personal details of every citizen, today the same is done with powerful machines using powerful AI algorithms. Surprisingly, the data is not collected by the government, rather by commercial companies. Initially for profit, but the prospects are too dangerous. We find ourselves too exposed with technology that knows our behavior all too well. And the technology never forgets; all the data is stored forever and there is no escape unless one does not use a computer! These are scary prospects. In oppressive countries like China, the government does attempt to collect such information and be able to attempt to violate our privacy more and more and use such predictions to regulate our behavior. Such prospects are scary.

The lack of regulations, part because the technology is changing so swiftly, part because the regulators can't follow) allowed various companies to take advantage. Consequently, because of the immense power of computing and effective AI algorithms, our computers became personal destinations, targeting individual messages, trying to sell us or influence our political or otherwise decisions.

All this is so new that politicians, mostly still the generation of the "industrial revolution" can't follow the progress and this ignorance is threatening the social structure via technology.

6.7 ARCHITECTURE

"Architecture is the art, which so disposes and adorns the edifices raised by man… that the sight of them contributes to his mental health, power and pleasure."

John Ruskin

"Architecture is really about well-being. I think that people want to feel good in a space … On the one hand it's about shelter, but it's also about pleasure."

Zaha Hadid

The history of architecture is a magnificent edifice of human ingenuity and imagination, driven by the need for practical, comfortable and beautiful physical structures and communities. Most of the structural need was always in utility; but structures have additional purposes, among them reflection of power, authority, pride, aesthetics, comfort and confidence. Architecture is therefore the art of utility and a structure should first be practical, functional and serving its purposes. Many historian and anthropologists consider communities as civilization only if it had developed architecture and great structures.

Architecture embraces many disciplines, but specifically in art and engineering, hence combines functionality and aesthetics. Its evolution could only have progressed with the genius designers who could combine these disciplines, as far as the technology of construction and materials would support. Then, human imagination was added to the drive for purpose (functionality) and glory. From the early pyramids, through the gardens of Babylon, the Hellenic temples, the magnificent Roman monuments and roads, to the Gothic cathedrals, the Renaissance concept of the "City as Art" and the modern marvels, architecture has progressed in style and complexity; it evolved to express the need and the imagination of the age. From the early Egyptian or Mesopotamia monuments, to the intricate and convoluted modern designs of surfaces and interiors, say by Frank Lloyd Wright or Frank Gehry, the path of progress incorporated higher imagination, complexity and awareness; structures that command respect, inspiration and awe. No doubt, technology (from the Roman arch to modern materials and computer-aided design, CAD) provided freedom to the architect, but it was their imagination that fired the rise of complexity as history has unfolded.

Without exception, great civilizations, no matter where or when on earth, always produced great architecture. Some were public gardens, while others served public functions, religious temples or utility structures (aqueducts, amphitheaters, bridges, roads) that have been functional and inspiring for locals and visitors. Rulers and priests wished to build monuments and the people were elated to be represented by these magnificent structures where they could worship or be proud of their community. The process was not linear and the style forever changing.

The pyramid builders were bold, daring and thinking monumental, in Egypt and central America. The Romans were great builders; their daring is still amazing. Immense roads, bridges, amphitheaters and aqueducts were undertaken and completed as marvels of their civilization. Many of them so fundamentally sound that they are still in use today. During the Middle Ages, the Romanesque, heavier style was replaced by the magnificent, elegant Gothic with the vast spans and spires reaching to heavens. During the age of the Humanists in Italy, when man's centrality "replaced" God's, humanists wished to restore and surpass the glory of the Greco-Roman civilizations. New construction techniques were invented and with them new dimensions and styles. The projects erected by the young artists-architects (Brunelleschi, Andrea Palladio, Bramante, etc.) leave us stunned. They were fantastic to behold, producing magnificent symmetry, soaring structures with increasingly complex surfaces that strike the visitor to these days. When freedom of the mind was liberated from dogma, there was no limit to what they dared to do. And if the past was thought along the lines of simple geometrical shapes, modernity has dared beyond; complex shapes are now employed for utility and aesthetics. Why be constrained to simple geometrical forms if we can use a much wider array of complexity? In modernity, architects also added new materials, which freed the planners to design even more elaborate and daring structures. Recently the computer is making inroads into architectural designs, allowing more complexity of surfaces and structure. Of course, modernity introduced another level of abstraction to architecture as it has to all arts. The rise of complexity in architecture is clear, as computer modeling, materials and imagination, allow more abstraction with better materials and functionality.

TECHNOLOGY

The Neolithic people of the Levant used mud-straw clay bricks for building dwelling and burial sites. In the Mediterranean, we find more complex structures using large boulders (the Megalithic temples in Malta are just one example; also found in Ireland, the Caucasus and other locations). Soon thereafter, the Egyptians started to build the pyramids some 4500 years ago. The gravitation towards geometrical shapes is rather natural, the math of antiquity was more geometrical than algebraic (Descartes invented Descriptive Geometry only in the 17th century). The exact building techniques, the materials used - most likely brought from the lower Nile - has been speculated upon for a long time. We know little about the architects or the organization of the masses that did the job, but these were projects of vast scale, admired even in modernity for size and scope; how did they manage such resources? The pyramid was a monument for the ruler and the state, a sign of force and perhaps divination and the burial sites of the Pharaoh. Their existence already points to a high civilization that could muster the planning, resources, manpower and organization to erect such monumental structures. The pyramid of Giza towers to 482 feet, the tallest structure man built for most of our history. It took thousands of years after the first pyramid to build the Hanging Gardens of Babylon, possibly by Nebuchadnezzar at the beginning of the 7ᵗʰ century BCE. We have no evidence of their exact location or structure, but the description given - perhaps somewhat mythical, as there is no archeological evidence for the gardens - already demonstrates more intricate design, with mud and bricks that already included hanging gardens within the physical structure.

The Greek civilization evolved on a different path, with the city and its citizens taking an unusual position of intense participation that evolved during the 4-6ᵗʰ century BCE (Solon to Pericles, the Athenian golden age). Geometric thinking was central to their civilization. It was Plato after all that inscribed the following at the entrance of his academy, "*Let no one ignorant of geometry enter.*" Ancient Greek civilization demonstrates clear civic-architectural (call it city-planning) structure, with the Agora, amphitheaters and the Acropolis, all to serve the community, not just the a few. Much of this archeology exists or has been reconstructed throughout Greece, Italy, Asia-Minor and the Mediterranean. Some of the facilities are still functional, they were built to be beautiful, powerful and to last. The Greeks, masters of geometry, were naturally attracted to geometrical shapes as their mathematicians started to analyze and understand the nature of curved Geometry, Apollonius of Perga (262-190BCE) already coined the terminology for the Ellipse, Parabola and Hyperbola. Both Apollonius and Archimedes (287-212 BCE), two of the greatest ancient mathematicians, were very close to using calculus in their math, which could have revolutionized architecture even more and Archimedes already calculated to very high accuracy (orders of magnitude better than the Bible). And they already knew how to calculate areas and volume of curved bodies - great tools for designers. The technological shortcomings of the age, especially before the invention of the Roman arch, limited span or openings. Some of the structures were very large, and these required dense columns, hence limitation on functionality. The circle was widely used, especially in the magnificent amphitheaters, demonstrating functionality, aesthetics and excellent acoustics. Even today, performances are held in these locations without the need for electronics and amplification. During the Hellenistic period, the overall structure of houses and temples consisted of "upright posts and horizontal beams" for structural support of the massive weight.

Building disciplines and practices were based on experience rather than theory. The math for modeling strength and pressures had to wait another 2000 years. Stone masonry decorated the structures and embellished the Doric, Ionic and Corinthian columns. Building materials were mainly stone, clay, wood and plaster. The Pantheon, built in the times of Pericles some 2,400 years ago is still a marvel of architecture, aesthetics and inspiration for modern designs.

The next evolution of architecture and construction, in shape and scope, happened during the times of the Romans, perhaps history's great builders. The Romans made extensive use of the Roman arch, since then a fundamental structure in architecture; these enabled larger spans and open spaces. The size, scope and range of their construction projects, of which many are still functioning, include roads, aqueducts, bridges, baths, civil buildings, amphitheaters, walls (the Hadrian wall is 117 Km long), triumph arcs and are still an amazing witness to the structural durability and integrity of the design. These are spread all over the Mediterranean in so many locations.

When the Empire collapsed in the 5-7th century CE, the lack of central power to maintain the roads and infrastructure resulted in neglect and deterioration. Many of the structures, specifically theaters, arenas and aqueducts continued to be used, until modernity (the aqueduct in Segovia, Spain was still functional 50 years ago). We are still using Roman building techniques only modernity offers an additional array of materials, mostly glass, metals, fortified concrete and modeling tools that help the designer and allow the engineer to check forces and stability. There are speculations that the Roman cement had advantages over ours, especially in watery environments.

Computer simulation tools today allow the improvement of stability and sturdiness against earthquakes, which was mostly done by adding robustness, thickness and more support in the past.

Romans started to establish architecture as a professional discipline with written literature. Vitruvius' (75-15 BCE) books (10 volumes, more like 10 chapters) on architecture have survived (rediscovered by the humanist Pogo Bracciolini 1414CE). The arch (arc), which the Romans perfected, freed the designer and the imagination and it was to become one of the greatest inventions in the history of construction. Marvelous curved structures were possible. Bigger openings allowed additional imaginative and functional possibilities through the realization that curvature adds stability and strength. This architectural style held in the west, until the High Middle-Ages and later gave way to the Gothic.

In the meantime, the Byzantine Empire and the Muslim civilizations continued the evolution of the construction discipline, adding their own styles during the Middle Ages, while the west was slumbering. In the Byzantine Empire, magnificent palaces and churches were erected, first among them the Hagia-Sophia (consecrated 537CE). In addition, the Empire managed to equip the city with walls that held every attempt to break in, until the development of powerful artillery and the city's fall to the Ottomans (1453CE). Structures increased in their geometric complexity. Brick and plaster were used in addition to stone, in the decoration of important public structures. Classical design order themes were used more freely and imaginatively. Mosaics replaced carved decoration as demonstrated magnificently in Venice, Constantinople and Ravenna. Large complex domes (cupola) rested upon massive piers, while the windows (glass - Alabaster windows is a Roman invention) allowed filtered light through thin sheets of Alabaster, to be later replaced by tainted glass. The magnificent Muslim architecture in Cordoba, Seville and Granada, in addition to Baghdad, Damascus and Iran, demonstrates the influence these civilizations exerted on one another and the cross- fertilization that occurred as their designs became more intricate. The grandiose structures were locations of worship, state rituals, accommodations for the rich and a source of pride and power. A visitor to Constantinople, Cordoba or Baghdad could not withhold their astonishment as demonstrated by chronicles they left. Those cities, centers of commerce, quickly established themselves as hubs for the exchange of merchandise and crossroads for civilizations. There is a sense of safety and security in massive structures.

The Gothic architectural era (the term Gothic initially indicated pejorative disrespect), from the 12th century to the 16th, has gifted us with architectural marvels of the highest degree. Its origin was in the later Romanesque style coupled with pre-Renaissance ideas, with larger ambitions, open spaces and soaring dimensions. At a peak, stood the Notre Dame or the Chartres cathedrals, both of immense intellectual and aesthetic value coupled with very complex designs, interiors and spatial vision. In certain ways, the architects and the builders stretched their imagination and techniques to a zenith that remains unsurpassed. These were possible, due to certain technological advancements, but also due to rising church authority, ambitions and the changing world-view of open spaces and capabilities, combined with a certain spiritual Renaissance of the 12th century (see ref. 43). These created the need for bigger, higher structures, with more openings and free space to inspire the believers and for the glory of God. The structures literally soared to the skies, their spires extending the reach with such beauty and extravagance that it commands awe and spirituality. The magnificent Milano cathedral, built over some six centuries, is witness to the sophistication, complexity and symbolism of such a masterpiece. Some of the arches became pointed, the ribs supporting the roof assumed a specific character and the buttressed ribs were added for strength and support and allowed higher and larger open spaces. Much of the structural support was learned from experiences as the mathematical models were not yet available, but experience coupled with devotion and genius produced monuments that have stood the test of time. The stained-windows told the biblical and mythical stories on marvelous tainted glasses. It was a new and glorious style. Many of these buildings were churches, cathedrals, and monasteries, but the style was also employed in palaces, castles, town halls and even universities that were born at that time. What followed, in the 17-18th centuries, was the Baroque style of architecture and then the "late Baroque" or Rococo, highly ornamented and luxurious.

In terms of design intricacy and attention to detail and embellishment, the Baroque and the high-Baroque achieved a certain zenith, very much as their music. Focus on luxury and embellishment overtook functionality, to please the higher echelon of society. These designs were usually very expansive and expensive and as a statement of wealth and power. A new trend had to emerge that allowed better economy and a certain simplification was required as the Enlightenment started to affect thought and taste. The middle class was rising (18-19th centuries) and with it, new potential for markets and innovations. The wasteful designs had to give way to more functionality, but also at a higher individual complexity. Architecture always advanced in tandem with art and building techniques.

After the 16th century, advances in the technology of building techniques started to liberate the architects and their designs started to follow the natural progression of all the other arts – towards more abstraction. This concept came to fruition only in the last two centuries, concurrently with other art forms, but started earlier with the advance of the scientific and artistic disciplines. New materials, especially metals and combinations of advanced traditional styles, coupled with rising needs, required innovation and expansion in utility. Large train stations, factories and warehouses emerged as well as hospitals and administrative centers. In the US, skyscraper technology required complex engineering and some pre-fabrication, itself a new concept at the turn of the 20th century. New schools and fashions were developed to support the new generation of designers who were now in better-established academic institutions. Concurrently, scientific progress started to put better analysis tools in the hands of the engineer. Material started to be added, like composites and glass, and these provided more tools and flexibility for the designers. Soon, architects started to design much more than structures and industrial design became an independent profession. City planning emerged as a discipline for the design of existing and the future Megapolis. Other disciplines had to be integrated, like sociology, public health and transportation. Architecture became the integrative engineering-art form, like opera (or musical), integrating more disciplines as it evolves.

Architecture entered the age of industrialization. Construction techniques started to form standards along with the professional terminology and drawings that had to comply with international specifications and safety standards. Large construction projects, be it for dwelling or office, had to use industrialization for cost and time.

The Victorian style (2nd half of the 19th century in the UK) was more conservative, drawing on classical styles, but in other places, styles like Bauhaus ("Form follows Function") emerged, focusing on functionality and aesthetics.

Cast iron and steel materials became popular and a neo-classicism style emerged too.

MODERNITY

During the 19-20th century, construction technology advanced so fast that immense projects could be erected relatively quickly because of the detailed documentation, industrialization, design and construction standards. For example, the skyscraper was possible due to industrialization and standardization of the metal structure. Those had a steel frame that supported the external walls. Some early skyscrapers had a steel frame that enables the construction of load-bearing walls. The technology that started around the 1880s, evolved later to skyscrapers characterized by large surface areas of windows, making the building look like a glass structure. Pre-fabrication allows both economy and ease of manufacturing off-site.

Some of the later architects insisted on designing every detail of the structure, including furniture and household items (even ash-trays) and were involved in industrial designs. Frank Lloyd Wright, Alvar Alto, Louis Sullivan, Corbusier and Louis Kahn are some of the designers that influenced the style of the 20th century and beyond. The magnificent glass designs of Alvar Alto, still popular since the 30s, the various furniture designs of the Bauhaus (a new Bauhaus museum has recently opened in Weimar to celebrate its centennial), show the liberation, imagination and abstraction of the designer coupled with functionality. The Bauhaus was born in Germany early in the 20th century (Walter Gropius), which immensely influenced future styles. Bauhaus was seeking simplicity, functionality and utility; the clean line of the Bauhaus style can still be observed in cities across the world; industrial design became a staple. Designs had to be practical and useful with the affordability that comes with mass production. Simplicity was tantamount to design principles, rather than embellishments. The growing middle class created a vast market but supported only the economy of moderate pricing. While the Romans used a certain type of "glass window," mostly Alabaster, industrial glass became a prominent building material only in the 19th century.

Figure 16: Vancouver glass waterfront

During the 20th century, with much better math modeling and materials, architectural genius shone. The circular designs of Frank Lloyd Wright (like the magnificent Guggenheim Museum, NYC), the new columns of the Johnson Wax headquarters and the integration of Falling Water villa demonstrate the freedom and complexity the artist-genius could accomplish. The later improvement of design tools and the advent of the computer, complete 3D rendering, became possible and with them very powerful modeling and more freedom of design. The architect became free and the results are stunning as is demonstrated by projects around the world, bridges (Calatrava), facilities (Calatrava, Gehry), cultural centers, housing, concert halls (Gehry, Jean Nouvel) and monuments. Technology cuts building time by orders of magnitude, while automation and industrial designs are soaring. This genius was extended in later years by the very complex surfaces and spaces so typical to the designs of Frank Gehry or Gaudi earlier. As time progressed, the technology of building provided almost complete liberty to the designer and the results are magnificently convoluted surfaces reflecting a complete freedom of expression and marvel of design that is both complex and abstract. The great scientific and technology advances and the rise of complexity and abstraction have aided modern architects. The modern CAD must aid this level of complexity – computer-aided design by enabling visualization, modeling surfaces and tensions and in many cases, industrialization.

Figure 17: Guggenheim Bilbao, by Frank Gehry

Although, somewhat outside of the traditional architectural space, the magnificent Sagrada Familia temple/statues/basilica in Barcelona (considered by some to be genius, or a bit of a kitsch by others) must be mentioned herein. The Spanish architect Gaudi, an unusual genius, put together a plan for a shrine, or a temple of faith and human ingenuity. The façade is a complex series of statues with an extremely complex interior as is typical of Gaudi's work. This project is still ongoing for Gaudi died many years ago. Not a style favored by everybody, especially those who prefer the simple-line, the monumental project has continued now for more than a century but progress is significant.

With the rise of affordability, modern architecture focused on housing, space design and the combinations of apartments and homes. City real estate became too expensive and apartment house complexes were erected in many suburban neighborhoods. It appears that even such complex multi-apartment homes can be designed with taste and integration with the environment while providing some economy; housing is expensive everywhere and the home usually the great family expense. Our parents, in 1920s Eastern Europe, still did not have in-house plumbing and toilet; this is now unthinkable and many homes include multiple bathrooms to serve the convenience and privacy of the family. The home, our castle, has become a complex space that accommodates many of our needs, from cooking and hosting, to privacy and comfort, with the many electronic devices now in every home. Better materials, greater insulation and temperature control are now required by the need to conserve energy and convert the home to an energy harvesting facility. Solar energy for water heating and for home energy (worldwide) has become a major industry that will replace traditional energy (coal, oil, natural gas) rather quickly. Various electronic devices provide security, cameras, utility and monitor, lighting and appliances, for better economy and convenience. With both partners working, some from home, the functionality of the home must change for function and comfort.

From the cognitive angle, architecture is an engineering, social, communal and art form that evolved from caves to monuments. The history of architecture is the history of mind over matter, the subjugation of gravity to the imagination, devotion, artistic impressions and whims of the human spirit. Over the last five thousand years, the discipline has gone through many phases, but its thrust has always been toward the subjugation of the forces of nature to human imagination and intelligence, with increased spatial utility and complexity. Architecture endures and allows us to appreciate the achievements of civilizations. If architecture's traditional focus was primarily on aesthetics and grandeur, the modern schools stress functionality first. If the building functions well, then aesthetics is part of this function. A nice, comfortable house is the traditional value of every civilization – see Zaha Hadid above. Definitions and functionality have changed over the generations, but a certain value, of functionality and aesthetics always stays.

The great structures of yore, Pyramids, Greek, Roman, Byzantine, Muslim or in the Yucatan peninsula, China, India or the Inca, among so many others, remain forever monuments to the greatness of human spirit. Architecture was always a staple of the civilization that built it.

Architecture is a practical discipline, the art of site choosing, resource planning, structural force calculation, functional details, designing and erecting structures and communities. Later it became the domain of "all the disciplines": social, political, ideological, economic, national, etc. City planning is indeed an extreme example inter-disciplinary considerations that has to do with much more than the structure. In modernity the many considerations include, in addition to the normal, considerations for water utilities, infrastructure, air and pollution, noise-pollution, land usage and open spaces.

Architecture continued to evolve along the same lines as the arts and be influenced by them, with increased complexity and abstraction. Architectural monuments became the symbol and pride of their civilizations and the markers of their advancement. Today many of us travel the world to see such monuments, from the cities or Egyptian pyramids, Greek and Roman urban centers and monuments, Gothic cathedrals and glorious structures of immense volume, complex spaces with ritualistic interpretations.

Then, in modernity, the vast Megapolis that are becoming the great civic centers of the world and the rising cities of the far-east, use pre-fabrication and many green spaces. The new planned cities, especially in China and India, expecting perhaps a billion souls moving from the villages to cities, are using the modern structural techniques, city planning concepts, new materials, complex design, computer modeling tools and sometimes complex and intricate surfaces.

Architecture was always grounded in a certain reality because the structures that could be pondered on paper eventually had to be erected. Brunelleschi had to erect the famous dome in Florence and Frank Lloyd Wright needed to prove that his columns would hold the weight (Johnson Wax headquarters, 1936-39).

The clear path of architecture, from glory to functionality and Cognition has accelerated in modernity, while enabling the usage of more materials, modeling tools and freedom of imagination for the architect and city planner.

7. CONCLUSION

"We can do what we will, but not will what we will."

Arthur Schopenhauer

"We know more than we can tell."

The "Polanyi Paradox"

The history of civilization is a matter of just 300-400 generations. Our genetics change constantly, but not fundamentally during such short time span. This epoch is biologically short, but culturally quite long. If long, why was our progress not more linear, faster? Were there natural hindrances to our advance? Did these emerge from natural or cultural consequences? What can we learn from our hesitations, from the numerous steps back, or from the vast cognitive progress of modernity?

Some 25 centuries ago, almost simultaneously, few breakthrough civilizations emerged almost in tandem: Buddhism that was seeking alleviation from suffering, Confucius that was teaching correctness and social responsibility, the Hellenics were teaching reason, science, aesthetics, math and the foundation of philosophy and Jewish teaching Monotheism and the rule of law. All within about 100 years! How and why did those happen almost simultaneously?

And what is the meaning of progress while religious fanaticism is spreading and we are not ready to own our responsibilities and keep violating the social contract with fanaticism and abusing the Earth, our only home? Are we witnessing a huge Cognitive revolution that is advanced and followed by a minority while the majority is still mired in religious wars, nationalist fever and human division based on frivolous beliefs? Is everything really "relative" and Punk music equal to Bach's quality?

We know from fossil records that our biology has not changed much during the rise of civilization, a time span of few thousand years. However, in recent studies we are finding out that the brain is endowed with an amazing "Elasticity," with the ability to change and adapt in ways we still do not fully understand. We might not be smarter than we were 2,500 years ago, but we can deal with a much more complex world. What we know today is that some 2000 years ago, literacy rate was only for 2-3% of the population and this has not changed much for 1500 years (world literacy was still <15% in the year 1800). Today, universal literacy is within reach; illiteracy is now a curse that exists only in few places on earth.

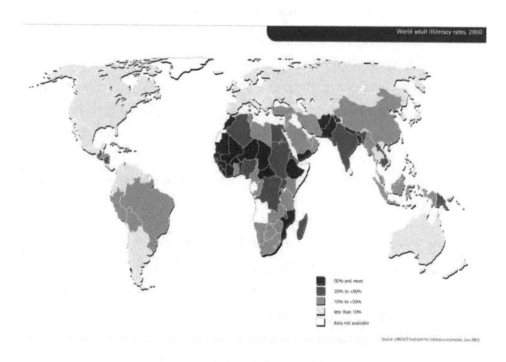

Figure 18: World illiteracy (circa 2000CE)

What has changed? Much did, but we specifically note three fundamental trends:

a. Our civilization has evolved towards a more cognitive and complex world-view and lifestyle. Ideas, knowledge and intelligence take central position; everything is becoming increasingly "mental" and complex. Machines have replaced much of the hard work, while study, research and R&D have become prominent in the interests of people, nations and societies. We are replacing "stuff" with symbols, images and cognitive actions. The more advanced nations turn to services and information processing, away from manufacturing and manual labor.

b.   Many more people participate today than before. The rise of political freedom and meritocracy has enabled the joining of millions into the creative brain-pool of humanity. Leaders have recognized the advantages that mass-education brings.

c.   Our physical challenges, mostly food and health are being replaced by cognitive. Our physical progress, in food production, healthcare and longevity have been swift due to automation and mechanization while the cognitive challenges have come to the fore.

Ours are probably the best times. And yet, some will argue that times could be better, that we are squandering many opportunities for a better world, better equality and better consciousness to our environment. What is becoming clear, is the centrality of Ideas, Thought and Complexity in the annals of human evolution and specifically since the rise of modernity, hence the importance of education. Some of us may even speculate that Complexity is a feature of the universe[318,319]. And we continue to be infinitely inquisitive; just listen to the marvelous questions that children come up with, those that continue to amaze us by both their simplicity and complications.

While we are by nature egotistical and self-serving, we are also creatures driven by a sense of humanity and morality. Morality is of course, not natural; it is rather a wholly human socio-cognitive invention, perhaps driven by natural forces. There have been many disturbances on our "civilized" path: Attila, Tamerlane, Pol Pot or Stalin are extreme manifestations, but eventually they have been washed by the tide of history, even if at the cost of great suffering and tragedies. History requires patience; let the process evolve before we come to conclusions. History is not linear or deterministic, rather a complex process pulled by a million forces that are not always logical, humane or benevolent. One could speculate, based on a long past, that history is mysteriously affected by the magical "morality-wand;" we did recover from Attila, Timur, Hitler and so many others; but there is no magical-wand. Much of the recovery was by sheer luck, sometimes it was razor thin. Our ability to have recovered in the past is no guarantee for the future, there is no "morality-wand". We have been warned.

Traditionally, a personal instinct, religion and religious institutions were the guardians of our morality, but in the 18th century, harking back to the Hellenics, they have been supplemented by philosophy. The American and French revolutions were eventually driven by the ideas of the Enlightenment and these were progressive, universal and cognitive. Perhaps the result of the Great War (1914-1918), our world-view and dreams have been farther shuttered, as was our faith in the leadership. WWI was indeed a monumental catastrophic western event not only because of its carnage, but also because of the lost dreams with not much to replace them, but Materialism. On this path, we also lost religion as western societies started to secularize, away from our traditions. And the west, which has dominated the planet, influenced all. Thus we are threading away from traditions towards a more materialistic and secular views. Technology is fostering many threats by forces that have proven to be pushing us to division and conflict as the 21st century unfolds. With progress come threats that did not exists before: plastics, pollution, GW (seems to be the effect of the last 150 years of industrialization) and materialism. Let us not forget the immense influence that technology has had on modernity and the adverse effects it can have in the future because of the power it might yield in the hands of the few, sometimes driven by envy, hatred or fanaticism.

We have acquired a tremendous amount of knowledge during these few thousand years. Part of this knowledge was accumulated experiences, towards formulating laws: Science, Art, History, Law and Humanity. Consequently, we are in a different state of mind, one that is more open to new ideas yet no less influenced by the past, our environment and the cognitive-cloud. Our brain has been endowed by other fantastic gifts: curiosity and the endless thirst for knowledge. We are finding that our future is coupled with knowledge and that knowledge is a quest unto itself, beyond its applicability. Knowledge gives us power and drive, but we also need to know because "we need to know". We have discovered that the more we know the more vistas are open for questioning and understanding. Knowledge and complexity grow as we march into the future and expand our understanding.

Not everybody was elated by the achievements of modernity, especially in matters of socio-political world-view. Rousseau was an early critic of civilization, so was David Thoreau. One of the more influential thinkers on the threshold of the 20th century, Friedrich Nietzsche, was one of many who passed serious critique on modernity and the ethics of what we call the Judeo-Christian civilization. Nietzsche adored the pre-democratic Greek, which he called the Dionysian-civilization that was driven by instinct and natural powers, the one that was replaced by Platonic-Christian ethics of morality and compassion. Nietzsche had a certain disgust for the homogeneity of modernity and the conformity that comes with democracy and popular religion. Like many others that he influenced - the Anarchists, Foucault, Derrida, Sartre or Ayn Rand (are we sacrificing quality for compliance, diversity?), he thought that western civilization had drifted towards mediocrity, towards focusing on the weak, rather than on the strong, the unique. He is not the only thinker to reject the world-view of history driven by reason, compassion and our adoration of our liberties, a matter that always comes with a price. We are however at a point of no return. Living in nature and being self-sufficient is a solution for few. Our achievements (Rousseau, after all, sent his children to the orphanage) are due to our coming together and erecting civilizations and social-order. Nietzsche notwithstanding, the decadence he mentioned is also a sign of better humanity, of compassion and recognition of the duty to help the weaker.

The most critical challenge facing us today is over-population. Most of the others we face, be it political or environmental, stems from too many of us, the density, the consumption, the pollution we cause! We have no solutions for this conundrum. Religious and political institutions have been silent on the issue, part of which is caused by an impressive rise in longevity. Who will complain about that?

In the developed world, the last few centuries witnessed the rise of social awareness, social revolutions and the immense increase of wealth and its spreading. There are growing numbers of jobs, mostly in services and particularly for the better educated. Our lives, art, tools and science are becoming increasingly complex. If the world has been painted for most of us in Newtonian physics, using Euclidian geometry and intuitive laws, we are learning that the world is much more complex and the math (or geometry) necessarily to comprehend it, of a different level. We find that we can muster the laws of the universe, but not understand or comprehend why they work. There is a limit to our scientific knowledge and that critique is fundamental to our progress. The more we know, the more we find to explore and the more complex it becomes. And this complexity has spread to all we do, from science and art to the economy and the spiritual life. Even the day by day is becoming complex and not easy to manage and fit, by many.

Yet, with all the praise of knowledge and reason, we also acknowledge that the mysteries of life are richer, mysterious; Mystery of Mysteries[327]. That forces we do not understand control our lives, still running mostly as an automata. That the great leaps are achieved by a certain genius or spark that cannot be explained. This is exactly what Wilde meant when he said, *"Education is an admirable thing, but it is well to remember from time to time that nothing that is worth knowing can be taught."* We have learned that science and art require a certain "craft," personal skill that cannot be defined yet. Michelangelo "seeing" David in the marble rock, Beethoven "hearing" the Eroica from within the classical paradigm, or Newton intuiting Kepler laws from the universal law of Gravitation, are just a few brilliant examples. As if they knew even before the work started. But human knowledge and wisdom is a river and, to participate, we must swim in its flow. Some of us are capable of leaping in a way that is not understood, nor is it just the result of knowledge or reason. Shared knowledge is our path to enlightenment; but then, life is even richer than science and knowledge.

There is a sense of decline in the west. Once asked about western civilization, Gandhi shrugged his famous response: *"I think it would be a good idea."* Indeed, at its best, it is a magnificent dream, at its worse, a horrible nightmare. Yet, the product of the hybrid between the pagan Greco-Roman and Christianity has taken us to a long path, including better equitability (never before have so many lived so well) and knowledge. We live in a world where hundreds of millions, even billions, enjoy life quality with housing, excellent services, mass transportation and a great variety of tourism (perhaps the largest industry today) and vacations, public education and safety.

But all civilizations that rise also decline. The old world is tired, while the new seems to hesitate. The combination of lost values, decadence and failing leadership are evident. Oswald Spangler[113] was not the first to prophesize the decline. Indeed, why should we adore western civilization as the one central "Sun?" We know that before modernity, other civilizations led and contributed mightily and they can do so in the future. We have learned some humility and to appreciate other civilizations as we are witnessing the rise of the Asian powers and their massive historical contribution. Especially in the east, the civilizations focused on the mind, its exercises and centrality much before the west. Indeed, the later western thinkers were heavily influenced by eastern philosophies (Schopenhauer, Nietzsche, Heidegger). However, in-spite of Spangler and his prophecies (*Decline of the West*), the west is still a leading civilization with its science, technology, art and wealth creation. So is its political and scientific influence. Only today, the west is more open, sharing and students from all over the world are welcome in western universities and think tanks, to learn and contribute. They bring the influence of their civilization in a world that is much better connected than ever before. No doubt, with the western lever and their own styles, other civilizations are now rising to compete, to contribute. We all know that the center of gravity continues its western move and South-East Asia (China/India) representing almost half of humanity, demand their share under the sun.

When the Napoleonic era was over, in-spite of the ideas of the Enlightenment, the revolutions and the bankruptcy of the old world, monarchs, emperors and tsars still ruled Europe and the old world. But the American Revolution, in-spite of fits and starts, managed to hold; it became a beacon. A European style east, blended by a pioneering spirit of the west, a continent of new style was forming. A new nation was rising, amalgam of races, styles and religions powered by a wonderful Constitution rose to monumental ambitions. A true Democracy of its own style, affected by the ideas of the Enlightenment and a long English tradition, was rising across the pond. The nations of Europe rose again in 1848, only to be squelched again by their old leadership. In America, a mighty civil war would tear the nation apart in order to fulfill the dream of "*all men are created equal*" and later linger towards including "all women" (1919 federal voting rights) too. However, the manifest destiny ambition of a young nation could not be stopped and it was perhaps only symbolic that the US completed the construction of the Panama Canal, to assert itself as a world power (1914). At about the same time, the European powers decided to commit suicide and launched World War I. Indeed, emperors and dynasties were eventually swept away in wars and revolutions. Alas, it proved to be only the introduction to a far more horrific conflict (WWII) that eventually changed the face of the west and the world.

These wars and conflicts also led to the prioritization of science and technology. Vast budgets were invested with the realization that these eventually won wars; they also produced economic power, wealth and progress.

The result is a new world with an average of $10K/capita world average GDP.

No doubt, a more complex world brings its own risks and dangers.

Some of us, with Libertarian political views, have rejoiced in the rise of the large corporations of modernity and their ability to challenge the political hierarchy. Large corporations are not new, but there is a difference. The large modern corporations are mostly cognitive; they are about owning and controlling cognitive properties, Ideas and Data. They invest in the most innovative concepts: AI, Quantum Computing, Genetics, Cloud Computing and those that have the potential to shape the future. Consequently, they will be much tougher to control. This is no more about land or resources, their power and property rest in the Cloud and they can operate from anywhere, anytime. Their power is in the mind, it is the ultimate power of modernity. They are also becoming richer than Crassus, which adds to their power and influence.

Do we have reasons to think that the new corporations will be more benevolent, more socially responsible than the democratically elected political hierarchy? Based on their behavior and thirst for wealth at all cost, one must doubt it and there is an additional danger: corporations are not democratic. The socio-political power they wield will not be offered for debate or choosing and might prove to be socially unacceptable. In the meantime, progress is so swift that political leaders can't follow the technology and therefore leave the field without regulation. This increases the power of corporations even farther. We are already witnessing the gigantic monopolies of corporations like Facebook or Google and there is no stopping.

We have made enormous technological progress and we have begun to understand the building blocks of life itself. We tinker with gene therapy and life modifications. Our machines already perform many functions that until recently, were considered exclusively human and companies like Deep Learning (a Google company) promise to make them a bit more universal, rather than just being able to perform a single task.

But machines do not think, not like us; they have no consciousness or social responsibilities. We, on the other hand, know, and know our place in the world. We live in a make-believe world, something still elusive for any machine. There is no humanity without such a make-believe worlds and it is not clear how machines will interact in our world, when they become more autonomous. Machines, after all, have no soul[321], no morality and no consciousness. They do not know that they are, they just follow algorithms. We are not an algorithm.

Globalization is a conflicted system by its nature. On the one hand, we are most comfortable in our own community; the language, cultures, currency and customs are known and convenient. We care more about our community. On the other hand, the value of globalization has been acknowledged for a millennium and specifically in the last century. Our communications and transportation gave globalization an immense advantage in politics, economy and culture. Thus, globalization is here to stay and we must make room in our little shell for this force because the planet has shrunk and we have global responsibilities. Therefore, the task is to find a balance between our natural tribal urges, fears of the unknown and the real needs of our community and the planet. In addition to economic advantages, many global challenges call for coming together. We have to decide in what way and how to regulate our integration.

One of the dangerous trends only touched-on in this work is the "monetization" of the Cognitive-Cloud. Computing power and AI has made every political campaign, every fund raising and marketing effort, use the tools of the web. The Facebook scandal regarding Cambridge Analytica[314] (the psychological characterization and sale of some 87 million non-complying - actually many more - naive Facebook users) is just the tip of the iceberg. Our privacy has been lost to financial, political and social causes we never agreed to be part of; some of them, via local or international agents are trying to affect our politics and behavior maliciously. Technology is also emerging as a dangerous tool in non-democratic regimes. We are losing our privacy and freedoms.

Specifically in the US, where the web operates almost without any regulations, the situation is critical because matters become only more complex and politicians, many of them from an older generation, have no real grasp of this revolution.

We have learned that our progress depends on our institutions. Among the many institutions we formed, the most critical today is education, our legacy to the next generation. This is the main tool we have to spread knowledge and provide opportunities to many, while improving the prospects of all because the more we know, the better our probability of success and capacity to adjust to a fast changing world.

Certain disciplines are becoming so complex that it takes the length of a career to fully grasp them. Maturity comes at a later and later age, but our peak mental capacity is usually reached when we are young. This is forcing the natural solution; knowing more and more about less and less. We should be careful not to educate towards too narrow knowledge and mindedness. We have seen that technocrats tend to ignore certain responsibilities. The scientists that change the world must be involved in politics and the consequences of their progress. For this, they must be widely educated[339].

We should abort the KISS = "Keep It Simple, Stupid" concept too, while we have a natural tendency to simplify our models, the fact is that we are marching towards a more and more complex world. Our models become mightily complex, no matter if in medicine, transportation, finance, education, weather or cosmology. We must learn to live with this complexity and not leave it in the hands of few.

In the last century we can also point to other fundamental political changes:

1. Monarchies and Empires were replaced by mostly elective systems.

2. The position of the women changed, political, career and gender relations improved.

3. The relative decline of the west and liberation from colonialism.

4. Equalization. The rise of the Asian powers, China, Japan, and India.

5. The rise of world wealth and better overall distribution.

6. The realization of our violation of the earth and world efforts to contain the danger.

7. Globalization. Both economic integration and the mixing of peoples improve economies, communication and understanding.

While we are facing rising challenges, there is no doubt that we have created a vast legacy, so much beauty, knowledge and benevolence and so many reasons to look forward with expectations and hope. Our progeny is left with a complex world but also one pregnant with promise and good hopes.

Civilization and Humanity are not just the great monuments we erected: the Symphony, the Museum, the Bridge, the Dam or the Sport Arena. Civilization is mostly in our day by day: our responsibilities, the education we provide our children and the stories we tell them when we tuck them in. Civilization is also the way we treat other creatures, nature, the planet and one another.

Civilization is becoming more complex but continues to require our defense and attention every day. We were given dominion over the earth, it is both a promise and a responsibility.

BIBLIOGRAPHY

1. Charles Darwin: On the Origin of Species by Means of Natural Selection, 1859.

2. Stephen Jay Gould: Ever Since Darwin, ISBN-10: 9780393308181.

3. E. H. Carr: What Is History? ISBN-10: 9780394703916.

4. Yuval N. Harari: Sapiens - From Animals to Gods.

5. Francis Fukuyama: The End of History and the Last Man. ISBN-10: 0743284550.

6. Samuel Huntington: The Clash of Civilizations. ISBN-10: 1451628978

7. Johan Huizinga: The Waning of the Middle-Ages. ISBN-10: 0486404439

8. Jakob Burkhardt: The Renaissance in Italy. ISBN-10: 9780140445343

9. Arthur Schopenhauer: The World as Will and Idea.

10. Noam Chomsky: The Essential Chomsky. ISBN-10: 9781595581891

11. Ernst Mach: Popular Scientific Lectures. ISBN-10: 1313055190

12. Edward Gibbon: The Decline and Fall of the Roman Empire. ISBN- 10: 0307700763

13. Henri Pirenne: Mohammed and Charlemagne.

14. Stephen Jay Gould: Hen's Teeth and Horse's Toe. ISBN-10: 0393311031

15. Pierre Teilhard de Chardin: The Human Phenomenon.

16. Kissinger: Diplomacy. ISBN-10: 9780671510992

17. Kissinger: A World Restored.

18. Wikipedia: https://en.wikipedia.org/wiki/Money

19. Rupert Sheldrake: The Presence of the Past. ISBN-10: 1594773173

20. Isaiah Berlin: Karl Marx.

21. Isaiah Berlin: The Roots of Romanticism. ISBN-10: 9780691156200

22. Paul Johnson: The Birth of the Modern.

23. Ian Kershaw: Hitler - A Biography.

24. Ernest Kanterowicz: The King's Two Bodies.

25. New thinking: The evolution of human cognition.

26. http://rstb.royalsocietypublishing.org/content/367/1599/2091.full

27. John La Monte: The World of the Middle-Ages.

28. Jared Diamond: Guns, Steel and Germs.

29. Collin Campbell: The Romantic Ethic and the Spirit of Modern Consumerism.

30. Thomas Kuhn: The Structure of Scientific Revolutions. ISBN-10: 9780226458120

31. AMA 3.0: James C. Bennett and Michael J. Lotus.

32. Christine Fielder, Chris King (2006). "Sexual Paradox: Complementarity, Reproductive Conflict and Human Emergence". LULU PR. p.156. ISBN 1-4116-5532-X

33. Joseph Conrad: Heart of Darkness.

34. Howard Zinn: A People's History of the United States. ISBN-10: 0062397346

35. Howard Zinn: A People's History of American Empire

36. Thomas Payne: Common Sense. ISBN-10: 9780486296029

37. Encyclopedia Britannica.

38. Isaiah Berlin: Personal Impressions. ISBN-10: 9780691157702

39. Kenneth Bartlett: The Renaissance, Great courses seminar.

40. Isaiah Berlin: The Proper Study of Mankind.

41. Isaiah Berlin: On Liberty. ISBN-10: 9780199249893

42. David Abulafia: Frederick II - Medieval Emperor.

43. Von Kleist: Michael Kolhaas.

44. Charles Homer Haskins: The Twelfth Century Renaissance.

45. Joseph Strayer: Medieval statecraft and the perspectives of history.

46. Paul Johnson: The Birth of the Modern.

47. Paul Johnson: Modern Times.

48. Barbara Tuchman: The Guns of August.

49.   Barbara Tuchman: The Proud Tower.

50.   Nicholas Wade: Before the Dawn - Recovering the Lost History of Our Ancestors. ISBN-10: 9780143038320

51.   Alex Ross: Listen To This.

52.   Craig Venter: Life at the Speed of Light. ISBN-10: 0143125907

53.   Alex Ross: The Rest is Noise

54.   Justin Barrett: Cognitive science, religion and Theology

55.   Paul Johnson: The Intellectuals.ISBN-10: 9780061253171

56.   Marsilius of Padua: The Defensor Pacis.

57.   Dante: De Monarchia.

58.   Arnold of Brescia – Apostle of Liberty. ISBN-10: 9781625649249

59.   Thomas Mann: Doctor Faustus.

60.   P. J. Proudhon - The general Idea of Revolution.

61.   Mikhail Bakunin – God and the State.

62.   Paul Krugman on sovereign debt: http://neweconomicperspectives. org/2014/10/paul-krugman-still-believes-teh-debt-can-problem-u-s.html

63.   Julian Jaynes: The Origins of Consciousness in the Breakdown of the Bicameral mind. Houghton Mifflin Publishing, 1976, ISBN 0-395-56352-663.

65.   Noam Chomsky: The Essential Chomsky.ISBN-10: 9781595581891

66. Noam Chomsky: On language.ISBN-10: 1565844750

67.   Stephen Hayes: Get out of your Mind & into your Life.

68.   Steven Pinker: The language Instinct. ISBN-10: 0061336467

69.   Justin Barrett: Cognitive Science, Religion and Theology.ISBN-10: 159947381X

70.   Nicholas Wade: Human Culture, an Evolutionary Force. New York Times, March 1, 2010. http://www.nytimes.com/2010/03/02/ science/02evo.html?pagewanted=all HYPERLINK "http://www. nytimes.com/2010/03/02/science/02evo.html?pagewanted=all&_r=0" & HYPERLINK "http://www.nytimes.com/2010/03/02/science/02evo. html?pagewanted=all&_r=0"_r=0

71. Steven Pinker: How the Mind Works.

72. Steven Pinker: Language, Cognition, and Human Nature: Selected Articles. ISBN-10: 0199328749

73. William Jones, Languages: https://en.wikipedia.org/wiki/William_Jones_(philologist)

74. Michael Polanyi: Personal Knowledge, Towards a Post-Critical Philosophy.

75. Leonard Susskind: Stanford MOOC, on Classical Mechanics.

76. Steven Goldman: Scientific Wars, seminar. Great Courses.

77. Steven HawKing: A Short history of Time.

78. Paul Davis: The Mind of God

79. Thorstein Veblen: Theory of the Leisure Class, ISBN-10: 9780199552580.

80. Roger Penrose: The Emperor's New Cloths. ISBN-10: 9780198784920

81. Thomas Hobbes: Leviathan.

82. Otto Weininger: Sex and Character.

83. Teofilio Ruiz: The Terror of History.

84. Richard Feynman: The Character of Scientific law. ISBN-10: 0262533413.

85. Heinrich Hertz: The Principles of Mechanics.

86. Bruno Latour: Science in Action

87. Michel Foucault: The Order of Things. ISBN-10: 0679753354

88. Malcolm Gladwell: The Tipping Point.

89. St. Augustine: Confessions.

90. St. Augustine: The City of God.

91. New World Encyclopedia – web service.

92. Calvin, William H (1998): Competing for Consciousness: A Darwinian Mechanism at an Appropriate Level of Explanation.

93. William Calvin - Ephemeral Levels of Mental Organization: Darwinian Competitions as a Basis for Consciousness.

94. Derek Bickerson: Roots of Language. Karoma Publishers. ISBN 0-89720-044-6.

95. Bickerton, Derek, (1984). The language bioprogram hypothesis, in:

Behavioral and Brain Sciences, 7, 173-221.

96. Derek Bickerton, William Calvin: Lingua ex Machina: Reconciling Darwin and Chomsky with the Human Brain, (2000).

97. Ken Mogi: Darwin and Consciousness, 2008, http://origin-of-consciousness.blogspot.com/2008/04/darwin-history-and-consciousness.html

98. Thomas Nagel: Mind and Cosmos, Oxford University Press, 2013.ISBN-10: 9780199919758

99. Allen Orr: Awaiting A New Darwin, The New York Review of Books, February 7, 2013 (review and critic on ref. 98)

100. Lawrence Krauss: Universe from Nothing. ISBN-10: 1451624468

101. Jan Swafford: Anguish and triumph (Beethoven).

102. Daniel Lieberman: The Story of the Human Body. ISBN-10: 030774180X

103. Niall Ferguson: Empire: How Britain Made the Modern World. ISBN-10: 0141007540

104. Niall Ferguson: The Ascent of Money. ISBN-10: 0143116177

105. Niall Ferguson: The Great Degeneration.

106. H. Kissinger: World-order (2014).

107. Fukuyama: The Origins of Political Order.

108. Richard Dawkins: The Selfish Gene.ISBN-10: 0198788606

109. Thomas Piketty: Capital in the 21st Century.

110. Israeli podcast (Hebrew), Ran Levi, on Indo-European language.

111. John Julius Norwich: A Short History of Byzantium.

112. Joseph Campbell: Myths to Live By.

113. Oswald Spangler: Decline of the West.ISBN-10: 0195066340

114. Ross King: Brunelleschi's Dome.

115. Machiavelli: The Prince.

116. Eric Hoffer: The True Believer.

117. Ian Kershaw: Hitler – a Biography.

118. Peppered Moth: https://en.wikipedia.org/wiki/Peppered_moth_evolution

119. The Federalist papers.

120. http://www.academia.edu/2077108/The_Significance_of_Schopenhauers_Perspective_on_Music

121. Robert Craft: Conversations with Igor Stravinsky.

122. Yuval Harari: Homo Deus: A Brief History of Tomorrow.

123. Malcolm Gladwell: The Story of Success.

124. Wikipedia: https://en.wikipedia.org/wiki/Great_Man_theory

125. The Economist: October 31th to November 6th 2015 issue.

126. Daniel Belinski: The Deniable Darwin.

127. Baldassare Castiglione – The Book of the Courtier (1508-1528).

128. Nick Lane: The Vital Question: Energy, Evolution, and the Origins of Complex Life. ISBN-10: 0393352978

129. John McWorther: The Story of human Language. Teach12.com course.

130. John McWorther: The Language Hoax.ISBN-10: 0190468890.

131. A J. Heschel: God in Search of Man.

132. Niall Ferguson – The Abyss.

133. Freeman Dyson: Origins of Life. ISBN-10: 0521626684

133. Freeman Dyson: Dreams of Earth and Sky. ISBN-10: 1590178548

134. Adam Smith: The Wealth of Nations.

135. John Julius Norwich: Absolute Monarchs (2012).

136. Ernest Kanterowitz: Frederick II.

137. Foundation of Western Civilization – lecture series The Great Courses.

138. J. J. Norwich: A history of Venice.

139. Shakespeare: The merchant of Venice.

140. Friedrick Hayek: The Road to Serfdom.

141. David Agus: The Lucky Years.

142. Bill O'Reilly: Killing England.

143. Mark Mazower: Governing the World: The History of an Idea, 1815 to the Present.

144. JayabrataSarkar: Debating a Post-Westphalian International Order.

Mainstream Weekly, 5/2015.

145. John Julius Norwich: Empire under the Sun (The Normans in Sicily).

146. Doctorow – Ragtime. ISBN:0-449-21428-1.

147. https://www.youtube.com/watch?v=BiKfWdXXfIs

148. http://www.desmogblog.com/nobel-prize-winner-ivar-giaever-resigns-american-physical-society-over-global-warming-stance

149. T. S. Eliot: The Wasteland.

150. Philip Daeleader: Early Middle-Ages, Great Courses seminar.

151. Raymond Trevor Bradley: Charisma and the Social Structure. ISBN-10: 1583480021

152. Paul Davis: The Goldilock Enigma.

153. John Gribbin: in Search of the Big Bang.

154. Steven Greenblatt: The Swerve.ISBN-10: 9780393343403.

155. OrlyGoldwasser: How the Alphabet Was Born from Hieroglyphs.

156. Benedict Anderson: Imagined Communities (2006).

157. Teo Ruiz – The Terror of History.

158. Ian Swafford: Beethoven, Anguish and Triumph (2014).

159. Rousseau: The Major Political Writings of J J Rousseau.

160. Cesare Beccaria: On Crimes and Punishments. ISBN-10: 0521479827.

161. Alan Charles Kors – Birth of the Modern Mind, Teach12.com seminar.

162. Sean Carroll – The Big Picture: On the Origins of Life, Meaning, and the Universe Itself.

163. Steven Johnson – Emergence.ISBN-10: 0684868768.

164. Voltaire: Candide.

165. Voltaire: Letters from England.ISBN-10: 0486426734.

166. Umberto Ecco: The name of the Rose.

167. Bernard Lewis: The Crisis of Islam.

168. Bernard Lewis: What Went Wrong?ISBN-10: 9780060516055.

169. Bernard Lewis: The Religion and the People. ISBN-10: 0134431197.

170. Lucretius: De Rerum Natura.ISBN-10: 0872205878.

171. Tom Wolfe: The Painted Word.

172. John Mortimer: The Rumpole Omnibus.

173. Bashevish-Singer: Satan in Gorai.

174. Tom Wolfe: The Kingdom of Speech.

175. Marvin Minsky: The emotion Machine. ISBN-10: 0743276647

176. Michael Beschloss: Presidents at War (2018).

177. Alex Ross: The Rest is Noise (2011). ISBN-10: 0312427719

178. Balzac – The Talisman.

179. http://galileo.phys.virginia.edu/classes/152.mf1i.spring02/KeplersLaws.htm

180. Siddhartha Mukherjee: Genes - an intimate history.ISBN-10: 147673352X.

181. Michael Lewis – The Undoing Game.ISBN-10: 0393354776.

182. John Julius Norwich: Sicily.ISBN-10: 0812995171

183. Arthur Schlesinger: The Cycles of American history. ISBN0-395-45400-x

184. Stephen Jay Gould: Eight Little Piglets. ISBN0-393-31139-2

185. Voltaire on King David - https://ebooks.adelaide.edu.au/v/voltaire/dictionary/chapter148.html

186. Roger Crowley: Empires of the Sea.ISBN-10: 1400066247.

187. https://en.wikipedia.org/wiki/Pirah%C3%A3_language

188. http://www.bing.com/videos/

189. Michael Corbalis: The Recursive Mind.

190. Fritz: http://www.pnas.org/content/111/20/7224.full

191. https://en.wikipedia.org/wiki/List_of_largest_cities_throughout_history

192. https://www.scientificamerican.com/article/the-surprising-origins-of-evolutionary-complexity/

193. Daniel W. McShea, Robert N. Brando: Biology's First Law: The Tendency for Diversity and Complexity to Increase in Evolutionary Systems. ISBN-10: 0226562263

194. Carl Sagan: Brocca's Brain.

195. Carl Sagan: The Dragons of Eden.

196. https://en.wikipedia.org/wiki/Mercury_(planet)#Advance_of_perihelion

197. Zalman Shneur: The Gaon and the Rabbi.

198. Rodney Stark: How the west won, The Neglected Story of the Triumph of Modernity.

199. Bertrand Russell: The Problems of Philosophy.

200. Henry Kissinger: A World Restored.

201. Heinrich Boll: The Clown.

202. David Thoreau: Civil Disobedience.

203. John Halperin: Eminent Georgians. ISBN-10: 0312176856.

204. http://www.marketsandmorality.com/index.php/mandm/article/viewFile/415/405

205. https://en.wikipedia.org/wiki/Universal_grammar

206. John Locke: Two Treaties of Government.

207. John M. Siracusa: Diplomacy.SBN-10: 9780199588503.

208. Plato: The Republic.

209. https://en.wikipedia.org/wiki/Wave_equation

210. "You can do anything with bayonets...except sit on them." Our French Daily Reckoning correspondent, Philippe Bechade, quoted Talleyrand to make his point. The French foreign minister under Napoleon explained that seizing a city was a very different matter from holding it. For the latter, you needed at least a minimum of cooperation from the citizens. You had to sit down with them and make a kind of peace. And you couldn't sit on bayonets.

Then again, "Napoleon never ordered a bombing of a wedding on pretext that enemy soldiers were in attendance...certainly not based on dubious intelligence available."

211. John Julius Norwich: Four Princes.

212. Robert Payne: The history of Islam. ISBN: 0-88029-562-7

213. Roger Crowley: 1453.

214. David Abulafia: The Great Sea.

215. John Julius Norwich: The Middle Sea.

216. Attributed to the last words of an Israeli hero, Josef Trumpeldor, inspired by Horace.

217. The Origin of Language and Communication https://trueorigin.org/language01.php

218. James Hurford: The Origins of Language (Oxford Linguistics). ISBN-10: 0198701888

219. Kevin Stroud: The History of the Alphabet (MP3 file).

220. Christine Kennealley: The First Word. ISBN-10: 0670034908

221. Big Data Revolution: https://www.youtube.com/watch?v=bIY3LUZ7i8Y

222. Deep Mind: https://www.youtube.com/watch?v=PSZw8egM2Is HYPERLINK "https://www.youtube.com/watch?v=PSZw8egM2Is&feature=youtu.be" & HYPERLINK "https://www.youtube.com/watch?v=PSZw8egM2Is&feature=youtu.be" feature=youtu.be

223. http://www.u.arizona.edu/~clin/professional/papers/origin_of_syntax.pdf

224. David Eagleman: Brain and Reality, https://www.youtube.com/watch?v=WvXYQ1QSFV4

225. Barbara Tuchman: The March of Folly.

226. John McWorther: https://www.youtube.com/watch?v=UmvOgW6iV2s

227. Paul Davis: Information and the nature of reality. ISBN-10: 1107684536

228. Nancy Isenberg: White Trash.

229. P. J. O'Rourke: Thrown under the Omnibus.

230. Maimonidas Creed: https://en.wikipedia.org/wiki/Maimonides#13_principles_of_faith

231. https://en.wikipedia.org/wiki/Voyager_Golden_Record

232. https://simple.wikipedia.org/wiki/Higgs_field

233. Global Warming opposition: https://topdocumentaryfilms.com/great-global-warming-swindle/

234. Phyllis Rose - Parallel Lives.

235. Allan Bloom: The Closing of the American Mind.

236. Plato: Sophist.

237. Steven Goldman, Great Courses lectures on Scientific Wars.

238. Churchill: The Gathering Storm.

239. https://en.wikipedia.org/wiki/Gravitational_wave

240. https://www.nobelprize.org/nobel_prizes/physics/laureates/2011/advanced-physicsprize2011.pdf

241. https://www.nytimes.com/2016/02/12/science/ligo-gravitational-waves-black-holes-einstein.html

242. https://en.wikipedia.org/wiki/Sokal_affair

243. Robert Greenberg: Mozart Chamber Music, Great Courses seminar.

244. Claude Shannon: https://en.wikipedia.org/wiki/Information_theory

245. https://en.wikipedia.org/wiki/List_of_tallest_buildings_and_structures

246. Victor Frankl: Man's Search for Meaning.

247. Paul Hoffman: Archimedes' Revenge. ISBN 0-449-21750-7.

248: Niall Ferguson: Civilization

249. Nietzsche: Beyond Good and Evil

250. Nigel Hamilton: Commander in Chief.

251. McAfee: Machine, Platform, and Crowd. ISBN-10: 039335606X

252. Christie Wilcox: https://blogs.scientificamerican.com/science-sushi/evolution-the-rise-of-complexity/

253: Resonance Academy: https://academy.resonance.is/the-rise-of-complexity/

254. Daniel Kahneman: thinking Fast and Slow.

255. Amos Oz: In the Land of Israel (essays on political issues) ISBN 0-15-144644-X

256. Paul Johnson: History of the Jews.ISBN-10: 0060915331

257. Paul Johnson: Renaissance. ISBN-10: 0812966198

256. Philip Radcliff: Beethoven's String Quartets. (1965)

257. Ferguson/Zakaria: Is This the End of the Liberal International Order?

259. FDR: https://en.wikisource.org/wiki/The_Four_Freedoms_speech

260. Steven Runciman: The Sicilian Vespers.

261. Marshall Eakin: Conquest of the Americas, Great Courses seminar.

262. Paul Kennedy: The Rise and fall of the Great Powers, ISBN 0-394-54674-1

263. Steven Runciman: The Fall of Constantinople, 1453.

264. Roger Crawley: 1453: The Holy War for Constantinople.

265. Edwin Bernhard: Maya to Aztec, Great Courses seminar.

266. Food Timeline, http://www.foodtimeline.org/vegetables.html

267. Big Data: https://en.wikipedia.org/wiki/Big_data

268. Niall Ferguson: The Square and the Tower (2017).

269. Block-chain: https://www.youtube.com/watch?v=KP_hGPQVLpA

270. Block-chain: https://www.youtube.com/watch?v=Pl8OlkkwRpc

271: Queuing Theory: https://www.youtube.com/watch?v=rSZWig173xM

272: Allan C. Guelze: Making History, Great Courses lectures.

273. W. S. Churchill: Memoirs of the Second World War.

274. Johan Huizinga: The Waning of the Middle-Ages.

275. Isaac Bashevis-Singer: Satan in Gorai.

276. Saul Bellow: More Die of Heartbreak.

277. Paul Johnson: Mozart- A Life.

278. The Economist – March 12, 2018 issue.

279. Alan Jacobs: How to Think.

280. Isaac Bashevis-Singer: A Friend of Kafka.

281. Charles Baudelaire: The Flowers of Evil (Les Fleurs du Mal). ISBN-10: 0199535582

282. Peter Stearns: A Brief history of the World, teach12.com series.

283. William McNeill: Plagues and Peoples. ISBN-10: 9780385121224.

284. First words: The surprisingly simple foundation of language – New Scientist, May 2017.

285. Skinner vs. Chomsky: https://noam-chomsky.wikispaces. com/~Chomsky+vs+Skinner~

286. Douglas Murray: The Strange Death of Europe.

287. Robert Wright: Nonzero - The Logic of Human Destiny. ISBN-10:

0679442529

288. Pedro Domingos: The Master Algorithm.

289. Robert Greenberg: Beethoven String Quartets, teach12.com seminar

290. Jay Winik: The Great Upheaval.

291. Yuval Harari: https://www.youtube.com/watch?v=XOmQqBX6Dn4&t=13s

292. A. Y. Heschel: Man is Not Alone.

293. D. Chopra: The Path to Love.

294: John Mortimer: The First Rumpole Omnibus.

295. Geoffry Villehardouin: The Conquest of Constantinople.

296. Joseph de Maister: Considerations on France.

297. Tom Stoppard: The Coast of Utopia.

298. Simon Winchester: The Perfectionists.

299. Friedrich Nietzsche: Beyond Good and Evil

300. Daniel Robinson: American ideals, founding a "Republic of Virtue"; Great Courses series.

301. Yuval Harari: 21 Lessons for the 21st century

302. https://en.wikipedia.org/wiki/Gaia_hypothesis

303. Christopher Clark: The Sleepwalkers. SBN-10: 0061146668

304: Deism: https://en.wikipedia.org/wiki/Deism

305. Hugh Ross & Fazale Rana: Origins of Life - Biblical and Evolutionary Models Face Off (2004).

306. Bill Moyers with Joseph Campbell: https://www.amazon.com/The-Heros-Adventure/dp/B07BC2VHHJ/ref=sr_1_1?ie=UTF8&qid=1542251632&sr=8-1&keywords=bill+moyers

307. Unberto Eco: Baudolino.

308. Jonathan Philips: The 4th Crusade and the Sack of Constantinople.

309. https://en.wikipedia.org/wiki/Thomas_Francis_Meagher

310. Innocent III - Vicar of Christ or Lord of the World? ISBN: 0-8132-0783-5

311. https://en.wikipedia.org/wiki/Marsilius_of_Padua

312. Bernard Lewis: The Middle East. ISBN-10: 0684832801

313. Sykes-Picot: https://en.wikipedia.org/wiki/Sykes%E2%80%93Picot_Agreement

314. https://en.wikipedia.org/wiki/Cambridge_Analytica

315. Joachim Fest: Hitler (1960)

316. Richard Wrangham: Catching Fire (on cooking) ISBN: 978-0465020416

317. Stradivarius competition: https://www.nationalgeographic.com/science/phenomena/2014/04/07/stradivarius-violins-arent-better-than-new-ones-round-two/

318. Complexity: https://www.edge.org/response-detail/26783. Also Leonard Susskind delivered a 3-lecture series on the matter in October 2018.

319. Leonard Susskind: https://pitp.ias.edu/sites/pitp/files/lecture-1.pdf

320. GW "terror": https://www.youtube.com/watch?v=zqIt93dDG1M&t=8s

321. Oscar Wilde: The Fisherman and his Soul.

322. https://en.wikipedia.org/wiki/Guidonian_hand

323. Robert Reich: The Common Good (2017).

324. Ephraim Emerton: The Late Middle Ages.

325. Mark Lehner: The Complete Pyramids: Solving the Ancient Mysteries (1997)

326. Michael Ruse: The Gaia Hypothesis. ISBN: 978-0226731704

327. Michael Ruse: Mystery of Mysteries. ISBN 0-674-46706-x

328. Malaria: https://www.newsweek.com/malaria-gene-editing-crispr-mosquitoes-1135871

329. Paul Davis, in New Scientist magazine, January 30, 2019

330. Roger Crowley: The Conquerors (2015).

331. https://en.wikipedia.org/wiki/Neume

332. https://www.smithsonianmag.com/smart-news/stradivarius-violins-dont-sound-better-newer-models-study-says-180963222/

333. Jamie Metzl: Hacking Darwin, 2019.

334. Jerusalem: Simon Sebag-Montefiore, 2019.

335. Israel Finkelstein: The Bible Unearthed: Archaeology's New Vision of

Ancient Israel and the Origin of Its Sacred Texts, ISBN 0-684-86912-8.

336. Daniel Kahneman: Thinking Fast and Slow.

337. Skinner - Whitehead: https://www.ncbi.nlm.nih.gov/pmc/articles/PMC2223160/

338. Plato: The Republic.

339. Fareed Zakaria: In Defense of Liberal Education. ISBN-10: 039335234X

CPSIA information can be obtained
at www.ICGtesting.com
Printed in the USA
LVHW100750071120
671026LV00038B/758